Retailing: Challenge and Opportunity

Retailing: Challenge and Opportunity
Second Edition

Robert F. Hartley
Cleveland State University

Houghton Mifflin Company   Boston
Dallas   Geneva, Illinois   Hopewell, New Jersey   Palo Alto   London

Infra-red photography on cover photo and chapter openers by Sharon Fox

Printed in the U.S.A.

Library of Congress Catalog Card Number: 79-88102

ISBN: 0-395-28185-7

Contents

Preface

Like the first edition, this second edition of *Retailing: Challenge and Opportunity* assumes that the student has some interest in a career in retailing, even though this interest may be more curiosity than firm resolve. Accordingly, a strong effort is made to present the challenges, opportunities, and excitement of retailing. The challenge of vying with competitors—of trying to anticipate, counter, and surpass their moves—can make one's work absorbing. In addition the intriguing reality of retailing profit centers affords high visibility for one's efforts, which can lead to rapid promotions for competent men and women.

We have attempted to give students an intimate acquaintance with important tools and techniques that they can use in their retail careers. For example, an entire chapter deals with supervision. Graduates who enter retailing will quickly find themselves in supervisory positions, where their success will be governed largely by what they can get done through people. As a result, they will need guidance about effective supervisory and management techniques, which we attempt to provide.

Department stores typically have received the most emphasis in retailing texts. While this aspect of retailing is important, opportunities lie in many other areas, in many different kinds of firms. Accordingly, we have presented a broad view of retailing and its diverse operations, in particular, the opportunities and challenges of self-employment.

Pedagogy

A major effort has been made to go beyond the strong pedagogical features of the first edition, to make the book highly stimulating and discussion-oriented, and to involve the reader as fully as possible. Discussion questions, projects, and role plays appear at the ends of chapters. Throughout chapters, innovative and creative thinking is encouraged with mini-cases and their "For Thought and Discussion" questions.

End-of-chapter material geared to stimulating discussions and critical, creative thinking includes:

Discussion Questions—Many of these are "thought" questions that cannot be answered by simply quoting from the book.

Projects—These provide a feel or perspective that will lead the student beyond the book into the real world of retailing.

Exercises in Creativity—These are designed to stimulate creativity and innovative thinking, attributes badly needed in the business world and invaluable in retailing.

Retailing in Action—These are role-playing situations in which the student is placed in real-world problem situations and asked to evaluate and recommend practical solutions.

Twelve new longer cases are provided, two at the end of each part of the book. These permit students to come to grips with realistic problems—ones they may soon face in the business world—and to develop practical remedies in the critical, yet constructive and supportive, environment of the classroom.

Other pedagogical features include a summary and a list of key terms at the end of each chapter. At the end of the book an extensive glossary of retailing terms is provided.

Organization and Content

Retailing is organized traditionally. Part 1 presents a general perspective of retailing. Topics include opportunities and careers in retailing, as well as the nature and scope of retailing, with particular attention to how it is changing. Chapter 3 is devoted entirely to self-employment prospects, including an in-depth examination of franchising as one of the more assured routes to successful entrepreneurship. Chapter 4 treats current issues facing retailers: consumerism, environmental problems, community relations, government relations, and ethical and social responsibilities. Retail executives can no longer afford to ignore such matters.

Part 2 is devoted to planning the retail enterprise. Chapter 5 considers the important preliminary aspects of establishing a business: defining the desired store image and target customers, then designing a retailing mix and strategy to best reach the defined market. Chapters 6 and 7 deal with store location, design, and layout.

Part 3 introduces the student to the management of people. The organization and structure of the firm and the functions of the personnel division are covered in Chapters 8 and 9. Chapter 10 concentrates on the important topic of supervision.

Merchandising, the basic foundation of retailing, is covered in Part 4. The objective is to introduce students to important merchandising tools and techniques in as clear and uncomplicated a manner as possible. Four key chapters deal with assortment planning, buying techniques, price setting and adjusting, and merchandise control.

Part 5 explores advertising, sales incentives, display, personal selling, and customer service in Chapters 15, 16, and 17. Chapter 18 concerns store operation and gives considerable attention to the major problem of shrinkage and how it can be minimized.

The last section of the book, Part 6, is devoted to retail accounting and expense control, in Chapter 19, and tools to improve decision making—the computer and retail research—in Chapter 20.

The following are specific changes from the first edition:

Material is completely updated.

Lengthy new cases—twelve altogether—have been added at the end of each part.

A complete chapter is now devoted to self-employment prospects.

Chapters on merchandising and control have been expanded.

The section on social issues has been made more concise and placed in a single chapter.

End-of-chapter material has been expanded to include key terms, summaries, and additional problems.

A glossary of terms is included at the end of the book.

Mini-cases have been highlighted graphically for clarity.

Acknowledgments

Many have contributed to this book: students, colleagues, businesspeople, and government officials. During thirteen years in retailing, I have been exposed to a wide variety of managerial styles, some worthy of emulation.

I particularly want to acknowledge the help of my colleagues at Cleveland State University Donald W. Scotton and Ronald Zallocco. For their help in providing meaningful suggestions and reviews, I would like to thank Gordon L. Wise, Wright State University; Carol Morris, University of San Diego; Elizabeth Helseth, City College of San Francisco; Dale Helwick, Lorain County Community College; James Moore, Community College of Denver, North Campus; Michael D'Amico, University of Akron; V. F. Ferrini, Jr., Montgomery Ward; and Ted Creighton, The Complete Runner.

Any errors or omissions are, of course, mine.

R. F. H.

Retailing: Challenge and Opportunity

1

Retailing in Perspective

1 You and Retailing

A PERSONAL NOTE TO THE STUDENT

In this second edition of *Retailing: Challenge and Opportunity,* as in the first edition, it seems fitting to suggest what I hope you may gain from the book and from a study of retailing. You may be asking: Is this a field of work I should think seriously of entering? Would I like it? Would it give me a good living? You should be better able to answer these questions by the end of the course.

Throughout the book, as questions or problems are posed, each reader is invited to participate in responding. This is a textbook about a fairly complex subject. There are many techniques and practices that you will need to know if you enter the field of retailing. Also, certain philosophies and concepts are worth knowing because they will help to enlarge your perspective, and perhaps stimulate your imagination.

A major theme of the book is that *retailing abounds in opportunities.* They lie all around, in small independent ventures as well as in large firms. Reference will be made to actual persons and how they achieved success. Some of these people were real innovators, while others were simply alert to opportunities and had the courage to take a risk.

The second theme of the book is that *retailing as an occupation is exciting and interesting.* Perhaps as you wade through the intricacies of markup, turnover, and open-to-buy calculations, you will not agree. But the variety of work in retailing, the fresh problems, the working with people, the chance to use imagination and creativity, can be intriguing. Of course, retailing, like any occupation, is not all rosy or easy. Later in this chapter we will look more closely at the good and bad points of retailing.

As you study this book, be open-minded about the opportunities and challenges of a career in retailing. Note the tools and techniques available for better operation. But note also that neither retailing nor any other occupation offers a guarantee of success with a minimum of effort.

The average shopper sees only one aspect of retailing: the point of purchase. Shoppers seldom realize the behind-the-scenes activities and planning required to bring about the condition—having the right merchandise at the right time and place, in the right quantity, and at the right price. Retailing seems far more simple than it really is.

Along with this common notion about retailing goes a related one: that no particular ability or knowledge is required. Anyone, presumably, can manage a retail store. But each year thousands of businesses opened by marginal retailers go bankrupt. This represents an economic cost to our society, as well as a heavy burden on the families involved.

Opportunities, however, do abound in retailing. They usually are found in responding to the needs of consumers. Some of these needs you can easily identify. Others require more imagination and a "feel" for certain factors.

OPPORTUNITIES FOR FRESH IDEAS IN RETAILING

There is always room for the change maker and *innovation.* We usually think of the innovator as an independent retailer, but innovators may thrive in large organizations too. However, many businesses are operated unimaginatively, "the way we have always done it." This kind of situation presents an opportunity for the aggressive person who is willing to break out of the rut of tradition.

Need for Innovative Thinking

The nature of retailing is *competition,* competition to win the attention and patronage of customers. To rise above mediocrity, a firm must distinguish itself from its competitors through its merchandise, its service, or some other aspect of its operation. It must build for itself a distinctive image. And creative thinking helps in finding opportunities.

Even worse than missed opportunities is the nearsightedness of retailers who permit severe competition to get started. The following are a few examples of such myopia:

Traditional hotel-keepers did not develop motels until the success of motels forced hotels to enter the field.

Drive-in movies were not pioneered by the great movie chains.

Two major retailing "revolutions"—supermarkets and discount stores—rose and flourished while traditional retailers, until too late, were complacent and scornful.

Just as innovation enables a firm to distinguish itself and become a viable and successful undertaking, so can imaginative thinking help the individual surpass fellow workers. So many aspects of retailing lend themselves to strong doses of *creativity:* for example, displaying and merchandising goods; promoting them; developing new and unusual treatments with fixtures, store and departmental layout and decor; and finding new ways to improve operational efficiency. In almost all retail jobs, in all types of firms, the challenges and the need for innovative thinking are ever-present.

IMPEDIMENTS TO INNOVATION   We have to recognize, however, that major innovations may not always be welcome. Large organizations in particular tend to resist change. Usually, such organizations have developed vested interests and both executives and employees fear that relationships, authority, and privileges will change for the worse if some innovation is adopted. Unfortunately, organizations also develop a tendency to remain engrossed in routine matters, rather than developing a wide perspective.

All organizations (but especially older and larger ones) are vulnerable to these faults, but retailers typically have been the worst offenders. Partly, this is due to the large proportion of family-owned businesses in retailing. While certain family-owned businesses do not lack keen and aggressive executive talent, others have been reluctant to move away from traditional ways. This situation, however, is changing today as newer managers, receptive to change, are assuming control.

William Batten's story is an extreme example of one man's courageous attempt to convince the executives of a staid and conservative major firm that innovation and aggressive action were long overdue. It is one of the best-known examples of a person laying his career on the line in an attempt to revitalize the thinking of a firm.

RETAILING PROFILE—*William Batten: Standing Up for a Conviction*

In 1957 William Batten was assistant to the president of the J. C. Penney Company. He had started with the company as an "extra" salesman twenty-six years before, and had come a long way. Now he staked everything on what he saw was a desperate need for change in the old conservative company. Up to then Penney had been a cash-only chain of stores selling softgoods (apparel, bedding, piece goods, and other textile-based merchandise). Jumping over the head of the president (his boss), Batten sent a memo to the board of directors bluntly telling them that the company was more in tune with the way things *were* than the way they were *going to be.*

The next year the board made Batten president, and the Penney Company began changing into credit, auto service centers, discount stores, hard goods (such as appliances and furniture), mail order, and, later, supermarkets and a drugstore chain.

Sources: For more detail, see "What's Good for the Country . . . ," *Forbes,* May 15, 1971, p. 66; and Robert F. Hartley, "J. C. Penney Company—Unchanging Policies," in *Marketing Mistakes* (Columbus, Ohio: Grid, 1976), pp. 19–30.

For Thought and Discussion

1. Would you take such a risk? (Before you answer this, place yourself in Batten's position. He was no longer a young man with job mobility; he had spent a working lifetime with this company, and was fairly high in the organization; overall, he had a lot to lose.)

2. What do you think would be the consequences of such a memo in some firms?

STIMULATING CREATIVITY IN THE RETAIL FIRM   Many innovations come from small entrepreneurs who may have little more than an idea. They are willing to take a chance because they do not have much to risk. A firm that is growing rapidly also becomes accustomed to change. Until increasing size and sheer cumbersomeness begin to slow the growth and open-mindedness of an organization, change tends to produce more change. Creative people are often attracted to a fast-growing, progressive firm.

To stimulate *creativity,* top management must encourage it. More than lip service is required. If ideas invariably wind up in an inactive file, an employee loses all incentive to suggest improvements.

Finding Unique Approaches to Retailing

The payoff of innovative ideas is their successful test in the marketplace. Often the innovative idea is nothing particularly unusual. Success can come in simple trappings, and from unlikely innovators. For example, one unlikely innovator achieved success at age seventy: Colonel Sanders with his Kentucky Fried Chicken. He appealed to consumers' desire for convenience by offering a take-home dinner at reasonable prices.

There are better ways of tapping opportunities than stumbling on a new approach by accident. For example: (1) One should be alert to changing consumer tastes and wants; and (2) one can identify unique needs of certain types of consumers who may not presently be adequately served.

We know that the age group between twenty-five and forty-four is rapidly increasing. We know that consumers today have more education, more leisure time, more affluence than formerly, that they are concerned with consumer protection and reliable buying information. We also know that many consumers prize physical fitness, freedom of movement, and the casual look. We know that the average customer wants convenience. Leisure time is precious, and shopping is no longer the adventure it was to other generations. All these subtle and obvious changes in the market are being translated into unique retailing offerings by alert merchants.

Sometimes success can be found in responding to the needs of relatively small groups of consumers. We will encounter examples of discovered opportunities throughout the book. Some of these will involve small-scale retailers; others, major firms.

SUCCESSFUL RETAILING STRATEGIES—*Reaching Untapped Markets and Unusual Customers*

Example 1   The current popularity of the outdoors has spawned retail activity in campers, trailers, and other recreational vehicles. This has led to the rapid growth of firms ranging from manufacturers to campground chains. There was a lag, however, in recognizing backpackers as a good potential market.

Appalachian Outfitters started in a basement in a small town about twenty-five miles from Washington, D.C. In only three years it became the largest backpacking, canoeing, and kayaking outfitter in the eastern United States. Although some twenty stores in the Washington metropolitan area stocked backpacking paraphernalia, this was a sideline to the more expensive camping equipment—for all except Appalachian Outfitters. Within three years Appalachian Outfitters had twenty-two employees, many of them expert backpackers and wilderness campers. Customers converging on the sprawling store in the small town caused weekend traffic jams.

Source: "Out to Oakton to Get Away," *Washington Post,* December 30, 1971, pp. Di and De. © The Washington Post.

Example 2   Speed and Briscoe Truck Stop caters to truckers who ply I-95, one of the heaviest traveled nonurban stretches of interstate on the East Coast. Speed and Briscoe does over $5 million of business a year. Their goods and services include fuel, free showers, clothes, motel rooms, repairs, telegraph facilities, food, a barber shop, and a general store with goods ranging from reflectors to dolls, from socks to stereo tapes. At any one time, upwards of a hundred tractor-trailer rigs may be parked on the fourteen-acre paved lot. In the fifty-mile stretch from Richmond to Fredericksburg, Virginia, there are five other modern truck stops, descendants of the "greasy spoon" diesel stops of twenty years ago, meeting truckers' needs twenty-four hours a day.

In 1966 there were 900 truck stops in the United States; by 1972 there were 1,900; estimates are for 3,800 by 1980. While hundreds of these are "mom and pop" family operations, increasingly they are growing larger and more sophisticated, and are offering a greater variety of goods and services. Perhaps the largest and most complete truck stop is Transport City which sprawls over 51 acres near Atlanta and offers truckers practically everything but beer and hard liquor: "Drinking and driving don't mix."

Sources: "Truck Stops Go Modern," *Washington Post,* January 10, 1972, pp. C1 and C3. © The Washington Post; and "In Georgia: Footnotes from a Trucker's Heaven," *Time,* February 19, 1979, pp. 6–7.

For Thought and Discussion   What are the untapped markets in your community? How would you go about assessing their potential for a successful business?

CAREERS IN RETAILING

Retailing has huge personnel needs. Over 14 million people are employed in some aspect of retailing. That is almost 17 percent of the total civilian employees on nonagricultural payrolls. Furthermore, for those who seek occupational independence, the self-employment opportunities in retailing are many and varied (as we will see later in this chapter and in more detail in Chapter 3). Even in tight employment markets, demand for retail workers, and especially for retail executives, is ever-present. Retailing offers nearly the largest pool of employment opportunities of any field of endeavor. Well over a million of those employed in retailing are college graduates.[1]

Don't Be Fooled by Relatively Low Starting Salaries

College students often view careers in retailing negatively because the starting salaries with some retail firms are lower than those in industry. General business and retailing salaries, in particular, are distinctly lower than those in the technical fields, such as engineering and accounting. For example, the engineering specialty most in demand, petroleum engineering, offered starting salaries averaging $1,653 a month for June 1978 college graduates; most other engineering specialties averaged several hundred dollars a month below this. In contrast, the lowest average offer to bachelor's degree graduates was $871 for graduates in the humanities. Business-related disciplines showed average offers of $1,124 for accounting and $993 for general business, and somewhat less for retailing.[2]

[1] *Occupational Outlook for College Graduates* 1977–78 (U.S. Department of Labor, Bureau of Labor Statistics, 1978), p. 12.
[2] The salary figures are from the College Placement Council, *News Release,* August 22, 1978, p. 3. They are based on "CPC Salary Survey: A Study of Beginning Offers." "The beginning salary data reported are based on offers (not acceptances) to graduating students in selected curricula and graduate programs during the normal college recruiting period, September to June. The Survey covers job openings in a broad range of functional areas, except teaching, within employing organizations in business, industry, and government. The data are submitted by a representative group of colleges throughout the United States."

Don't be misled by the lower starting salaries for retailing positions, lower, particularly, than those in engineering and other technical fields. With the rapid promotions that come to capable people, a retail salary earner often forges ahead of his or her nonretail counterpart in a few years. Retail executive compensation frequently includes a bonus arrangement based on sales and profit results for the executive's areas of responsibility. This arrangement can add substantially to base salaries and allows good performance to be specifically rewarded. Top retailing executives are among the highest-paid business leaders. Middle-management levels are also well compensated. Buyers usually earn between $12,000 and $40,000 a year, although top buyers for large department stores and chains can earn upwards of $50,000 a year. Salaries of store managers vary widely depending on the size of the store; most range from $10,000 to $100,000.

What Does Retailing Offer as a Career?

Career opportunity in retailing may be likened to an iceberg; certain aspects of it are visible, but the bulk of the work lies beneath the surface. The retailing operation may be self-service and may culminate at the checkout counter, but a host of management, buying, and planning activities are behind the scenes. Many of these are interesting jobs handled by well-paid executives.

In retailing you may work for someone else, possibly a large firm, such as Sears, Penney, Macy, or K mart. The other possibility is self-employment, being confronted with all the risks and rewards of having your own firm. Each type of career offers certain attractions, as well as drawbacks. As you can imagine, each appeals to a somewhat different personality.

IN A LARGE FIRM   The large retail firm offers a *diversity of jobs;* many different skills are needed. A partial listing of specialized job requirements for a large department store or chain is:

Managers (of everything from departments to stores, warehouses to offices)
Accountants
Systems analysts
Marketing researchers
Buyers
Merchandise controllers

Fashion coordinators
Industrial engineers
Artists
Copywriters and layout people
Traffic and transportation experts
Credit officers
Real-estate specialists
Architects
Financial executives
Personnel executives
Education and training directors

Even physicians and nurses are needed in a large store, as are detectives and "protection" agents. Such diversity offers many avenues of opportunity and exposes a person to many types of people. This can be a broadening experience.

Some of the most exciting and even glamorous jobs in retailing fall in the merchandising sphere. Buyers and merchandise managers seek out and bring to their stores the vast array of consumer goods offered in our society, from furniture to high fashions, from toys to imported artifacts. Though they are not typical, some buyers travel to Europe and other parts of the world in search of distinctive merchandise to offer their customers. New York City is a focal point for many merchandise-procurement activities.

The opportunity to *get into management quickly* appeals to ambitious people. Retailing needs many managers—department managers, section managers, division managers, floor managers, and store managers. New employees, especially if they have college training, can often become responsible rather quickly for large-volume operations and supervision of the personnel involved. For example, one major department store corporation, in its recruiting brochure, notes that after a week and a half of indoctrination, an employee may be ready to start as a supervisor and may progress to assistant buyer a year or so after that.[3] As assistant buyer you manage selling space within a department, help direct the merchandise activities of salespeople, serve as liaison with suburban stores, and are responsible for reordering certain kinds of goods. It usually takes three to five years to achieve buyer rank in a large department store. Other routes to management are in operations, control, sales promotion, and personnel divisions.

[3] "You Won't Get a Job at Ohrbach's—Unless You're Pushing for a Career," *Executive Recruiting Manual* (New York: Ohrbach's).

Working conditions in most retailing jobs are good, but there are unattractive aspects. Let's look at the less attractive features first. The hours in retailing are frequently long. Stores are open to serve the public, and this often requires being open on Saturdays and one or more nights a week. More and more stores are even opening on Sundays and holidays. The greater reliance on shifts, however, is bringing hours more in line with those of other occupations.

Most retail employees enjoy pleasant physical surroundings. Stores are designed to attract customers and to make their visit comfortable so that they will come frequently and stay to shop. While office space (such as that for buying offices) may be cramped in order to maximize selling space, the general environment is far superior to that of a factory or many other job surroundings. Other advantages retail employees have are discounts on merchandise, first choice of sale items and new goods, and the sense of being in the heart of things, whether downtown or in a shopping mall.

The retail job involves working with others—customers, fellow workers, subordinates, stockroom personnel, maintenance people, suppliers, and advertising and display specialists—and the variety of personal contacts is more stimulating than the isolation that many office jobs require. One can develop leadership and social skills that may be expressed in such nonbusiness activities as church work, community projects, charity drives, and educational programs.

Variety of work characterizes retail jobs. Changes in seasons and in merchandise bring fresh and interesting challenges, as do differences in customers, in business conditions, and even in ordinary job requirements. For example, one day in the life of a department-store buyer may involve the following activities:

Conducting a training class for salespeople

Reviewing personnel records of subordinates

Coaching an assistant buyer in some aspect of display and merchandise presentation

Talking with customers on the sales floor to get feedback on certain new merchandise

Consulting with the advertising department and the fashion director

Giving attention to a problem in the stockroom concerning merchandise

Strolling through competing stores, over an extended lunch hour, to note any new merchandise and displays

Talking with sales representatives of manufacturers and wholesalers

Reviewing stock records

Evaluating merchandise samples

Writing orders for new and replenishment goods

Beginning the preparation of long-range promotional and merchandise budgets

Visiting branch suburban stores to bring them up to date and help with problems

Now let us look at an incentive for a career in retailing that is particularly important for the person who has ability and is eager to get ahead. A person's *effectiveness is easily measured* and is more visible than in almost any other kind of work. Retail management jobs usually are broken down into *profit centers*. The manager, then, is responsible for the sales and profitability of a particular department or store. Sales figures tell how well he or she does the job. Performance can be measured against industry norms, other profit centers in the firm, and previous periods of time. Here are two examples:

A large department store may have as many as two hundred departments in its merchandising division. Each department is an individual profit center. The managers running them are, in effect, creative entrepreneurs who are accountable for the operation and for the profitability of their own business.

A chain store, be it a small shoe store or a Sears or Penney type of department store, is also a profit center. The store manager is responsible for his or her own store and sales and profitability are easily measured and compared with other similar units in the chain.

Such tangible evidence of job performance is lacking in most jobs in finance, in accounting, and in personnel. For example, the direct contribution of the personnel executive to the profits of a store is virtually impossible to measure; and the cost accountant may develop error-free reports, but his contribution to sales and profits is also unlikely to be measurable.

The highly motivated man or woman can move ahead quickly. Many retailers are opening new stores, and introducing diverse types of merchandise and services. Their need for aggressive and capable executives is great. Few other occupations afford the *advancement opportunities* found in large retail organizations. As one example, look at Table 1.1 for the growth of S. S. Kresge Company and its K mart stores in recent years.

As the first K mart store was not opened until 1962, such growth brought about a large demand for trainees and executives. The chain

TABLE 1.1   THE GROWTH OF K MART

Year (as of January 31)	Number of K marts In Operation	Stores Added Each Year
1979	planned 1,546	planned 180
1978	1,366	160
1977	1,206	271
1976	935	132
1975	803	130
1974	673	93
1973	580	94
1972	486	75
1971	411	73
1970	338	65
1969	273	57
1968	216	54

Source: S. S. Kresge published reports.

trains store managers in a five- to six-year on-the-job program and has 4,000 in training. The average K mart store has 75,000 to 95,000 square feet of nonfood selling space. Sales for each unit are in the millions of dollars. In 1976 alone, K mart promoted 310 assistant store managers to store-manager positions and hired 27,000 additional people to support one of the greatest yearly expansions ever achieved by a major retailer.[4]

Opportunities for women are better in retailing than in any other area of the business world. While some women have done spectacularly well in advertising, this industry employs relatively few people (fewer than 500,000). In retailing, though, women in many department and specialty stores fill one-third to one-half of the buying and executive positions. They are prominent as publicity and fashion directors and in personnel and training positions. A few women reach major executive levels—for example, Macy's New York promoted five women to vice presidential rank a few years ago. On the other hand, some major chain

[4] As reported in *Chain Store Age,* General Merchandise Edition (June 1977), 81.

organizations have done little to urge women toward executive positions.

The success of some women in retailing is at least partially due to the fact that women shoppers predominate in most retail stores, especially department and specialty stores. Women buyers and executives tend to have more rapport with such customers and more understanding of their preferences, especially in fashion goods. Many able women are attracted by the excitement and glamor of these jobs. Since their performance is readily measured by the sales and profits of their departments, top-management recognition and promotion can follow.[5]

OPPORTUNITIES IN SELF-EMPLOYMENT   Many retail firms are small. Some are owned by one person or by two people in a partnership. Self-employment, owning one's own business, is a dreamed-of goal for many persons. It offers satisfactions that can never be achieved by working for someone else.

For some persons there is an irresistible challenge in giving up the relative security of a large firm for the risks and rewards of operating their own business. The desire for independence and freedom from bosses can be overpowering. Self-employment also affords the challenge and fascination of building a business, both its physical assets and its standing in the community. A successful entrepreneur may have something tangible to leave his children and may be able to bring them into the business.

And the monetary rewards? As you might imagine, these can range from meager subsistence to great wealth, as a small business grows to a large one. Many entrepreneurs find it desirable to plow money back into their growing businesses, rather than spending it in other ways.

RETAILING PROFILE—*Quick Success in Self-Employment*

David Pensky and Richard Hindin, two men in their twenties, started Britches of Georgetown ("fine clothiers since 1967"). Their credit was so bad they had to build the interior of their 700-square-foot store themselves. Because they could not afford much merchandise, they would triple-fold slacks, with tissue paper between the folds, to make it appear they had more stock than they did.

[5] For recent specifics on women executives in retailing, see Karen R. Gillespie, "The Status of Women in Department and Specialty Stores: A Survey," *Journal of Retailing* (Winter 1977–1978), 17–32; and Kate Kelly, "Room At the Top," *Stores* (February 1978), 36–38.

After one year of operation—featuring "elegant informal wear" and high-fashion men's clothing—they had grossed $120,000. They began looking for additional sites and in a few years had opened four additional stores (including The Snooty Fox, operated by the mother of one of the partners, which stocked posters, novelties, and psychedelic gear).

Sales in two years had reached over $800,000; in the third year they were close to $1.5 million. Pensky and Hindin became one of the largest sellers of Pierre Cardin shirts in the United States. Some 270 dozen were sold in the fall season alone, at prices starting at $15. Interestingly, the two partners had first met in their high school days when they operated fireworks stands together.

Source: "Fancy Britches Spark a Boom in Georgetown," *Washington Post,* March 3, 1969, p. D1. © The Washington Post.

For Thought and Discussion

1. Are there any dangers in expanding this fast?
2. In what ways does operating fireworks stands provide good training for future entrepreneurship?

We must recognize that for every such success story, there are many mediocre ventures and some failures. But the opportunity is there for those with the motivation, perseverance, and confidence to pursue it.

DISADVANTAGES OF RETAILING CAREERS   Now let's spell out some negative aspects of a retailing career. It is worth noting that most of the disadvantages are particularly evident in the early years. The result is that many able people are discouraged and leave the field. Retailers vary widely in how effectively they seek and motivate able trainees and junior executives. Some retailers still have the traditional view that "hard work is really what counts."

Starting pay in retailing, as we have seen, is lower than in many other occupations. Fortunately, this is changing, with the large retailers recognizing that they must compete with other firms and industries in attracting the best people. As noted earlier, working hours still tend to be longer than in many other occupations, and usually include some night and weekend hours. While unions for rank-and-file retail workers have usually reduced the work week to forty hours (by staggering hours), management people often find their own hours difficult to stagger.

Some stores have poorly organized training programs. As a result, the trainee may become discouraged and unwilling to wait for greater responsibilities and more interesting assignments. Retail work in the beginning can be boring—the tediousness of stock counts, the monotony of folding and arranging merchandise thrown askew by impatient customers, the constant restocking of counters during busy days. But what job doesn't have tedious and aggravating moments?

Employment with a retail chain may require relocating frequently. This is a drawback for some trainees and executives, but others welcome the changes of scene and the chance to witness different operations.

We have noted that a person's performance can often be evaluated by the profit-center division of responsibilities. For the able, this is a decided advantage, but for the not-so-able, it is a disadvantage. Strong pressures may be exerted for better performance, and this is not always a comfortable situation.

While the rewards can be great in retailing—in accomplishment, compensation, and an interesting career—we should recognize that not all people find them so. Success requires initial patience, hard work, and determination. And for the person bent on self-employment, we should note that even J. C. Penney failed in his first venture.

■ **Summary**

Let's review briefly the major thoughts in this chapter:

1. Retailing abounds in opportunities for the innovative firm or individual. But many retailers are not alert and eager for change and they may become vulnerable to a competitive innovator, as conventional camping equipment stores were to Appalachian Outfitters.
2. Some new approaches were developed almost by accident, but opportunities are better tapped by (a) being alert to changing consumer tastes, and (b) identifying certain consumers with unique needs who are not being served adequately.
3. Although a retailing career has a poor image among college students, careers in retailing offer some unique and powerful advantages. This is true for both men and women, in large firms or in their own businesses. Most of the disadvantages of retailing are prevalent in the first few years of work.

We invite every student to weigh the pros and cons of retailing according to his or her own ambitions and interests. The author's strong conviction is that retailing offers an exciting and interesting career, one well paid and satisfying.

■ **Key Terms**

Creativity   Self-employment
Innovation   Working conditions
Profit centers

■ **Discussion Questions**

1. Why do large firms typically tend to resist change?
2. Why does innovation often come from the small firm or individual, rather than from the large, established firms?
3. How can consumers' desire for more leisure time be a source of retailing opportunity?
4. What is a profit center? Can you give some examples of retail profit centers? What are the implications of profit centers for executives and trainees?
5. In considering individuals for promotion, what means would you use to evaluate the performance of:
   a. a personnel executive
   b. a cost accountant
   c. a display manager
   d. a buyer
   e. a store manager
6. Why are opportunities for women so good in retailing?
7. How would you weigh the pros and cons of a retailing career, based on your knowledge today?
8. What types of individuals do you think are best suited for a career in retailing? Why?

■ **Project**

Talk to a buyer, merchandise manager, or store manager of a large retail store. Ask how he or she feels about the job, its opportunities, and its satisfactions—and its negative features also. Then talk to the owner of a fairly successful small retail firm regarding the same points. Compare and contrast their attitudes toward their jobs. Can you offer an explanation for any differences?

■ **Exercise in Creativity**

You are the department manager of a medium-sized Penney store (sales are about $1 million). James Goodenough, the manager, approaches you one day. "Gladys, we need to come up with more imaginative promotions. The big new Sears and K mart that just opened are digging into our business pretty badly. We need somehow to make shopping more exciting in this store."

Puzzled, you respond, "But what can we do that is really different? Our promotions and key merchandise are planned by the regional and New York offices."

"We still can use some imagination. Gladys, the January White Sale will be here in three weeks. Do you think we can come up with some creative ideas to make this a more successful promotion than it was last year—even with our new competition?"

"I don't know, but I'll see what ideas I can come up with."

"Not only you, Gladys. I'd like to encourage all of our people to stimulate their creative juices. By the end of the week I'd like you to draw up a plan, including meeting schedules and topics, for seeing if we can't involve our people in producing some good, innovative ideas."

How would you stimulate employee creativity in this store? Give general guidelines and specific suggestions for the White Sale three weeks away in your stimulation plan.

■ **Retailing in Action**

John Chancy has asked Bob Kautious to go into partnership with him in opening a restaurant. John's wife and mother are both accomplished cooks, but his experience is limited to distributing soft drinks for a local bottler. Bob is an assistant buyer in the men's clothing department of the largest department store in town.

The site has been selected. While it is not ideal, it should be adequate. Financing will present no immediate problem, since John and his wife have some money saved up, and so does Bob.

Several things bother Bob in making such a decision. He has just been promoted to assistant buyer of a larger department and expects within two or three years to be promoted to buyer, if he stays. While he is working rather normal hours now, he can see working many more hours in the new business, since the restaurant would be open nights and Sundays. He is not sure if the rewards will be worth the risks; it is not so much that he expects the business to fail, as that he fears it may not produce enough to give two families a satisfactory income.

But John says: "This is a great opportunity, Bob. As we get this thing going, we can expand into other outlets. This is the time for us to make our move. In another few years, when the kids come, it will be too late."

Bob turns to you as a good friend for advice. What would you advise him? Why? Is there any other information you would want to know?

2 Dimensions of Retailing

Retailing is a major influence in our economy and our society. It's aim is to satisfy the needs of people like you and me in the most efficient and convenient way possible. But retailing is not static. On the contrary, it is dynamic; it changes as new ways are found to better satisfy customers. Retailing's ever-changing scene can provide intriguing challenges and myriad opportunities. In this chapter, we will look at aspects of the nature and historical evolution of retailing, some of the personalities involved, and some of the emerging trends.

NATURE OF RETAILING

Retailing involves selling goods and services to the ultimate consumer. But not all selling of goods and services is retailing, since some buyers are industrial purchasers of raw materials, parts, factory supplies and equipment, and partially processed items. Some buyers are wholesalers and retailers themselves, who are buying for *resale* to ultimate consumers.

We usually think of retailers as having stores, but they need not. Door-to-door selling, such as that done by Fuller Brush or Avon sales representatives, is also retailing. The vending machine is another type of retailing. So is the firm that solicits business and handles all transactions by mail. Some of the largest retail firms, such as Sears, Montgomery Ward, and J. C. Penney, do substantial mail-order and telephone-order business through their catalogs.

Retailing is labor intensive: it takes a large number of retail employees to produce the sales dollars a manufacturer, for example, might produce with a smaller work force. But what about self-service? Hasn't this made retailing less labor intensive? Table 2.1 shows the trend in full-time employment in retailing since 1950 and compares it with the total labor force.

As Table 2.1 shows, automation in retailing is still remote. Even self-service, which became more prevalent after discount stores came on the scene in the 1950s, has not appreciably cut down on the proportion of retail workers in the total labor force. On the contrary, since 1950 the proportion of retail workers has risen from 15.2 percent to 16.9 percent of the total civilian nonagricultural labor force.

The overall purpose of retailing is to provide goods and services wanted by consumers. This means that, if customers are to be satisfied and the business is to be successful, the retailer should consider how

TABLE 2.1   TREND OF EMPLOYMENT IN RETAILING, 1950–1978

	1950	1960	1970	1978
Number of employees on non-agricultural payrolls (000)	45,222	54,234	70,920	85,760
Number of employees in retail trade (000)	6,868	8,388	11,225	14,496
Percentage of retail workers in total civilian non-agricultural labor force	15.2	15.5	15.8	16.9

Sources: U.S. Department of Labor, Bureau of Labor Statistics, *Employment and Earnings* (February 1978), 57; and *Employment and Earnings* (January 1979), 75, for preliminary figures for 1978.

best to blend incentives for shopping. The following *shopping incentives* are sometimes called patronage factors to denote the reasons why customers shop certain stores:

Convenience—of hours, of location, of shopping ease

Assortment of merchandise—whether a wide variety, or limited

Quality and fashion level of goods—generally a shopping incentive at the high-quality and high-fashion end

Price—generally important at the lower end, as "lowest prices," or "lowest prices consistent with dependable quality"

Services—such as credit, delivery, return-goods privileges, home decorator assistance, and a courteous and knowledgeable sales staff

Excitement—as conveyed by promotional efforts, use of celebrities, fashion shows, and tent and moonlight sales

You can see that one store cannot provide all these ways to satisfy customers. For example, a store with the lowest prices can hardly offer the widest variety of services and the highest quality of goods. Nor is it likely to offer a wide assortment of goods; rather, it must seek the "best sellers" so that inventory costs can be kept moderate. The store with high prices, on the other hand, can afford to carry a greater variety of goods and more "fringe" items, so that customers have more to choose from in each product category.

Finding different ways of satisfying current consumer needs also represents opportunities for new or existing retailers to carve out new business. For example, discount stores first entered the retail scene competitively in the 1950s by offering lower prices, as well as the convenience of night and Sunday shopping, and ample free parking. We will refer to these ways to satisfy customers again in later chapters.

HISTORICAL PERSPECTIVE

We may get some idea of the opportunities awaiting the innovator in retailing as we look at the historical evolution of retail institutions in the United States. Change has been rather rapid. The retail environment of today is scarcely recognizable when compared with that of a century ago.

In colonial days, shoppers used small, specialized shops, such as cobblers, candlemakers, and tailors. On the frontier there were trading posts. Established on main routes of travel, some of these trading posts

This is an example of a traditional general store operating today. Note the variety of merchandise. Under what conditions do you think an old-fashioned store can compete with modern retail outlets? (Peter Angelo Simon Photo Researchers, Inc.)

were major goals of wagon trains as they crossed a sparsely populated and often hostile land. Probably the first retail selling in most of America was done by peddlers:

> *At the outset they walked. Those of more stature rode horseback and the even more prosperous rode in wagons or carriages. . . . The peddler's life was strenuous, lonely, and hazardous. When the opportunity developed or "when they found the right place or the right girl," many were happy to settle down as storekeepers. Many dry-goods stores (so called to distinguish them from those which sold liquor or "wet" goods) were started in this way.*[1]

Later, the trading posts and some of the dry-goods stores evolved into general stores that featured a wide variety of merchandise. Though these general stores were not organized by departments and had crude fixtures and merchandise, they served the needs of the community. In rural areas, you can still find descendants of these old general stores, usually at crossroads.

By the last decades of the nineteenth century, population had grown and was concentrated in major cities. This created opportunities for

[1] Tom Mahoney and Leonard Sloane, *The Great Merchants* (New York: Harper & Row, 1966), p. 5.

some of the major types of retailers that we know today. Department stores, variety stores ("five-and-ten-cent stores"), general merchandise chains, mail-order houses, and large specialty stores came into being in the late 1800s. Many entrepreneurs, whose names are familiar to us today, were starting their dynasties in humble circumstances near the beginning of the twentieth century. S. S. Kresge, F. W. Woolworth, Montgomery Ward, and Marshall Field are some examples.

RETAIL GIANTS—*James C. Penney*

He was a minister's son, one of twelve children. When twenty-seven years old, he opened a dry-goods store in a small mining town, Kemmerer, Wyoming. The year was 1902. It was his second venture in entrepreneurship. His first, a butcher shop in Colorado, had failed. Failure was predicted for this enterprise also. The store was only one room, twenty-five by forty feet, and it was off the main street. Penney and his wife lived in the attic overhead. Their furniture was made from packing cases. Water had to be carried from a Chinese restaurant a few doors down the street. But the biggest difficulty was that nearly all local trade was on credit, at stores owned by the mining companies. Penney was selling strictly for cash.

But he offered such values that his customers were willing to pay cash. The store opened at 7 A.M. on weekdays and 8 A.M. on Sundays, and remained open as long as there was a miner or sheepherder on the street. Sales for the first year were $28,898. The J. C. Penney Company grew from this point.

Source: For more detail, see Norman Beasley, *Main Street Merchant* (New York: McGraw-Hill, 1948).

For Thought and Discussion   Do you think Penney would have been successful if he had started such a store in a larger city, such as Denver, Omaha, or Salt Lake City? Why or why not?

Most of the other "great" merchants had similar beginnings, for the American market was ripe for innovative changes. But was opportunity for innovation gone after these first giants made their starts? Not at all. Major innovations were to come long after department stores and chains were well established by the great merchants.

The supermarket became popular in the late 1930s. It had a major impact on the form of food stores, which until then had been small with limited assortments, clerk-served, and located in populated areas where foot traffic was heavy.

RETAIL GIANTS—*Michael Cullen*

As an employee of a food chain in the late 1920s, he foresaw a need for grocery stores to adapt to the growth of the automobile age. His suggestion was to develop large self-service stores on a cash-and-carry basis, surrounded by parking space and located outside high-rent districts, and featuring mass displays of groceries at low prices, with heavy advertising to promote sales volume.

His employer wouldn't buy these ideas, and Cullen quit and in 1930 opened what is generally acknowledged to be the first supermarket, King Kullen, in Jamaica, New York. It was an immediate success. Two years later he had eight stores with sales of almost $9,000,000.

For Thought and Discussion   What happened to Cullen and his supermarkets in later years? (Research the literature.)

Even major chains like A & P were profoundly affected by this change in grocery retailing. In 1930, A & P had 15,709 stores; three-quarters of these were later to be abandoned as this largest food chain switched to the supermarket idea.

In the late 1950s, discount stores began to have an even greater impact on the existing retail structure than supermarkets had two decades before.

RETAIL GIANTS—*Eugene Ferkauf*

After returning from World War II service as a sergeant, he went to work in his father's two small luggage shops in Manhattan. But he wanted to test his theory that he could boost sales substantially by chopping the conventional 40 percent markup in half. In 1948, with $4,000, some of it supplied by his father, he rented a second-floor walkup on East 46th Street and began selling luggage at a discount. Soon he added appliances, pricing them at slightly above cost to draw traffic. They sold as fast as he could get them in the store. In two years, he had a $2,000,000 business and began opening other stores. And Korvette began the growth which was to make it the biggest-volume discounter.

Source: For more detail on Ferkauf and Korvette, see Robert F. Hartley, *"Korvette–Indigestion from Growth,"* in *Marketing Mistakes* (Columbus, Ohio: Grid, 1976), pp. 31–44.

For Thought and Discussion By the early 1960s, not much more than ten years after it began its rapid growth, Korvette was faltering. What lessons can be learned from this?

Discount stores began in austere surroundings, with few amenities, and practically no services. Their early customers saw garments hung on pipe racks, while the store itself might be housed in an abandoned factory building. But the prices were substantially lower than those of conventional retailers. Many customers were willing to put up with crude surroundings to save money. Discount stores today have shed most of their early austerity. Many now provide some services, such as credit. They are a major part of the retail scene, although the "discounts" aren't nearly as striking as they once were.

Other newcomers have been *specialty stores.* These stores (or shops or boutiques) offer one or very few lines of related merchandise, but carry depth within such lines. While specialty-type stores have existed almost since the first retail institutions, today there are many more products that are handled in such stores. Examples are lamps and shades, wigs, jeans, backpacking equipment, and records. As customers become more affluent and acquire a taste for distinctiveness, such small specialized stores will continue to flourish.

There is room in the market place for big generalized stores and small specialized ones, for high-price stores and for cut-price ones.

CLASSIFICATION OF RETAILERS

Since there are so many different kinds of retailers, some sort of classification is necessary for analysis and comparison. A useful way to classify retailers is (1) by ownership, (2) by categories of merchandise handled, and (3) by various nonstore methods of retailing. In the following discussion, we will consider the major forms of retailing coming under each of these classifications.

Classification by Ownership

The major forms of retail ownership are:

1. Independent retailers
2. Corporate chains
3. Consumer cooperatives
4. Leased departments
5. Franchised operations
6. Government-owned stores

INDEPENDENT RETAILERS   Independent retailers often are single-store operations run by an individual or by partners. Such enterprises are often small, but large retail firms can also be independent; that is, they are not part of some larger group of stores such as a chain. An independent department store can, however, have one or more branches. In that case it is known as a multiunit organization.

CORPORATE CHAINS   A chain is a string of stores under single ownership, carrying similar merchandise; all the units have a similar motif, and are managed by a central headquarters. Buying and operational policies are centralized. As a result, the individual store units reap the benefits of mass buying. In addition, central headquarters can supply expert accountants, display personnel, advertising staff, computer specialists, and architects and designers. Major chains may carry most of their merchandise under their own brands, rather than the brands of manufacturers. A few examples of chains are J. C. Penney, Sears, S. S. Kresge, Walgreen, and Kroger.

CONSUMER COOPERATIVES   Sometimes a group of consumers will band together to operate a retail store, usually hiring a manager. Such *consumer cooperatives* strive to offer their members lower prices, and this may be reflected in a year-end "patronage" dividend, whereby a percentage of each member's expenditures in the coop is returned. Historically, cooperatives have been much stronger in Europe, especially Scandanavia, than in the United States. Only in states such as Minnesota and Wisconsin, where there are large Scandinavian populations, have cooperatives made much headway. The advantage of lower prices usually has not been that significant for members.

Cooperative chains are described in the next chapter. These are associations of independent retailers who are able to compete more effectively with the corporate chains by buying and merchandising as a group.

LEASED DEPARTMENTS   A specialized department operated within a store by someone other than the management of the store is a *leased department.* Many leased departments are operated by chain organizations that lease space primarily in department stores, discount stores, and supermarkets. So tied in with the image of the store is the typical leased department that most customers do not realize there is a difference in ownership.

The lessee is responsible for the merchandise and management of the particular department. Usually the lessor, or store, is paid a flat rental charge, a percentage of sales, or some combination of the two. In department stores, leased departments are often beauty salons, shoe-repair shops, and florists. Discount stores frequently lease their grocery operations to someone more expert in handling such merchandise. Some discount firms in the early 1960s (the years of their most rapid expansion) even leased major departments like shoes, clothing, auto accessories, jewelry and cameras, and restaurants and snack bars. The discount operator could thus finance expansion into additional stores more rapidly than would otherwise be possible, since his inventory investment would be lessened.

A store may find certain disadvantages in the leasing arrangement. It loses some control over pricing, promotional efforts, and sales help. And there is often the nagging thought that more profits might result from not leasing. Retailers—and especially discounters—as they acquire more capital and a larger staff of capable executives, tend to take over these departments themselves.

The lessee, of course, benefits from the customer traffic generated by the other departments in the store. Using the store's fixtures and services leaves the lessee free to concentrate on specialized merchandise lines. However, there are some perils.[2]

RETAILING ERRORS—Overextension by Allied Supermarkets

Allied Supermarkets was chosen in 1963 to become the supermarket licensee in practically all future Kresge K marts. At the time this seemed a great coup for Allied, with K marts destined to be the fastest growing and largest

---

[2] For a discussion of some of the conflicts between lessees and lessors, see Burton Elliott, "The Licensor/Licensee Relationship—A Critical Element for Success," *Retail Control* (April-May 1976), 19–27.

discount operation in the world. But the agreement with Kresge required Allied to open a supermarket wherever Kresge chose to open a K mart. This wide dispersion of stores often forced Allied to rely on higher-cost local wholesalers. And the rapid opening of new stores placed severe capital demands on the firm. Other stipulations were that it must price its goods so as not to be undersold, and that it not carry many nonfood items that tend to raise profitability (since the K mart stores were stocking them). All in all, the leasing agreement with Kresge seriously limited the flexibility and autonomy of Allied.

The result was that sales soared from under $400 million in 1963 to over $1 billion in the fiscal year ending June 30, 1970. But profits declined so rapidly that the firm began operating in the red and the dividend had to be eliminated. The firm continued to incur serious losses year after year, despite major retrenchment. Finally, on November 4, 1978 it went into default and filed under Chapter XI of the Federal Bankruptcy Act.

Sources: For more detail on the dilemmas of Allied Supermarkets, see "Growing into Trouble," *Forbes*, June 15, 1970, p. 50; and "Supermarkets and Wholesalers," *Forbes*, January 8, 1979, pp. 137–138.

For Thought and Discussion

1. What lessons can be learned from this?
2. Do you see any way that Allied might have been able to cope with such a "great opportunity"?

FRANCHISED OPERATIONS   A franchise is a contractual arrangement in which the independent franchisee agrees to operate a business according to a prescribed format. Through franchising, an independent retailer benefits from affiliation with an already accepted name and product or service. The following firms are franchised operations: McDonald's, Burger King, Holiday Inn, Midas Muffler, National Car Rental. Many gasoline stations and most auto dealers are franchised. Franchising will be discussed in more detail in the next chapter.

GOVERNMENT-OWNED STORES   Stores provided by the military for its personnel and dependents are post exchanges (PXs) and commissary stores. PXs carry a fairly complete line of goods and services, although some categories of goods have specific price limitations within the continental United States. Commissary stores handle groceries and are similar to commercial supermarkets. These stores offer goods and services at much lower prices than can be obtained elsewhere and military personnel regard the stores as a fringe benefit.

Some eighteen states, including such large ones as Michigan, Ohio, and Pennsylvania, operate stores that sell liquor for off-premises consumption. These state-owned monopolies generate $9 billion of the $36 billion of annual alcohol sales in the United States. Unfortunately, these stores are often sources of patronage and inefficiency, and the public suffers from poor product selection, inconvenient stores, and higher prices than in the free-market or "open" states.[3]

Classification by Merchandise Handled

Retailers are commonly classified by the type of merchandise they handle. Some retailers carry a wide variety while others limit themselves to one category, such as wigs, or to a few closely related categories, such as men's furnishings. The major merchandise classifications of retailers are:

1. Department stores
2. Discount stores
3. Supermarkets
4. Variety stores
5. Specialty stores

DEPARTMENT STORES *Department stores* carry many categories of goods, including furniture and appliances, wearing apparel for the family, and household linens and dry goods. Such goods and services as gourmet foods, pets, travel arrangements, and bridal services may also be offered. Department stores usually provide their customers such services as delivery, credit, gift wrapping, and home decorating. These stores are the largest retailers in size. A store must have at least twenty-five employees to be classified as a department store. Examples are Macy, Dayton Hudson, Rich's, Carter Hawley Hale Stores, Marshall Field, and Sears.

DISCOUNT STORES The difference between discount stores and department stores is lessening today. When discount stores began moving

[3] For more information on the drawbacks of these state-owned monopolies, see "Prohibition's Last Revenge," *Forbes,* January 22, 1979, pp. 42–43.

onto the retail scene in the late 1950s and 1960s, they offered a wide
variety of goods at prices considerably lower than those in conventional
department stores. To do this required that they have plain surroundings, provide few if any customer services, and usually stock only the
best-selling sizes and styles within product categories. Many discounters today have upgraded their stores and merchandise, and have consequently given up much of their price advantage.

In the early days of discounters, their great growth and their severe
price competition caused consternation among more conventional retailers. The discount phenomenon even became known as the retail
revolution. To defend against this "discount threat," some of the major
retailers started their own discount subsidaries. Today, with superior
management and financial resources backing them, department-store or
variety-store corporations own most of the major discount chains, as
Table 2.2 shows.

SUPERMARKETS *Supermarkets* are large departmentalized food stores.
They usually feature self-service shopping and have check-out counters. Most supermarkets also offer such nonfood items as drugs, wom-
en's and children's accessories, and housewares, since these items typically carry a higher profit than most foodstuffs and are readily "picked
up" by shoppers. Most supermarkets are chains, but some are independently owned. Examples are A & P, Winn-Dixie, Safeway, Grand
Union, and Stop & Shop.

VARIETY STORES Originally called five-and-ten-cent stores, variety
stores today have traded up; some goods even sell for over a hundred

TABLE 2.2   PARENT COMPANIES OF MAJOR DISCOUNTERS

Parent Company	Discount Subsidiary
Kresge	K mart
Woolworth	Woolco
J. C. Penney	Treasury
Federated Department Stores	Gold Circle
	Gold Triangle
Dayton Hudson	Target Stores
Allied Department Stores	Almart
	Hunter
May Company	Venture

dollars. However, variety stores still concentrate on lower-price categories of merchandise. The distinction between larger variety stores and department stores is somewhat hazy. The Bureau of Census, in classifying retail statistics, may be governed by whether the store operators view themselves as a variety store or a department store. Examples of variety stores are S. S. Kresge, G. C. Murphy, and F. W. Woolworth.

SPECIALTY STORES   A wide variety of stores can be described as specialty stores. In contrast to stores that offer many lines of merchandise, specialty stores are limited line.[4] They may, however, carry a larger assortment of goods within a merchandise line than does the large department store or discount store. Possibilities for such specialty stores are almost endless: shoes, women's apparel, men's clothing, appliances, furniture, imported gifts, wigs, greeting cards, and even unisex items. Some limited-line stores are independent. But chain organizations are prominent with shoes, drugs, and to a lesser extent, women's apparel. Food stores, restaurants, lumber and building-materials dealers, and those who service and sell automobiles are limited-line retailers who have a major impact on total retail sales. (See Table 2.3, on page 34.)

Nonstore Methods of Retailing

While nonstore retailing accounted for only 2.5 percent of total retail sales in the 1972 Census of Business, this still amounted to over $11.5 billion (see Table 2.4, on page 35). And this figure is understated, since many vending machines, which are regarded as nonstore retailing, are located in stores and have their sales reported under store sales. Vending machines, catalog or mail-order selling, and door-to-door (or direct) selling are the major kinds of *nonstore retailing.*

VENDING MACHINES   For certain merchandise lines, such as cigarettes, candy bars, and soft drinks, the *vending machine* (or merchandising machine) is a major retailing method. The great advantage of vending machines is their convenience. They are placed in heavy-traffic locations and can be used as long as the buildings themselves are open. Vending machines, however, are high-cost operations. They require greater stocking time and repair labor than nonmachine operations.

---

[4] A distinction that is sometimes made is to use the term *specialty store* for a shop that carries women's apparel. The term *limited-line,* then, is reserved for other stores carrying such goods as men's wear, appliances, and hardware.

Their prices are usually higher than prices for the same goods purchased elsewhere—often from 15 to 50 percent higher. Obviously, not all kinds of goods can readily be sold by machines.

CATALOG RETAILING   Mail-order selling, or *catalog retailing* dates back to the beginning of mass selling in this country, the end of the 1800s. Sears, Roebuck (1886), and Montgomery Ward (1872) were started as mail-order retailers. With the expansion of railroads and postal service, they served a widely scattered market, and offered lower prices and wider assortments than other retailers could. It might appear today that catalog selling is hardly necessary, with stores so convenient to most of us. But this is not the case.

While catalog selling no longer dominates the retail scene, it still is robust. In fact, it is growing faster than retail trade in general, in large part because of the increase in working couples who have little time or inclination for leisurely shopping. Customers can even order by telephone, which makes shopping still more convenient. The five major catalog companies are Sears, Ward, Spiegel, Aldens, and Penney. But many other retailers woo telephone and mail-order business through newspaper ads and special promotional mailers. This is especially commonplace during the Christmas season. Even nonretailers are entering this business. For example, Hallmark Cards, the noted greeting card company, put out a nationwide catalog for the 1978 Christmas season featuring women's apparel, accessories, and gifts. For 1979, it planned total mailings of 3,650,000 catalogs.[5]

Catalog retailing offers the customer the convenience of leisurely examining the catalog and ordering at home, often from a wider variety than is available in the store. For example, the Sears semiannual catalog has more than 150,000 items.

DOOR-TO-DOOR SELLING   While *door-to-door selling* is only a small part of total retail sales, it is far from dead. Actually, it seems to be growing faster than total retail sales. Precise figures are not available for this present-day successor to the old Yankee peddler, but the industry is estimated to have doubled its sales in the last five years. There are some counter-trends, however. Home delivery of milk by dairy companies has been abandoned; it is simply too costly for a low-markup item. But for goods with high markups, such as cosmetics, toiletries, encyclopedias, and specialty housewares, the potential seems to be increasing. J. C. Penney Company has trained over five hundred "decorator-consultants" to sell a complete line of home furnishings in the home.

[5] As described in "Hallmark Goes into Mail Order," *San Francisco Chronicle,* Dec. 4, 1978, p. 26.

Many furniture and department stores have rug and furniture salespeople or "home decorators" who, upon invitation, take their samples to customers' homes.

The most successful door-to-door seller in terms of profitability and sales growth is the cosmetic manufacturer-retailer, Avon Products. The relative success of its retailing strategy can be compared with that of Revlon, another aggressive cosmetic manufacturer, which sells through retail stores, particularly department stores. In the five years before 1971, Avon had achieved an annual sales growth rate of 15.1 percent, notably outstripping the 8 percent growth rate for Revlon. In recent years, the relative growth rates have reversed for the billion-dollar competitors; Avon could only achieve a five-year average sales growth of 11.1 percent from 1973 to 1978, while Revlon was averaging a sales gain of 19 percent a year.[6]

Usually, door to door is a more expensive way of selling than going through stores. It is expensive to train salespeople, and there is often a high turnover, so that recruiting and training are continual. Travel costs are involved, and perhaps a car or truck has to be furnished. But the major cost is that each salesperson can make only a limited number of contacts; therefore, the volume of sales available to cover expenses may be rather low. Despite this, the Fuller Brush representative is still around, and Tupperware parties have helped to pay many a student's way through college.

Sometimes an innovative approach to the market can be made through the door-to-door route. An example is Girl Scout cookies. Some 100 million boxes of cookies, averaging $1.25 each, are sold each year door to door by some 2.5 million Girl Scouts.

SCOPE OF RETAILING

Number of Establishments

Table 2.3 shows the number of retail establishments, their total sales volume, and the per-store sales volume. To remove the influence of inflation, these sales-volume figures are expressed in 1957–1959 dollars. It can be seen that the number of establishments remained about the same for some thirty years from 1939 to 1967, although total retail sales and sales per store both rose substantially.

Table 2.3 shows that during the years of deep depression in the

[6] As reported in "31st Annual Report on American Industry," *Forbes*, January 8, 1979, p. 100.

TABLE 2.3   NUMBER OF RETAILERS AND SALES, 1929–1972*

| | | Volume of Sales (in 1957–1959 dollars) | |
Year	Number of Establishments	Total Sales (millions)	Average Sales per Store
1929	1,476,365	$ 80,955	$ 54,834
1939	1,770,355	86,864	49,066
1948	1,769,540	155,753	88,019
1954	1,721,650	181,590	105,474
1958	1,788,325	198,258	110,862
1963	1,707,931	228,868	134,003
1967	1,763,000	280,289	164,110
1972	1,913,000	337,961	176,665

* *Note:* 1972 *Census of Retail Trade* statistics are the latest available at the time of this publication. While a Census of Retail Trade was taken in 1977, the results have still not been disseminated. However, we have no reason to think that the 1977 statistics will show appreciable change from the trend shown in this table.

Sources: U.S. Department of Commerce, Bureau of the Census, *Census of Business, Retail Trade,* 1972 (Washington, D.C.: U.S. Government Printing Office). Alaska and Hawaii are not included in figures prior to 1963.

1930s, when many businesses were going bankrupt, the number of retail firms increased substantially—to almost the highest total ever recorded before or since. How can we account for this? The answer lies in a phenomenon of retailing which accounts for its great attraction to would-be entrepreneurs and also for its great inefficiency. It is *easy to enter* retailing. Many small retail stores can be opened with a minimum of investment and experience. The able and ambitious as well as those seeking a "last resort" may attempt to start a retail business. During the depression years of the 1930s, many who lost their jobs invested whatever money they had accumulated in retail ventures in the hope of maintaining a means of livelihood.

Relative Importance of Retail Firms

Table 2.4 shows retail sales by type of firm, as designated by the U.S. Census, for the last several decades. While all categories of firms

TABLE 2.4   RETAIL SALES BY SELECTED TYPE OF FIRM, 1948, 1958, 1967, 1977

Type of Outlet*	Sales (billions)			
	1948	1958	1967	1977
Food	$ 29.2	$ 49.2	$ 70.3	$156.3
Automotive	20.1	31.9	55.6	143.7
Filling stations	6.5	14.2	22.7	56.5
Eating and drinking places	10.6	15.3	23.8	63.8
Apparel and accessory stores	9.7	12.6	16.7	33.5
Department stores	9.4	13.4	32.3	71.6
Lumber and building materials group	11.1	14.3	17.2	38.0
Furniture and appliance stores	6.6	10.1	14.5	34.5
Variety stores	2.5	3.6	5.4	8.0
Drug and proprietary stores	4.0	6.8	10.9	22.4
Main order (department store merchandise)			2.7	6.8
TOTAL (in nonconstant dollars)	128.8	200.4	310.2	708.3

* U.S. census definitions

Sources: Census of Retail Trade, 1972. Alaska and Hawaii are not included in figures prior to 1967. Figures for 1977 are from the *Statistical Abstract of the United States,* 1978, p. 841.

increased their sales during this period, the relative importance of the automobile in our economy is particularly noteworthy. Automotive-group sales, and the related sales of the filling station group, accounted for 28 percent of all retail sales in 1975, up from 20 percent in 1948. The importance of food retailers is also evident, as they accounted for 22.5 percent of total retail sales in 1975.

Table 2.5 shows how the top twenty business firms in the United States rank by sales. Four of the twenty largest firms are retailers, although no retail firm approaches the size of General Motors, Exxon, Ford, or American Telephone & Telegraph.

Table 2.6 shows the rank by dollar profits of the six most profitable retail firms. The profitability of retailers appears to compare rather badly with that in other industries. Sears, the most profitable retailer,

TABLE 2.5   TWENTY LARGEST U.S. CORPORATIONS BY SALES, 1978

Rank	Company	1978 Sales (millions)
1	General Motors	$63,221
2	Exxon	60,333
3	Ford Motor	42,784
4	American Telephone & Telegraph	40,993
5	Mobil	34,736
6	Texaco	28,608
7	Sears, Roebuck	23,486
8	Standard Oil of California	23,232
9	IBM	21,076
10	General Electric	19,654
11	International Telephone & Telegraph	19,399
12	Gulf Oil	18,069
13	Standard Oil of Indiana	14,961
14	Chrysler	13,618
15	Safeway Stores	12,551
16	Atlantic Richfield	12,298
17	K mart	11,813
18	Shell Oil	11,063
19	U.S. Steel	11,050
20	J. C. Penney	10,845

Source: Forbes, May 14, 1979, pp. 234–235. Reprinted by permission of FORBES Magazine from the May 14, 1979 issue.

ranks only 10th among all firms. Safeway, the most profitable food retailer, ranks 15th among all firms in sales, but is only 144th in dollar profits.

This suggests that retailing is not very profitable, compared to other kinds of business. But the relatively poor profit performance of retailers is not quite as negative as it might appear. Investment required in retail stores, their fixtures, and goods for sale is usually not nearly as great as the investment required for manufacturing firms. Therefore, the important measure of profitability, the return on investment, is more favorable for retailers.

TABLE 2.6   RANKS OF TOP SIX RETAIL FIRMS IN DOLLAR PROFITS, 1978

Rank in Profitability Among All Business Firms	Retailer	Net Profits (millions)
10	Sears, Roebuck	$906
43	K mart	344
60	J. C. Penney	276
62	Dayton Hudson	265
97	Federated Department Stores	198
144	Safeway Stores	146

Source: Forbes, May 14, 1979, pp. 240–247. Reprinted by permission of FORBES Magazine from the May 14, 1979 issue.

The true measure of the profitability of any investment is the *return on investment*—the interest, dividends, or profits we get for the money invested. This is true whether the money is in a savings and loan association paying 5 percent interest or in a business where it may realize more. But note that in the examples below return on investment is not the same as net profit as a percentage of sales.

Retailer		Manufacturer	
Sales	$10,000,000	Sales	$10,000,000
Investment in store, fixtures and merchandise	2,000,000	Investment in plant, equipment, raw materials, and goods in various stages of completion	10,000,000
Net profit percent of sales	5	Net profit percent of sales	10
Net profit dollars	500,000	Net profit dollars	1,000,000
Return on investment	$\dfrac{500,000}{2,000,000} = 25\%$	Return on investment	$\dfrac{1,000,000}{10,000,000} = 10\%$

In this example, the retail operation is much more profitable, despite its lower net profit, since the money invested in the retail business is much less than that required for the manufacturer.

CHANGES IN RETAIL INSTITUTIONS

In this chapter, we have described how the major types of retail institutions evolved in the United States. For an explanation of why these changes occurred in modes of retailing, let us first examine the *wheel of retailing* theory. Despite certain flaws and exceptions, this theory does account for most of the important changes that have taken place. As we shall see, it also suggests possible emerging opportunities.

In this section we will also discuss the retail-life-cycle theory, a more recent view of how retailing changes, and scrambled merchandizing, an important trend in the current development of retailing.

FIGURE 2.1 ENTRY AND MOVEMENT OF DEPARTMENT STORES AND DISCOUNT STORES ON THE WHEEL OF RETAILING

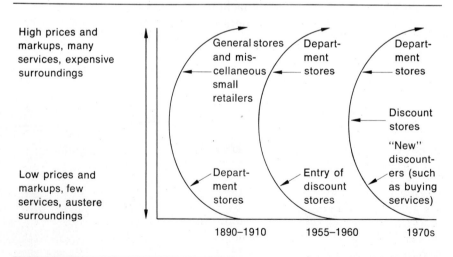

If the wheel is considered to be turning slowly clockwise in the direction of the arrow, then the department stores around 1900, and the discounters later, came on the scene at the low end of the wheel. As it turned slowly, they moved with it, becoming higher-price operations, and at the same time leaving room for lower-price types of firms to gain entry at the low end of the wheel.

The Wheel of Retailing

New types of retail firms may enter the marketplace as low-status, low-markup, low-price operations. However, as they become successful, they open more elaborate stores and offer more services. As a result, their costs grow and they have to charge higher prices. In turn, they also become vulnerable to new low-status, low-markup, low-price retailers, and the cycle begins again. Figure 2.1 shows this cycle for department stores and discount stores.

The theory accounts for the entry of discount stores in the late 1950s and 1960s and for the coming of supermarkets in the 1930s. Further back, in the late 1800s and early 1900s, the development of department stores, mail-order houses, and the various kinds of chain stores can be explained by the theory.

On the other hand, vending machines, which generally have higher costs and higher selling prices than other retail operations, are not explained by this theory; nor are *convenience food stores,* those "junior supermarkets," which are small, easily accessible, and open long hours. These stores afford convenience of place, hours open, and quickness of shopping. They have grown from 500 in 1957 to over 27,500 in 1977, though they offer prices substantially higher than those in nearby stores. The success of vending machines and of these convenience food stores shows that many consumers today are willing to pay a higher price for ease of shopping.[7]

RETAIL CONTROVERSY—How Much is Convenience Worth?

We, as consumers, usually pay more for convenience, whether it be the instant cake mix, the pack of cigarettes from a vending machine, or the food purchased at a convenience food store. But how much more are we willing to pay for convenience? 10 percent? 20 percent? 33 percent? 50 percent? even more?

How much more are you willing to pay for the cold beer or soft drink at the ball game on a hot afternoon?

[7] "Convenience Stores: A $7.4 Billion Mushroom," from the March 21, 1977 issue of BusinessWeek, pp. 61–64. © 1977 by McGraw-Hill, Inc., New York, NY 10020. All rights reserved.

How much more are you willing to pay for a loaf of bread, a six-pack of pop, and some ice cream at a nearby convenience food store, to avoid going to a more distant supermarket with longer checkout lines?

There has been no definitive research that we know of to determine at what point consumers will resist higher prices and forgo convenience. Undoubtedly, this varies according to the individual, the occasion (the hot afternoon at the ball park), and the product.

We do know this: in its 7,600 stores the largest convenience-food-store chain, 7-Eleven, charges prices 25 percent, or more, above nearby supermarkets'. And it has boosted its sales from $179 million in 1961 to $3 billion in 1978, with profits soaring 20 percent annually. The president of the firm comments, "We have a reputation for being so damned high in price that when people come in, they simply expect to pay more."

Sources: "The Threat to Southland's Growth," from the October 28, 1972 issue of BusinessWeek, pp. 60–62; "Convenience Stores: A $7.4 Billion Mushroom," from the March 21, 1977 issue of BusinessWeek, pp. 61–64; "Southland: Moving Downtown with its 7-Eleven Stores," from the October 30, 1978 issue of BusinessWeek, pp. 180–185; and "Despite High Prices and Sparse Selection, 7-Eleven Stores Thrive," *Wall Street Journal,* May 1, 1979, pp. 1 and 17.

For Thought and Discussion

1. How much more are *you* willing to pay for convenience?
2. Do you think a tolerance of higher prices would increase as you became more affluent? Why or why not?

Does this apparent flaw in the wheel of retailing theory make it invalid today? Not at all. As most discount stores evolve into higher-cost operations, the way is opened for other modes of retailing. Not all of these are new. *Warehouse retailing,* for example, has been around for a long time. In the 1930s it was a predecessor of the supermarket, and in the 1940s and early 1950s it was an early form of discount store. Today, warehouse stores are increasing again, in such fields as foods, furniture, carpeting, appliances, building materials, and even toys. Lower costs resulting from low-rent, isolated buildings and sparse customer service yield customer savings, for example, 10 to 15 percent on grocery bills.[8] Four rather different types of retail institutions are also entering the wheel at the low-price end: group buying services,

[8] As reported in "Fisher Foods Turns 10 Stores into 'No-Frills' Facilities," *Wall Street Journal,* January 18, 1979, p. 2.

limited-assortment food stores (which may also be warehouse stores), hypermarkets, and discount-catalog showrooms.

GROUP BUYING ORGANIZATIONS   United Buying Service Corporation (UBS) is the largest group buying organization. Group buying gives individual consumers the price advantages that only large customers, such as car rental companies, formerly had. UBS guarantees a seller a certain volume of sales; in return, the seller agrees to sell to UBS members at a price just enough over cost to make a profit. Besides cars, a variety of other products are handled—cameras, stereos, kitchen appliances, furs, furniture—some 10,000 items in all.

LIMITED-ASSORTMENT FOOD STORES   These are "bare bones" operations that are able to offer customers significantly lower prices. They are similar to warehouse stores, but are usually smaller; some 8,000 to 9,000 square feet, compared to typical supermarket sizes of 25,000 to 30,000 square feet. Their unique strategy is to offer a greatly reduced assortment of merchandise. For example, the average store may contain fewer than 600 items, in contrast to the 8,000 to 10,000 handled by the typical supermarket. Thereby, inventory costs are substantially reduced. Customers are usually required to bring bags and pack their own groceries. Other cost savings result from eliminating individual-item pricing, check cashing, and frilly equipment and fixtures. It is estimated that limited-assortment stores numbered over 500 in 1979, almost double those operating in 1978.[9] The best known stores of this type are Jewel Company's Jewel-T stores and Kroger's Buy-Lo stores.

HYPERMARKETS   Also called hypermarche, the hypermarket handles both food and general merchandise, and is, essentially, a combination of supermarket, discount store, and warehouse. Hypermarkets were introduced in this country from Europe, along with the idea of stocking merchandise in huge stacks at prices 10 to 15 percent below normal retail prices. They emphasize great sales volume and try to offer the lowest possible prices. A merchandise assortment limited only to top-demand items (called cherry picking), together with their no-frills approach, aroused glowing predictions of success for hypermarkets in the United States.[10] However, to date, U.S. consumers have not responded well to the hypermarket concept.

[9] For more detail, see "Limited-Assortment Stores," *Marketing News,* December 29, 1978, pp. 1 and 3.
[10] See, for example, "An Overview: Europe's Hypermarkets," *Discount Store News,* December 10, 1973, p. 6; and E. B. Weiss, "Department Stores and Hypermarche Competition," *Stores* (June 1974), 40.

DISCOUNT-CATALOG SHOW ROOMS   In contrast to hypermarkets, *discount-catalog show rooms* have been one of the hottest trends in retailing today. These discount catalogers have comfortable show rooms that give customers the chance to look and touch before buying. The catalogs feature top-of-the-line, branded merchandise and concentrate on items with traditionally high markups, such as jewelry, gifts, luggage, cameras, and small appliances. There is little or no newspaper advertising, and pilferage rates are low. As a result, the new discounters can offer better prices than conventional discounters can. Best Products Company is the largest firm in this field and has some 15,000 nationally advertised products. Twenty years ago, the forerunner of Best was a small, wholesale, mail-order school-book business in Richmond, Virginia. Then came the idea of setting up a small display at the warehouse and opening it to the public. By 1978 Best had 53 stores doing business of $526 million in a growing industry worth nearly $6 billion.[11]

The Retail Life Cycle

Not as widely known as the wheel of retailing theory are a number of other theories regarding changes in retail institutions. Most of these are beyond the scope of this book. However, a recent view of changes in retailing observes that retail institutions have a life cycle—from birth to growth to maturity to decline—just as products have. This *retail life cycle* has four phases:[12]

1. Innovation—to improve price and convenience, or create other advantages that differ sharply from the past
2. Accelerated growth—with rapid increases in sales, but with cost pressures occurring near the end of the period
3. Maturity—during which competitive inroads occur from other forms of retailing
4. Decline—which sometimes can be avoided by a shift of strategy or emphasis

[11] For more detail on the rise of Best Products Company, as well as on the future promise of catalog-showroom merchandising, see "I Can Get It For You Wholesale," *Forbes,* September 4, 1978, pp. 47–51.
[12] William R. Davidson, Albert D. Bates, and Stephen J. Bass, "The Retail Life Cycle," *Harvard Business Review* (November-December 1976), 89–96.

The retail life cycle today may well be getting shorter as competition becomes more aggressive and innovative. Consequently, we may expect to see more institutional changes in the future.[13]

Scrambled Merchandising

Scrambled merchandising is the prevalent practice among firms of adding nontraditional lines of merchandise (usually with a higher markup and profit) to their regular assortments. Thus, in the supermarket, a wide assortment of nonfood items may be carried, ranging from toys, housewares, and health and beauty aids, to pantyhose. Many drugstores now stock cameras, hardware, auto accessories, jewelry, even camping equipment and lawn furniture. The oil companies are adding convenience food stores to gas stations. Many stores today are taking on the characteristics of the old general store, stocking all manner of unrelated merchandise under one roof.

Scrambled merchandising poses an interesting set of management problems. Competition among the various types of retailers tends to increase. For example, a hardware store, the traditional source for lawn supplies such as grass seed and fertilizer, now faces competition from variety stores, supermarkets, discount stores, drugstores, and even convenience food stores and gasoline stations. It is also becoming difficult for a store to maintain its individuality and to have a loyal group of customers.

The newest wave of scrambled merchandising is to add services rather than product categories. For example, in Peoples Drug Stores, a 375-store operation in nine Eastern states, customers now can draw money from an automatic check-cashing machine, take a blood pressure test, or pick up a frozen dinner. The addition of services has successfully repositioned faltering retailers as neighborhood-oriented convenience health-care and food centers.[14]

---

[13] On the other hand, some researchers predict less change. They contend that stores currently tend to maintain a permanent position in their environment as they evolve into more traditional types of retailers, thus restricting opportunities for new retail enterprises. See Dillard B. Tinsley, John R. Brooks Jr., and Michael d'Amico, "Will the Wheel of Retailing Stop Turning?" *Akron Business and Economic Review* (Summer 1978), 26–29.

[14] "Peoples Drug: Adding Services to Keep a Recovery Going," from the January 22, 1979 issue of BusinessWeek, pp. 72–73. © 1979 by McGraw-Hill, Inc., New York, NY 10020. All rights reserved.

THE SEARCH FOR DIFFERENTIAL ADVANTAGE

A *differential advantage* occurs when a firm has achieved some degree of distinctiveness from its competitors. This may result from the particular location, the services offered, the brands and product mix carried, special customers appealed to, or some other characteristics. (Appeal to special customers or market "segments" will be discussed in greater detail in Chapter 5.) Every retailer wants to be reasonably secure from competition. Most successful retailers today have achieved a differential advantage, whether by accident or through careful appraisal of market opportunities. To the extent that such an advantage can be achieved, the firm is insulated from competition.

Some stores have consciously sought to appeal to a particular type of customer, one who was ignored or overlooked by most retailers. Lane Bryant successfully achieved a competitive advantage by emphasizing custom-sized clothing for women who had trouble finding their sizes in other stores. Less successful retailers have not been able to develop a distinctive image. They may have been poor imitators. Or they may have scattered their efforts, rather than focusing on a single image or single type of customer.

■ Summary

The marketplace is complex. There is room for many different kinds of retailers to prosper; some do not even need stores. This diversity reflects the variety of goods and services wanted by customers. That is, some want convenience in shopping, others are more concerned with lowest prices, while still other consumers will patronize those stores offering the greatest range of choice.

In the past, the retail environment has witnessed significant changes in the types of retail institutions. Some of the innovations, such as discount stores and supermarkets, have caused consternation among other retailers. The retail scene is still changing today, though not on such a massive scale as in the past. But the search for differential advantage is yielding enough change to show that the retail environment is dynamic and offers ample opportunity for those who can find new ways of satisfying customers. Despite the competition of large firms, small businesses still find opportunities. The next chapter will focus specifically on the problems and opportunities in small retailing.

■ **Key Terms**

Catalog retailing	Retail life cycle
Consumer cooperatives	Return on investment
Convenience food stores	Scrambled merchandising
Department stores	Shopping incentives
Differential advantage	Specialty stores
Discount-catalog show rooms	Supermarkets
Discount stores	Vending machines
Door-to-door selling	Warehouse retailing
Leased departments	Wheel of retailing
Nonstore retailing	

■ **Discussion Questions**

1. Is a store or place of business essential to retailing? Why or why not?
2. What are some ways that a retailer can appeal to a customer's desire for convenience?
3. Is it likely that a store can appeal to customers through both lowest prices and widest assortments of merchandise? Through lowest prices and convenience?
4. Why are department and discount stores willing to lease certain of their departments to outsiders?
5. Contrast a specialty store and a department store. Can a specialty store be part of a chain?
6. During the depression of the 1930s, when many businesses were going bankrupt, the number of retail firms increased substantially. How do you explain this phenomenon?
7. What induces discounters to go to more elaborate and higher-cost operations? Do you know of any that have not done so? What do you think has kept them from following the trend?
8. What is scrambled merchandising? Why is it so prevalent today?
9. Discuss some ways in which a store can make itself distinctive and gain a differential advantage.

■ **Project**

Visit two chain and two independent stores; each pair should carry the same types of merchandise, for instance, one chain food store and one

independent food store. Compare and evaluate the chains and independents as to:

Employees' courtesy and product knowledge
Attractiveness and neatness of merchandise and displays
Freshness of stock
Customer traffic
Your general impressions of their efficiency and profitability

What conclusions do you draw from these comparisons?

■ Exercise in Creativity

How many products do you think might be successfully retailed door to
door? What are some that would be impossible to merchandise in this
way? What do you conclude are the characteristics a product has to
have if door-to-door selling is to be successful? (Try to think of nontraditional products, rather than those, such as brushes, cosmetics, and
encyclopedias, that are commonly sold door to door.)

■ Retailing in Action

A friend, Jason Trye, owns a small camera store near the campus. He is
an expert photographer, but lately he has not been faring well with his
business. He blames declining sales on a new K mart discount store that
recently opened on the outskirts of town and has a camera department
offering merchandise at discount prices.

"I just can't compete with them on prices since they're able to buy in
such large volume. It seems that all my customers come in to have me
explain the features of the various cameras. But then they don't buy
here; they go over to K mart," Jason ruefully explained.

Jason asks for your advice. How can his independent camera store
compete against the large, price-cutting retailer?

3   Self-Employment Prospects

In Chapter 1 we touched briefly on the opportunities in self-employment. Usually we think of self-employment and small business as synonymous. Even highly successful self-employment enterprises are small when compared with corporate giants. But one, two, or three generations ago, the largest firms were small businesses started, perhaps, by either a single entrepreneur or a partnership. As the businesses prospered and grew, they incorporated, and eventually they became the major firms we know today. In this chapter, we will take a more in-depth look at the opportunities and the risks in self-employment; we will also investigate a major franchising trend, encouraging self-employment.

AN EXAMPLE OF SELF-EMPLOYMENT— CHALLENGES AND ACCOMPLISHMENTS

To begin, let's examine in some detail how a young couple decided to start their own store, how they struggled through the early months, and how they achieved the great satisfaction of developing a prospering enterprise. The problems they encountered, the lessons they learned, and the significant payoff are applicable to many other small retail ventures.

Ted Creighton was an instrumental-music teacher in a Cleveland elementary school. He was also a runner. With declining enrollments and tight school budgets, teaching in many places is becoming frustrating. Because of this, or perhaps because Ted was just ready for a change, he decided to go into business for himself. And he correctly assessed the mushrooming popularity of running as a national pastime. Thus, in September 1976 he began planning to open a store specializing in running shoes and other paraphernalia for runners. He found a small shop to rent for $175 a month in an older commercial area along a busy suburban street.

Ted had no business experience. However, he read all the books on small business management he could find in the public libraries and at the Small Business Administration (SBA) office. He also attended several months of clinics and workshops sponsored by the SBA. His biggest problem, however, was obtaining the necessary financing. He and his wife, Linda, had $2,000 in savings to use, but Ted believed that he should have $5,000 more for inventory and fixtures. The SBA would not help him with financing, and five banks turned him down, saying that this type of business was too seasonal and without sufficient sustained potential. Finally a bank in the vicinity of his proposed store, desiring to reduce vacant storefronts in the area, lent him the money.

On February 19, 1977, the store was opened in the midst of one of the coldest and snowiest winters in Cleveland history. Ted called the store The Complete Runner. Ted continued to work as a teacher, getting to the store about midafternoon. Linda, by placing their two small children in nursery school, was able to run the store until Ted arrived.

The small enterprise encountered problems right from the start. Ted soon discovered that he was seriously undercapitalized; he had started on too much of a "shoestring." He should have tried to borrow more money. He had to turn down the opportunity to carry one important and popular brand of shoes, Nike, because he simply could not finance the additional inventory. For all of 1977 he struggled with supply problems and was often unable to get enough shoes to meet the ever-increasing demand. Ted's assessment of the boom in running was proving correct, and the manufacturers of running shoes simply were not able to produce enough. As a small and very new retailer, The Complete Runner was at the bottom of the list for preferential treatment. Delivery of some orders took six months.

Still, sales were improving. Ted, a dedicated runner himself, participated in all the local running events. He began sponsoring and supervising bimonthly "fun runs" in nearby parks. He gave special merchandise discounts to members of running clubs. His little store became the center for up-to-date information on area running activities.

More and more people became interested in running; the popularity of running was certainly evident from the sales of *The Complete Book of Running,* by James Fixx, which was number one nationally on the nonfiction best-seller list for month after month. As more women became interested in running, Linda helped organize Cleveland Women Running, a club that met weekly for running and other activities. And permeating the entire operation of the store was the personal and knowledgeable treatment that Ted and Linda were able to give their customers. This was most valuable in the fitting of shoes (the pounding that feet take in running makes the correct fitting and choice of footwear of paramount importance). Customers also appreciated knowledgeable advice about the purchase of other running gear.

Throughout 1977, the Creightons took no money from the store; they plowed back everything they made into stock. By January 1, 1978, the original inventory of less than $7,000 had grown to $35,000. Sales for the first year of operation reached $70,000: $20,000 more than the Creightons' most optimistic forecasts. Net profit was $12,000, or 17 percent of sales. By spring 1978 weekly sales were averaging $4,000, and Ted could project sales for the full year of $150,000 to $175,000. Fearful that other competitors would enter the growing market, he opened another store, on the other side of town, in April 1978 and was able to stock it with $20,000 of inventory. In June 1978 Ted left the teaching profession to devote full time to his growing enterprise.

Several things can be noted from this example of a successful small-business venture. First, while Ted Creighton had no experience in small-business management, he tried hard to become as familiar with it as he could by reading books and attending seminars conducted by the SBA.[1]

Second, while Ted made one of the more common mistakes of

---

[1] For a guide to sources of information on small business ownership, see Joseph C. Schabacker, *Small Business Information Sources* (Milwaukee: University of Wisconsin, National Council for Small Business Management Development, 1976).

beginning entrepreneurs—undercapitalization—he was able to overcome this rather quickly. Inadequate stock probably delayed his potential growth by six months, but his business did well enough to enable him, with time, to build up an adequate inventory. Since Ted still had an income from teaching, he and Linda needed none of the store's profits for personal living expenses. Consequently, all of it could be reinvested in the business.

Third, Ted had a regular job to fall back on in case of failure and could afford to face the risks encountered in the crucial early days of a business. Ted did not give up his teaching job until the success of the business seemed assured.

Fourth, any business, but particularly a small business, has a better chance of prospering if it can offer something unique to prospective customers. The Complete Runner excelled in the difficult art of meeting the needs of runners; it became the meeting place for runners, the place to find out about running clubs, about area races, about the newest techniques and products for serious runners.

Finally, Ted recognized an emerging trend—the jogging boom—and capitalized on it. Rapid growth resulted.

Small businesses do succeed without meeting all of the above conditions. However, as we will see in the following sections, many others fail because of ill-conceived ventures, inadequate experience, and insufficient financial resources.

VIABILITY OF SMALL RETAILERS

While there are many small retailers, large firms dominate and are becoming more powerful. Figure 3.1 shows the decreasing percentage, since 1929, of small retail stores (defined as having annual sales under $100,000) in proportion to total retail stores and total retail sales. In 1939, almost 97 percent of all retail stores were small retailers; by 1972 (the last year for which we have reliable statistics at the time of publication), only 59 percent of all stores were small ones. But the trend is even more striking when one looks at total retail sales. In 1939, small retailers accounted for almost 58 percent of all retail sales; by 1972 small retailers made only 8.5 percent of total retail sales. Obviously, big firms today do the bulk of retail trade. (While the increasing dominance of the big firm is unmistakable, we should note that these comparisons are not quite as bleak for small retailers as they at first appear. Because of inflation, a $100,000 small retailer today is much smaller than twenty, thirty, or fifty years ago.)

FIGURE 3.1 PROPORTION OF SMALL RETAILERS (ANNUAL SALES
            UNDER $100,000) TO TOTAL RETAIL STORES AND SALES

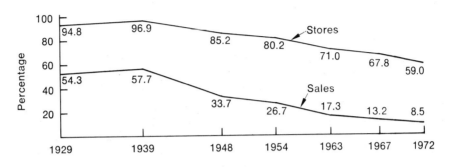

Source: U.S. Census of Business, Retail Trade for years indicated

Table 3.1 shows sales by size of establishment. Here we can see that, at the time of the census, there were still many more small retailers than large ones. Over 516,000 or 30.2 percent of all retail stores had sales of less than $30,000, even though this same 30.2 percent produced only 1.6 percent of total retail sales.

High Mortality of Small Retailers

Many underfinanced, poorly qualified people enter retailing and fail. Over half of all business failures are retailers, particularly those with the smallest sales volumes and those in the first two or three years of operation. Table 3.2 shows the age of retail establishments that failed in 1974.

Once again let us emphasize the fundamental reason for retailers' vulnerability to failure: small retailing is the easiest business field to enter. Financial requirements are minimal for certain "mom and pop" operations (even Ted Creighton could start what was later to become a thriving business with a mere $2,000 of personal capital and $5,000 of borrowed funds), and the belief persists that anyone can run a restaurant or grocery store. Ease of entrance entices both the able and ambitious, and the incompetent and desperate, to embrace retail business ownership.

The direct causes of failure range from lack of experience with the product or service being offered, to lack of well-rounded managerial

TABLE 3.1   RETAIL SALES BY SIZE OF STORE, 1972*

Size of Store (annual sales)	Stores		Sales Volume	
	Number (thousands)	Percent-age of Total	Sales (millions)	Percent-age of Total
$1,000,000 and more	74	4.3	$224,597	52.5
$500,000–$999,999	71	4.2	48,823	11.4
$100,000–$499,999	556	32.5	118,221	27.6
$30,000–$99,999	492	28.8	29,326	6.9
$29,999 and less	516	30.2	6,673	1.6

* *Note:* The 1972 *Census of Retail Trade* statistics are the latest available at the time of publication. While a Census of Retail Trade was taken in 1977, the results have not been disseminated at this time. We think it reasonable to expect that the 1977 statistics will show small retailers having declined still further in importance.

Source: Census of Retail Trade, 1972.

TABLE 3.2   AGE OF RETAIL FIRMS THAT FAILED IN 1974

Age	Percentage
One year or less	2.1
Two years	16.1
Three years	22.3
Total three years or less	40.5
Four years	15.6
Five years	10.1
Six years	6.1
Seven years	4.4
Eight years	3.1
Nine years	2.8
Ten years	2.0

Source: The Business Failure Record, 1974 (New York: DUN AND BRADSTREET, INC., Business Economics Department, 1975), p. 10.

experience, to simple incompetence. Such flaws usually manifest themselves in inadequate and undercontrolled financial records. Diminishing cash, declining sales, excessive inventory, increasing uncollectible customer accounts, and mounting debt are thus neglected by management. Small businesses often keep poor records and overlook the importance of sound accounting practices. The presence of inadequate and untrained personnel partly explain this. Another reason is that the accounting operation is performed after the fact, and the daily grind of managing other phases of the operation may seem more important.

RETAIL CONTROVERSY—*Should Small Entrepreneurship Be Restricted to the Able and Experienced?*

We know that most businesses fail because inexperienced, unqualified people undertake marginal ventures. Their failure is both an economic cost to society and an emotional blow to themselves and their families. Should government screen would-be entrepreneurs or impose standards (perhaps financial, educational, and experiential) to lessen the chance of business failure?

Pro

Would eliminate most marginal businesses and reduce business failures.

Would make marketing and retailing more efficient, and perhaps result in lower, more competitive prices and better-satisfied customers.

Con

Would arbitrarily deny opportunity to those who could not meet the standards.

Might increase the welfare burden since some marginal businesses at least provide a living for those not otherwise employable.

Would involve the government in greater control and would flaw the free-enterprise system.

For Thought and Discussion

1. Can you think of any other pros and cons on this issue?
2. How would you vote on imposing standards and limitations on entrepreneurship? Why?

Relationship of Small Firms to Large Firms

How can small retailers survive? We tend to be awed by the power and efficiency of large organizations. But this can be a mistake. Smaller firms, whether retailers or producers, have a freedom and flexibility of action that no large firm has. Furthermore, as noted in Chapter 1, many large organizations have difficulty coping with major change. The small, hungry firm can lead in innovative approaches to retailing, as did the discount store, and the supermarket before that. Thus, while large organizations may have certain advantages because of their size and the availability of capital, smaller firms also have advantages because of their size and their lower overhead. Consider the advantages and disadvantages of small retail businesses as compared to larger firms.

Small retailers can have the following advantages over their larger counterparts:

1. Growth potential is greater because a successful small operation may have a virtually boundless market. It can expand in size or through additional outlets. Almost all large retailers had humble beginnings, sometimes only one or a few generations ago.

This small, imaginative retail business caters to a market that developed only a few years ago, but is now very lively. Success in entrepreneurship can come from being the first to anticipate changing customer needs. (Cambridge Alternative Power Co., Inc.)

2. More flexibility is possible, since advantageous changes in policy and operational procedures can be made quickly. The larger firm is usually restrained by red tape and SOP (standard operating procedures).

3. Close contact with customers affords the small retailer better opportunities for assessing market demand.

4. The personalized service that can come from the small retailer–customer relationship is attractive to many consumers who are put off by the impersonality of large firms.

5. The small firm can have certain cost advantages over larger competitors. Family members may contribute time. There is no need for a large staff.

6. Not the least of the advantages is the entrepreneur's total commitment; typically, the economic future of entrepreneurs, the education of their children, and the well-being of their families, are vitally linked to the success of their businesses. This leads to a level of commitment hard to duplicate in any form of hired management.

However, the small firm also faces these serious disadvantages:

1. Costs of acquiring merchandise are frequently higher, since small retailers cannot purchase on a large scale.

2. Small firms are often financially vulnerable. Even when enough money is available to meet normal needs, it may be insufficient for small firms to take advantage of cash discounts, special purchase opportunities, expansion possibilities, and the like. Loans are usually more difficult to obtain and tend to be available only at higher rates than for larger businesses.

3. Specialized managerial aids, such as marketing research, computer access, and detailed record keeping, are less possible because of more limited resources. There may even be a lack of general managerial ability.

4. Lack of resources often limits promotional efforts to circulars, display signs, or inconspicuous newspaper advertisements, which are less effective than more expensive methods.

5. The small firm that wants to expand often has difficulty obtaining the able trainees and executives needed to do so. Larger firms, with formalized training programs and good reputations, are usually more attractive, even though they sometimes pay less.

Now let's look at an important tool of analysis for persons contemplating a new venture.

RETAILING TOOL—*The Break-Even Analysis*

The *break-even analysis* is valuable in making go/no go decisions about new stores, new products, and new strategies. It is useful in determining which of several alternative decisions is best. It is highly recommended for assessing the wisdom of opening a new business at a specific site and time. A break-even analysis can be shown graphically as follows:

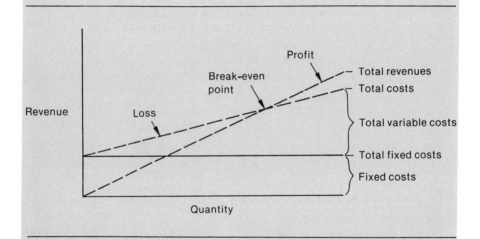

Below the break-even point, the venture suffers losses; above it, the venture becomes profitable.

Example   You are contemplating going into business for yourself. You have found a location that you can rent for $500 a month; an investigation of probable utility charges suggests that they should average $300 a month. You estimate that salaries, supplies, and miscellaneous expenses should cost about $70,000 for the first year. Interest on the loans you can procure for remodeling, for the necessary furniture and fixtures, and for inventory requirements will total $7,000 a year. You think you should be able to do about $150,000 in sales the first year. Information gathered from potential suppliers indicates that your markup will average 40 percent of your selling prices. Based on these estimates and figures, should you open this business at this time and place?

$$\textit{Formula} \text{ Break-even point} = \frac{\text{Total fixed costs}}{\text{average margin or markup percentage}}$$

Fixed costs

$500 × 12 =	$6,000	rent
$300 × 12 =	3,600	utilities
	7,000	interest on loans
	70,000	other expenses
	$86,600	total fixed costs

$$\text{Sales needed to breakeven} = \frac{\$86,600}{.40} = \$216,500$$

With sales estimated at $150,000, your prospective new venture will incur a substantial loss that will probably force it into bankruptcy. Furthermore, in planning fixed costs, you made no provision for advertising or other promotional efforts, which would probably be necessary to gain initial customer interest. Advertising and promotional efforts would, of course, add to the fixed costs.

Now, you can see some problems with this analysis. While the costs may be fairly well estimated, the 40 percent margin is harder to forecast without prior experience in this type of business. Especially troublesome is the estimate of sales, which the prudent would-be entrepreneur should approach conservatively.

Therefore, while break-even analysis does not remove all the problems and risks from these decisions, it does permit a systematic evaluation of profit consequences given certain reasonable conditions. As such, it can be a valuable tool indeed.

For Thought and Discussion

1. In the above example, estimate that sales will increase to $250,000 if you commit $10,000 to advertising and promotion. Should you then decide to go or not go?
2. Does a new business venture have to break even or make a profit for the first year to be worth going into? Discuss.
3. In the above example, did you have any other alternatives?
4. How would you go about making an estimate of sales for a new business venture such as this? Be as specific as you can.

Defenses of Small Retailers

Four defenses or competitive responses are available to small retailers attempting to compete effectively against larger firms:

1. Help from trade associations
2. Assistance programs of wholesalers
3. Wholesaler-retailer cooperative and voluntary chains
4. Franchising

We will briefly describe the first three and then look at franchising in more detail.

TRADE ASSOCIATIONS   A *trade association* is a group of firms with common business interests that meets to discuss problems, shares operating and market information, and sometimes attempts to influence public opinion and legislation in its favor. Some trade associations are powerful lobbying bodies: an example is the National Association of Food Chains, which often speaks for the supermarket industry.

Other trade associations are composed mainly of small firms that benefit from contact with other, progressive firms (who are noncompeting since they are not nearby) and from management aids that can be provided under the auspices of the association. Sometimes there is an opportunity for group purchasing of store supplies and display material. In general, the small retailer can benefit from exposure to similar firms with similar problems. Even small retailers, when united, can exert influence on suppliers and legislators. They can also sponsor certain marketing research efforts, which none could afford to do alone.

ASSISTANCE PROGRAMS   Wholesalers, and occasionally manufacturers, have found it advantageous to offer *assistance programs* to retailers. Usually, these have been geared to small retailers, since big retailers typically mistrust the advice of wholesalers. (Often they test the profit feasibility of bypassing wholesalers altogether.) Sometimes wholesaler representatives help in setting up displays, providing signs, taking inventory, and training retail salesclerks. Some wholesalers' salespeople have even been called counselors. Relationships between wholesalers and small retail customers can be mutually beneficial and frequently turn into long-lasting associations.

COOPERATIVE AND VOLUNTARY CHAINS   Cooperative and voluntary chains have more formal types of affiliations with wholesalers. Retailers may band together to form retailer-owned *cooperative chains*. The independent retailers involved may set up their own wholesaling organizations or find wholesalers to work with them, thereby more effectively matching corporate-chain prices. This is most common in the food industry, where Associated Grocers and Certified Grocers are the largest such associations.

Wholesalers most frequently sponsor affiliations of small retailers. These *voluntary chains* usually involve contractual arrangements under which the wholesaler and a number of retailers agree to coordinate their operations, usually under a common name and operational format. The wholesalers provide various services, including advertising aids, accounting records, store location research, and layout plans; they may even furnish field supervisors. With the combined buying power thus obtained, prices can be competitive with corporate chains. Sometimes the association may even market items under its own private brand, such as IGA (Independent Grocers Alliance) and Super Valu. Other examples of wholesaler-sponsored chains are Ace Hardware and some Western Auto, Rexall, Walgreen, and Gamble stores.[2]

FRANCHISING

While franchising is not new, it has grown prodigiously in the last fifteen years. *Franchising* is a contractual arrangement in which the franchisor extends to independent franchisees the right to conduct a certain kind of business according to a particular format.

This definition may sound like the voluntary chains described in the last section. Franchising is somewhat different, however, in that voluntary chains tend to work with existing retailers, whereas franchisors prefer to work with new entrepreneurs whom they train and get established.

The three basic types of franchising arrangements that have developed, and some well-known examples of each, are described below. You can see how important it is that all franchised outlets be readily identifiable as members of the group and have a common trade name. Without such rigid adherence to a successfully developed format, a McDonald's franchisee, for example, could gain little from the customer acceptance of the product mix, the cleanliness, and the fast service developed from exposure to other McDonald's stands. Similarly, unless the franchisor institutes careful controls and checks to assure that quality and service are being maintained in all outlets, a few

[2] For specifics on how affiliation with a wholesaling-and-service operation such as Super Valu can enable an independent supermarket owner to compete effectively against the big chains, see "The Independents' Best Friend," *Forbes,* February 1, 1977, pp. 47–49.

careless operations can result in a bad customer perception of all such outlets.

Types of Franchising Arrangements

MANUFACTURER (FRANCHISOR) AND RETAILERS (FRANCHISEES)   A manufacturer may franchise a number of retail outlets to sell its particular brand and products. This is one of the oldest franchise arrangements.

Examples: This arrangement is particularly prevalent among outlets for passenger cars and trucks, farm equipment, shoes, paint, earth-moving equipment, and petroleum. Virtually all new cars and trucks are sold through franchised dealers, while an estimated 90 percent of all gasoline is sold through franchised independent retail service stations.

MANUFACTURER (FRANCHISOR) AND WHOLESALERS (FRANCHISEES) A manufacturer may franchise independent wholesalers.

Examples: This arrangement is most common in the soft-drink industry. Most national manufacturers of soft-drink syrups—Coca-Cola, Pepsi-Cola, Seven-Up, Royal Crown, and so on—franchise independent bottlers, who then serve the retail markets.

SERVICE SPONSOR (FRANCHISOR) AND RETAILERS (FRANCHISEES) Rather than a product, the major component of these arrangements is a service. While the franchisor may provide some manufacturing and wholesaling functions, the major contribution is a carefully developed, promoted, and controlled format.

Examples: This is the most common type of franchise today. Examples are many and include Holiday Inn, Howard Johnson's, McDonald's, Dairy Queen, Avis, Hertz, Kelly Girl (employment franchises), Kentucky Fried Chicken, and H & R Block (income tax preparation).

Growth of Franchising

Franchising dates back to at least 1898, when General Motors established its first independent dealer to sell and service automobiles. By 1910, franchising was the principal method of marketing automobiles and petroleum products. By 1920 it was being used by food, drug, variety, hardware, and automotive-parts stores. The major growth of franchising began after World War II. Take, for example, soft ice cream: in 1945 there were 100 soft–ice-cream stands in the United States; by 1960 there were almost 18,000.

FIGURE 3.2 AN ADVERTISEMENT FOR FRANCHISING OPPORTUNITIES

BRING THIS AD - SAVE 50¢
BE YOUR OWN BOSS!
Shop the all new 1979

OWN YOUR OWN BUSINESS EXPO

June 1-2-3 CONTINENTAL REGENCY - 500 Hamilton Blvd.
EXPO HRS: Fri. & Sat. 11 A.M. to 8 P.M. Sun. 11 A.M. to 6 P.M.
SHOP A GREAT SELECTION OF NEW FRANCHISES, DISTRIBUTORSHIPS, SERVICES, FACTS ABOUT BUSINESSES.

Tired of working for others? Worried about inflation? Act now to secure your future! Become your own boss! Come to the Expo and shop a great marketplace of new franchises, distributorships and services. Talk to many representatives about opportunities for men or women. Investments range from $1,000 to $100,000.

FREE! **SEMINARS ON SUCCESS IN BUSINESS 11 A.M. & 3 P.M.**
EACH SEMINAR WILL COVER THESE & OTHER TOPICS

- HOW TO SUCCEED IN BUSINESS
- DO'S & DON'TS OF STARTING A BUSINESS
- HOW TO BORROW MONEY
- HOW TO RECOGNIZE A GOOD BUSINESS
- WORKING FOR SOMEONE OR YOURSELF
- FINDING ASSETS YOU DIDN'T KNOW YOU HAD
- PROS & CONS OF INCORPORATING
- SOLE PROPRIETORSHIP VS PARTNERSHIP
- NEW BUSINESS TRENDS FOR '79
- ADVANTAGES WOMEN HAVE IN BUSINESS
- BUSINESSES YOU CAN START FOR UNDER $1000
- PLUS MANY OTHER VALUABLE IDEAS

$3.00 ADM. Includes Exhibits, Buyer's Guide & Seminars
For Exhibit Info call SHULMAN PROMOTIONS 513/948-1900

50¢ Present This Coupon At Expo & Receive 50¢ Off Reg. $3.00 Admission 50¢

Source: Courtesy of Shulman Promotions, Inc.

Franchise sales of goods and services was about $275 billion in 1978, and this was equal to 30 percent of all retail sales. There are almost half a million franchise establishments in the United States, and these employ over 4 million workers.[3] Figure 3.2 shows an advertisement promoting franchising opportunities which has appeared in many major cities. Sources of information about franchising are available in most libraries. The U.S. Department of Commerce, for example, has an

[3] U.S. Department of Commerce, *Franchising in the Economy,* 1977–1979 (Washington, D.C.: Superintendent of Documents, U.S. Government Printing Office, 1979), pp. vi, 1.

annual *Franchise Opportunities Handbook,* which gives specific information about hundreds of franchising concerns; it also provides a checklist for evaluating a franchisor. This book is available from the Superintendent of Documents, U.S. Government Printing Office, Washington, D.C., 20402.

As a specific example of the opportunities and growth possible through franchising, consider the franchisor Colonel Harland Sanders.

RETAILING PROFILE—*Colonel Harland Sanders*

With his long-time restaurant forced to close because of a new highway, Sanders took five frozen frying chickens, a special cooker, and some flour and spices, and attempted to interest restaurant managers in his method of high-temperature cooking. Acceptance was slow. He gave franchises away; he leased cookers; he supplied, at cost, paper napkins and buckets with his picture and the Kentucky Fried Chicken name on them.

After three years he finally made some headway. And then the idea caught on. In eight years he had sold over 500 franchises. He received five cents for each chicken sold by these restaurants and his revenues were over $2.3 million a year. In 1962, at seventy-two years of age, he expanded the business to include take-home sales. In 1964 he sold the entire business for $2 million. By 1968 sales were over $250 million and there were over 1,500 outlets. His age when this all began? Sixty-five.

Sources: For more detail, see "Life Begins at 65," *Forbes,* May 15, 1966, p. 36; and "Cooking Up Profits, Southern Style," *Business Week,* June 24, 1967, pp. 176ff. For more recent data concerning Kentucky Fried Chicken, see "America's Eating-out Splurge," *Business Week,* October 27, 1975, pp. 45–51; "Fast Food Franchisers Squeeze Out the Little Guy," *Business Week,* May 31, 1976, pp. 42–48; and "Smaller Fast-Food Chains Feel the Brunt of Big-Three Companies' 'Burger War'," *Wall Street Journal,* February 20, 1979, p. 40.

For Thought and Discussion

1. You are probably all personally familiar with Kentucky Fried Chicken. What particular factors do you think account for its success?

2. Do you think that another fried chicken franchisor could be as successful with a different strategy?

Advantages from the Franchisor's Viewpoint

A major advantage for the franchisor, and probably the key reason for the rapid growth of this kind of retailing, is that the franchisor can expand with only limited finances, since the franchisees are putting up some or most of the money. Consequently, expansion can take place almost as rapidly as entrepreneurs can be induced to invest in the franchise system. As a name becomes well known—as Kentucky Fried Chicken became—almost the only limitations to growth are the need to screen applicants, to find suitable sites for new outlets, and to develop the managerial controls necessary to assure consistency of performance. During the late 1960s, the period of most exuberant growth, some franchisors were tempted to shirk these operational requirements.

Another major advantage is that franchisors can normally obtain conscientious people to operate the outlets, since franchisees are entrepreneurs with a personal stake, rather than hired managers. A further advantage for the franchisor is being able to bypass big retailers in marketing efforts, thereby maintaining better control of product and distribution.

Advantages from the Franchisee's Viewpoint

The major advantage that franchising offers the entrepreneur is a lower risk of business failure (or, to put it another way, more chance of success). The franchise provides a unique product or service that is handled exclusively in a given area, such as McDonald's hamburger outlet, a Midas Muffler shop or, if the resources are available for investment, a Holiday Inn franchise. The type of outlet will probably already have a proven consumer acceptance and perhaps wide recognition. The franchisee can also benefit from proven managerial and promotional techniques and from the group buying power that is afforded.

An example is Butler Brothers (now part of City Products Corporation), which administers over 2,400 franchised Ben Franklin variety stores. All Ben Franklin stores are given assistance in site selection, store layout, and leasing arrangements. Advertising suggestions and mats are provided for local advertising, while all units benefit from national advertising by Butler Brothers. Prospective franchisees are extensively trained in all aspects of retail operation. A zone manager supervises from ten to twenty of these independent stores and reviews inventories, offers display suggestions, helps with any bookkeeping problems, provides a variety of other assistance as needed, and updates store people on new merchandise and trends. A basic control system, consisting of stock checklists and seasonal records, is also provided for all stores.

Undoubtedly, franchising has improved the competitive viability of small business by better training individual entrepreneurs and providing them with some of the sophisticated management and accounting techniques of larger firms. More than this, some marginal applicants have been weeded out and refused franchises.

Disadvantages from the Franchisee's Viewpoint

Even so, there are inefficient and marginal operations, even among franchises. A franchisee may chafe at the franchisor's attempts to enforce the controls deemed necessary for the success of the whole franchise system. And he or she may resent the franchisor's insistence that the stipulated proportion of merchandise and supplies be purchased through the franchisor.

Some franchises are overpromoted and oversold. Perhaps the franchisor (who may be pursuing rapid growth at the expense of a solid foundation) has promised more managerial aid and efficiency of operation than can be delivered. Sometimes there are too many similar franchise outlets in a given area. This is becoming especially true of fast-food franchising. One wonders how many hamburgers, buckets of chicken, and donuts can be consumed by an average family.[4]

The costs of obtaining some franchises are not low. A McDonald's franchise may cost $250,000 to start, while a motel may require well over $1 million. However, the diversity of franchising does provide for most levels of investment; a person with limited means can obtain an H & R Block income tax preparation service for around $1,000. Furthermore, a person can enter most franchised businesses with less cash investment for fixtures and equipment than a conventional business would require, because credit help is available from the franchisor.

Successful franchise operators may also face a nagging thought: how much more might their profits be if they did not have to pay a certain percentage of their revenues to the franchisor?[5]

Prospective franchisees should keep in mind that, as in almost all ventures, there is the possibility of either intentional or careless over-extension of resources by the franchisor. There are a few fly-by-night franchisors who take the franchisee's investment, then can't, or won't, hold up their end of the bargain. It behooves the would-be franchisee, when dealing with a little-known franchisor, to investigate the integrity

[4] For an early 1979 view of fast-food chain competition, see "Smaller Fast-Food Chains Feel the Brunt of Big-Three Companies' 'Burger War'," *Wall Street Journal,* February 20, 1979, p. 40.
[5] For a detailed overview of the nature of franchising, see Donald W. Hackett, *Franchising: The State of the Art* (Chicago: American Marketing Association, 1977).

and financial resources of the franchisor, perhaps through the Better Business Bureau or through Dun & Bradstreet.

Trends in Franchising

It is probably true that the major growth of franchising is over, and that it created some excesses and abuses. A more mature phase of development seems both probable and desirable. With the best locations for franchises already filled, franchisors now are buying out some of their independent franchisees. For example, by 1977 Kentucky Fried Chicken (now a subsidiary of Heublein, Inc.) had 795 company-owned outlets and 3,398 franchised outlets in the United States; five years earlier it had only 250 company-owned outlets.

Attaching the name of a celebrity, usually from the entertainment or sports world, to a franchised operation has proven insufficient to guarantee success in the absence of sound management. For example, Joe Namath fast-food restaurants and Eva Gabor wig salons were two of a number of celebrity-backed operations that flopped.

A trend toward multi-unit franchises is emerging, with a number of franchisees becoming good-sized companies themselves. Several things account for the popularity of the multi-unit franchise concept. Parent companies (franchisors) find it much easier and more efficient to deal with major franchisees, who not only have more financial muscle than smaller franchisees, but also have a proven success record. Furthermore, dealing with just a few large franchisees reduces the complexity of paperwork and procedures for the franchisor.

The greatest growth of franchising in the United States today is occurring in the service sectors, such as lawn service, income-tax preparation, home cleaning and repairs, and even hair-styling shops for men and women:

Called Command Performance . . . for 10 or 12 hours a week of management, there is a potential yearly pretax operating profit of 20 to 30 percent of sales, or $50,000 or better on a total investment running only $50,000 to $80,000.[6]

An increasing number of real-estate brokers are becoming franchised operations, gaining the benefits of management and staff training programs, interoffice referrals, access to financial services, and nationwide advertising and promotion under a single banner. In 1975 there were

[6] "Profits in Unisex Hair-Styling Shops Lure Franchise Buyers With Limited Spare Time," *Wall Street Journal,* May 8, 1978, p. 38.

only 3,808 franchised real-estate offices; by 1977 their number had grown to 11,449; by 1980 it is estimated that there will be approximately 22,000.[7]

Large corporations have begun entering the field of franchising. Sears and Montgomery Ward have franchised catalog stores in small towns. Swift has a chain of Dipper Dan Ice Cream Shoppes, and Olin Corporation has set up commercial gun shops. Pet, Inc., bought Stuckey's chain of roadside stores; General Foods controls Burger Chef; Pillsbury acquired Burger King; United Fruit has both A & W Root Beer and Baskin-Robbins Ice Cream stores.

Franchising is expanding into foreign markets. A Department of Commerce survey found that in 1977, 244 U.S. franchising companies had 14,217 outlets spread throughout most countries of the world. This was a 15 percent increase in the number of units in just one year. Fast-food restaurants lead U.S. franchises in foreign countries with 68 percent of their foreign outlets in Canada, Japan, and the United Kingdom.[8]

Social Benefits of Franchising

As noted, franchising gives individuals the opportunity to go into self-employment and to do so with some assurance of success because of competent managerial backing. Some individuals have a strong psychological drive to accomplish something significant, and building one's own business can be highly satisfying.

Perhaps franchising's biggest social deficiency has been its slowness in providing opportunity for business ownership among blacks and other disadvantaged racial and ethnic groups. This situation is improving, however. The number of minority-owned franchised outlets increased 11 percent in 1977 over the previous year, and 38 percent over 1975, according to a Department of Commerce survey. However, the total number of outlets owned or leased by blacks, Hispanic Americans, American Indians, and Orientals is still meager; out of 192,081 outlets of reporting firms in 1977, only 4,758 were minority owned.[9]

Women, on the other hand, seem to be getting heavily involved in franchising. A recent study showed that, of those firms reporting, women either owned outright or shared in the ownership and manage-

[7] Department of Commerce, *Franchising in the Economy, 1977–1979*, p. 5.
[8] Ibid., pp. 5–7.
[9] Ibid., pp. 7, 35, 45.

ment of 37.4 percent. Projections were that women would become even more heavily involved in the future.[10]

■ Summary

The last four decades have seen a steady trend toward the dominance of large retail firms. But this does not mean that small business is no longer feasible for people interested in independence and the challenge of building their own businesses. Because of lower overhead, smaller retail establishments have the advantage of greater flexibility in response to market demand. A business owner has far greater motivation than a hired manager. A small retailer can also give more personalized service and have more direct contact with customers. Franchising, in particular, offers better assurance of success for small entrepreneurs, although some independence will be sacrificed. The great diversity of opportunities in franchising—with investment requirements ranging from minimal to hundreds of thousands of dollars—enables individuals of widely different means, backgrounds, and inclinations to experience the triumphs and frustrations of operating their own businesses.

■ Key Terms

Assistance programs	Franchising
Break-even analysis	Trade associations
Cooperative chains	Voluntary chains

■ Discussion Questions

1. Why are small retailers so vulnerable to business failure?
2. What benefits can a small retailer gain from a trade association?
3. What is the difference between a cooperative chain and a voluntary chain?
4. Why is it important for a franchisor to institute controls and checks over franchised operations? Does this make the franchisee's position more or less attractive?
5. What might be some reasons that a franchise company would fail, despite the advantages of having a celebrity's name?
6. Frequently, persons starting and operating their own businesses find themselves working much longer hours than they ever would for someone else.

[10] Shelby D. Hunt, "Women and Franchising," *Business Topics* (Spring 1978), 25–28.

a. Evaluate this tendency from the point of view of your own inclinations.
b. Discuss the reasons for it.
c. Evaluate the possible consequences for the individuals involved, as well as for the general conduct of the business.

7. What factors would you say account for McDonald's franchising success?
8. If you were to think about opening a business, would you rather buy out an existing business or start a new one? Evaluate the pros and cons of these two approaches to self-employment.

■ Project

Investigate two franchise operations in your community that deal with the same type of goods or services. Compare and contrast them as to what it takes to start in the way of money and experience; potential profits and risks; general operational restrictions and advantages; general level of success and competitive advantage; and the franchisee's satisfaction or dissatisfaction with the franchisor and company policies. For example, you may want to compare McDonald's with Burger King, or Howard Johnson's with Holiday Inn, or perhaps some service operations, such as Kelly Girl with Manpower, Inc.

■ Exercise in Creativity

How many opportunities for small retail businesses do you see in your community? Be prepared to defend your ideas, and be as innovative as possible.

■ Retailing in Action: Role Play

Your father owns an older motel that for many years has been moderately successful. In recent years, however, several franchised outlets of major motel chains, notably Holiday Inn and Ramada Inn, have opened in the same general area. With their modern facilities, and especially their free reservation service, they have drastically cut into your father's business.

"I wanted to have a thriving business for you to step into," he tells you. "But now it looks as if I may have to sell out or close up. I can join a motel association such as Quality Courts or Western Motels, and this would help us compete better with the motel chains. But I don't think I can afford the remodeling to bring it up to their standards. What do you think I should do?"

4 Environmental Factors Affecting Retailing

In the last decade a new dimension has been added to the American business scene by social and environmental issues. These issues are varied: consumer agitation against deceptive advertising, poor quality of products, flimsy warranties and guarantees, concern about pollution, inequities in the ghetto, and minority employment and training. These issues affect all firms. They involve retailers more than manufacturers because the retailer is "on the firing line," in direct confrontation with consumers. Customers' unhappiness with products and services, even when the retailer is not at fault, rebounds to the store's detriment. In extreme cases, consumer resentment of dishonest practices has resulted in businesses being looted and burned.

Consumers seek the best value for the fading purchasing power of their dollars, and the issues they raise should concern retailers now and in the future. If the public image of retailing is darkened, so is the reputation of those engaged in it, and so is its attractiveness as a career. There is another reason for not taking these issues lightly: a rising trend of governmental influence and intervention in business. This stems mostly from consumer complaints, the publicity these are receiving, and the voting power of consumers. The result may make retailing more costly and more complex in the years ahead. Constraints are being placed on businesses; absolute freedom of operation is no longer possible. But opportunities are presented for the firm and the entrepreneur who are responsive to the nuances of the marketplace.

CONSUMERISM

Consumerism may be defined as consumer dissatisfaction and public outcry about the products and practices of the marketplace.

Areas of Consumer Complaint

While consumers have spoken out in protest against many practices, most of their complaints refer to two categories of malfeasance:

1. Practices aimed at preventing consumers from making the most rational choice of a product or service
2. Failure to stand behind products and services and to handle customer problems in a satisfactory manner

These may seem to be easily correctible problems, but that is not the case. They are complex. Tradition is on the side of their continuation. The profit motive underlies such practices and interferes with their correction.

Here are some specific examples of complaints:

1. *Hiding or distorting consumer buying information*

    Deceptive packaging: preventing value comparisons with fractional-weight packages and distorted quantities

    Deceptive advertising: misleading product claims, unsupported contentions and comparisons, exaggerations, or insufficient information for a customer to make an informed buying decision

Deceptive pricing practices: creating an illusion of value not war-ranted by the quality, or showing a false "reduction" from an "original" price

Deceptive credit charges: attempting to obscure what customers are paying for credit (a practice that has been attacked by the Truth-in-Lending Law)

Deceptive promotional practices with games and contests: abusing both the prizes offered and the method of selecting winners

2. *After-sales repudiation*

Murky and deceptive warranties: offering meaningless product backing and buyer protection, for example:

A Dispoz-a-Lamp sold in a retail store for 66¢. While it was an unfamiliar product, it had a "guarantee." Closer inspection of this guarantee, usually made after the product was bought, revealed that if the light failed to work properly, all the customer had to do was send it back to the factory in Connecticut together with $1 "to cover postage and handling charges."[1]

Poor service on defective goods: failing to repair defective items like cars or TV sets

Poor-quality products: resulting in 30 percent consumer dissatisfac-tion with automobiles, 35.5 percent with color TVs, 19.7 percent with stereos, and 18.9 percent with lawn mowers, according to one study[2]

Unsafe products—ranging from cigarettes to lemon furniture polish that smells like soda pop, fabrics that explode into flames, toys that cut children, electric steam vaporizers that scald infants, and drugs with dangerous side effects

Are retailers absolved from blame for some of these problems? After all, it is the manufacturer, not the retailer, who makes cleaners that smell like soda pop. But if any retailer thinks he can truly "pass the buck," he is mistaken; customers invariably hold the retailer to blame for stocking and selling such items. And consumers are justified in this accusation. The retailer is acting as the purchasing agent for customers.

---

[1] Bill Gold, "The District Line," *Washington Post,* March 20, 1972, p. D10. © The Washington Post.
[2] William R. Thomas and F. Kelley Shuptrine, "The Consumer Complaint Process," in *Southern Marketing Association Proceedings,* ed. Barnett A. Greenberg, 1974, p. 293.

The store should do the initial screening and put pressure on manufacturers to eliminate bad practices.

There is another category of consumer abuse: outright *fraud*. While fraud is not as widespread as complaints about defective goods or services, it does exist, particularly with products and services where there is *no repeat business* and no need to cultivate customer loyalty. Used cars and home repairs are most vulnerable to fraudulent practices. Fraud is particularly prevalent in ghettos and with low-income consumers. Such practices can range all the way from misrepresenting a product as new when it is really old, to taking a down payment or complete payment for a product and never delivering. It is not uncommon for naive customers to sign sales contracts with blank prices and terms to be filled in later by the seller, with any figures desired.

Causes of Consumer Militancy

These abusive practices are not new in the marketplace; they have simply been unrecognized or ignored. But this apathy is changing. Consumers today are better educated and more affluent. As a result, they are more discerning, less easily swayed, more skeptical, and less easily satisfied. They do not tolerate lack of information about the products they buy. They are unwilling to accept products that wear out before they should, or service and adjustment "runarounds," in which neither retailer nor manufacturer is willing to accept responsibility and correct defects.

Ralph Nader and the attention he received served to trigger and sustain such consumer resentments.[3] Many books and newspaper and magazine articles also fed this discontent.[4] The spiral of inflation has been a factor, as many consumers saw prices rising faster than take-home pay, while quality and service continued to erode.

At the same time that consumers expect and demand more, we find that American business is responding less. The retailing environment has become more impersonal, more out of touch with customers. The rise of self-service and discounting, along with the high cost of trained service personnel and the impersonality of the computer, reflects this trend.[5]

[3] Nader and his influence are described in "The U.S.'s Toughest Customer," *Time,* December 12, 1969, pp. 89–98.
[4] For example, Senator Warren Magnuson and Jean Carper, *The Dark Side of the Marketplace* (Englewood Cliffs, N.J.: Prentice-Hall, 1968).
[5] For more analysis and discussion of the scope and causes of consumerism, see George S. Day and David A. Aaker, "A Guide to Consumerism," *Journal of Marketing* (July 1970), 12–19.

Two consumers carefully check merchandise prior to purchase. More than ever before, consumers today seek product quality and freedom from defects. They are less inclined to trust a dealer and more willing to expend effort to try to find the best buy. Retailers should be willing and able to describe the technical features and performance of their products for a discerning customer. (Arthur Grace/Stock, Boston)

Extent and Trend of Consumerism

Consumerism can be dated from the mid-1960s. Two influential books were Rachel Carson's *Silent Spring*[6] and Ralph Nader's *Unsafe at Any Speed*.[7]

As a result of the rash of consumer protests in recent years, many laws relating to consumer protection have been passed by federal, state, and local governments. Consumer-protection offices or departments have been set up within city, county, or state governments. Many states have a prosecutor in the attorney general's office devoted to consumer fraud cases. And there has been support, although insufficient for passage, for legislation to consolidate consumer-related matters in a cabinet-level Department of Consumer Affairs, to assure permanent consumer representation at top levels of government.

[6] *Silent Spring* (Boston: Houghton Mifflin, 1962).
[7] *Unsafe at Any Speed* (New York: Pocket Books, 1966).

Retailers' Role in Consumerism

Retailers' attitudes toward consumerism can generally be classified as follows:

1. Unconcerned, apathetic, and willing to ascribe all devious practices to other "small and marginal" retailers
2. Obstructive to all contemplated legislation that attempts to give consumers better information and better buying assurances
3. Constructive in efforts to cater to consumer desires for better information and treatment

RETAILER APATHY AND UNCONCERN   In the past this has been the most typical attitude of retailers. Many thought that consumer dissatisfaction and militancy were characteristic of a small minority of consumers—"the chronic complainers"—and therefore not worthy of concern. And there is no doubt that many customers complaints and returns of merchandise do come from a minority of "repeaters."

Most retailers acknowledge that some abuses and deceptive and even fradulent practices take place. It is easy to blame the marginal firms, those that operate at the threshold of legitimacy. For example, small furniture stores have been known to collect orders and prepayment from customers, and then suddenly and quietly go out of business "under cover of darkness." Even if bankruptcy papers are filed, major creditors get first crack at whatever assets remain. The buyers are out of luck, left waiting for prepaid deliveries of furniture that never arrives.

However, abuses and deceptive practices are not limited to marginal firms. Much consumer frustration results when retailers refuse to stand behind defective products, especially automobiles, appliances, and furniture. Recently, we saw the conclusion of one of the more celebrated cases of a manufacturer and its dealers trying to escape responsibility for a defective product. Firestone Tire & Rubber Company, after almost a year's controversy, finally yielded to the pressure of the National Highway Traffic Safety Administration and recalled some 13 million of its Firestone 500 steel radial tires. The company gave in, in the face of newspaper revelations that in 1975 its own tests showed frequent blowouts under heat and stress.[8] In a similar case, also in 1978, Ford Motor Company reluctantly agreed to correct a gas-tank

[8] "Goodyear's Solo Strategy," from the August 28, 1978, issue of BusinessWeek pp. 66–70. © 1978 by McGraw-Hill, Inc., New York, NY 10020. All rights reserved.

defect in its Pinto, which had received widespread public attention for a tendency to burst into flames in rear-end collisions.

Puffing by which a product's attributes are exaggerated in advertisements and personal selling, is not uncommon in retailing; at times it can reach deceptive extremes. For example, a customer may be assured by a salesperson eager to make a sale that expensive carpeting will last for twenty years, only to have it begin to unravel in a year.[9]

RETAILER OBSTRUCTION Some retailers—the largest ones—have tried to block consumer legislation aimed at providing consumers with better shopping information. These efforts are a prime example of unresponsiveness to the needs of the marketplace.

Perhaps never has obstruction been more evident than in the opposition to revealing true interest rates on customer charge accounts. In 1968 the Truth-in-Lending Law was finally enacted. This requires lenders and sellers to reveal the true annual interest rate of consumer loans and credit buying, including revolving charge accounts. For years this legislation was bitterly opposed by finance companies, car dealers, and big retailers. (The initial sponsor of the legislation, Senator Paul Douglas of Illinois, tried to get the law through Congress for six years, until he retired in 1966.) Retailers who had heavily promoted their revolving charge accounts with a "service fee" of $1\frac{1}{2}$ percent a month were particularly strong in their denunciations of such disclosures. (A monthly rate of $1\frac{1}{2}$ percent adds up to 18 percent annually.) The opponents of such legislation warned that the economy would suffer from less-rapid expansion of consumer credit and that the consumer needed to be "protected" from full disclosure in order to continue that progress toward material well-being. The flaw in this argument is shown by the lack of decline in consumer use of credit since the Truth-in-Lending Law, despite the disclosure of 18 percent interest rates.

Unit pricing, another way of providing consumers with better shopping information, was also bitterly opposed by some retailer groups. Unit pricing is retailers' posting of prices by the ounce, pound, or similar standard measure, which helps shoppers make better price comparisons. Concerned consumers had long proposed it as a remedy for the confusion of varied packages and fractional weights. In 1966 the Fair Packaging and Labeling ("Truth-in-Packaging") Act was finally passed. But bitter opposition succeeded in watering down the bill, so

[9] Some puffing has been accepted by governmental and legal officials as simply the enthusiastic representation of a product. The boundaries at which puffing exceeds tolerable, modest exaggerations are hazy. The Federal Trade Commission is now taking a more severe stance on unproven advertised claims.

that a pocket calculator was often still required to figure out the best buy amid the maze of prices and package sizes in the supermarket.

The governments of New York City and Massachusetts were the first to enact legislation making unit pricing mandatory for food products and other low-price consumer products, such as drugs and health and beauty aids. Despite dire estimates of how much unit pricing would add to the cost of supermarket operations, the costs of setting it up and maintaining it have turned out to be so small that prices are not affected. At the same time, stores are better able to promote their own brands by showing them to be a better buy compared with nationally advertised brands. Today, without any legal requirements, some supermarket chains have adopted unit pricing in an attempt to gain advantage over their competitors and to establish a better public image.

The effectiveness of unit pricing has been somewhat spotty. Early studies indicated that most consumers did not use it. This was especially true in low-income areas (where consumers would seem most in need of getting the best value for their money). About one out of three consumers in middle-class areas apparently used it to some extent. A more recent study, involving a nationwide sample of 2,334 shoppers, found that 70 percent were now using unit pricing frequently. The percentage was even higher near the top of the socioeconomic ladder.[10]

CONSTRUCTIVE RETAILER EFFORTS   Not all retailers have opposed or disregarded consumerism issues. Some have turned a constructive attitude into a competitive advantage and gained a reputation as socially responsive firms. One of these is Stop & Shop.

SUCCESSFUL RETAILING STRATEGIES—Responsiveness to Consumerism at Stop & Shop

Consumer boards of directors—composed of householders who are young and old, rich and poor, black and white—meet regularly to air gripes and suggestions to Stop & Shop executives. There are some fifty-two of these consumer boards with one thousand men and women communicating at all levels of management. Suggestions have led to the use of clear-plastic meat trays for greater visibility, special floor heaters to take the chill out of frozen-food aisles, and more ethnic foods in highly concentrated ethnic neighborhoods. Redesigned labels on store-brand items show caloric con-

---

[10] Robert Dietrich, "Some Signs of Our Times: On the Road to Smarter Shopping," *Progressive Grocer* (November 1976), 43.

tent and nutritive value. Color-coded meat labels give instructions for the best cooking methods. "Miniminders," wallet-sized cards that enable a shopper to calculate unit prices, are offered to customers.

A special inventory was made of 5,400 grocery items, and 52 turned out to be more expensive in the "economy" size than in smaller sizes. The company immediately cut its prices on the larger sizes and then pressured suppliers to lower their prices. In 1978, a quality-control department made over 2,000 inspections of stores, and even of suppliers of private-brand merchandise, to assure that they were maintaining quality levels. In these and other ways, Stop & Shop had pursued an aggressive marketing strategy compatible with consumer desires for a fairer shake in the marketplace.

Sources: "A Shoppers Forum Bags Goodwill," from the January 31, 1970 issue of Business Week, p. 52. © 1970 by McGraw-Hill, Inc., New York, NY 10020. All rights reserved. And Stop & Shop annual reports for 1976, 1977, and 1978.

For Thought and Discussion   As an executive of Stop & Shop, how would you counter an assertion that these actions are strictly public relations gestures and really superficial?

In addition to the *nutrition labeling* provided by Stop & Shop, *open dating* of food has become more commonplace. About 70 percent of food retailers now clearly mark their merchandise with the last date on which it should be sold. Consequently, consumers can determine the freshness of the products they are buying.[11]

A positive approach to consumerism can also foster more informative advertising. Some retailers are beginning to recognize that they should act as the consumer's representative or agent: "We should be impatient with manufacturers of products that endanger the health and safety of the consumer public; we should demand improved quality."[12]

A retailer stands to benefit in many ways from being responsive to customers' complaints. The store gains good will, which leads to customer loyalty, with its repeat business and favorable word-of-mouth advertising. A good public image may result in a strong competitive position and will probably attract new customers.

Responsiveness, however, requires more than just a "gut" feeling or feedback gathered by talking with a few employees or neighbors. An

[11] Charlene Price, "The Consumers and Open Date Labeling," *National Food Situation* (September 1976).
[12] From a speech by Harold Brockey, president of Rich's of Atlanta, reported in "The Age of Magnificent Discontent," *Stores* (March 1972), 18.

objective measure of customer satisfaction is needed. How do most firms attain this?

MEASURING CUSTOMER SATISFACTION   Unfortunately, most firms do not have good measures of how satisfied their customers are with their products and services. Many do not even attempt to analyze this. Or, if they do, the measurement factors are flawed. Sales and market-share results, for example, are indirect measures. Many other things, such as the economy, competition, and weather, affect sales and market share. Furthermore, sales and market-share results do not measure degree of satisfaction; for example, customers may be greatly pleased or merely tolerant of the store, its merchandise, and its service.

Opinions of salespeople tend to be biased and overly optimistic. Unsolicited consumer responses, the occasional letters of complaint directed to top executives, seldom represent customer attitudes in general, since they come from the vocal minority of customers, those most difficult to satisfy or most desperate to have their complaints heard. Many dissatisfied customers and their friends simply take future business elsewhere, without fanfare. In addition, there is a natural tendency in all organizations to insulate higher executives from complaints. Consequently, the full extent of customer dissatisfaction does not filter up to responsible executives. Unless a system is established to monitor customer feedback, tabulate it, and analyze and act upon it, such data are fragmented and lost.

In Chapter 20, customer attitude surveys are discussed. While these surveys are not difficult to make, care should be taken to make them systematic and objective. For ascertaining customer satisfaction, such direct measures of customer attitudes are superior to the indirect measures of profit, sales, and market share.

BETTER BUSINESS BUREAUS   For decades, retailers and other local businesses have directed group efforts toward self-regulation of deception, fraud, and other abuses. Nationwide, there are 146 *better business bureaus*. These are independent, nonprofit operations funded by local business concerns in each community. Their fundamental purpose is to monitor, investigate, and correct deceptive advertising and business practices. They respond to customer complaints and try to resolve disputes between firms and customers. They also provide educational materials to consumers, give trade-practice advice to businesses, and report offenders to appropriate law enforcement agencies. The better business bureaus work closely with government consumer-protection agencies. While they can exercise no strong coercive power, they can usually induce legitimate businesses to clear up any misunderstandings or questionable practices, because of the threat of adverse publicity that can come from blacklisting by a bureau.

RETAILING IN THE GHETTO

The ghetto environment has bred the worst abuses by marketers and retailers. Deceptive practices have been common and have dissipated the already meager purchasing power of ghetto consumers.

The ghetto consumer is far more vulnerable to high-pressure tactics, exorbitant prices, and shoddy merchandise than is a middle-class counterpart in the suburbs. Ghetto residents usually have insufficient cash because of low-paying jobs or meager welfare checks. Accordingly, they have to buy on a "hand-to-mouth" basis. They often have not had much opportunity to learn how to manage money and therefore tend to be considered poor credit risks. The typical ghetto consumer lacks the mobility to shop in stores outside the ghetto, because of the lack of a car, poor bus service, or a reluctance to brave the unfamiliarity of the outside world. Consequently, these consumers tend to be chained to the inefficient and abusive retailers who characterize much of the ghetto marketplace.

Retail Stores and Their Practices in the Ghetto

We find few chain stores or big retailers in the ghetto. Generally, when a supermarket-chain outlet or a Sears, Penney, or Woolworth store is in the ghetto, it is because the ghetto gradually expanded and grew around a store that was already there.

Most ghetto stores are small. They are usually drab, dirty, and rundown. There is little need or incentive for the owners to refurbish them because competition does not require this and the ghetto consumer is in no position to shift business outside the ghetto. Merchandise typically is of inferior quality, often "seconds" (with some seconds and flawed goods passed off as first quality). A visitor might be surprised at the number of stores handling furniture and major durables such as appliances. The explanation is that low-income people tend to measure success by what one can buy; the formal term for this practice is *compensatory consumption*. Prices for appliances and furniture are high, much higher than for similar brands and styles sold outside the ghetto. For example, a TV set that sells for $129 in a nonghetto store may sell for more than $200 in a ghetto store.

Why would anyone pay such prices? Part of the answer lies in the characteristics of the ghetto consumer: lack of expertise in the buying situation and inability or disinclination to shop around and compare prices. But the greatest reason is this customer's need for readily available credit. Retailers outside the ghetto rarely will accept what they view as such a poor credit risk. But the ghetto merchant is ready to fill this need—for a price, of course.

There has been considerable public controversy regarding food prices in ghetto and nonghetto branches of the same firm. Evidence from a number of research studies is contradictory.[13] In view of this widespread publicity, it is doubtful if many large food chains would leave themselves vulnerable to criticism by deliberately pricing differently. What is more evident, however, is that the ghetto stores of a chain carry lower quality, less fresh, and less clean products. For example, vegetables and fruits may be shriveled and bruised, and meats stale and of less desirable cuts.

The ghetto has spawned special adaptations of credit. It is offered by almost all merchants there, in spite of the high risk involved. "No money down," "A dollar down and a dollar a week," are frequently encountered signs. Credit charges are as high as the law allows and sometimes more. With the inherently high risks, various controls are commonplace. Some of these controls, which make credit in the ghetto possible, are described in Table 4.1.

"Hard-sell" techniques are commonplace. Customers are relatively few, and merchants tend to exert strenuous efforts to prevent their leaving a store without a purchase; and customers typically have no return-goods privileges, even if the goods prove defective. Table 4.2 describes some common sales practices in the ghetto. Of course, these undesirable practices are not limited to retailers in low-income areas. However, their greatest abuse occurs in the ghetto.

Opportunities in the Ghetto Market

It is not easy to do business in low-income areas: the environment intrudes and overwhelms. Large firms and chains have shied away,

[13] For example, Charles S. Goodman, "Do the Poor Pay More?" *Journal of Marketing* (January 1968), 18; U.S. Department of Labor, Bureau of Labor Statistics, National Commission on Food Marketing, "Retail Food Prices in Low and Higher Income Areas," *Special Studies in Food Marketing,* Technical Report No. 10, June 1966; and Burton H. Marcus, "Similarity of Ghetto and Nonghetto Food Costs," *Journal of Marketing Research* (August 1969), 365–68. For a comprehensive review of the overall low-income market, see Leonard L. Berry, "The Low-income Market System: An Overview," *Journal of Retailing* (Summer 1972), 44–63, 90; and Marcus Alexis and Clyde M. Smith, "Marketing and the Inner City Consumer," *Journal of Contemporary Business* (Autumn 1973), 45–80.

TABLE 4.1 TYPES OF CREDIT CONTROLS IN THE GHETTO

Balloon note	Prescribing small payments until the end, when a large final payment is required. The final payment is often beyond the means of the debtor, thereby facilitating repossession.
Repossession of merchandise	Taking back merchandise—usually furniture or appliances—when installment payments are in arrears. Such merchandise then can be resold (sometimes even resold as new).
Lien against property	A court judgment by which a defaulting customer can have his property attached by the creditor.
Lien agains wages (garnishment)	A court judgment by which a delinquent customer can have his wages (or a certain part of them) attached in payment of his debts. Since some employers do not hesitate to fire employees rather than submit to the nuisance of a garnishment, this is a particularly serious action.
Discounting paper	A note or sales contract sold to a third party, such as a finance company. The third party then becomes the innocent "holder in due course," and the debtor is bound to continue the payments, regardless of satisfaction or the state of the goods purchased. (Recent federal legislation has now made third-party creditors liable for shoddy merchandise.)
Flexible credit	A more positive type of credit control that may be practiced by merchants who want to achieve good will in their neighborhoods and who know their debtor customers. It allows for an occasional missed payment and may permit payment adjustments for certain contingencies.

partly because of the risks of pilferage and vandalism, which result in higher insurance costs. But ghetto stores of a chain also have higher operating costs because the per-capita sales average only one-half the sales in a suburban store. Thus, twice the traffic is needed to produce the same total sales. This results in more wear and tear and a need for more help.[14]

[14] Donald S. Perkins, "The Low-Income Consumer—A Human Problem and a Selling Problem," Executive Lecture Series, March 2, 1970, University of Notre Dame; and Louis S. Allen, "Making Capitalism Work in the Ghetto," *Harvard Business Review* (May–June 1969). Three bibliographies that provide references on minority marketing are *A Selected Bibliography of Readings and References*

TABLE 4.2   UNDESIRABLE SALES PRACTICES IN THE GHETTO

Bait and switch	Enticing customers into a store by an ad or window display offering a very low price. The advertised goods are either "sold out," or else are shopworn and broken, so that the customer is switched, perhaps with high-pressure tactics, to more expensive items.
Multiprice stores	The goods in these stores carry no price tags. The salesperson varies the price according to how naive the customer appears or how much he or she might be able to pay.
"Tossover" selling technique	Turning "difficult" customers over to another salesperson. The second salesperson exerts fresh pressure on the customer to buy the merchandise.
Misrepresentation of merchandise	This may vary from misrepresenting product performance to claiming that the particular item is new when it really is not.
False comparative prices (fictitious list prices)	A misrepresentation of the regular before-reduction price. For example, "Was $19.95, now $11.88," when in truth the item was never sold at $19.95, nor was it worth that price.
Fictitious sales	A misrepresentation of goods as being salepriced, when they really are not.

An area of low per-capita income would seem to offer little potential for business. Nonetheless, the growing population and the ever-increasing concentration of black consumers in the center city can be fruitful for those merchants willing to adapt to this market. Furthermore, competition in the ghetto is vulnerable to retailers offering bigger, cleaner stores; honest values; and improved services. Where such stores have built or remodeled in ghetto locations, they have

Regarding Marketing to Black Americans, 2nd ed., ed. Milton M. Pressley (Greensboro, N.C.: Center for Applied Research, 1976); *Marketing and the Black Consumer: An Annotated Bibliography,* eds. Thomas E. Barry, Michael G. Harvey, and Michael E. McGill (Chicago: American Marketing Association, 1976); *The Economics of Minorities: A Guide to Information Sources,* ed. Kenneth L. Gagala (Detroit: Gale Research Co., 1976).

Not all sales are legitimate. Abuses occur particularly with "fire sales," "going-out-of-business sales," and the like. A store may remain open month after month, constantly replenishing the stock but never altering the "Everything Must Go!" theme. Some cities now require that retailers obtain licenses before running such sales, with the final closing date of the firm or the sale specifically indicated. (Michael Ginsburg/Magnum)

helped to beautify the inner city and bring a new sense of pride to people tired of dilapidated and dirty buildings.

Businesses that have successfully tapped the ghetto market have done so with a specially tailored program, one distinct from those of nonghetto stores in merchandise, promotional efforts, and credit requirements. It requires no great perceptiveness to see the desirability of selling black dolls or advertising on black-oriented radio stations. Similarly, in a Puerto Rican, Mexican American, or American Indian ghetto, the need to tailor advertising and merchandising to these consumers should be obvious. With Spanish-speaking customers, salespeople who speak the language and advertising through local Spanish-language radio stations can be very effective.

The need for changed credit policies is often less evident. The established ghetto merchants who offer exorbitant prices and shoddy goods do provide relatively liberal credit. The reputable retailer entering the ghetto may need to experiment with more flexible credit policies if the consumer is not to remain chained to the existing system.

ENVIRONMENTAL PROBLEMS: RETAILERS' INVOLVEMENT

The major environmental problems facing us today have been well publicized. They concern pullution of our air, our water, and our land. This contamination comes from giant steel mills, from paper mills, from oil spillage, from the exhausts of millions of cars. It also comes from ordinary people: careless picnickers who dump refuse and motorists who throw beer cans by the side of the road. Can retailers escape responsibility for these environmental problems?

Problems of solid-waste disposal should concern retailers. Packaging materials—paper, cans, bottles, and other containers—account for major disposal efforts. So do such things as food wastes (garbage), newspapers and magazines, discarded toys and tools, rags, furniture, and a variety of other items from Christmas trees to old tires and appliances. We throw away annually such astronomical amounts as 48 billion metal cans, 26 billion glass bottles and jars, 4 million tons of plastic, and 30 million tons of paper.[15] While some of the metal cans are tin, which rusts away in ten to fifteen years, many are aluminum and can last practically forever.

Retailers also have a stake in the depletion of our natural resources, particularly trees, from which paper and many packaging materials come. Furthermore, retailers sell the laundry detergents that pollute our waters, and other products, such as pesticides, that have ill effects on our environment that are not yet fully known.

So, while no single group—packaging companies, manufacturers, consumers, merchants, solid-waste handling agencies—can be blamed for the problems we face, the efforts of all are necessary if the situation is to be improved. Without positive and responsive efforts, our monumental environmental problems may become uncorrectible.

There are some specific things that responsible retailers can do for environmental improvement. They stand in a strategic position of

[15] David Pinto, *How to Make Ecology Work for You* (New York: Chain Store Age Books, 1972), pp. 123–124.

influence between suppliers (who usually are manufacturers) and users. While retailers can seldom coerce, they can influence suppliers by choosing which products to stock and how much space and effort to devote to selling them. Merchants can influence consumers by their choice of brands and which products to emphasize through pricing, display, and advertising.

RETAILING CHALLENGE—*Arousing Consumer Environmental Involvement*

King Soopers, a highly successful Denver-based supermarket chain, has disseminated brochures, booklets, and pamphlets designed to involve citizens in ecology. The firm has run ads asking such local groups as the Boy Scouts, Campfire Girls, Girl Scouts, YMCA, and other organizations to help fight pollution. King's tells them what they can do. And, often as not, these groups take up the challenge.

Even though it is only a small regional chain (forty-nine stores, but dominating the Denver market with 48 percent of the grocery business there), King's has gained a national reputation as a leader among retail ecologists. It has also gained a considerable reputation for its consumer consciousness. For example, its refund policy is so liberal that, in addition to giving a customer's money back for a defective product, it will also pay for the customer's time.

Sources: David Pinto, *How to Make Ecology Work for You* (New York: Chain Store Age Books, 1972), pp. 84–86; "Dillon Cos.: It Couldn't Be Done, But They Did It," *Forbes,* October 16, 1978, pp. 120–122.

For Thought and Discussion

1. "What real good does it do for me to persuade my customers to buy returnable bottles instead of throwaways? This only makes more work for me and more inconvenience for them. And how is what I do going to have any significant effect on the environment?" Evaluate this statement.
2. If one retailer refuses to stock canned beverages and throwaway containers, and insists on returnable bottles, but competing merchants do not, what is the consequence likely to be? Is there a solution?

Retailers can do at least the following things to promote a better environment:

1. They can push their suppliers to avoid nonreusable containers made of metal, glass, or plastic.
2. They can encourage their customers, through persuasion and price advantages, to buy reusable containers, such as soft-drink bottles, and impress customers with the need for pollution control.
3. They can develop incentives for their customers that encourage systematic disposal of wornout products, perhaps through trade-ins and scrap rebates.
4. They can take an active role in persuading manufacturers to develop recycled paper products and promote these in their stores. Recycled paper towels, tissue, napkins, and the like can save thousands of trees.
5. Finally, and as a last recourse, retailers can refuse to stock products that would cause disposal or pollution problems for which there is no apparent solution.

Some retailers are moving in these directions; many are not. In certain areas, retailers are obstructing efforts of citizens to eliminate sources of pollution. In 1970, Bowie, Maryland, was the first city in the nation to impose a local ordinance banning the sale of nonreturnable and nondisposable containers; in 1972, Oregon became the first state to act in a similar manner. But some retailers balked, complaining of the burden of handling returnable bottles and cans, even though cleaner highways, parks, and beaches would result.

COMMUNITY RELATIONS

Retailers have been leaders in community relations in many cities. They have served as chairpersons and workers for United Fund drives, hospital drives, and a host of other charitable activities. Retailers are represented on chambers of commerce and better business bureaus. They serve on community committees and boards dealing with urban and suburban problems. They are involved with cultural activities and organizations. Such service to the community is not limited to the merchant who has deep roots there. Major retail chains often insist that their managers and lesser executives play an active role in the community. Chains may even pay membership fees and provide ample time away from the job for such involvement.

Indicative of the prevailing attitude of retail executives is this quotation: "There is the real need to participate generally in civic, cultural, and charitable activities of our communities. . . . We have the obligation to 'put back' into the community as well as 'take out' of it."[16]

Retail executives have been involved with the National Alliance of Businessmen, an organization aimed at bringing unemployed and underprivileged individuals into the mainstream of society. Some executives have retired early or have been given leaves of absence to devote their time to social and environmental problems.

Opportunities in Community Relations

Numerous possibilities exist for retailers to make a contribution in public and community affairs. The following examples show what some retailers are doing:

1. Employing and training disadvantaged minority-group members to help reduce unemployment and the number of welfare recipients
2. Giving advice and counsel on consumer credit uses and abuses
3. Providing management help and financial assistance to minority businesses, especially in their first months of operation
4. Sponsoring consumer education conferences for newlyweds, ghetto and other disadvantaged consumers, and home economics teachers
5. Maintaining cultural centers in stores for exhibitions of local talent in the arts
6. Providing scholarships and charitable efforts in depressed areas
7. Promoting special projects for cleaning up the environment and recycling containers
8. Offering summer job opportunities, as well as regular part-time jobs, for high school and college students
9. Sponsoring special service clinics and promotions dealing with drug abuse, accident prevention, and so on[17]

The Importance of Good Community Relations

Some retailers see a community-relations commitment as an expression of appreciation for the patronage that makes their enterprise a success. Some feel that they have an obligation to the community. Other

[16] Brockey, "Age of Magnificent Discontent."
[17] For example, Allan L. Korn and John Zoller, "Businessmen Back Summer Jobs," *Stores* (September 1972), 12.

retailers may approach community relations more selfishly; they hope to gain good will, prestige, and tolerance by government bodies. These public-service efforts tend to be contagious; competitors, not wishing to be outdone, may also join in such endeavors.

Of course, the direct short-run benefits to a participating retailer are not obvious. The retailer cannot pinpoint a contribution to net profit. For example, how does a Penney store manager, who is an active member of the chamber of commerce and has directed a charitable fund-raising drive, directly benefit the J. C. Penney Company?

But a broader, longer perspective shows that a retailer should have a strong interest in the well-being and healthy growth of the community, which can create more optimism in the community and a greater total business potential. Community efforts, then, benefit both the firm and the community.[18]

RELATIONS WITH GOVERNMENT

Business today faces increasing governmental regulation. Numerous local and national law regulate competition, furnish protection to consumers, and provide a spur for equitable and honest dealing.

Federal Laws and Regulations Affecting Retailing

In the past, most major laws affecting marketing have dealt with maintaining competition and have directly affected big manufacturers and their dealings with their customers. Such major laws as the Sherman Act, the Clayton Act, and the Robinson-Patman Act only indirectly affect most retailers, and they serve to help small businesses. It is true that fair trade laws and chain-store–restrictive legislation have strongly affected retailing, but these were state, not federal, laws.

However, with the attention given consumer protection today, retailers face many federal laws, both passed and pending. For example, in the credit area alone, four major pieces of federal legislation have been passed.

1. The Consumer Credit Protection Act of 1968 (also called the Truth-in-Lending Law), discussed earlier in this chapter, stipulates the following:

[18] For more discussion, see M. C. Burke and L. L. Berry, "Do Social Actions of a Corporation Influence Store Image and Profits?" *Journal of Retailing* (Winter 1974–1975), 68–72.

    a. Information on how finance charges will be applied, and what the equivalent annual interest rate is, must be provided to the buyer.

    b. Unsolicited credit cards cannot be sent to prospective customers.

    c. The cardholder's liability is limited to $50 if the card is lost or stolen.

2. The "Fair Credit Reporting" Act, effective April 25, 1971, controls credit bureau practices in the formulation and use of consumer credit ratings. It permits a consumer to examine his credit file and dispute any inaccurate information.

3. The Fair Credit Act of 1975 requires retailers to inform customers of their rights in questioning their bills, and where to send inquiries. It also reverses the traditional doctrine of the "holder in due course." Under this doctrine a third party holding a credit contract (for example, one turned over to a credit agency by a retailer) had no obligation for the merchandise received by the customer. The customer was obligated to pay the creditor even if the merchandise was shoddy or defective. This was a rather common phenomenon in the ghetto.[19]

4. The Equal Credit Opportunity Act, effective June 1, 1977, bars sex discrimination in judging a credit application. Lenders' reports to credit bureaus now must include the names of both spouses so that the wife can share in the credit rating. Before, widowed or divorced women often were unable to obtain credit; they had no credit rating because credit reports were in the husband's name only.[20]

It is, of course, impossible to describe here the myriad federal laws that can have some effect on retailers. But several should be briefly noted. Shopping center developers face considerable restraints from a number of environmental-protection laws: the Clean Air Act of 1970, the National Environmental Policy Act of 1970, and the Federal Water Pollution Control Act of 1972. The Occupational Safety and Health Act (OSHA) of 1970 is major legislation affecting retailers as well as all other kinds of businesses. It is designed to improve the safety of workers, and it imposes many standards that add considerably to the costs of doing business, as well as to the expense of constructing new retail stores.[21]

---

[19] "A New FTC Rule Irks the Banks," from the May 24, 1976, issue of BusinessWeek, p. 35. © 1976 by McGraw-Hill, Inc., New York, NY 10020. All rights reserved.

[20] "Married Women Get a Credit Rating," from the June 6, 1977 issue of BusinessWeek, pp. 28–29. © 1977 by McGraw-Hill, Inc., New York, NY 10020. All rights reserved.

[21] OSHA has been greatly criticized. Businesspeople don't criticize the intent of the act, but they feel that its enforcement has involved too much nitpicking and costly interference, without improving worker safety all that much. See, for example, "Accident Statistics That Jolt OSHA," *Business Week,* December 11, 1978, pp. 62–66.

Regulatory agencies of the federal government have been vigorous in attacking alleged deceptive practices, whether by the retailer or by the manufacturer. The *Federal Trade Commission (FTC)*, in particular, has assumed a strong role as a consumer watchdog.

RETAILING ERRORS—*"Deceptive" Practices Resulting in Government Intervention*

Sears' Advertising Problems   In November 1977, the Federal Trade Commission issued a complaint against Sears for making deceptive and unsubstantiated claims for the cleaning performance of its Lady Kenmore dishwashers. Statements in the ads that were challenged were: "The do-it-itself dishwasher. No scraping. No prerinsing. . . ." The FTC maintained that there was no reasonable basis for these claims, that demonstrations did not prove the alleged cleaning ability, and that the claims were inconsistent with the owners' manual, which instructed consumers to presoak and firmly scour cooked- or baked-on foods.

Only a year earlier, Sears had another run-in with the FTC, that time over alleged bait-and-switch tactics, in which it offered sewing machines, washers and dryers, and other major home appliances at low prices to induce prospective purchasers to visit Sears' stores. Salespeople then disparaged the advertised low-priced items and attempted to sell customers higher-priced models.

The AAMCO Automotive Transmission Case   The FTC issued a complaint against AAMCO, a franchisor of automotive transmission rebuilding and repair shops. It alleged that AAMCO's advertisements were full of misrepresentations, such as the following: "$23 removal and inspection service for transmissions," "free towing service," "easy credit terms," and "lifetime" guarantees. The FTC also charged that AAMCO instructed its dealers to disassemble transmissions unnecessarily, thereby forcing the customer to pay undisclosed charges to reassemble the transmission to its former condition in the event he or she resisted the pressure to buy a new or rebuilt one.

Sources: Cases described in "Legal Developments in Marketing," *Journal of Marketing* (July 1978), 120; (April 1977), 106; (January 1971), 82.

For Thought and Discussion

1. How would you defend such practices from the viewpoint of the retailers involved?
2. Is the bait and switch necessarily a deceptive practice that should be curbed by the FTC?

Another form of federal regulation, control of prices and wages, is most common during wartime, but may also be imposed during other times of booming inflation. While such controls are controversial, impose hardships, and curtail some profits, the objective—to stabilize the economy—cannot be questioned. Disagreements focus on how this can be done best.

State and Local Laws Affecting Retailing

Many state and local laws affect retailing. Most of these are restrictive in some way. Many reflect entrenched special-interest groups in state and local communities and are aimed at keeping out or restricting competitors. Frequently, the large corporation or "outside-owned" chain or discounter is the target of the enactments. Table 4.3 shows the major types of such restrictive legislation. Many of the provisions aimed at restricting competition were enacted in the 1930s when small merchants' fear of big firms, and especially of chains, was at its peak. The influence of such laws is waning today in most states; the state fair-trade laws, in particular, were repealed by federal legislation as of March 1976.

However, consumer-protection legislation is increasing. Some states are prohibiting "giveaways" and other promotions. Some prohibit the use of trading stamps. New York City led the way in enacting consumer-protection laws to crack down on deceptive sales practices, and merchants and high-pressure, door-to-door salespeople who prey on ghetto residents. In 1974, the federal government mandated a three-day "cooling off" period for all door-to-door sales involving over $25. This gives the customer three business days in which to cancel the contract and receive a full refund of all money paid. Most states have laws to insure truth in advertising; some have laws against bait advertising and misleading prices. Hazardous products and toys have been banned by some state and local ordinances.

ETHICAL AND SOCIAL RESPONSIBILITY

The area of business activity that involves ethics and social responsibility is murky at best. *Ethics* is concerned with standards for right conduct. *Social responsibility* refers to the sense of responsibility a firm has for the needs of society, over and above its commitment to maximizing profits and stockholder interests. There are widely differing viewpoints

TABLE 4.3   RESTRICTIVE STATE AND LOCAL LAWS AFFECTING
RETAILING

Type of Law or Regulation	Provision
Zoning	Restricts the location and types of stores in a community.
Licenses	Certain types of stores, such as liquor stores, and certain occupations, such as accounting, law, barbering, and medicine, require licenses. Allegedly, licensing enforces certain standards, but in reality it limits competition.
Blue laws	Restrictions on store hours and on Sunday selling.
"Green River" ordinances	Restrictions on activities of salespeople representing nonlocal firms.
Chain-store taxes	Taxes on chain stores, usually graduated according to the number of stores operated in the particular state.
Unfair-trade practices acts	Prohibitions against using loss leaders and offering goods at or near cost.
Fair-trade laws	Requirements that retailers not sell particular branded products below a certain designated "fair-trade" price. All such state laws were repealed by federal legislation in 1976.
Consumer-protection laws	Various state and local laws aimed at protecting consumers from deceptive practices or dangerous goods.

about what is ethical and unethical, and the extent of social responsibility that a firm should demonstrate.

Ethics and the Law

There are some who equate ethical behavior with legal behavior: "If it's not against the law, it's ethical." But this attitude condones many of the shady little deceptions that a scrupulous person would condemn, such as exaggerated claims, overuse of the word *sale*, hiding the fat and gristle of a cut of meat, and so on. Then there is the produce manager of a certain supermarket who decides to get rid of a lot of half-rotten tomatoes by including one, with its good side exposed, in every tomato six-pack.

There may be merit in the position that ethical behavior should go beyond the law, that the law only codifies the bad conduct that society feels most strongly against. On the other hand, perhaps not all behavior that is against the law should be considered unethical, as, for example, remaining open on Sunday despite blue laws.

Ethics and Profits

Many businesspeople assume that the more strictly one interprets ethical behavior, the more profits must suffer. Certainly, the loss that the produce department in the example might incur by throwing away the spoiled tomatoes will be prevented if customers can be induced to buy them without realizing they are bad. And a firm that reduced its cigarette promotion in the interest of consumers' health would probably suffer lower profits.

Yet a strong argument can be made that scrupulously honest and ethical behavior is better for business and for profits. Well-satisfied customers tend to bring repeat business. A firm's reputation for honest dealing can be a powerful competitive advantage. Even during the ghetto riots of the late 1960s, a store that was gutted was sometimes next to an untouched store, the influential factor being the store's reputation for honest or dishonest dealings. Ethical conduct is compatible with maximizing profits *in the long run*. In the very short run, the unscrupulous operator may do better.

How Much Social Responsibility?

Basically the question of social responsibility is one of priorities: Where does a firm's primary duty lie? to its stockholders? its customers? its employees? society in general? Unfortunately, these different interests are often not best served by the same policies. For example, stockholders obtain the greatest benefits from profit-maximization policies, whereas society may not. Yet, we are increasingly recognizing that business firms owe something to the community in which they make their living.

The following are some major issues of social responsibility:

Downtown decay

Abandonment of the ghetto

Minority hiring

Education of and communication with the general public, and with ghetto consumers in particular

Product safety and product quality

DOWNTOWN DECAY   In most U.S. cities, the move to the suburbs and the increasing concentration of lower-income people in the central city has resulted in downtown business districts' losing business and decaying. Major retailers faced with crime, grime, and congestion have either closed out their downtown stores or downgraded them by refusing to put in fresh investment or renovation. With the heart of a city stricken, a much-needed tax base is lessened. Thus, as the taxes are raised for businesses remaining in the city, the incentive to relocate becomes greater, and the cycle continues, gaining momentum.

What is the responsibility of major retailers in this situation? Do they owe any moral obligation to the area that nurtured their growth and present success? As with many ethical and social-responsibility issues, opinions differ widely. A few retailers are plowing in fresh investment downtown. Gimbels East, New York City's first new full-line department store in more than half a century, and one of the country's tallest to date, opened in downtown New York City on 86th Street. Marshall Field built a second store on North Michigan Avenue in Chicago. And a new Bullock's opened in downtown Los Angeles.

Sometimes, in the desire to meet civic responsibilities, a firm may go too far. Take the Higbee Company of Cleveland, one of the largest independent big-city retailers. Attempting to stimulate the city's growth, management poured time and money into civic affairs and urban redevelopment. But the downtown redevelopment projects lost money and the company's main department store also began suffering from more aggressive competitors. By 1979, earnings were not sufficient to cover the annual dividend, and the heavy borrowing had created a seriously troubled retailer.[22]

ABANDONMENT OF THE GHETTO   We have noted the inclination of most large retailers, especially chains, to leave the ghetto market to

[22] "Perils of Not Minding the Store," from the January 15, 1979 issue of BusinessWeek, pp. 56–58. © 1979 by McGraw-Hill, Inc., New York, NY 10020. All rights reserved.

marginal retailers and direct their energies instead to the affluent suburbs. This raises the question: Should a retail chain open stores in ghetto areas, even though past experience has shown that such outlets often lose money? But perhaps another question is more relevant: How can marketing strategy and operational efforts be adjusted to better tap the potential existing in the ghetto? The first question reflects a negative, even a defeatist, attitude. The second suggests that a firm can provide a much-needed social service and still make money.[23]

MINORITY HIRING   Employing disadvantaged, perhaps underqualified, minority workers is a social responsibility that can benefit the employer. The training problems may be greater than with more experienced employees. If employees are inexperienced, the demands on the firm are greater; personnel training costs may be higher; and there is some danger of customer dissatisfaction because of less knowledgeable and, perhaps, less tactful employees. The disadvantages may be offset by gains from tapping a new labor pool and from enhancing the firm's rapport with its minority customers. And the real success of conscientious minority hiring, training, and follow-up is a more livable and prosperous community. As with other social-responsibility issues, the decision to take positive action may be made altruistically, but there are also tangible gains.

EDUCATION AND COMMUNICATION   A socially responsible firm can lead in fostering consumer-education programs, in helping consumers of all ages and races to make more knowledgeable buying decisions. While such a stance means that any practices bordering on deception, exaggeration, or misinformation must be discarded, the gains in customer good will and an improved public image can be substantial.

PRODUCT SAFETY AND PRODUCT QUALITY   Problems with products may seem more the responsibility of the manufacturers who make them than of the retailers who sell them. But socially concerned retailers can hardly hold themselves above such matters. It is difficult to be aware of all product quality and safety problems in the goods handled. Still, when defective products come to their attention, either through their own observation or the complaints of customers, retailers can certainly take a strong position against the products, and against the manufacturers who supply them.

---

[23] For a comprehensive treatment of this topic and of ghetto marketing in general, see Alan R. Andreasen, *The Disadvantaged Consumer* (New York: Free Press, 1975).

Furthering the Social Contribution of Retailing

Opportunities for a social contribution by retailers extend beyond what has been mentioned. Consider the contributions of Pier 1 Imports, Inc., in the international arena.

In 1966 Pier 1 started business. Five years later it had grown into the largest chain of import stores in the United States, with sales of over $39 million from 196 stores. The strategy that made all this possible also brought new, even undreamed of, prosperity to scores of tiny villages in remote, undeveloped corners of the world. Cottage industries have been organized to mass-produce handcrafted items such as cricket cages and carved elephants from Kenya, dried blowfish from Taiwan, Mexican piñatas, brass pots, wicker tables and chairs, and wooden bowls from the Philippines. One small farming community in Rumania crafts 10,000 wicker chairs a year "in the winter when they can't work in the fields." One supplier in Mexico transformed a small shop in the back of his house into a factory employing more than fifty workers. An entire village in Kenya carves wooden animals for Pier 1. By 1977 Pier 1 had some three hundred stores and was budgeting $4 million in advertising. Many items that made the company's stores unique ten years before were now carried by discounters, drug stores, and department stores. As a result, Pier 1 began molding a new image as a chain of specialty stores featuring decorative home furnishings, accents, and gift specialties.[24] But the impetus it had given to overseas cottage industries caused them to mushroom.

Not all retailers concern themselves with the broader aspects of how to help society. But as the Pier 1 example shows, profitability need not suffer for social causes; the responsive retailer may discover opportunities instead.

■ Summary

Today's retailer can hardly ignore a new dimension in the environment surrounding business. This is true for small retailers; it is even more true for larger ones. Consumers and government have become less apathetic, more demanding, more critical, and less tolerant of selfish business practices. In this chapter, we focused on some of the more important issues and problems that face retailers, namely, dissatisfied consumers (consumerism), sales in the ghetto, the environment, community and government relations, and the more intangible issues of

[24] "Pier 1: A Retailer for Cottage Industries," from the October 2, 1971 issue of BusinessWeek, pp. 58–59. © 1971 by McGraw-Hill, Inc., New York, NY 10020. All rights reserved; and "Pier 1 Molding New Image with Spokeswoman," *Advertising Age,* November 21, 1977, p. 80.

ethical and social responsibility. The use of the word *issue* is well advised, since many of the situations described in this chapter have no all-acceptable solution. Opinions differ; what may satisfy one group of people, such as environmentalists, may be rejected by other groups who want convenience, stability, and low prices.

As we have seen in this chapter, however, the issues of consumerism and environmental protection can afford retailers opportunities to differentiate themselves from competitors by being more responsive to a changing environment. Some retailers and other members of the business community show apathy or selfish disinterest for social and environmental issues. The result may be increased governmental intervention and regulation. Retailers are especially involved in certain areas of social responsibility: How much do they owe the community that sustains them? Yet the possibility exists that altruism and involvement in community improvement may cause profits to suffer and jeopardize the viability of a firm, or at least the satisfaction of its stockholders.

■ **Key Terms**

Bait and switch	Garnishment
Balloon note	Licenses
Better business bureaus	Lien against property
Compensatory consumption	Nutrition labeling
Consumerism	Open dating
Ethics	Puffing
Fair-trade laws	Social responsibility
Federal Trade Commission (FTC)	Tossover selling technique
	Unit pricing
Fraud	Zoning

■ **Discussion Questions**

1. With what types of products and services is outright fraud most likely to occur? Why?
2. What is puffing? At what point would you say that puffing becomes deceptive? Can you give any criteria for determining this?
3. Do you think sales and market share results provide a good measure of customer satisfaction? Why or why not? How about letters of complaint?
4. If ghetto stores charge much higher prices than stores outside the

ghetto, why don't their customers simply shop where prices are better?

5. Bait-and-switch tactics are common in retailing. In fact, most retail advertising focuses on the lowest-priced item, with the expectation that some customers will be "traded up." At what point do you think bait and switch becomes dishonest and deceptive?

6. Would you say that a firm that violates a blue law, and thereby incurs a fine, is acting unethically? Why or why not?

7. "My employees are welcome to do community-relations work on their own time. I can't afford to have them doing so during working hours." Evaluate this position.

8. Why do you think retail chains have encouraged, and in some cases insisted on, local managerial participation in community organizations and activities?

9. How can the extent of customer good will toward a store be measured?

10. In view of the publicity given to crimes committed with guns, do you see any ethical questions for a firm that continues to sell handguns, especially so-called Saturday night specials?

■ Project

Check for consumer-help organizations in your community. Ascertain how long they have been in operation, their specific functions or objectives, and how many customers they have benefited. Evaluate their effectiveness. How could they be more effective?

■ Exercise in Creativity

The general manager of a regional chain of drugstores (which also carry a wide range of nondrug items) wants to improve the public image of his firm. A research study has found the chain to have a cold, impersonal, cut-rate, generally negative image. You have been asked to help the firm develop its image as a responsive retailer, one concerned with the environment and other social problems. What steps would you recommend for acquiring such an image?

■ Retailing in Action

Richard Mayan is a buyer of curtains and draperies for a growing discount-store chain that presently has seven stores. Drapery hardware is a subdepartment with merchandise that sells steadily from a twenty-foot wall display furnished for each store by the manufacturer. Because of the display and the many different items needed for a complete line, most of this merchandise is bought from only one supplier.

Since Richard has been in the department, another drapery hardware manufacturer has been pressuring him: "Even if you won't put us in all your stores, at least try us in a few."

Richard has investigated the company and its products and can find no appreciable differences in prices and quality. However, the manufacturer's representative says, "My boss has authorized me to buy you two new suits—anything you want—if you will let us put our display and goods in two of your stores."

What should Richard do? What would you do?

Would he be acting unethically if he took up the offer?

Would you change your opinion if the goods in question were of inferior quality or higher in price?

Where should one draw the line on payola?

Cases for Part One

MORGAN FURNITURE AND APPLIANCE STORE—Marketing Practices in the Ghetto[1]

Sam Morgan has graduated with a degree in business administration from a prominent university. His father has long been trying to persuade him to come into the family business, which is a furniture and appliance store in New York's Harlem. The father, nearing sixty, wants to slow down from the six-day-a-week job and gradually turn responsibility over to his son. Despite the fact that the profits from the store give the Morgan family a comfortable living in an affluent suburb and enabled Sam to graduate from a prestigious university, certain aspects of his father's operation trouble Sam badly. "This is the only way that business can be done in the ghetto," his father has always dogmatically maintained.

The Morgan store occupies a choice location on a corner. Consequently, it has a double exposure: two windows facing each of the two moderately busy, intersecting streets. Mr. Morgan believes this permits him to almost double the sales he would have with a noncorner location. And he uses his windows to advantage. One window on each side of the corner entrance usually features a complete room of brightly colored furniture—perhaps a $77 bedroom suite, or a complete living room for "only $99." The other two windows often do not carry price tags, but display color TV sets and other appliances, along with big signs such as "Friendly, Easy Credit!" Sale streamers are pasted on all four windows and on the doors as well. Mr. Morgan believes, "Our customers want to shop where they feel welcome, where there is always a sale, and, of course, where they can buy on credit."

Inside the store, most merchandise does not carry a price tag. "I find it better to be somewhat flexible in my pricing," Mr. Morgan acknowledges. "Some people can't afford as much as some others, so I try to adjust to what I think they can afford—within limits." Sam knows that his father charges high prices; sometimes he is appalled at the customary $100 to $200 difference over what a downtown department store might charge. For example, one day while he was in the store a black-and-white TV set sold for $349; he recalled having seen the same brand and model displayed at $169 in one of the larger downtown stores.

[1] Adapted from a case in Robert F. Hartley, *Marketing Fundamentals* (New York: Dun-Donnelley, 1976), pp. 563–566.

"I have to charge more," his father explained. "I only buy these one at a time, so I pay a lot more. Then my credit losses—most customers buy on credit—run up to 25 percent. My insurance charges are higher. I have to worry about being robbed. All these things add to my costs of doing business."

The customers are mostly black, with a scattering of Puerto Ricans. Most of them have low-paying jobs and are or have been on welfare. They do not have cash, and if they are to buy any furniture or appliances, they must have credit. They are poor credit risks; the bigger downtown stores refuse to take the risk. But Morgan's is willing to, for a fee (as are most other stores in the ghetto).

Mr. Morgan pushes his installment sales, even though he doesn't believe that the 18 percent annual interest rate—the maximum allowed by law—yields much if any profit; most of the interest is eaten up by collection costs, attorney's fees, and uncollectable-account losses. "We push credit because every installment customer is a future customer. He has to come into the store to make his weekly or monthly payments. Often he sees something else to add to his account." The office is on the second floor, so the customer has to go all through the store to make his payment.

Bad-debt losses do run fairly high. But, considering the low incomes of the customers, these losses could be much worse. Morgan does not discount his installment contracts to a finance company, preferring to make his own collections. He is reluctant to grant credit to those who do not have wages that can be attached in the event of nonpayment, although he will consider doing business with welfare recipients, employees of the federal government, and others who cannot be garnished, if they have a large downpayment. He attempts to be firm but flexible in his collection methods. If a customer occasionally misses a payment, he will not immediately repossess, but will send a polite reminder letter. In this way he hopes to avoid losing a customer. And he is always sympathetic to any unusual problems a customer may have. With time, though, dunning can become much harsher. Threatening letters will be used, as well as phone calls (if the customer has a phone). Morgan may also contact the employer to remind him or her of the extra bookkeeping involved if a garnishment is required, and to suggest that the employer use some persuasion to get the delinquent employee to pay up. Morgan has no qualms about taking a case to court; and he wins most of these cases by default, since the customers are generally unfamiliar with legal procedures.

Another aspect of the operation troubles Sam Morgan. The four sales-people his father employs are masters of the bait and switch. The customer coming in for the $99 living room set displayed in the window will often be adroitly "switched" to a higher-priced, better-profit set. "I would not keep these men if they could not use the hard sell. Our customers need a push. They appreciate having their decisions made for them. If we don't do it here, they'll go to some other store, and someone else will give them the hard sell," Mr. Morgan maintains.

Sam also observes that if one salesclerk is not able to close a sale with a particularly difficult customer, then a wink to another salesclerk, or sometimes to Mr. Morgan, results. The customer is then turned over to someone else to prevent a hasty departure. This tossover technique is often effective in crumbling a customer's defenses. As Sam's father says, "We only get ten to twelve customers on a normal day in here; we can't let any of them get away. Competition is too keen. There are forty or more stores like us in this area."

Sam's father does very little advertising. Most of the promotional efforts are through window displays that emphasize 50 percent discounts and other appealing "bargains." Mr. Morgan explains, "Most of these Puerto Rican customers can't read English (some can't even speak it). And most of the blacks either aren't able to read, or else hardly ever buy a newspaper."

Sam ponders whether or not to join his father. He feels ashamed of some of the practices his father and other ghetto merchants are using and thinks there must be a better way. At the same time, the low turnover, the high costs of insurance, and the need to furnish credit at substantial risk, are all obstacles to using more legitimate methods of operation. There is always the danger of rioting and looting, although this seems to have lessened in recent years. However, robberies and muggings are increasing. And there is a social stigma in being a ghetto merchant: you are criticized by your neighbors at home and often hated by your customers for selling shoddy goods and forcing the everlasting monthly payment.

Questions

1. What do you think Sam's decision should be? Why?
2. Would you change the Morgan operation? How?
3. Where would you draw the line regarding ethical conduct in this case?
4. How can more legitimate retailing practices be financially viable in the ghetto environment?

GEORGE'S JEWELRY—Small Store Seeking to Make a Change

George's Jewelry is a small neighborhood store located in an older Chicago suburb. Since it began operations in its present location, sales have climbed only slightly.

1971	$59,273
1972	62,154
1973	63,051
1974	64,150

1975	64,858
1976	65,397
1977	65,208
1978	65,876

In the last two years the neighborhood has begun to change. A number of robberies have taken place nearby, and the store itself has been broken into twice. Many of the better customers are moving away from the area, and this in turn has hurt sales. Faced with this dismal situation, the owner, Mr. Koriakis, is considering whether or not to relocate his jewelry store.

Shortly after World War II, George Koriakis immigrated to the United States, having learned his watch-repair skills from his uncle. Soon after arriving in Chicago, he opened his first jewelry store about two miles from downtown on a main traffic thoroughfare. Over the years he built up a large following of loyal customers and a very successful business. His success could be traced to two factors: the personal service he gave his customers, and the excellent watch-repair work he did. However, in the mid-1960s the neighborhood began deteriorating, culminating in his being robbed and injured so badly that he spent several months recovering. After that he closed his store and relocated in an older, middle-class suburb. Although he practiced the same business philosophy in his new store, he was never able to build up as large a clientele of loyal customers as he had previously.

The stagnant sales of the present store can be attributed partly to changes in the retail jewelry business itself. Competition from discount stores, department stores, variety stores, and catalog showrooms is forcing many smaller retailers out of business.

Mr. Koriakis is seriously considering relocating in a suburban shopping center. He finds that the rent for a 20-by-40-foot store in one such center would be $650 per month. This does not include the following additional estimated expenses: $35 a month for maintenance; $90 a month for utilities; $75 a month for comprehensive insurance; and $40 a month for miscellaneous expenses. Furthermore, a five-year lease is required, and 4 percent of gross sales over $100,000 is collected by the lessors. Mr. Koriakis is also considering relocating in a larger, more prestigious shopping center. But there the rent alone would be $950 a month.

In recent years a unique concept in shopping centers has developed: the "Enclosed Shopping Village." Existing vacant buildings, usually abandoned discount department stores, are subdivided into as many as 155 individual stores within the one large building. Two of these "villages" have recently opened in the Chicago area. The subdivisions are leased on the following basis: the landlord pays all utilities, maintenance, and security costs; the shopkeeper signs a one-year lease with a two-year option and receives three 8-foot-high paneled walls, and three electrical outlets. The front of the shop is left open and the shopkeeper is required to close it at his own expense to his own taste. The hours that the "village" is open are 6:00–10:00 P.M. on Thursday and Friday, 12:00–10:00 P.M. on Saturday, and 12:00–6:00 P.M. on Sunday, for a total of twenty-four hours a week.

Rents range from $229 a month for a 10-by-10-foot unit, to $550 a month for 15 by 20 feet. Furthermore, the lessor collects no percentage of sales. The only additional cost to the shop owner is a $45-monthly advertising charge, which goes toward a $150,000-a-year overall advertising and promotional budget for the village. The population within 3.7 miles of the village in which Mr. Koriakis is interested is 487,000, and the developer estimates that customer turnout will range between 14,000 and 22,000 each week.

Questions

1. Mr. Koriakis expects gross profit (before expenses) to be 50 percent of sales, and his expenses, other than occupancy costs, are $16,000, which includes his salary, or draw. What sales volume will he have to achieve to make a profit in the first shopping center he is considering?
2. What sales volume will he have to achieve to break even in the 10-by-10-foot shop at the village?
3. What disadvantages do you see in locating in the village?
4. On balance, what is your recommendation to Mr. Koriakis? Why?

2

Planning the Retail Enterprise

5 Aiming Retailing Efforts: The Retailing Mix

The neighborhood or city where a retailer operates is seldom homogeneous. Customers differ in their characteristics and attitudes. For the small corner grocery, the differences may not be significant, but for larger stores drawing from a wide area, the market consists of a number of customer groups or *market segments*. For example, the homeowner and the renter are part of two significant market segments with different buying habits and needs. A market area can be divided into those consumers who have low incomes or are attracted by sales and low-end merchandise, and those who have higher incomes and want better-quality goods to choose from.

How a firm uses its merchandise, prices, services, and promotional efforts to cater to particular customers is called the *retailing mix*. The components of the retailing mix will be discussed later in this chapter. First, the image of the store must be considered.

IMPORTANCE OF STORE IMAGE

Store image is the way a particular retailer is viewed by customers. Customers seldom verbalize an image until they discuss where they like to shop. Then a store image may appear in such remarks as: "They have the friendliest clerks there," or "Their meat doesn't look as good as ____'s."

A retailer's image is a result of the way business is carried on, the location, and the physical appearance of the store. The major elements in a consumer's view of a store are:

The location of the store

Its size, newness, type of fixtures and displays, width of aisles

Type (age, social class, grooming, and so on) of salespeople and other store employees, and their friendliness, courtesy, and merchandise knowledge

Frequency of advertising and the style of ad layout (whether cluttered, heavy with headlines and sales pitches, or subdued, with much white space)

Number and genuineness of "sales"

Quality and type of merchandise; how it is packaged, displayed, and priced; the brands carried

General atmosphere of store, whether dark or well lighted, whether noisy or subdued, whether cheerful or somber, clean or cluttered, friendly or impersonal

After-sales experience with the store and its merchandise: honesty and dependability; handling of adjustments and complaints.

Probably one of the most serious deficiencies of any retail firm is not having an image.

What happens to the retail store that lacks a sharp character, that does not stand for something special to any class of shoppers? It ends up as an alternative store in the customer's mind. The shopper does not head for such a store as the primary place to find what [he or she] wants. Without certain

*outstanding departments and lines of merchandise, without clear attraction
for some group, it is like a dull person.* [1]

In recent years, a major retail chain, some seventy years old, expanded
without a clear objective of what it wanted to be, and met disaster.

RETAILING ERRORS—W. T. Grant Company: Lack of Distinctive Image

In June 1975, with almost 1,200 stores and sales approaching $2 billion,
Grant ranked in the top half-dozen U.S. merchandisers, in the company of
K mart, Marcor, Penney, Sears, and Woolworth. But Grant faced serious
problems. It was in financial jeopardy; indeed, on the verge of bankruptcy.
It had lost a staggering $175 million in 1974 and had already lost $54
million in the first quarter of 1975. Furthermore, it owed hundreds of
millions of dollars to banks and other creditors. The end came in February
1976 when Grant, after seventy years of proud existence, was forced into
bankruptcy and liquidation. It was one of the largest firms ever to go
bankrupt.

While the direct cause of the Grant calamity was reckless expansion in
the early 1970s, a major source of its problems was that it expanded without
having a definable and distinctive image in the minds of shoppers: "You
walk into their stores and you don't know whether they're trying to be a
discounter or compete with Sears and Penney . . . they're almost imageless."

Sources: For more detail, see "Notes of Grant Creditors' Panel Filed, Show Firm's Effort to
Avoid Bankruptcy," *Wall Street Journal,* June 21, 1976, p. 5; Robert F. Hartley, "W. T.
Grant—Ill-conceived Expansion," in *Marketing Mistakes* (Columbus, Ohio: Grid Publishing,
1976), pp. 45–56.

For Thought and Discussion

1. What image do you think Grant should have aimed for?
2. How might it have gone about developing such an image?

Image is not an easy thing for a firm to improve or to change. Later in
this chapter, we will consider some positive things a firm can do to
capitalize on its potential and thereby achieve a desired image. But
before a firm can decide what image it wants to project, it must

---

[1] This statement is not new, but comes from the original study of the importance of store image by
Pierre Martineau, "The Personality of the Retail Store," *Harvard Business Review* (January–
February 1958), 50. The statement is as valid today as it was when first published.

determine who its target customers are. Only then can it build an image that will attract such customers effectively.

THE NEED FOR TARGET CUSTOMERS

No store can be all things to all people, despite claims to this effect made by a few large department stores. Invariably, a certain type of customer will be attracted by a firm's location, goods, prices, salespeople, services, and so on. The same features that attract some customers will alienate others. Perhaps this is best illustrated by a discount store that attracts certain people because of low prices, informality, and the convenience of parking. The typical customer of a high-fashion department or specialty store, on the other hand, would be repelled by "popular" prices and styles, and the lack of services and other amenities.

With many retailers, the attraction of certain types of customers is more accidental than planned. Other retailers, however, analyze their customers and consciously exert efforts to continue to attract them, or shift policies and appeals to attract other customers with more long-term potential. For example, a major department store in Chicago analyzed the characteristics of its customers—income, family size, age, and so on. Appallingly, it found that it did not have its share of the young marrieds with growing families and mounting merchandise needs. Instead, the bulk of its charge accounts were with older couples and individuals, many of relatively high incomes, but with decreasing needs. The store hastily reassessed its policies in an effort to attract middle-class families.

In Chapter 20 we will explore retail research and how characteristics of customers are determined. At this point, let us establish that a firm should know who its *target customers* are and which consumer groups it is best—and least—able to serve. The retailer opening a new store or an additional store has a better chance of success if it can be learned *which consumer groups are best served by existing retailers and which are least well served.* The latter consumers may represent the best potential for a new store.

MARKET SEGMENTATION

A total market is divided into various segments or groups. The people within each segment are similar in their wants and their reactions to sales appeals and product offerings. In other words, a large and diversified consumer market is composed of smaller subgroups that are rather homogeneous but may differ greatly from other groups. A moment's reflection will reveal how greatly groups can differ, even though they reside in the same geographical area. For example, college students comprise one very important segment for some retailers and some manufacturers of consumer goods. Yet the interests of this group differ greatly from the interests of the young married group, or of couples with children, a suburban home, and a sizable mortgage.

Reason for Segmentation Strategy

If a retailer chooses target segments carefully and appeals to them effectively, the result will be a far more profitable marketing strategy

This store appeals to a specific and narrowly defined market. Such a speciality store offers greater depth of merchandise and more personal service than larger, multiline stores usually do. Will a specialty store always have a competitive edge? (Ray Ellis/ Photo Researchers, Inc. and Lady Madonna Maternity Boutique)

than trying to please all consumers. By tailoring all merchandise and promotional efforts toward a selected group of customers, a store can offer a greater variety of goods and better service, and can zero in on target customers with effective promotion. Target customers will then more likely be satisfied and loyal customers.

For a segmentation strategy to work, three things are necessary:

1. Target customers or segments must be identifiable.
2. They must be a large enough group and have sufficient purchasing power to be attractive to the retailer.
3. They must be reachable by promotional efforts, special merchandise, and service offerings.

The college market generally meets these requirements. It is easily identified; the potential purchasing power is substantial; and promotional efforts can be directed through college publications and other media that are widely read or heard.

On the other hand, some consumer segments are difficult to reach or are too small. For example, how could one effectively identify and reach consumers who need corrective footwear? Or who like to try new things? Or who tend to have high brand and store loyalty?

SUCCESSFUL RETAILING STRATEGIES—*Lane Bryant: An Example of Effective Market Segmentation*

Lane Bryant is a chain of 213 retail stores, as well as a mail-order business. In 1977, its sales were $333 million, most of them to hard-to-fit women. "We discovered fringes of consumers who were not being well serviced, and we began to develop clothing to satisfy them."

The initial growth of Lane Bryant can be at least partly attributed to mass merchandisers' trimming their stocks of large-size dresses—leaving them to Lane Bryant—to better cater to youth and diet-conscious adults. Lane Bryant offers great depth in sizes 16 and 18, sizes for tall girls, chubby girls and teens, short stouts, and other custom sizes.

The success of Lane Bryant has stirred other retailers to re-examine these neglected customer segments. Still, Lane Bryant remains the volume leader in merchandising efforts toward hard-to-fit women, with sales having increased 45 percent and profits, 34 percent, since 1970.

Sources: "Bless 'Em All . . . ," *Forbes,* December 1, 1971, p. 75; "Taking Maternity Leave," from the June 1, 1974 issue of BusinessWeek, p. 67, © 1974 by McGraw-Hill, Inc., New York, NY 10020. All rights reserved. And from Lane Bryant annual reports.

For Thought and Discussion

1. Do you think the discount stores and department stores erred in neglecting this market segment? Why or why not?
2. At this time, how vulnerable do you think Lane Bryant is to competitive inroads?

Practical Ways to Segment

Lane Bryant segmented on the basis of customer sizes, or, to put it another way, by physical characteristics. The easiest way to distinguish significant groups in the marketplace is by using *demographic factors.* These are certain statistical characteristics of the population that identify the composition of consumers within a particular trading area. The following are the most popular:

1. Age   Children, youths, adults, the elderly
2. Sex
3. Size of household   Single individuals, couples, families with various numbers of children
4. Nature of housing   Single-family dwellings, multiple-family dwellings; owner, renter
5. Income
6. Education
7. Occupation   Professional and technical, managerial, white collar, blue collar, farmers, housewives, unemployed
8. Race   White, Negro, Oriental, Hispanic American, American Indian
9. Religion
10. Social class   Lower-lower, upper-lower, lower-middle, upper-middle, lower-upper, upper-upper

Besides these demographic bases, for which market statistics are readily available through governmental and other agencies, other bases help account for demand variations. Not all are easily identifiable or practical to isolate and reach, but where this can be done, a retailer has a powerful marketing tool. Examples of other bases for segmentation are:

1. Fashion interest	Tendency toward leadership or conformity
2. Physical charactristics	Like those Lane Bryant chose to use as a major base for segmenting
3. Leisure-time interests	Gardening, sailing, running
4. Benefits sought	Economy, status, dependability
5. Brand- and store-loyalty tendencies	Inclination toward strong or shifting loyalties

While they are less practical for the average retailer, there are various psychological attributes by which people can be segmented:

1. Extroverts and introverts
2. Conservatives and radicals
3. Leaders and followers
4. Impulsive and deliberate
5. Self-confident and unsure
6. High achievers and low achievers

These by no means show all possible ways of grouping or segmenting people.[2] Nor is it always useful to use such means of segmentation. One would not attempt to present products specifically to extroverts or introverts, for example. However, psychological segmentation some-times can be effective. The manufacturer of a deodorant may direct his advertising to people who are psychologically unsure of themselves and require a product to give them confidence.

Most large retailers will not appeal to only one segment. Some departments of a store appeal to certain customers—such as those of middle income—while other departments are geared to a higher-income group. However, as we will discover later in this chapter, some coordination of the retailing mix is needed so that various departments and activities of a store (pricing, merchandise lines, advertising, caliber of salesforce) are not working at cross-purposes.

---

[2] The whole field of consumer behavior, which draws on research findings and techniques from psychology, sociology, anthropology, and other behavioral disciplines, is aimed at identifying and reaching consumers, individually and in groups. Many of these concepts can be of use to retailers, particularly those of communication, opinion leadership, motivation, perception, and cognitive dissonance. For a recent text introducing the basic concepts of consumer behavior, see Gerald Zaltman and Melanie Wallendorf, *Consumer Behavior* (New York: Wiley, 1979).

Neglected Market Segments

Sometimes certain categories of consumers are relatively neglected. Retailers tend to be followers or conformists, rather than innovators. This has resulted in a concentration of retailers in suburban locations, to the point, in many communities, of saturation: there are too many similar stores competing for the same customers. Other market segments are neglected. Two such relatively neglected categories of consumers are the rural market and the Spanish-speaking market.

THE RURAL MARKET SEGMENT   Small rural towns (which we will define as nonsuburban communities of under 25,000 people) have considerable homogeneity in attitudes and buying habits. Research has found that these rural consumers are dissatisfied with their shopping environment.[3] While most believe they face higher prices than would be the case in bigger cities with more competition, this is not the major source of their dissatisfaction. They are unhappy with the small assortment of goods and with the slowness of local merchants in stocking new items.

One might think that such rural consumers could satisfy their major shopping requirements in periodic trips to larger cities. Few of these small towns are more than two hours away from major shopping centers. But apparently only a minority avail themselves of big-city shopping. Most hesitate because of the congestion and complexity of large cities and the unfamiliarity and impersonality of the stores there.

This situation suggests opportunity for retailers to better serve this large segment of consumers. Stores carrying large assortments of goods might find a substantial market here. They might draw customers from neighboring small towns as well. Stores in major cities might direct promotional efforts and special "courtesy" privileges, such as free parking and shopping tours, to their rural hinterland to encourage periodic shopping trips. Although the growth rate in such small towns is not comparable with the burgeoning suburbs of most cities, such towns represent a sizable market, one rapidly increasing in per capita income. Perhaps more important, competition is far less keen than in the major centers of population.

THE SPANISH-SPEAKING MARKET SEGMENT   This market seldom receives retailers' attention. In size it comprises some 11 million consumers, 6 percent of our total population. Furthermore, it is concentrated

---

[3] Robert F. Hartley, "The Perceived Importance of Price in Small-town Shopping Behavior," *Southern Journal of Business* (April 1970), 24–32.

This retailer caters to a specific ethnic group, one generally neglected by larger retailers, and has thereby been able to achieve a differential advantage. (Paolo Koch/Photo Researchers, Inc.)

in New York City, Miami, the Mexican border area, and California. Its growth rate is greater than that of the white English-speaking majority. And it is relatively homogeneous. It is easy to reach through Spanish-language radio stations, newspapers, magazines, TV stations, and movie houses.

Most of the retailers who presently vie for this market are marginal firms, usually run by members of the group. For example, in New York City alone there are 5,000 small Hispanic grocery stores (*bodegas*) and 750 drugstores (*farmacias*). To tap this market effectively, retailers need a special retailing mix and strategy. Spanish-speaking employees are required and differing customs, needs, and attitudes must be considered. But the potential is great for retailers who are willing to bring efficiency and broader merchandise offerings into this market.

OTHER NEGLECTED MARKET SEGMENTS Some other market segments tend to be neglected. Senior citizens and people who have

recently moved are ignored by most retailers. While few retailers can
afford to limit target markets to these groups, they do represent potential for extra business.

Senior citizens (those over sixty-five) make up almost 11 percent of
the population—some 23 million Americans. This segment is increasing twice as fast as the population under sixty-five. But for all their
numbers, these older Americans remain one of the most neglected
minorities in our country. While their individual incomes are low
(averaging about half the average income of the younger group) they
still represent an enormous market, which is bound to grow as pension
programs expand their coverage and benefits. We know that elderly
consumers tend to be more cautious than younger ones, more set in
their preferences, and are shrewder comparison shoppers. Yet, how
many retailers consciously seek to attract these consumers through
special products, facilities, services, and promotional efforts?[4]

The "movers" also represent a sizable market, one even more neglected than the elderly. For one representative year, 1977, the breakdown into percentages of the total population of those who had and had
not moved within the last two years was as follows:[5]

Nonmovers (still in same house as in 1975)	72.6%
Movers (to a different house)	
In the same metropolitan area	12.9%
In a different metropolitan area	13.6
Movers from abroad	1.0
	———
Total movers	27.5%

(The percentages do not add up to quite 100% because of rounding.)

In numbers 54,620,000 people moved to a different house in the
two-year period from 1975 to 1977; 29,959,000 of these moved some
distance, at least to a different city, and some 2,000,000 of these moved
from abroad. The retailing opportunities from such mobility are
significant. These people have to acquire new shopping habits, sometimes new product and brand preferences. Accumulating information
about the new economic environment becomes important. An alert
retailer who welcomes newcomers and provides them with helpful

[4] For an examination of the potential of sixty-five–and-over consumers, see Betsy D. Gelb,
"Exploring the Gray Market Segment," *Business Topics* (Spring 1978), 41–48.
[5] *Statistical Abstract of the United States,* 1978, Mobility Statistics, p. 39.

information wins new customers. But in most communities a large percentage of newcomers go unrecognized during their frequently difficult adjustment period.

Recently, some furniture manufacturers and retailers have begun appealing to this segment of the market. Customer-assembled furniture, known as K-D (for "knock-down"), is sold unassembled and packed in cartons. K-D furniture is in great demand among customers who want to save and also want ease of moving. Such furniture can be disassembled and loaded back into original cartons, making moving quicker and less espensive.[6]

WAYS TO SATISFY CUSTOMERS—
THE RETAILING MIX

In Chapter 2 we noted that customer needs and wants—the reasons why a customer tends to shop at a particular store—can be considered under these categories:

Convenience of shopping
Merchandise assortment—breadth and depth
Quality and fashion level of merchandise
Prices
Services
Store excitement

If retailers correctly appraise their target customers, they can adjust merchandise and services accordingly. To a large extent the various combinations of merchandise and services are *controllable* by the retailer. Stores can stay open evenings and on Sundays (unless prohibited by city or county blue laws); merchants can decide to stock low-priced or expensive goods; to offer many services or a bare minimum; to have frequent sales, style shows, and other excitement-creating events, or none. The way in which these goods and services are combined by a particular retail store is the *retailing mix*. A good retailing mix provides a high degree of satisfaction for target customers and results in customer loyalty.

[6] "The Upswing in Knock-Down Furniture," *Business Week,* September 18, 1978, pp. 61–64.

Components of the Retailing Mix

Of course, the components of the retailing mix exist to a greater or lesser degree in every store. For example, one store may offer more shopping convenience than another, but a third store may offer still more. Figure 5.2 on page 122, depicts these components on a scale by which stores can be compared and contrasted.

CONVENIENCE OF SHOPPING   From the consumer's viewpoint, convenience involves time, place, and effort. A store open every night and also on Sunday is certainly more convenient than one open only from 9:30 to 5:00. While discount stores had several powerful attractions when they made their great inroads into the existing retail structure, not the least of their appeal came from their longer shopping hours and ease of parking.

If a store is located close to the customer, it has more "place convenience" than one far distant. This factor helps account for the rush to the suburbs by many retailers.

Less effort needed for shopping is another aspect of convenience. In an attempt to counteract competition from convenience food stores (7-Eleven, Li'l General, Minit Markets, to name a few), many supermarkets have fast check-out lanes limited to those customers with only a few items. But even so, shopping in a big store usually requires more effort and time.

MERCHANDISE ASSORTMENT: BREADTH   A store with many lines and departments of merchandise has *breadth of assortment*; a narrow-line store is a specialty store. Two trends in retail establishments are evident: many stores that carried limited lines, such as groceries or drugs, are expanding their lines through scrambled merchandising and are thereby offering a broader assortment. On the other hand, specialty stores and boutiques are prospering through offering such narrow assortments as wigs, pets, lamps and shades, and jeans.

MERCHANDISE ASSORTMENT: DEPTH   *Depth of assortment* refers to the variety of colors, styles, sizes, and prices that a retailer offers in a given line. Such depth explains the popularity of specialty stores. For example, a shopper wanting a large assortment of wigs and expert knowledge of them would probably go to a specialty store, not a discount or department store. Figure 5.1 shows the difference between merchandise breadth and depth and how these vary for typical discount, department, and specialty stores.

Merchandise depth and breadth are seldom found in one store,

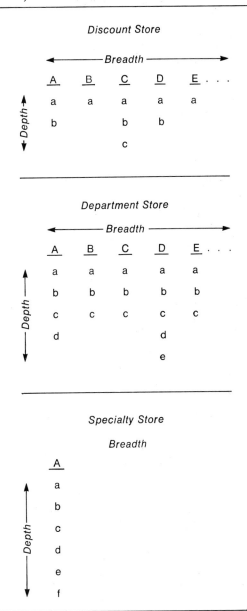

With the capital letters representing the number or breadth of product lines, and the small letters depicting the choices in any one product line, it can be seen that discount stores are wide and shallow in merchandise assortment. Specialty stores, at the other extreme, have few product lines, but much more depth in the few they carry. The typical department store falls between these two extremes, having a broad assortment with many merchandise lines, and medium depth in each line.

although the biggest department stores approach this. But even a department store faces limits of space and investment. The customer interested in one-stop shopping will find the department store or discount store to be an efficient choice. But a specialty store offers customers greater variety in a small line.

QUALITY AND FASHION LEVEL OF GOODS   Quality and fashion are important attractions at the high end: high quality and newest fashions. While quality in a product is often difficult for a shopper to determine, price lines and brands carried are major reflections of quality in the customer's mind. Fashion refers to a particular style that has become accepted. A high-fashion store offers the newest fashions before they have become popular (that is, widely accepted). Stores like Bergdorf-Goodman, Bonwit Teller, Neiman-Marcus, and Marshall Field have international reputations for the quality and fashions they offer their elite customers. At the opposite end of the scale, discount stores and salvage stores offer distress merchandise and other low-end merchandise.

PRICE   It might seem that price would be directly related to quality and fashion level of goods. And to an extent it is. Higher-quality goods and newest fashions usually command higher prices. However, good quality may be available without the highest prices. *Private brands,* which are retailers' own brands (described in Chapter 12), usually are priced lower than nationally advertised brands. For example, the private-branded appliances of Sears, Penney, and Montgomery Ward are often priced far below the highest-price brands and yet are of adequate and even superior quality. Often the difference in price between highest- and lowest-price items does not accurately reflect the difference in quality. Some grocery chains are even introducing *no-brand generic products* priced below both nationally advertised brands and private brands.[7] These products are not purported to be of the highest quality. Still, their retailers maintain that they are acceptable, without the assurance of a reputable brand.

The major appeal of discount stores is their low prices. Many other stores direct the bulk of their promotional efforts, especially their newspaper advertising, to "sales" and particular goods offered at special low prices. Most supermarket advertising promotes low-price specials or leaders, designed to attract customers to the store so that they may then buy other regular-price items. *Leaders* are items sold at a below-

[7] "No-Brand Products Enter Chains in New York and Ohio Markets," *Advertising Age,* March 6, 1978, p. 2.

average markup—sometimes even near cost—in order to attract customers to the store.

Despite the overwhelming commitment by many retailers to low prices as the major promotional tool for advertising and display, not all consumers appear to view price as all that important. The poor—the very consumers who should be most price conscious—do not always seek out the best values, because of ignorance and apathy. Other consumers tend to view convenience, merchandise quality and assortment, and friendliness of clerks as more important than price.[8]

CUSTOMER SERVICE   Many things come under the rubric of *customer service:* friendly and well-trained salespeople, credit, delivery, trading stamps, gift wrapping, bridal consulting, interior-decorator consulting, return-goods privileges, baby-sitting availability, alterations, workroom activities, and handling of customer complaints and merchandise corrections. Even the store itself, its decor, pleasant surroundings, restroom facilities, and air conditioning, are a form of service. Department stores usually provide the most services. Discount stores generally have the least, although this is changing somewhat.

Services involve expense, and full-service stores necessarily charge higher prices. As discount stores entered the market with a minimum of services and often the barest of decor, they were able to significantly undercut the prices of department stores. Department stores then were often forced to cut back on some of their services or to charge for certain ones, such as delivery and alterations.

EXCITEMENT AND CHANGE   Some stores are continually seeking ingenious and innovative ideas to attract customers and make their shopping interesting and exciting. Some examples are Santa Claus landing by helicopter, flower shows, fashion shows, import-goods spectaculars, exhibitions of various kinds, use of celebrities to meet customers and sign autographs. Sometimes these excitement-creating activities are sponsored by an entire shopping center rather than an individual store. Some stores attempt to create an urge to buy by continually holding special sales, dollar days, anniversary sales, and the like. Customers may be encouraged to come to the store by frequent shifting of displays and departments. Games and contests may be used to make shopping more intriguing. Discount stores and other promotional retailers use truck or

[8] A sampling of studies supporting this conclusion are F. E. Brown and George Fisk, "Department Stores and Discount Stores: Who Dies Next?" *Journal of Retailing* (Fall 1965), 15–25; Robert F. Hartley, "The Perceived Importance of Price in Small-town Shopping Behavior," *Southern Journal of Business* (April 1970), 24–32; Mary Joyce and Joseph Guiltinan, "The Professional Woman: A Potential Market Segment for Retailers," *Journal of Retailing* (Summer 1978), 59–70.

FIGURE 5.2 COMPONENTS OF THE RETAILING MIX

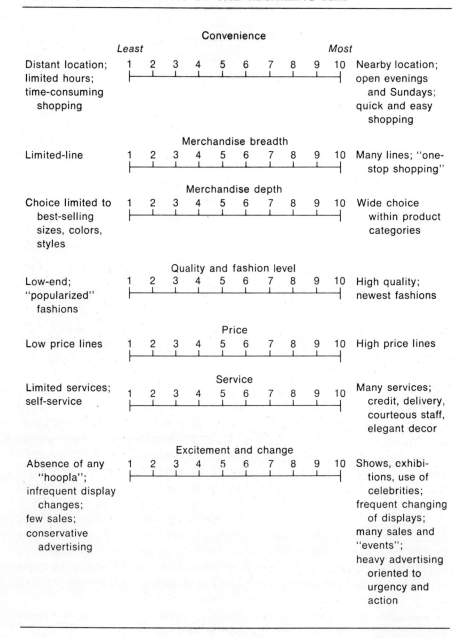

Convenience

Least   *Most*

Distant location; 1 2 3 4 5 6 7 8 9 10 Nearby location;
limited hours;   open evenings
time-consuming   and Sundays;
shopping   quick and easy
                                                  shopping

Merchandise breadth

Limited-line   1 2 3 4 5 6 7 8 9 10 Many lines; "one-
                                                  stop shopping"

Merchandise depth

Choice limited to 1 2 3 4 5 6 7 8 9 10 Wide choice
best-selling   within product
sizes, colors,   categories
styles

Quality and fashion level

Low-end;   1 2 3 4 5 6 7 8 9 10 High quality;
"popularized"   newest fashions
fashions

Price

Low price lines   1 2 3 4 5 6 7 8 9 10 High price lines

Service

Limited services; 1 2 3 4 5 6 7 8 9 10 Many services;
self-service   credit, delivery,
                                                  courteous staff,
                                                  elegant decor

Excitement and change

Absence of any   1 2 3 4 5 6 7 8 9 10 Shows, exhibi-
  "hoopla";   tions, use of
infrequent display   celebrities;
  changes;   frequent changing
few sales;   of displays;
conservative   many sales and
  advertising   "events";
                                                  heavy advertising
                                                  oriented to
                                                  urgency and
                                                  action

trailer sales, sometimes in their parking lots. Even tent sales are used to generate excitement and an aura of special bargains.

Other stores are staid and conservative, and shun such "hoopla." For certain target customers, this is the best strategy. Infrequent display changes, perhaps only one or two "clearances" or "anniversary" sales in the year, contribute to a subtle image of high quality and status which some customers demand.

Retailing Mix Scales

Figure 5.2 shows the various components of the retailing mix, scaled from least to most. For example, a store can offer varying amounts of convenience to its customers. In Figure 5.2 you can plot this on the scale from 1 (least) to 10 (most). Convenience food stores would be near the top of the convenience scale, around 10, since they offer nearby locations and long shopping hours. At the other extreme is the traditional downtown department store, perhaps open only one night a week, with poor parking facilities and tedious shopping.

DESIGNING A RETAILING STRATEGY

By studying how well existing retailers are satisfying customers, one can detect the strengths and weaknesses of competitors. This technique may show where the best opportunities lie. For example, discount firms found a vast market opportunity, with most existing retailers ranking low on the convenience scale and high on the price scale. Many customers wanted ease of shopping—convenience of both parking and hours open—as well as the attraction of lower prices, and were quick to shift their patronage when discount stores opened.

Finding a Differential Advantage

While discount stores are now commonplace, within any particular market area there are some stores that are not offering the variety and depth of merchandise that many customers would like to select from. (This, as we noted earlier in this chapter, is the situation in many small rural towns.) In many places, stores have gone overboard in self-service. Better-informed salespeople or goods that are not prepackaged might attract some customers. For example, some perceptive retailers are opening meat markets where customers can select the particular cut of meat they want, or have the butcher cut it for them, without being limited to packaged meat in the supermarket.

RETAILING TOOL—*Analyzing Competition by Retailing Mix Scales*

Stores in a given community or shopping area can be ranked according to the *retailing mix scales* in Figure 5.2. Such an evaluation can be made through personal observation or, if one is new to the area, by questioning a few knowledgeable people. It is not difficult, but it does require a systematic investigation of all competitive stores if it is to be worthwhile.

Example   A buyer in a department store is interested in opening her own store, an infants' and children's store, in one of the growing suburbs. Upon carefully looking over the situation, she sees three stores that are presently carrying enough children's goods to be competitive. Using retailing mix scales, she ranks the competition as follows:

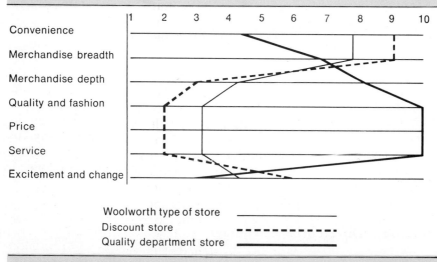

Woolworth type of store
Discount store
Quality department store

The differences are significant among these stores. Since the area is a fairly typical middle-class neighborhood, the buyer correctly sees the opportunity to fall between the two extremes. In particular, she decides to feature medium-price and medium-quality goods and to offer expert selling help, as well as specialized services such as baby sitting, credit, courtesy coffee, play equipment, and a new-mother register.

While she sees the need to generate excitement and change, how to do it on a continual basis escapes her in the beginning. She promises herself she will make a concerted effort to do as much of this as practical for a small store. Some ideas she is considering are baby and children's pictures, a contest for the most photogenic, collaboration with a neighborhood children's dancing studio for promotional efforts, and a special drawing for expectant mothers.

For Thought and Discussion   You can analyze competition in your community by using these retailing mix scales. Assume the role of a prospective retailer interested in entering your community with (1) a supermarket, (2) a women's clothing store, (3) a shoe store, and (4) a department store. What retailing mix do you think would be most successful for each of these stores? Why?

As we noted in Chapter 2, a retailer needs to search for a differential advantage to achieve a unique niche among competitors. While imitation of a competitor may sometimes be wise, it may prove too dangerous if the competitor is well established. Imitation of some successful retailing operations in noncompeting markets in other cities or states could be more fruitful. The successful retailer is always seeking new ideas and new ways to attract customers.

AVOID DIFFUSION OF EFFORTS   A store should gear its prices, merchandise, services, and promotional efforts to its target customers and the image it wants to establish. For example, there is a connection between store layout and ad layout: clutter in one connotes cheapness and bargains, an image best tied in with clutter in the other. Personnel can also be used for effect. For example, harried, even surly, help may in fact convey the store's intended bargain image: the employees are busy with so many customers that they do not have time to give good service, and expenses are being cut to the bone to provide the lowest prices. Table 5.1 depicts appropriate coordination of retailing efforts in order to achieve the desired consistency of image or impression.

Desired consistency is lacking in some stores. The various components of the retailing mix may be working at cross-purposes. For example, a store may wish to cater to customers who want high-quality products, are willing to pay the prices for such goods, and also want courteous and knowledgeable service from salespeople. Such a store will be diffusing its efforts if the quality and training of sales personnel are inconsistent, or if advertising stresses the lowest-price items and sales. Lack of resources may sometimes hinder such a store in seeking its target markets. Money available for investment may be insufficient to provide the elegance that some customers would expect.

Figure 5.3 shows the elements of the retailing mix diffused and imperfectly directed to the target market. In medium- and large-size stores, different people are in charge of buying merchandise, display and advertising, and personnel and services. Continual efforts are needed to make sure that everyone's activities are coordinated and directed to the same objectives.

THE UNCONTROLLABLE FACTORS Certain *uncontrollable factors* also affect retail business. But management should try to recognize them, so that it can adjust expectations and strategy accordingly. The major uncontrollable variables the retailer faces are:

Consumer attitudes—especially how these may be changing

Political and legal environment—how laws and regulations, or their possibility, are constraining

Economic situation—the state of the economy, whether prosperity or recession, and any local conditions

Technological and competitive framework—any shifts in present ways of doing business

The weather—any unusual conditions that can greatly influence sales of seasonal goods

In the past, retailers have been notoriously shortsighted in recog-

TABLE 5.1 APPROPRIATE COORDINATION OF RETAILING EFFORTS

Factor	For a Bargain Image	For a Classy Image
Ad layout	Cluttered	White space
Floor layout (discussed in Chapter 7)	Grid	Free flow
Prices	Low	High
Promotional emphasis on prices	Heavy	Restrained
Salesforce	Limited in number and customer awareness	Customer and service oriented

Source: Suggested by Professor Michael d'Amico, University of Akron.

FIGURE 5.3 DIFFUSION OF RETAILING EFFORTS

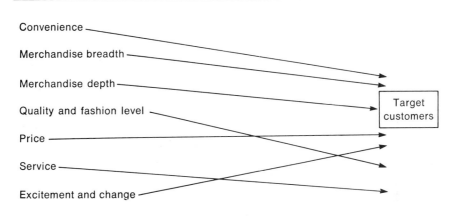

nizing and adjusting to these factors (except for the weather). The force of consumerism did not emerge on the retail scene all at once and unheralded. Increasing consumer resentment of deception and garbled information came about gradually, amid newspaper publicity, magazine articles, and popular books. Consumer attitudes change slowly, but it is a mistake to think they are unchanging.

The political and legal framework tends to lag behind changes in social attitudes, but it does follow them. We are seeing this today in government regulation against abusive practices. Former commonly accepted ways of doing business and advertising are being questioned and condemned. As we saw in Chapter 4, retailers have sometimes opposed pressures for strengthening the consumer's role, but it is a shortsighted retailer who takes this stance.

The economic situation has always been part of the environment in which business operates. Except during extreme peaks and valleys, it usually poses no severe problems. But inflationary pressures and looming recessions should be considered in planning for the future. Wage and price controls are sometimes imposed, placing constraints on operations and on profits.

Local conditions can impose problems or opportunities. Strikes, a major factory shutting down or moving into town, a military base closing or expanding—these drastically affect retail business.

Changes in the technological and competitive framework have, in the past, crept up unnoticed by most retailers. An overcommitment to services, to inefficient merchandising, to high markups, and a disregard for changing consumer needs opened the market to discounters.

Whether slowly emerging changes will be ignored again depends on the responsiveness of a new generation of retail executives.

Finally, what can the retailer do about the weather? Short-range forecasts are fairly accurate, but weather in the long term remains largely unpredictable. The best most retailers of seasonal goods can do is to plan for normal weather conditions and take advantage of the unexpected.

■ Summary

The dilemmas of firms that are still groping to find a distinctive image underline the importance of a distinctive store image. Target customers and market segmentation are ways for a firm to find a profitable place for itself in the marketplace. Several market segments are relatively neglected.

A competitive retailing strategy can be designed around the retailing mix. To be successful, a retailing mix must fit customers' needs, especially those needs that are not being satisfied by other retailers. In this way a merchant develops a distinctive image and a loyal body of customers, and is able to define clear-cut objectives in planning and coordinating all aspects of the retailing strategy.

■ Key Terms

Breadth of assortment	Private brands
Customer service	Retailing mix
Demographic factors	Retailing mix scales
Depth of assortment	Store image
Leaders	Target customers
Market segments	Uncontrollable factors
No-brand generic products	

■ Discussion Questions

1. Why is it important for a store to have an image?
2. Why is it so difficult for a store to improve or change its image?
3. While Welcome Wagon or a similar welcoming service is used in many communities to identify and solicit the business of newcomers, most merchants do not subscribe to it. Why is this? Why are the larger retailers, particularly the chain outlets, reluctant to subscribe to Welcome Wagon services?

4. Discuss the differences between merchandise breadth and depth. Can a store generally offer both? Which type of store will usually provide more merchandise depth—a department store or a specialty store? Why?

5. An air of excitement and change is one of the components of the retailing mix. Are there stores in your community that you would class as exciting? How do they generate this image?

6. How would you go about trying to improve your retailing mix? How successful would you expect to be?

7. Do you think a store can successfully appeal to all types of consumers? Do you know of any that do?

8. Are there any neglected consumer segments in your community? If so, why do you think they have been ignored by retailers? What would be a positive solution?

■ Project

Draw up retailing mix scales and rate and compare the major department stores, fast-food franchise outlets, discount stores, and supermarkets in your community. What blend of the retailing mix appears to be most successful? Do you see any gaps that might suggest competitive opportunity?

■ Exercise in Creativity

How would you go about creating a successful children's store? woman's apparel shop? supermarket?

■ Retailing in Action

You have been persuaded to join a group of three other entrepreneurs and to open a "singles" bar. Your town is rather average, with about 250,000 people. A state college with about 15,000 students is nearby.

What kind of image would you recommend to your partners for this enterprise?

How would you go about trying to achieve this image?

What difficulties would you anticipate?

6 Choosing the Location

Usually the most important decision a retailer makes is where to locate the store. A poor location limits the potential of a business.

A number of sophisticated formulas and models for analyzing and defining trading areas have been developed. Store saturation or competition in a given area can also be measured. But some retailers continue to make poor location decisions. Many small retailers court failure by rushing into this important decision without careful study of all relevant determinants.

THE ROLE OF LOCATION DECISIONS IN A RETAILING STRATEGY

As we saw in the last chapter, a retailing strategy involves selecting market segments or target groups of customers, and directing efforts toward attracting these customers. The location of a store is a vital part of the strategy. Such a decision, once made, can seldom be adjusted quickly. This makes careful analysis all the more important for location decisions.

No competent retailer would expect customers to come to an inaccessible or distant store, unless they are seeking antiques, art, other merchandise with unique characteristics, or very low prices, as in warehouse sales. Therefore, the location should be convenient for the target customers.

The store should be compatible with its shopping area and with the expectations of its customers. For instance, a store featuring high quality and the newest fashions in women's clothing should choose a site in harmony with this image and retailing mix. On the other hand, John's Bargain Stores, which feature low-end merchandise in austere surroundings, would be incompatible with a plush suburban shopping center.

The major type of merchandise that a store intends to sell should be considered in the location decision. *Consumer goods* are classified in most marketing texts as:[1]

1. *Convenience goods:* examples are cigarettes, bread, candy bars, and various other low-priced items for which a person normally does not want to devote much time or shopping effort. Impulse goods are sometimes given as a subcategory to denote items often purchased on impulse—the ice-cream bar from the vendor, or the candy bar or magazine at the checkout counter.
2. *Shopping goods:* an example is clothing, for which customers are willing to devote more shopping effort, and which they will want to compare with similar products and brands.
3. *Specialty goods:* certain brands of fine china, furniture, stereo components, and expensive ready-to-wear have unique characteristics or brand identification that make some customers willing to exert a special shopping effort.

Stores selling mostly convenience goods, such as grocery, drug, and variety stores, must be located close to customers, who will not ordinarily want to travel very far for such goods. Stores featuring shopping goods, and particularly specialty goods, will draw from wider areas.

---

[1] Some books list a fourth category, unsought goods, to denote those items that a customer is not motivated to seek. Such goods may be so new that potential customers are not familiar with them; or they may be goods and services like encyclopedias and life insurance, which must have aggressive promotion if they are to sell. For our purposes in this book, the distinction of convenience, shopping, and specialty goods is sufficient.

Sometimes a specialty-goods store may be able to draw from an entire metropolitan area. Since people usually like to shop around and compare before purchasing shopping goods, shopping-goods stores should try to locate near stores with similar products, preferably in a downtown or shopping-center location.

Location decisions, therefore, should take into account:

1. Target customers
2. Retailing mix to be employed
3. Type of consumer goods to be offered

A Good Location May Change

One of the serious risks of any location, no matter how carefully researched and selected, is that conditions may change so that profits decline or another location offers better opportunities. Population shifts occur, sometimes rather quickly. Competition, sometimes from a big new shopping mall, can affect traffic patterns. Even prestigious Fifth Avenue in New York City has experienced major changes.

Retailers need to re-evaluate existing locations periodically to determine whether conditions have changed or are likely to. Large chain organizations can open additional units as such shifts occur, but it is not always so easy to close existing units that have become marginal or unprofitable. Long-term leases and management reluctance to cut back often keep such stores open when profit potential has diminished. For the smaller retailer, moving involves serious costs: new fixtures, remodeling, often higher rent, and promotional efforts to attract new customers. These costs, along with the loss of old customers, may prohibit a move. Sometimes a less-than-optimal location has to be tolerated.

The Need to Open More Stores

Even worse than choosing a bad location is the failure to expand when appropriate. A small firm may find it advantageous to open additional stores in growing suburban shopping centers. For large firms, too conservative a policy can make it impossible ever to catch up with more aggressive competitors. Such was the error of Montgomery Ward in the years after World War II.

RETAILING ERRORS—Sewell Avery's Reluctance to Expand Ward's

Sewell Avery was at the helm of Montgomery Ward & Company during, and for some years after, World War II. A crusty autocrat, he ran the company with an iron hand and reportedly said (with some humor, we hope), "If anybody ventures to differ with me, of course, I throw them out of the window." In 1944 he challenged President Truman's authority to seize the Chicago plant of Montgomery Ward. A labor dispute had shut down the plant during wartime, and Avery had been unyielding. In a celebrated action, Avery was removed bodily from his office by two U.S. Army enlisted men.

Since Avery believed a postwar depression would lower the cost of labor and materials, he deferred expansion. Accordingly, Ward's maintained a large cash position, and sat on it. Sears, on the other hand, expanded vigorously during this period. Result:

	Sales (thousands)	Percent of Change	Operating Profit (thousands)	Percent of Change
Montgomery Ward				
1945	$ 620,969		$ 48,279	
1955	887,336	26	66,262	38
1965	1,697,390	90	29,200	−56
Sears				
1945	988,770		112,156	
1955	2,965,408	203	323,140	188
1965	5,740,034	96	507,772	57

As you can see, in the ten years from 1945 to 1955, Ward's, with no growth in number of stores, had a 26 percent total gain in sales, while growth-minded Sears vastly outstripped Ward's with a 203 percent sales increase. In the years after 1955, with Avery retired, Ward's tried to catch up and almost matched the Sears rate of sales growth from 1955 to 1965. But look at the effect on profits.

Source: For more detail, see Robert F. Hartley, "Fallacy of Conservation: Montgomery Ward—Effect of a No-growth Policy," in *Marketing Mistakes* (Columbus, Ohio: Grid, 1976), pp. 7–18.

For Thought and Discussion   What arguments would you have given
Avery to demonstrate that some expansion efforts would be needed after
World War II, even if his prediction of a major depression turned out to be
accurate?

SELECTING A LOCATION

Location decisions consist of:

1. Selecting a city or metropolitan area
2. Selecting a specific site
3. Terms of occupancy—whether to buy or rent

For the local retailer-to-be, the selection of the city may not be a
problem. The choice narrows down to the specific site and the terms of
occupancy. However, even the small retailer may find, upon analysis,
that a nearby city or suburb offers better opportunities than the local
surroundings.

For the chain or department-store corporation interested in expanding, the choice of metropolitan area is of major importance. Some
areas will be below average in per-capita purchasing power, or else the
trend in income and employment may show a limited or erratic potential. Other metropolitan areas may have too many stores in keen
competition.

Terms of occupancy also involve major decisions. Should a firm
build, or renovate an existing facility? Should it rent and thereby have
less control over the facility but more flexibility? Both alternatives can
be successful. Later in this chapter, we will examine some pros and cons
of renting and owning.

SELECTING A CITY OR METROPOLITAN AREA

A careful retailer seeking a location considers several aspects of an area:

1. Population factors, particularly size, characteristics, and income
2. The size of the trading area from which customers are drawn
3. The competitive situation for the particular kind of business

4. Various other factors, such as the labor situation (particularly unionism and the chance of lengthy or frequent strikes); dependence on one or a few major industries (with a consequent risk of economic cutbacks); any particularly onerous laws and regulations regarding store hours, pricing, licensing, taxation, and zoning; and traffic flow and the presence or absence of good arterial highways

In other words, a retailer must ask and find answers to such questions as the following: Are the population and income growing, declining, or growing more slowly than in other areas? Is the competitive situation fairly stable, or is it changing? Are the political and labor situations stable or uncertain?

Standard Metropolitan Statistical Areas (SMSAs)

With the movement of city populations to the suburbs, the U.S. census has developed a separate population classification, the *standard metropolitan statistical area (SMSA)*. Each SMSA usually consists of a central city and its surrounding suburbs. Data are gathered for 283 SMSAs and include statistics on population size and composition, employment, retail and wholesale trade, and personal income. Altogether, over 200 items are shown for each SMSA. Obviously, such data can be very useful in analyzing and comparing potential opportunities in various metropolitan areas.

Analyzing the Population

In addition to statistics supplied by the U.S. census for cities and metropolitan areas, other data on population, family size, income, home ownership, occupation, and the like are readily available from city-planning bureaus and chambers of commerce. Sometimes a major newspaper collects such data as a service to business. These statistics are usually broken down for different sections of a city, so that market opportunities can be more specifically assessed. The prospective retailer need only ask for such data; no research is involved.

TYPE OF MARKET INFORMATION AVAILABLE FOR ST. PAUL, MINNESOTA St. Paul is one metropolitan area where data relevant to business is easily accessible. Since 1945, the *St. Paul Dispatch–Pioneer Press* has conducted yearly surveys of St. Paul families as to:

Consumer preferences for leading brands in many product categories

Family characteristics: income group, occupation, age of children, education level, and dwelling-unit characteristics

Patronage factors: stores and shopping centers shopped for various categories of goods

"Favorite store" breakdowns by the area lived in, income, and age

The Chamber of Commerce supplies the following:

A listing of major retail facilities in the metropolitan area

An inventory of parking facilities in downtown St. Paul

Names of principal firms and their approximate employment

A map showing the area's census tracts (small, rather homogeneous subsections) of St. Paul and the racial breakdown, number of households, median income for families, and approximate total income in each tract

A breakdown of growth in various economic indices, such as total payroll, annual earnings per worker, employment, total retail sales, and bank deposits

SURVEY OF BUYING POWER   The *Survey of Buying Power* is prepared annually by *Sales and Marketing Management* magazine, a widely used business periodical. Figure 6.1 gives a representative page. This survey presents data and estimates on population, income, and certain categories of retail sales for city, county, and metropolitan areas in the United States and Canada. Since these data are updated each year, they furnish needed statistics between the ten-year censuses.

RETAILING TOOL—Using the Survey of Buying Power to Compare Market Potential of Several Trading Areas

Whether a small independent or a chain, a retailer considering expansion has to decide among alternative possibilities. Which suburban area or city has the best potential for this particular kind of store? The data supplied by the Survey of Buying Power can furnish several useful comparisons. To gain a feel for the usefulness of this tool, place yourself in the role of several different retailers.

Example 1   You are thinking of opening a children's apparel store in the Dallas, Texas, area. You examine the Survey of Buying Power for the

FIGURE 6.1 SURVEY OF BUYING POWER

SMM ESTIMATES	$$ EFFECTIVE BUYING INCOME 1977						
METRO AREA County City	Total EBI ($000)	Median Hsld. EBI	% of Hslds. by EBI Group: (A) $8,000–$9,999 (B) $10,000–$14,999 (C) $15,000–$24,999 (D) $25,000 & Over				Buying Power Index
			A	B	C	D	
DALLAS - FORT WORTH	**17,916,645**	**17,059**	**5.9**	**16.9**	**32.5**	**24.8**	**1.3544**
Collin	651,551	16,532	5.8	15.7	31.6	23.1	.0428
Dallas	10,585,931	18,133	5.7	16.2	32.2	28.4	.7918
• Dallas	6,103,912	16,620	6.5	17.4	29.0	26.5	.4813
Garland	869,599	20,334	3.8	14.5	44.0	29.4	.0652
Grand Prairie	385,058	17,445	5.0	19.8	39.1	22.1	.0274
Irving	760,370	20,140	4.1	14.5	41.2	30.2	.0559
Mesquite	394,156	19,758	3.4	14.9	49.5	24.0	.0331
Richardson	588,064	26,488	1.9	6.9	30.4	56.4	.0370
Denton	588,459	15,021	6.8	17.5	30.6	19.5	.0472
Ellis	284,755	13,477	6.9	17.0	29.1	16.1	.0212
Hood	52,578	9,521	6.9	16.0	23.7	8.7	.0045
Johnson	323,074	13,841	6.5	19.6	32.7	12.0	.0237
Kaufman	169,195	11,777	7.8	18.5	26.2	12.2	.0135
Parker	187,534	13,946	6.8	19.0	31.2	14.5	.0150
Rockwall	53,406	12,530	7.0	16.7	25.8	15.9	.0037
Tarrant	4,903,643	16,742	5.8	17.7	34.7	22.2	.3822
Arlington	842,907	19,468	4.6	15.7	39.1	28.4	.0678
• Fort Worth	2,296,201	14,690	7.0	19.3	29.9	18.9	.1934
Wise	116,519	13,125	6.1	18.5	30.2	12.3	.0088
SUBURBAN TOTAL	**9,516,532**	**17,957**	**5.1**	**15.9**	**35.7**	**25.4**	**.6797**

various suburbs that are part of this metropolitan area, as shown in Figure 6.1. You narrow your choice down to three suburbs, based on the following statistics relevant to your type of store:

	Age Groups		Population (thousands)	Median Household Effective Buying Income
	18–24	25–34		
Denton	24.8	15.8	99.9	$15,021
Arlington	18.5	21.1	119.1	19,468
Collin	11.7	19.6	105.3	16,532

TEXAS (cont.)
SMM ESTIMATES

POPULATION—12/31/77

METRO AREA County City	Total Population (Thousands)	% Of U.S.	Median Age of Pop.	% of Population by Age Group				House-holds (Thousands)
				18–24 Years	25–34 Years	35–49 Years	50 & Over	
DALLAS - FORT WORTH	2,642.8	1.2135	28.5	13.6	18.3	16.7	21.4	916.3
Collin	105.3	.0483	28.4	11.7	19.6	14.3	22.7	36.5
Dallas	1,452.9	.6672	28.2	13.2	19.3	17.1	19.9	503.6
• Dallas	825.0	.3788	29.2	13.6	17.8	16.8	22.9	300.1
Garland	132.6	.0609	26.3	11.5	23.5	18.0	11.6	40.7
Grand Prairie	61.7	.0283	26.4	14.8	20.1	16.3	16.3	20.4
Irving	109.7	.0504	26.3	13.8	23.3	17.6	12.1	35.4
Mesquite	66.5	.0305	25.7	10.3	25.3	17.4	9.2	19.4
Richardson	69.6	.0320	27.1	8.0	22.8	22.0	9.9	20.9
Denton	99.9	.0459	24.7	24.8	15.8	13.2	20.1	33.5
Ellis	53.1	.0244	31.9	10.8	13.9	14.5	31.2	18.4
Hood	10.8	.0049	38.3	8.5	11.6	15.4	38.0	4.3
Johnson	58.1	.0267	31.9	10.7	15.4	16.2	29.0	21.6
Kaufman	36.3	.0167	34.9	10.3	13.4	15.0	34.9	11.8
Parker	34.4	.0158	31.0	14.1	13.8	15.7	28.8	11.5
Rockwall	9.6	.0044	32.8	9.5	15.1	16.4	30.3	3.6
Tarrant	760.2	.3491	28.6	13.8	17.7	17.5	21.2	263.5
Arlington	119.1	.0547	26.0	18.5	21.1	17.4	13.6	40.4
• Fort Worth	365.6	.1679	29.9	14.1	16.0	16.2	25.7	133.2
Wise	22.2	.0101	33.9	9.6	14.7	15.7	32.6	8.0
SUBURBAN TOTAL	1,452.2	.6668	27.9	13.4	19.1	17.0	19.4	483.0

TEXAS (cont.)
SMM ESTIMATES

RETAIL SALES BY STORE GROUP 1977

METRO AREA County City	Total Retail Sales ($000)	Food ($000)	Eating & Drinking Places ($000)	General Mdse. ($000)	Furniture/ Furnish./ Appliance ($000)	Auto-motive ($000)	Drug ($000)
DALLAS - FORT WORTH	10,247,140	2,058,957	926,963	1,349,463	509,091	2,171,974	358,893
Collin	196,914	55,655	9,572	17,540	9,725	40,805	8,454
Dallas	6,089,372	1,109,941	623,212	782,336	331,921	1,234,330	184,174
• Dallas	4,137,261	656,186	487,299	535,970	225,150	868,821	110,725
Garland	474,491	104,245	31,574	50,018	32,576	120,662	16,428
Grand Prairie	167,843	45,757	17,167	6,411	7,290	33,422	6,340
Irving	401,409	104,701	24,565	59,994	18,414	87,646	13,063
Mesquite	287,188	53,463	16,482	98,485	4,897	23,128	5,883
Richardson	194,701	41,888	15,870	16,010	9,433	30,543	8,845
Denton	374,158	82,817	26,383	35,074	11,846	99,395	10,772
Ellis	128,813	31,058	7,843	7,445	5,052	36,782	11,181
Hood	36,492	8,635	2,188	1,250	459	15,808	493
Johnson	142,145	32,672	9,031	8,259	9,418	37,000	7,621
Kaufman	89,174	23,301	3,586	3,854	2,553	27,658	3,041
Parker	113,464	23,837	3,621	8,923	3,402	40,423	4,302
Rockwall	19,915	1,705	1,024		1,708	8,891	629
Tarrant	3,001,395	674,617	237,024	483,254	131,701	614,812	122,408
Arlington	593,163	134,264	46,685	115,755	19,024	142,176	22,015
• Fort Worth	1,730,983	334,738	145,657	270,480	89,251	359,627	83,394
Wise	55,298	14,719	3,479	1,528	1,306	16,070	5,818
SUBURBAN TOTAL	4,378,896	1,068,033	294,007	543,013	194,690	943,526	164,774

Of these three, Arlington looks most favorable to you. It has a younger population than Collin and, although it is not quite as young as Denton, the median income is considerably higher.

Example 2 You are the store-location research director for a chain of high-quality women's apparel stores. You decide that the following statistics from the Survey of Buying Power are relevant:

	Median Household Effective Buying Income	Population (thousands)	Buying Power Index
Garland	$20,334	132.6	.0652
Irving	20,140	109.7	.0559
Richardson	26,488	69.6	.0370

You have initially narrowed down the search to the three suburbs having the largest median effective buying income per household. In these terms, Richardson seems the clear choice. However, when you compare populations you have second thoughts, since Richardson is much smaller than the other two. You finally decide on Garland, which has a satisfactory median income, as well as the largest population of the three. Also, its buying power index is the highest of the three.

The *buying power index (BPI)* is sometimes used by itself to determine the relative potential of various counties, cities, and suburbs. It is a general index constructed from three weighted factors: effective buying income (weighted by 5), retail sales (weighted by 3), and population (weighted by 2). Based on the BPI, the potential for consumer goods in general is highest in Garland and lowest in Richardson, despite the higher median household income of Richardson. (The BPI is given in the last column of Figure 6.1.)

Population factors, important as they are, are only one type of data that should be considered in making location decisions. For example, the competitive situation certainly must be evaluated, as well as the trend of economic factors.

For Thought and Discussion

1. Do you see other data in the Survey of Buying Power that you think should be used in making these two location decisions?

2. Using Survey of Buying Power data for three nearby suburbs or counties in your area, compute their relative market potential for: (a) an automobile dealer, (b) a discount furniture store, (c) a high-quality furniture store, and (d) a toy store.

Analyzing the Trading Area

A *trading area* is the geographical area from which most customers are drawn. Three types of trading areas are important to retailers:

That of the store itself
That of the shopping center or district where the store is located
That of the city or metropolitan area

A small convenience-goods store, such as a corner grocery or drugstore, may draw customers from only a few blocks around. At the other extreme, a few prestigious downtown department stores, such as Marshall Field of Chicago or Neiman-Marcus of Dallas, may have charge customers from all over the world. Shopping-center trading areas also vary. Some old "strip" centers may draw from only a few blocks, while huge regional centers may pull customers from miles around.

Many large and expanding retailers have developed their own methods for plotting trading areas. Other sources, such as chambers of commerce, also plot trading areas. *The New Yorker* periodically defines trading areas for "quality merchandise" for some 130 cities. It uses four factors to determine the size of each trading area:

1. Accessibility of the city or its suburban shopping centers: highways, traffic congestion, parking facilities, even bus and rail traffic, are considered.
2. Delivery routes, especially free delivery by trucks on a regular schedule for large merchandise purchases.
3. Local shopping customs: shopping attitudes are surveyed, as is the location of charge-account customers.
4. Other definitions of the trading area are also considered—those from local newspapers or chambers of commerce—as are the SMSAs defined by the federal government.[2]

[2] *The Primary Markets for Quality Merchandise* (New York: Sales Development Department, *The New Yorker*).

Note that the pull of a trading area ordinarily is important only for shopping and specialty goods. Convenience-goods stores, as we have noted before, seldom draw from any sizable distance.

There are several methods for defining trading areas. One, Reilly's Law, is useful for determining the effect of competition between trading areas.

RETAILING TOOL—*Determining the Trading Area of a Shopping Center: Reilly's Law*

A retailer making a location decision is interested in the "draw" of a particular business district or shopping center. With a reasonable knowledge of the region from which the trading area pulls customers, a retailer can estimate total business potential and understand the characteristics (income, family size, occupation, home ownership, and so on) of the customer likely to be attracted.

Sometimes local chambers of commerce or newspaper advertising departments compile information on primary trading areas. Where satisfactory information is not available, useful estimates can be obtained by ascertaining what territory is regularly served by retail merchants' deliveries. Newspaper circulation figures also reflect the trading area. License numbers of cars in the shopping area can be listed. Merchants can find the addresses from official registration records and then plot them on area maps, thereby providing another estimate of the trading area.

Another type of analysis determines a trading area by means of a mathematical formula. *Reilly's Law* of Retail Gravitation predicts the draw of a particular town or shopping center against another town or shopping center according to the distance between and the respective populations. One modification used for shopping centers is

$$\left. \begin{array}{l} \text{Number of miles from shopping} \\ \text{center A to the outer limits} \\ \text{of its trading area in the} \\ \text{direction of shopping center B} \end{array} \right\} = \frac{\text{Miles to shopping center B}}{1 + \sqrt{\dfrac{\text{Sq ft floor space of B}}{\text{Sq ft floor space of A}}}}$$

Application   If shopping center A is 6 miles from B, and the respective sizes are A = 200,000 square feet of selling space, B = 800,000, then the limits of the trading area of A in the direction of B are

$$\frac{6}{1 + \sqrt{\dfrac{800,000}{200,000}}} = \frac{6}{1 + 2} = 2 \text{ miles}$$

Therefore, according to this formula, the trading area of A would extend 2 miles toward shopping center B. This same analysis can be made in every direction from a particular shopping center or city, and the limits of A might be computed as follows:

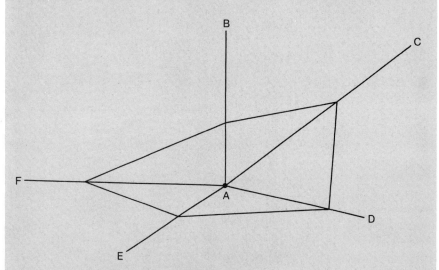

Source: Adapted from William J. Reilly, Research Monograph No. 4, University of Texas Bulletin No. 2944, Bureau of Business Research (Austin: University of Texas Press, 1929); and P. D. Converse, "New Laws of Retail Gravitation," *Journal of Marketing* (October 1949), 379–84. These concepts, while old, are still being used, although often with certain modifications.

For Thought and Discussion

1. What weaknesses do you see in Reilly's formula? What advantages?

2. Can you think of any modifications that might be desirable?

3. What other inputs might you want to use in determining the trading area?

4. Using Reilly's formula, compute the trading area of a major shopping center in your area. For miles in the formula, substitute driving time. In place of square feet of selling space, substitute population or sales volume.

Huff has developed a mathematical model similar to Reilly's, but Huff's model recognizes that patronage declines with distance; that is, the more distant a consumer is from a shopping center, the less probable it is that he or she will shop there. Therefore, the strength of a particular center's draw might range from .99 for people with $\frac{1}{2}$

mile, to 0.5 for those 10 miles distant.[3] However, neither Reilly's nor Huff's model recognizes the significance of other factors that can affect patronage decisions, such as image, accessibility, modernity, and even the presence of nonretail attractions, such as entertainment and medical facilities.[4]

Analyzing the Competitive Situation

As you can readily imagine, the number and kinds of competitors are important to any retailer. Even convenience-goods stores will find limited opportunity where there are nearby stores offering similar goods. As noted in the last chapter, competing stores can be analyzed to determine their retailing mix, their target customers, and whether any void exists that might offer opportunity for another retailer. You should realize, however, that with the present trend toward scrambled merchandising, competition typically comes from a variety of retailers.

It is customary to use the term *saturation* to denote the competitive situation in a particular area. If there are too many drugstores in a given area, this is an oversaturated condition. But grocery, hardware, or discount stores are not necessarily oversaturated in the same area.

Attempts have been made to quantify or reduce to a formula the degree of saturation. Some approaches are:[5]

1. Sales per square foot of existing stores: when sales per square foot are lower than in other localities, this suggests oversaturation.
2. The ratio of store vacancies to total number of stores: the larger the percentage of vacant stores, the more oversaturation has probably existed.
3. The number of consumers per retail establishment: a large number of consumers per retail establishment suggests an undersaturated condition.

Analyzing the saturation of supermarkets within a given area probably lends itself best to a quantitative approach.[6] First, merchandise is

[3] David Huff, "A Probabilistic Analysis of Consumer Spatial Behavior," in *Emerging Concepts in Marketing,* ed. William S. Decker, (proceedings of the winter conference of the American Marketing Association, December 27–29, 1972), pp. 443–461.

[4] The effect of differences in image on retail patronage has been researched by Thomas J. Stanley and Murphy A. Sewell, "Image Inputs to a Probabilistic Model: Predicting Retail Potential," *Journal of Marketing* (July 1976), 48–53.

[5] William Applebaum and Saul B. Cohen, "Trading Area Networks and Problems of Store Saturation," *Journal of Retailing* (Winter 1961–62), 38–39.

[6] An interesting effort to develop an index of saturation is described in Bernard J. LaLonde, "New Frontiers in Store Location," *Supermarket Merchandising* (February 1963), 110.

fairly standardized in supermarkets. Second, we can develop better norms as to what per capita expenditures for food will be.

Except for food retailing, most efforts at analyzing the competitive situation in a given area rely on a subjective evaluation of the strength of present competitors and any vulnerability they may have. But one should not ignore possible plans for entry or expansion by other retailers, especially by strong and aggressive ones. In the early 1960s, when discount stores were vigorously expanding into most metropolitan areas, the dominant department-store corporation in the Minneapolis-St. Paul area, Dayton's, publicly announced its intention to start its own discount-store subsidiary. Dayton's announcement caused most major discount-store chains to turn their attention elsewhere. Almost half a decade elapsed before major discount chains entered this sizable market.

Other Possible Factors

The kinds of industries in a trading area often indicate its economic and labor stability. A recent history of shutdowns and labor disturbances may forbode future vulnerability. Knowing how local businesses and industries are growing is useful in evaluating potential. The progressiveness of a city is an intangible thing, but it can be fairly well ascertained by looking at the efforts of the chamber of commerce or other organizations to attract new industries. Urban-renewal projects, highway and parking facilities, community-betterment programs, and the progressiveness of the school system also furnish clues about the business environment. Tax rates and any restrictive local ordinances (such as a limit on hours of business) should be considered. The bankers in the community may be conservative or they may encourage expansion; they may be familiar with the problems of retailers or unconcerned about them.

Seldom will all factors in a given area be favorable. But systematically evaluating the strengths and weaknesses of a community may prevent a costly mistake.

SELECTING A SPECIFIC SITE

Once the community or metropolitan area has been selected, the retailer must decide on the specific place for the business. Even in a city with great potential, a site that is not near main traffic patterns or that has inadequate parking or other negative features is a bad one.

The 100 Percent Location

Retailers speak of the *100 percent location.* This means the best location for a particular kind of store. A variety store, for example, thrives on customer traffic. It needs to locate where the greatest amount of foot traffic is flowing by. Some variety chains periodically conduct traffic surveys to count the number of persons passing certain spots. The count is compared with preceding periods; in this way changes in traffic patterns can be detected.

While the variety store needs a flow of foot traffic, the best location for a convenience-food store or a fast-food restaurant is a street carrying a large number of vehicles slowed down by traffic lights, so that turning off the street and coming out onto the street are not difficult.

Of course, not all stores can locate in a 100 percent location. There are not that many choice locations, and not all retailers can afford the cost of such locations. A site with less traffic may be entirely satisfactory for some types of stores: those carrying specialty goods for which customers will exert some shopping effort. Jewelry, sporting-goods, furniture, and bridal shops are examples. but such stores can locate *too* far out of the traffic and suffer for it.

Certain types of stores are called *generators.* They pull people in, sometimes from a considerable distance, and thereby contribute greatly to the traffic flow in their vicinity. Department stores and discount stores are such generators. In most shopping centers, the greatest customer traffic is near the major department store. Discount stores are usually isolated from other stores, but as long as they are easily accessible via streets and highways, they can generate sufficient traffic by themselves.

Traffic patterns vary even between sides of the street; one side usually has more pedestrian traffic than the other. Sometimes this is because of the character of stores on one side, but even weather can be a factor. In warm localities the shady side of the street is more popular; in northern cities in winter the sunny side may be choicest. A corner location is usually desirable, since it taps traffic coming from two directions. Some of these passersby may be delayed by traffic lights or waiting at the bus stop; the window display space available to a corner store can lure such traffic inside.

The 100 percent location results mainly from shopper traffic. But other factors deserve consideration in the site decision:

Transportation facilities
The adequacy of parking
The growth of businesses and facilities in the area

The intercepting qualities of the site
The compatibility of existing businesses
Possible negative features

We will discuss these in more detail in the sections to follow.

Accessibility of the Site: Transportation Facilities

With the maze of streets that characterizes most cities, we tend to take transportation facilities for granted. Yet they can attract to or detract from a particular site. In major cities, the nearness of public transportation (buses and subways) is important, especially for such consumer groups as the elderly. Congestion and variations in traffic during certain periods of the day or week are significant. For example, crowded streets that are made more crowded by shifts of factory workers or by baseball or football crowds can be detrimental. On the other hand, unless the site is part of a major shopping-center complex, it can be disastrous if most nearby traffic travels on freeways. Many a town or commercial area has watched business dry up as a superhighway bypassed the area.

The matter of accessibility is rather complex, however. Even a shopping center is at a disadvantage if it is not easily reached via major arteries, preferably superhighways. A nearby highway extends the range of customer draw.[7] Visibility for the store or shopping center from such a highway is also desirable. While local customers will be familiar with the store, visitors or out-of-town shoppers will not be.

The Adequacy of Parking

Related to the accessibility of a site is its parking situation. We know that the decline of downtown business is partly caused by the scarcity and expense of parking facilities. Many large department stores have attempted to improve the parking situation by constructing their own garages and ramps or by arranging for free parking at nearby lots. In most downtown shopping areas it is common to see signs calling attention to free parking with a purchase validation from a cooperating store. But it is difficult for downtown merchants to match the parking convenience of the newer suburban shopping centers. Even some of the older

---

[7] For a study of this, see Richard T. Hise and Jan P. Muczyk, "The Effect of Interstate Highway on Driving Times and Regional Shopping Center Drawing Power," *Journal of the Academy of Marketing Science* (Spring 1977), 126–133.

A passerby shows interest as a display window is set up. This store site has limited parking availability. Yet the Baskin Robbins ice cream store, which must have a good traffic location, indicates that this is normally a busy street. What might account for heavy foot traffic at a site like this one? (HUD photo)

shopping centers are suffering from overcongested parking facilities; this is especially true of the older strip centers.

Important as parking is to most retailers, there are still newly constructed parking facilities that are inadequate. Land is costly, and there is a temptation to skimp a little and paint narrower parking stalls so that more cars can be accommodated in the same space. Parking then requires more effort; sides of cars are chipped by doors opening and banging into them; and ease and comfort in parking are still lacking while prices continually rise.

The Growth of Businesses and Facilities in the Area

Most store-location decisions involve long-term commitments. Therefore, a retailer should consider whether the business district and the areas from which it pulls are improving or going downhill. New stores or buildings and modernization efforts are an encouraging sign. On the other hand, a lack of such efforts suggests that present facilities are becoming obsolete and that merchants intend to move to the suburbs as leases expire. New residential construction and new construction permits should be investigated. For larger cities, projected subway routes can provide a long-term indication of the viability of particular sites.

The Intercepting Qualities of a Site

A large store or shopping center draws customers from residential areas, from office buildings, and from the fringes of the shopping area. Stores or smaller shopping areas located *between* such a magnet and a source of its customers will intercept part of this business. In Figure 6.2, site A would intercept some of the business going to the major shopping center. This site would be attractive to a discount store, for example.

Even a small store can benefit from an interceptor location. Take the example of two candy stores of identical size owned by the same chain. One was about a block away from a large office building; the other was half a block away. The first was between the office building and the retail district, while the second store was in the opposite direction. The first store got more than twice as many customers as the one that was half a block closer.[8]

The Compatibility of Existing Businesses

Some businesses enjoy compatibility with each other; that is, they benefit from being close together. The major reason for this is shopping goods—shoes, clothing, furniture, even automobiles—for which many customers like to look around in different stores, to compare and choose from a wide variety. Customers are drawn to shopping centers having several similar stores. Although such stores compete with one another, they also attract a larger total of customers.

Other stores are complementary. For example, shoe stores, jewelry stores, and millinery shops complement dress shops. They offer related goods that a customer might want to shop for at the same time she purchases a dress. *Customer interchange* is the term used to describe the extent to which customers of one store become customers of a nearby store.

The cumulative drawing power of similar stores clustered together is

---

[8] This example appears in a classic book dealing with store location, Richard L. Nelson, *The Selection of Retail Locations* (New York: F. W. Dodge Corporation, 1958), pp. 81–82.

FIGURE 6.2 AN INTERCEPTING SITE

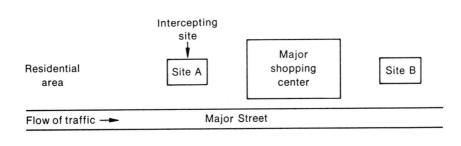

reflected in the tendency of large department stores to locate close together in downtown business districts. And large suburban shopping centers seek not one, but two, three, or more major department stores as tenants.

A well-planned shopping center attempts to maximize the benefits of compatibility. Tenants are chosen with this in mind, and the successful shopping center provides strong customer interchange. But not all retail stores are compatible.[9]

Certain types of stores are fundamentally incompatible: they detract from each other. An extreme example would be a motorcycle sales and service store located next to a high-quality women's dress store. But any stores that appeal to entirely different customers are hardly good neighbors. At best, there would be little customer interchange. At worst, the nearness of one store might jeopardize the patronage of some customers of the other stores.

The threat of unwelcome competition that discount stores posed for conventional retailers led to their being barred from many shopping centers. This is changing today. We are beginning to recognize that discount stores, far from taking business away from nearby merchants, actually generate more traffic for a shopping center and are often compatible with other stores.

Possible Negative Features in a Site

Certain things can be detrimental to a particular site and should be evaluated by the retailer in making a location decision. Vacant buildings

[9] For a more detailed treatment of the principle of compatibility, see Nelson, pp. 66–78. He presents an equation to quantify the increased business volume resulting from adjacent compatible outlets.

FIGURE 6.3 NEGATIVE FACTORS AFFECTING A SITE

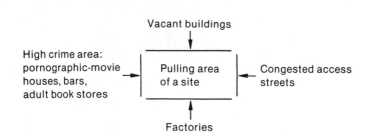

not only fail to contribute to drawing customer traffic, but also create an atmosphere of neglect and poverty. Poor sidewalks, smoke, or unusual noise from nearby factories can be detrimental. Proximity to a shabby bar or cheap movie house flaws a site. If the area is run down or poorly lighted, or if patrons may be bothered by undisciplined children, then business probably will suffer. Even a somewhat more intangible factor, the reputation of a particular neighborhood for crime or vandalism, will be a negative influence. Figure 6.3 graphically illustrates how negative factors can constrict the draw of a particular site.

TYPES OF SHOPPING AREAS

Central Business District

The central business district, or downtown, is the largest shopping area for most cities: the historical center of retailing with the biggest stores and the greatest assortment of merchandise. Though a retailer may have branch stores, the downtown store usually is the headquarters. The main-store buyers also buy for the branches.

The central business district is the heart of a metropolitan area. It is served by all transportation facilities, both private and public. Major banks, office buildings, and entertainment and cultural functions are usually downtown.

But downtowns have been losing business and decaying for decades. Often, the heart of a city is also the center of its oldest area, surrounded by deteriorating slums. In more than a few cities, customers are reluctant to venture downtown at night. J. L. Hudson, the huge downtown

The climate-controlled Minneapolis Skyway eliminates much of the conflict between pedestrians and autos, and also enhances shopping during a harsh winter. This is an excellent example of downtown rejuvenation. (Courtesy of Minneapolis Convention and Tourism Commission)

store in Detroit, was forced to close earlier at night because of waning business, but its suburban branches found it desirable to stay open on Sundays to handle an overflow of customers.

It might appear that the decline of downtown areas is inevitable, but this prediction may be too pessimistic. It is true that many retailers have a defeatist attitude about downtown locations and are reluctant to invest in them. For decades no new major retail store was built in a downtown location; many were closed. But now some major retailers are beginning to give downtowns another chance. Downtown merchants' associations are closing certain streets to vehicular traffic and turning them into shopping malls. More parking ramps are being built. And better mass transit, particularly subways, are helping some downtowns. In many older cities, restoration of existing industrial and commercial buildings is turning run-down, underused downtown areas into thriving commercial showcases.

Shopping Centers

The decentralization trend started in the 1920s, as stores began spreading out from the downtown core along main streets and fanning out into suburban residential areas. It was not until after World War II, however, that retailers began following the population shift to the suburbs in any great numbers.

First came the *strip center,* a string of small shops along a busy street, usually anchored by a supermarket. Strip centers served primarily the immediate neighborhood, with some transient business from passing motorists. Then came the larger *community center,* which included a small department store, or a Penney or Sears branch. In the mid-1950s the large *regional center* made its appearance. Often such a shopping center would have one or two department stores, along with scores of smaller shops and bountiful parking. Before long the enclosed mall enabled customers to shop in springtime comfort all year round. We will now examine the major types of shopping centers in more detail.

Types of Shopping Centers

STRIP CENTER (NEIGHBORHOOD CENTER)

Description: Merely a row of stores or a long building partitioned into stores. Parking, somewhat limited, is usually in front of the stores.

Street
Parking
Strip center

Comments: This older form of shopping center is still common. The stores typically are small and emphasize convenience goods: grocery stores, drugstores, bakeries, and service establishments such as barber shops and shoe-repair shops. This older form of shopping center suffers from congested parking and can seldom expect to draw customers from far away, especially when stronger shopping centers are within reasonable distance.

L-SHAPED CENTER (COMMUNITY CENTER)

Description: Usually a shopping-goods center. The focal point is a department store or large variety store. Parking is much better than at strip centers.

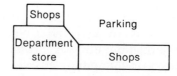

Comments: This is a newer form and generally a much larger shopping center than a strip center. Because of the shape, the total walk from one end to the other is shortened. Furthermore, this type of center is designed to attract traffic from two major streets instead of one. But it is vulnerable to newer, more attractive centers.

MALL CENTER (REGIONAL CENTER)

Description: This is the prototype for virtually all large centers. Two department stores typically are placed at either end, with smaller specialty stores between, and a pedestrian walkway in the center. In the newer centers, this entire complex is enclosed or roofed to create all-weather shopping, and benches, trees, fountains, and so on may be placed in the mall. Parking usually is on all sides. The larger malls have several floors of stores, each opening onto the mall.

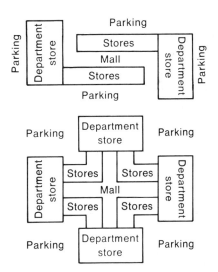

Many variations are possible with a mall center. For example, more department stores may be accommodated by adding wings.

Comments: This style appears in both old regional centers and the newest ones. It is comfortable and relatively convenient for customers. It is important, however, that major traffic generators, usually department stores, be placed at each end of the mall; otherwise traffic patterns will be uneven. Since these centers are oriented inward, the rear is presented to the streets; therefore, the exterior is not likely to be attractive.

HUB CENTER (REGIONAL CENTER)

Description: Northland in Detroit is the most famous example of this type of center. The department store is in a most advantageous position at the center of all the shopping patterns. Abundant parking usually surrounds the center.

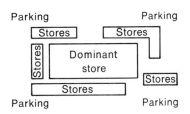

Comments: This pattern is not particularly popular today, especially since most of the newest and biggest shopping centers have three or more dominant department stores; the hub center really is suitable for only one dominant store.

SUCCESSFUL RETAILING STRATEGIES—*Giantism in Shopping Centers*

As shopping centers become larger, it seems reasonable to wonder if there must not be an ultimate limit to size. How far is the average customer willing to walk? How many levels of stores can be piled up without confusing the customer? How many cars can a parking lot accommodate before traffic congestion, finding a parking space and, later, finding one's car, and hiking to and from the stores will become too burdensome?

Yet some developers are building ever-bigger shopping complexes, and doing so successfully. For example, Woodfield opened 25 miles northwest of Chicago in 1971. At the time, it was billed as the world's largest enclosed multilevel shopping center. It cost $90 million to construct, has 2 million square feet of space, 215 shops and services, and 3 major department stores, including the largest stores Sears and Penney had ever built up to that point and the largest suburban store that Marshall Field had ever put up.

But Woodfield's claim was to be surpassed. In August 1976, Randall Park Mall, 2.2 million square feet and a $175 million undertaking, opened in the eastern suburbs of Cleveland, Ohio. It has 5 major department stores and almost 200 smaller shops and stores, with total plans calling for 6 department stores and almost 250 smaller stores. Randall Park quickly began drawing customers from as far as 50 to 60 miles away. Less than a mile down the road stands Southgate, an old but large strip center, which for 21 years had been the areas's largest shopping center. (A case involving Southgate's confrontation with Randall appears at the end of Part 2.)

Near these huge retail centers, other commercial, recreational, and cultural facilities are often developed. More and more, hotels, apartment houses, office buildings, churches, and theaters are causing the new giant shopping centers to become downtowns in scope.

Sources: For more detail about Woodfield, Randall Park Mall, and Southgate, see "Shopping Centers Grow into Shopping Cities," *BusinessWeek,* September 4, 1971, pp. 34–38; "Edward J. DeBartolo, The Pharaoh from Youngstown," *The Cleveland Magazine* (July 1976), 54–85; and "Shopping Center Boom Appears to be Fading Due to Overbuilding," *Wall Street Journal,* September 7, 1976, pp. 1, 10.

For Thought and Discussion

1. Where is a major shopping center (such as Randall, with sales projections of $200 million plus) likely to draw its business from?
2. Do you think a shopping center can be too large? If so, at what point do you think this is probable?

Free-Standing Stores Versus Shopping-Center Locations

Some large retailers have preferred to place certain of their units in *free-standing sites* (where no other stores are adjacent), rather than in the more customary shopping-center locations. Early discount stores frequently had no other choice, since they were banned from many shopping centers. S. S. Kresge Company, even when it had a choice, has favored free-standing units for its K mart stores. On the other hand, the discount operation of F. W. Woolworth Company, Woolco, favors shopping centers. Kinney Shoes and Robert Hall have consistently sought free-standing sites, in sharp contrast to most shoe and clothing merchants.

Sears was the first major retailer to open department stores in free-standing suburban sites. Today it has both free-standing units and units in shopping centers. While supermarkets are found in both types of locations, the bulkiness of merchandise and the necessity for convenient loading has led them to seek isolated locations even when they are in a shopping center.

RETAILING DISAGREEMENTS—*Should We Locate by Ourselves or with Other Stores?*

Arguments for Free-standing Stores

Rental costs are lower than in a shopping center.

Parking facilities are better, since no other stores will be creating demand for the same space.

There is more freedom of operation than there is under the rules and constraints of a shopping center.

There is less competition for a store that is itself a strong generator of business because of size, reputation, pricing, promotional practices, or the merchandise carried.

Some customers will be attracted because less shopping effort is needed and parking is more convenient than in a large shopping center.

Arguments for Shopping-Center Locations

For many goods, customers like to shop around; therefore, locating near other stores caters to consumer preferences.

The isolated store cannot expect to have as much traffic flowing by as it would have in a shopping center.

A well-managed shopping center can develop strong promotional and traffic-pulling efforts—special exhibits, entertainment, extravaganzas, and the like—that no store by itself can do on the same scale.

For Thought and Discussion

1. Can you think of any other arguments for these decisions?
2. Which arguments do you think are the most important?
3. Why do you think so few large stores have tried free-standing locations?

OCCUPANCY ALTERNATIVES

The retailer, large or small, may have another major decision to make after settling on a site: whether to buy or to rent? Renting involves a lease arrangement of some kind. Ownership assures permanent occupancy and allows the owner to change and modernize the site as desired. If property values rise the owner benefits.

However, the advantages of buying are often outweighed by disadvantages. More of a firm's resources must be committed to real estate; less is available for operating expenses and inventory. Even firms with sufficient capital often prefer to get the higher return from their money that is possible through renting. Some large retail chains build a store on a desirable site, then sell it to private investors and lease back the store, thereby freeing funds for further expansion.

Another major limitation of ownership is the loss of flexibility. Location decisions are not always correct. Even the best location may deteriorate in a few years, so that a change is desirable.

Types of Leases

For this discussion we shall consider leasing and renting as essentially the same. Usually a *lease* for a certain period of time is part of a rental agreement. Three types of leases are common:

Fixed rental or flat amount
Straight percentage
Percentage with guaranteed minimum

Under the fixed-rental lease the same rent must be paid regardless of sales or profits. This benefits the retailer whose sales increase. But a fixed-rental lease is risky if the potential of a site is overestimated or if business declines.

The straight-percentage lease permits the rent to fluctuate according to sales volume or profits. Especially when tied to sales, this is an equitable arrangement for both the lessee and the landlord. However, if the lease is tied to profits, the landlord may be at a disadvantage if an inefficient retailer rents the property.

The percentage with a guaranteed minimum protects the landlord from sharp declines in sales, and at the same time allows participation in the success of a tenant. It is a reasonable compromise between the fixed-rental and the straight-percentage arrangement.

Rent Variations

The large retailer often enjoys a powerful position with the landlord. For example, rent for major shopping centers typically runs from 1.5 percent of gross sales to 8 percent. The supermarket operates on a very low margin, and will average only about 1.5 percent of its gross sales on rent. While a Macy's, May Company, Sears, or other full-line department store will have a higher margin, it can drive a harder bargain. Such a department store may own its own property in the shopping center and pay the center nothing but a maintenance fee. If it leases rather than owns the space, rent may be held to 2.5 percent of gross sales. A variety-store chain, meanwhile, might pay 4.5 percent. Small specialty stores, which have the highest markups of all and the least bargaining leverage, usually pay 5 percent to 8 percent. The reason for the power of big retailers is their ability to generate traffic. They are the "anchor stores" that the shopping-center developer needs to make the facility successful.

Sometimes rents are calculated by square feet of space. For example, in Randall Park Mall tenants pay from $6.50 to $22.00 per square foot. Rents vary considerably between shopping centers. In Southgate, the old shopping center less than a mile from Randall Park, the same type of space can be had for $5.00 per square foot. Why would a prospective tenant pay the higher rent of Randall? It is warranted if the traffic generated by the newer and bigger center results in much higher sales.

■ Summary

The importance of the location decision cannot be overemphasized. Even the best merchant finds it difficult to overcome the drawbacks of a poor or deteriorating location. At the same time, the cost of buying or leasing the optimal site may be unreasonable. A compromise often has to be made. The retailer should approach this decision carefully, weighing the pros and cons of alternative locations, before going on to decisions about the physical appearance and layout for the store.

■ Key Terms

Buying power index (BPI)   Regional center
Community center   Reilly's Law
Compatibility   Saturation
Consumer goods   Shopping goods
Convenience goods   Specialty goods
Customer interchange   Standard metropolitan statistical
Free-standing sites   area (SMSA)
Generator   Strip center
Interceptor location   Survey of Buying Power
Leases   Trading area
100 percent location

■ Discussion Questions

1. For a store featuring specialty goods, location decisions are less important than for a store featuring shopping goods. Why?
2. Would the buying power index be important for locating a convenience-food store? Why or why not?
3. Would Reilly's Law be an important tool for locating a convenience-food store? Why or why not?

4. What is a 100 percent location? For what types of retail stores is it important? Why?

5. What is meant by an interceptor location? For what types of stores is such a location significant?

6. Give several examples of incompatible businesses. How does this relate to customer interchange?

7. Why is the strip center particularly vulnerable to competition from newer shopping centers?

8. What is the primary drawback of a hub center?

9. If you were a retailer contemplating expanding to other outlets, would you prefer buying or renting your store facilities? Why?

■ Projects

1. Determine what market information (of use for making location decisions) is available in your community from local newspapers, the chamber of commerce, and other planning groups. Evaluate the probable usefulness of this information for (a) small businessperson contemplating opening a new retail store, and (b) a discount chain contemplating entering the community.

2. Visit shopping centers in your city and note their strengths and weaknesses. Predict how each will fare in the next ten years, and why.

■ Exercise in Creativity

Visit several shopping centers that appear to be declining. What creative approaches can you come up with to give them new life? (Assume that the individual merchants might be induced to do some remodeling, but that extensive improvements are impractical.)

■ Retailing in Action

You have been asked by the owner of a camping-equipment store located near downtown to find another location in the suburbs.

How would you approach this location problem?
What information would you want?
Where would you obtain it?
Design a step-by-step plan for researching this decision.

7 Store Design and Layout

After selecting a site, the retailer must decide on the exterior and interior appearance of the store. The physical appearance should reinforce the entire retailing strategy.

When well designed, the physical appearance of a store serves two objectives: it is distinctive, and it is in harmony with the image being sought for its appeal to the target customers.

THE PHYSICAL APPEARANCE OF THE STORE IN THE RETAILING STRATEGY

Stores range from the veritable palaces of certain department and specialty stores to the crudely renovated warehouses of some low-end discount stores. All have a place, although such extremes may be less acceptable today than formerly. Discount stores originally came on the retail scene with the powerful price-saving image that is compatible with warehouses; but most customers today want a more pleasant shopping environment and sometimes are suspicious of efforts to convey a super–cut-rate operation. On the other hand, extravagant displays and decor may be viewed as wasteful, and the customer may suspect that they are reflected in exorbitant prices.

Between these two extremes, innovative merchants can find ample room to be different, to be creative, to generate flair. In nearly every community there are examples of successful businesses with unique approaches to exterior and interior decor. In particular, small boutiques have given a new flavor to shopping.

The physical appearance of a store should be harmonious with the taste of the customers being sought; it should also reflect the merchandise and services offered. There are dangers in being unresponsive to changing customer tastes. For example, some conservative old department stores took pride in maintaining their original store fronts and decor. Their executives pointed out that "this reflected the refinement and lack of garishness that are in keeping with the tastes of our upper-class, refined customers." But too many potential customers, including young ones with substantial purchasing power, thought such a point of view was outmoded.[1]

STORE DESIGN

A large retailer can maintain a staff of experts in store planning and building: architects, building and lighting engineers, designers, drafters, and other specialists. But the small retailer cannot afford such a staff. Most retailers are not likely to be expert in such matters, although they may have strong ideas of what they would like. Nor can they afford to hire consultants, although for major construction it is advisable to engage an architect to assure proper planning. For less ambitious projects, fortunately, the small retailer can obtain technical assistance at little cost.

Some leading manufacturers of consumer goods provide assistance in store planning. They do this because they believe successful retailers will contribute to their own success. Wholesalers often give advice, particularly about fixturing. The retailer who is a member of a voluntary

[1] For an example involving the biggest retailer of Canada, Eaton's, see "Corporate Rip Van Winkle," *Forbes,* June 15, 1971, p. 37; and "Venerable Store Begins to Swing," *Business Week,* September 9, 1967, p. 74.

chain or is a franchisee will receive design specifications that conform to association standards. Manufacturers of store fixtures and equipment will offer substantial help. Trade associations, such as the National Association of Retail Grocers and Menswear Retailers of America, give technical assistance to their members. Trade publications are a valuable source of information, especially about new developments.[2] The Small Business Administration (SBA) also provides advice.

Exterior Design Decisions

A merchant who wants to build a new store or remodel an existing one can choose from many alternatives. The decision is influenced by cost and by the amount of investment money available for the physical appearance of the store. The front of a store is of major importance: it should always be inviting, for it conveys the store's image and helps to attract customers.

WINDOWS   A primary decision is whether to have windows and, if so, what type. Retailers have traditionally thought that window displays attract customers and are thereby an extra selling tool. But there is evidence that this is not true for some stores today. For downtown department stores, window-shopping may be almost obsolete.

The problem is that big downtown stores are not set up for fast shopping, and the public wants fast shopping more today than twenty or thirty years ago. Especially is this desire for convenience important to noon-hour shoppers. For them, seeing an item in a window and taking time to find it in a large multi-floor store is just not practical.[3]

Free-standing suburban stores (those that are not located adjacent to other stores) also find that they don't really need windows. No pedestrians window-shop, since customers arrive by car and come into the store through the parking lot. Such stores can better use their window space for selling areas and save the cost of maintaining displays.

But while windows may be unimportant for some stores, for others they perform an important selling function. Small stores, especially those lining malls, where shoppers stroll leisurely by, need attractive windows with displays designed to woo shoppers inside.

[2] Examples of such publications are *Chain Store Age, Department Store Management, Stores, Progressive Grocer,* and the more specialized trade journals for menswear stores, jewelry merchandisers, and the like.
[3] E. B. Weiss, "Tapping Passing Traffic for More than Window Shopping," *Stores* (February 1972), 39–40.

ENTRANCES   Customer entrances should permit easy access. Recessed fronts are sometimes used to draw people off the sidewalk and to offer protection from the weather. Air-curtain doors having no obstructions provide an inviting, wide-open entrance. Other retailers, especially supermarkets, have doors that open automatically.

SIGNS   A sign identifies the store, provides information about the types of goods carried, and helps create an image. It can also give a distinctive touch. For multiunit firms, common signs identify all the units. Sometimes the sign is so prominent it dominates all other aspects of the building exterior. For example, the large Holiday Inn signs identify the units from a distance. Similarly, the orange roofs of Howard Johnson's restaurants have long been a distinguishing symbol.

PARKING   Adequate, convenient parking facilities should be part of exterior planning for many retailers who are not located in a shopping center, where parking is provided for by the developer. But parking is not important for some retailers located where pedestrian traffic is serviced by adequate public transportation. Many major cities are turning to subways; with congestion, pollution, and fuel shortages causing problems, public transportation should assume a far bigger role in the future.

Interior Design Decisions

The retailer with a creative flair has almost endless possibilities for the store interior. For example, more than fifty finishes may be selected for floors, ranging from wood and cork to rubber and marble; and there are endless varieties and patterns of carpeting. Colors, wall materials, ceilings—all these can be chosen to create an atmosphere that will enhance the appeal of the store.

Store fixtures and equipment also afford many possibilities. Some are more practical for one need than another. Whether a store is to be self-service or to use salespeople will determine the kind of fixtures needed. (We will look at the matter of self-service in more detail later in this chapter.)

Most interior design decisions require some technical expertise. For example, the matter of lighting is more complex than it may seem at first. Stores used to have a problem with dim lighting. But with the advent of fluorescent lighting about thirty years ago, using plenty of light became possible and retailers adopted this approach. Since then, however, it has been noted that casting everything in bright light prevents distinctiveness: nothing looks important or stands out. The trend therefore has shifted to more sophisticated lighting using a low level of fluorescent for basic illumination, while highlighting featured merchandise and displays with brighter light. Lighting experts can provide help in determining the type and extent of lighting needed to enhance the salability of merchandise.

Stores usually must provide air conditioning for customer comfort and employee productivity. If the store has more than one floor, vertical transportation must be furnished. For larger stores, escalators have gained wide acceptance, but some elevators are necessary for customers who are handicapped or have young children.

STORE LAYOUT

Store layout refers to the arrangement of merchandise, fixtures, and displays, including nonselling areas. Layout decisions involve many levels of retail executives. Even a junior executive makes or implements layout decisions within a department. The aisles, which regulate the flow of customer traffic, are of prime importance. Certain nonselling areas, for example, reserve-stock rooms, fitting rooms, and checkout counters must be carefully integrated with selling areas, to expedite selling.

The Importance of Layout

While a store's layout can be haphazard, retailers are finding it desirable to devote thought and planning to this aspect of their operation. Studies of customer-traffic patterns and the "stopping power" of various types of displays are useful. Layout is important for the following reasons:

1. It can guide the flow of customer traffic to all parts of the store, thereby giving the best exposure of merchandise.
2. It can provide stopping power for impulse buying.[4]
3. It permits the store to maximize the amount of sales space in relation to nonselling space.

---

[4] As noted in chapter 6, impulse buying refers to purchases customers make that are unplanned, and that result from suggestions they receive in the store, through either displays or a salesperson's comments.

4. It aids the customer in selecting and comparing merchandise.
5. Departments and merchandise categories can be placed and emphasized according to sales potential for maximum effect.

A layout should be flexible. Planning the layout can be a never-ending effort. The merchant wants the best layout possible within the existing facilities of the store but can never be sure that the optimum has been reached. The aggressive retailer, therefore, experiments with different arrangements. Each season requires layout changes. Furthermore, changing the layout periodically can keep a store fresh and exciting for both its customers and its employees.

Factors to Consider in Store Layout

Planning a store layout involves the following steps:

1. Determining the space available in the facility
2. Determining space needs for the selling and nonselling areas
3. Fitting space needs to available space to achieve a good traffic flow and maximum sales per square foot

The first step in planning the layout is easy. If there are no blueprints, the dimensions of the building can be measured. The last two steps are more complicated and require study.

The following should be considered in determining space needs:

1. Kind and extent of departmentalization
   a. Space requirements of departments
   b. Locations of departments
2. Traffic flow desired
3. Types of displays to be used and their space requirements
4. Extent of layout flexibility
5. Types of nonselling activities
   a. Space requirements
   b. Location requirements
6. Special provisions for self-service

We will discuss each of these factors in more detail in the following sections.

Usually the third step of fitting the selling and nonselling areas into available space involves compromise. Often a retailer does not have enough space. Typically, the receiving room and stockroom facilities are cramped. Less often a retailer may be confronted with too much space. In both cases, some compromise can be made. The retailer who has too much space might consider renting some out, perhaps as storage space for a neighboring firm. Or the excess may be used as nonselling space until such time as business warrants a greater investment in inventory and more space for selling. In any case, the negative image conveyed to customers by a large and half-empty store should definitely be avoided.

DEPARTMENTALIZATION

Departmentalization means that goods are grouped into sections, such as boys' clothing, shoes, sporting goods, and so on. In large stores, these categories of goods are bought by different buyers, and each department is run rather independently. For the small store, departmentalization may not be so formal. But it is still sensible to group and display similar kinds of goods together. Chapter 8 will discuss the important concept of departmentalization in more detail.

Space Requirements of Departments

A key factor in apportioning space to a department is its sales potential, which may be measured in relation to other departments within the store. Generally, the more sales potential a department has compared to other departments, the more space it should have. For example, a department store would not give its bath shop as much space as the men's department, since bath shop sales normally would be far less and it is not likely that adding more space to the bath shop would increase its sales.

Other factors can affect space allocation. Some types of goods simply need more space. Furniture, for example, requires a lot of space; so do lamps and shades. Toys and games need more space than most other goods, at least during peak season. At the other extreme, women's hosiery can be stocked and displayed in a small space; yet it is usually a high-sales-volume department.

Certain departments convey the fashion image of a store. They may be called *bellwether departments* because they are key departments in establishing a store's reputation. Women's and misses' dresses, coats, and sportswear are such departments. Typically, they are given more display space than most other departments.

SPACE-PRODUCTIVITY RATIO   The *space-productivity ratio* is the sales per square foot of selling area of a department or section. This ratio is commonly used in apportioning space among departments. Various retail publications and trade associations furnish retail operating ratios for different sizes and types of stores.[5] Thus, a retailer can measure a department's performance against an industry average.

For existing stores, such a comparison helps the retail executive spot and correct problems. For new or planned stores, space-productivity ratios can serve as a guide for allotting space to departments. Table 7.1 shows space-productivity ratios for certain selected departments in a median, or typical, store and in a superior store. The retailing tool in the next section illustrates how these data might be used in planning space for a women's sportswear department in a new store.

CAUTIONS IN USING SPACE-PRODUCTIVITY RATIOS   Planning by the average statistics for space-productivity ratios is a follow-the-leader method; it is imitative, not innovative. The performances of less-efficient firms lower these productivity averages; an aggressive firm may find its results considerably better than these figures. Also, such averages mute the influence of seasonal factors, which are important in some locations. For example, space productivity in women's coat sales will vary greatly between a store in Minnesota and one in Georgia. Still, average ratios are better guides for allocating space and measuring performance than hunches or haphazard judgments. And management can easily interpret the averages according to a firm's unique strengths and limitations.

THE MODEL-STOCK APPROACH   Another guide sometimes used for space allocation is the *model-stock approach.* The ideal assortment of sizes, styles, colors, price lines, and so on is determined. Then the amount of space needed to stock such an assortment is estimated. However, this is an arbitrary approach, which does not always help. For example, it is not unusual to find that the ideal assortment would require far more space than the store has. Then the ideal must be compromised.

---

[5] For example, various trade associations, such as the National Retail Merchants Association and the National Retail Hardware Association, furnish statistical comparisons. Various journals carry articles dealing with retail ratios. Two examples are the *Journal of Retailing* and the *Lilly Digest* (for drugstore firms).

TABLE 7.1 SPACE-SALES RATIOS

Department	Sales per Square Foot of Selling Space		Selling Area (Percentage of total division)	
	Median[a]	Superior[b]	Median[a]	Superior[b]
Total adult female apparel	$98	$106	100.0	100.0
Women's, misses', and juniors' coats and suits	106	134	18.0	24.1
Women's, misses', and juniors' dresses	85	104	42.3	47.4
Women's, misses', and juniors' sportswear	94	127	34.7	51.4
Total adult female accessories	118	123	100.0	100.0
Corsets and bras	134	157	16.6	18.0
Lingerie, sleepwear, and robes	106	135	23.8	27.3
Hosiery and gloves	176	228	10.5	12.4
Handbags and small leather goods	87	126	11.0	15.4
Millinery	100	135	11.9	16.1
Neckwear, scarves, belts, handkerchiefs, and umbrellas	96	127	7.4	9.1
Footwear	115	133	24.3	27.1
Total adult male apparel and furnishings	110	144	100.0	100.0
Men's clothing	174	194	57.1	59.0
Men's furnishings	127	181	48.0	56.9

Source: Department Store and Specialty Store *Merchandising and Operating Results* I (New York: National Retail Merchants Association, Controllers Congress).

[a] Midpoint of all stores surveyed.
[b] Superior to that achieved by 75 percent of stores surveyed.

RETAILING TOOL—*Planning Departmental Space and Estimating Sales*

Problem   Assume that a new department store is being built in the South. The entire second floor, 100 × 150 feet of selling space, is to be used for women's apparel. Calculate optimal space allocation for the sportswear department, and estimate sales.

Solution   The retailer can use the data in Table 7.1 or an updated version furnished by a trade association or some other group for this calculation. From Table 7.1, a store can use either median or superior percentages. Since this store is located in the South, sportswear probably will sell above the average. Therefore, it is decided to use the superior figure.

100 feet × 150 feet = 15,000 square feet of selling space for all of women's apparel

51.4 percent of 15,000 = 7,710 square feet for sportswear department, which would be about 70 feet × 110 feet

Looking at the Sales columns, we see that sales per square foot vary from $94 to $127. Using the more conservative $94, we can estimate sales at about

$$\$94 \times 7,710 = \$724,000$$

For Thought and Discussion   Examining the sales results of a men's clothing and a men's furnishings department, you find that the former had sales of $170 per square foot, while the latter had $198 per square foot. What would be your initial conclusion about space allocation? (*Hint:* Use Table 7.1)

Locating Departments

Not all space in a store is equally desirable. Obviously the upper floors of a multifloor store have less customer traffic than the first floor. But even first-floor locations differ in traffic; for example, those in the back of the store have less traffic than those in the front near the doors.

    Certain departments need customer traffic, since they carry many impulse goods or goods with low-unit prices for which customers will not exert shopping effort. These goods are weak generators that attract virtually no traffic on their own. Departments such as candy, hosiery, drugs and cosmetics, jewelry, accessories, gifts, and stationery tend to attract little traffic. Typically these departments also have high space-productivity ratios.

On the other hand, some departments are generators; they pull traffic. Furniture is a generator; so is a women's clothing department; so are most major departments in a store. For such merchandise customers are willing to exert more shopping effort. Most retailers place these generative departments in the less accessible parts of the store, assuming that customers will go to them wherever they are located.

In some departments unhurried shopping is important to customers. China, expensive jewelry, and some types of apparel are examples of contemplative goods. Such goods should be located where customers can shop leisurely without congestion.

TRAFFIC FLOW ALTERNATIVES

Three basic traffic flow patterns may be used: grid, free form, and boutique. Figure 7.1 differentiates these.

The *grid* pattern is the traditional store layout. It is much like a highway system, with a main artery and perhaps secondary and tertiary aisles that carry less traffic. It is relatively simple to plot the flow of customers as they enter and leave such stores, and thus determine the corners or ends of counters that have the most customer exposure. These "feature" spots are good places for impulse goods and new items that might produce extra sales. In some stores, various departments vie with each other for the privilege of having some of their "hot" merchandise so displayed. If the main aisle is wide enough, a gondola or small table may be placed there to further tap some of the traffic flowing by. Most stores that carry many relatively low-priced items tend toward the grid pattern. Supermarkets do; so do most variety, drug, hardware, and discount stores. For such stores, customer shopping habits practically force a grid arrangement. Furthermore the grid pattern is a relatively inexpensive layout.

Many shops and departments that feature style goods use various arrangements of the *free form* pattern. Most department stores use a combination of the grid and free form, according to the type of merchandise being presented. This provides variety in layout, making the store more interesting. A more recent trend in department and specialty store layout has been the *boutique.*

FIGURE 7.1 TRAFFIC FLOW PATTERNS

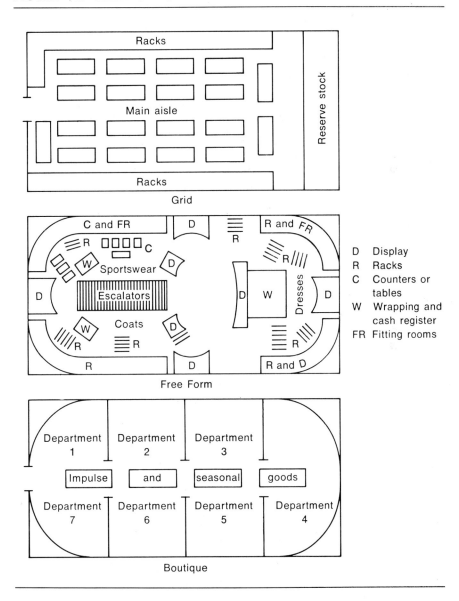

A view of a free-form layout pattern in a department store shows wide use of apparel racks and displays. Note the L'eggs display, strategically located to cater to impulse buying, yet taking up very little space. (Alex Webb/Magnum)

RETAILING STRATEGIES—*Boutique-style Merchandising*

This layout breaks up floor areas into a series of small specialty shops. The objective is to give customers a greater sense of personal attention, a more concentrated array of merchandise, and goods for unique areas of interest. Imaginative thinking can produce some startling changes in traditional departmental layouts. For example, eliminating the men's wear department and replacing it with a Man's World creates a shopping area that includes not only wearing apparel, but, also a smoke shop, a gift shop where men can find presents for friends and relatives, a greeting-card corner, and even a coffee corner with a TV set.

Themes for these boutiques are virtually unlimited. A few stores are testing Adam and Eve shops, devoted to birth-control devices. Other shops may carry unisex merchandise, for boy-girl couples who shop together. The names reflect the nontraditional orientation: Zoo's Who (fun furs), Kaboodle (junior sportswear), Spare Hair Shop (wigs), S'fari Room ("for the adventuresome pursuer of the unique"), and L'Arcade Elegante (high fashion).

Boutiques are a response to the reaction of many people against the bigness and impersonality of stores. Also, because of the increasing numbers of styles, the small shop makes shopping easier. Fun and excitement are vital ingredients of a boutique's success. Some shops have merchandise tumbling out of half-open drawers, enticing customers to rummage and discover.

Merchandising in these boutiques is, of course, different from that in conventional departments. Most shops offer goods that cross department lines, and may carry hats, purses, scarves, shoes, gloves, accessories, and whatever else it takes to complete the costume. Little depth of stock is carried. This means that a buyer must have a variety of sources available for small orders; and this can pose problems.

At the height of the boutique fad in the late 1960s and early 1970s, some department stores found themselves with a lot of little rooms. While sales often expanded as much as 15 to 20 percent over the traditional, more wide-open approach, very high selling costs also resulted. As with most things, moderation in boutiques seems to be desirable. Boutiques add the personal touch and offer interesting assortments of merchandise, but too many of them lead to unbalanced costs and a confused store image.

For Thought and Discussion

1. Are there boutiques in your local stores? How long have they been in operation? Can you estimate the extent of their success or lack of success?
2. What would you judge to be the necessary ingredients in the success of a boutique?
3. Would the successful buyer or manager of a boutique be likely to be successful in operating a major department? Why or why not?

THE EMPHASIS TO BE GIVEN TO DISPLAYS

In a grid pattern, displays are rather limited in number and there is little flexibility in their location and the amount of space that can be used. At the other extreme, the free form pattern permits the widest possible flexibility of displays and special features. Certain categories of goods benefit from displays more than others. Women's dresses, coats, and sportswear are particularly enhanced by attractive and timely displays. These displays can also contribute to the desired image of the store, whether it is low price, newest styles, flamboyance, or conservatism. Boutiques usually have their own distinctive modes of display, which are important in creating particular moods.

We will talk more about displays in a later chapter. For now it is worth noting that while displays take away from counters and selling space, thay also break up the monotony of merchandise presentation and are valuable in featuring or highlighting selected items. Even the supermarket, constrained as it is by the nature of its goods and the necessity for a grid pattern, can use imaginative and productive counter-end displays to increase impulse sales.

THE EXTENT OF FLEXIBILITY NEEDED

Some stores change their layouts and departmental arrangements frequently. Other stores hardly ever change. But there are several incentives for shifting layouts periodically:

1. It is desirable to keep a fresh appearance, so that customers will not become bored but will shop frequently and see what's new.
2. Special seasonal requirements force some departments, such as toys and gifts at Christmas time, to expand to maximize sales potential. Other departments, because of their lessened sales potential, can be reduced in space seasonally.
3. Boutiques necessitate flexibility. Those with poor sales have to be quickly phased out, while others may need to be expanded or modified.

Some stores are experimenting with flexible interiors that enable them to change layouts in as little as three hours. These usually take the form of modules with molded forms, prefabricated wall units, new ceiling systems, new flooring materials, and other technological innovations. Flexible interiors allow retailers to meet special merchandise requirements quickly, create desired atmospheres and generate an air of change and excitement.

A caution should be noted. In their eagerness to produce excitement, some retailers have found that continuous changing of layouts may confuse and irritate customers. And costs are involved, such as salaries, materials, and management time for planning and supervising.

NONSELLING DEPARTMENTS

Nonselling departments are usually placed in the least valuable parts of a store. For example, executive offices, the advertising department, parcel checking, accounts-receivable windows, and check-cashing services can be placed on upper floors or in the back of a single-floor store, Such locations for departments that have direct customer contact can increase customer circulation in the more remote parts of the store. Other nonselling operations have to be in less-remote spots. If self-service is used, check-out counters must be placed in prime spots near entrances. Dressing rooms, display windows, and escalators also take up choice selling space. The profit-conscious merchant keeps such intrusions to a minimum, and locates nonselling activities away from productive selling areas whenever possible.

Larger stores need more space for nonselling departments than do smaller stores. In one sense, this suggests a lack of efficiency; but large stores do perform more customer services. They have more staff and more specialization. They need space for the comfort and convenience of store personnel. Vertical transportation—elevators and escalators— also require large amounts of space.

SPECIAL REQUIREMENTS

The extent to which a store or department will use salespeople must be reckoned in layout planning. We are familiar with departments serviced by clerks behind a counter, such as women's hosiery. Men's and women's clothing usually have salespeople circulating through the department. The extreme in salesperson service is *salon selling,* usually limited to high-priced dresses and furs. The customer is seated and selected items are brought out or are modeled. The check-outs of the supermarket or discount store represent the extreme of self-service. A modification of self-service that some stores have adopted is decentralized cashier counters, which may be scattered throughout the store.

The various degrees of clerk service can be depicted on the following scale:

Salon	Clerk service behind counters	Roving-clerk service	Decentralized cashier stations	Centralized checkouts

←——————————————————————————————————————→

More salesperson service   More self-service

    Besides checkout or cashier facilities, self-service requires good *self-service fixtures*. Since there is normally no clerk to assist the customer, merchandise needs to be visible and identifiable. Packages, displays, and signs have to assume the selling function.

    Retailing has seen a major trend toward self-service or diminished clerk service. Most supermarkets and discount stores are completely self-service, as are many variety stores and even drugstores (except for prescription counters). Some major department stores, even prestige ones, are converting certain departments to complete or modified self-service. Self-service has even moved into gasoline stations. In Baton Rouge, Louisiana, self-service pumps began emerging in 1968. From then on, self-service gasoline has had a major impact on gasoline retailing. Projections are that by 1980, 25 percent of gasoline sales will be self-service. Many people, it seems, are willing to serve themselves to save one or two cents a gallon.

RETAILING CONTROVERSY—*Self-service or Not?*

Advantages of Self-Service

Selling costs are lower. A major incentive for self-service has been ever-rising labor costs. Furthermore, for most of the 1960s, stores had difficulty getting enough good people to provide the services deemed desirable and to obtain maximum sales. The success of discount stores and their serious price competition made cost reductions mandatory for many retailers; salaries were the major ingredient in costs of operation.

Some customers prefer self-service. They dislike being pestered by sales people. They tend to buy more when they shop leisurely.

Limitations of Self-Service

Some customers dislike the impersonality of self-service.

Some products, such as cameras, sporting goods, appliances, and furniture require the advice and service of salespeople.

Self-service demands more housekeeping, careful signing and price ticketing, and organized sizes. In their efforts to keep selling costs low, some stores neglect this and lose sales.

Shoplifting is easier where there are few store employees circulating on the sales floor.

Self-service, because of its wide use by discount stores, tends to create a low-price image in the minds of customers, which may be undesirable for a prestige store.

Conclusions   Self-service is no panacea. As we have seen, there are both pros and cons regarding it. And where a majority of similar stores have gone to self-service, there may be opportunity for the retailer who dares to be different. For example, a community might welcome an old-time butcher shop if most grocery stores offer only self-service, prewrapped meat.

For Thought and Discussion   Are there stores in your area that are prospering with personal service, while other similar stores are self-service? How do you account for their success?

THE DEPARTMENT'S INTERNAL LAYOUT

As you enter retailing, the space allocation and item arrangement within your department will probably be an important concern. Only as your responsibilities increase, or if you venture into self-employment, will you face overall store layout decisions. Success in developing departmental displays and layouts paves the way for bigger responsibilities.

The principles are the same, whether one is planning departmental or store layout. They are:

1. The traffic-pulling items (or departments) should be located so that they expose customers to other goods.
2. Merchandise (and each department) should be given prominence according to its estimated profit potential.

Of course, the highest sales volume does not necessarily produce the greatest profit. Supermarkets recognize this by displaying their own branded goods, which carry the highest profit margins, at eye level. Nationally advertised items that may generate more sales but give less profit are displayed in a less advantageous position. Certain bulky products may require more space than normal in proportion to their contribution to profit, and other fast-selling items, such as cigarettes, may be adequately merchandised with less space. But these are exceptions to the rule. An example of an error in placing items would be giving tooth powder, which produces only a small sales volume, the same space allocation as toothpaste.

What to Feature?

Every store and department has certain prominent locations that are exposed to the most customer traffic. In stores with a grid layout, these *feature locations* may be the ends of certain counters that face the front so that customers view them as they come into the store.[6] For stores with other layouts, these feature locations may be near main traffic aisles or perhaps near entrances and escalators.

The wise retailer is constantly changing the merchandise displayed in these prime locations. Since this is choice space, it is wasted if the items featured do not produce a certain level of sales. For example, a certain display counter may normally average $100 a day. To permit an item to occupy such space and produce only $10 a day would be a waste. Goods occupying such valuable space should be constantly monitored and quickly replaced if sales are not up to expectations.

In the search for the best goods for prime locations, good judgment and alertness affect departmental sales and profits. These locations also provide a testing ground for new merchandise. By exposing new items to peak customer traffic, a merchant can get fast feedback on salability, and reorders can be placed quickly on hot items.

How to Arrange Merchandise

Goods can be arranged for sale in various ways. For example, you can group men's suits by:

Price
Size
Fabric (worsted or synthetic fibers)
Style (double-breasted, single-breasted, mod, knits)
Color
Weight (winter weight, year-round weight, tropicals)

[6] For examples, see "Are You Wasting the Sales Appeal of Gondola Ends?" *Hardware Retailing* (September 1975), 148; and "Attract Sales with Exciting Gondola Ends," Ibid. (July 1975), 63.

Usually men's suits are arranged by size. The full range of the assortment is thus shown in one place, making selection easier for the customer. Customer convenience and ease of shopping are good guiding rules in merchandise arrangement.

But stores can test different arrangements. They may emphasize a special promotion on summer-weight suits by separating them from regular stock, or they may group suits by color, thereby adding variety to the shopping environment. When experimenting, one must watch sales carefully. If sales decline, change arrangements quickly.

THE NEED TO MODERNIZE

In today's environment, products, buildings, and fixtures become obsolete and newer and better replacements must be found. Sometimes the improvements bring long-term reduction in expenses, for example, escalators and self-service elevators eliminate the need for elevator operators. Sometimes such improvements are necessary to enable a store to simply maintain its image and prevent erosion of business.

Few retailers escape the need to modernize or rejuvenate their stores from time to time, although the small retailer may be tempted to procrastinate as long as possible. (Exceptions to this need for remodeling are the superdiscount stores and warehouse and surplus stores, whose cut-price appeal is enhanced by austere surroundings.) Modernization is usually necessary to keep abreast or ahead of competition or to keep a shopping area from deteriorating.

Technological improvements may sometimes force a retailer to invest sizable funds in the installation of new fixtures and equipment. Escalators and air conditioning, for example, became widespread, despite their cost, because the retailer without them faced a loss of business.

■ Summary

The exterior and interior appearance of a store can help produce a distinctive and attractive image. It can also give a competitive edge by drawing in customers. Of course, a retailer's design decisions are constrained by costs and the funds available for investment. But ingenuity can often overcome financial limitations.

Store layout is important in maximizing the sales productivity of the various categories of goods and selling departments. Each of three basic traffic flow patterns has its uses; no one pattern is advisable under all circumstances. Displays and featured items, when carefully planned, can improve sales volume in any store. Some retailers should consider self-service, but only when this is compatible with the merchandise offered, the desired image of the store, and the wishes of the target customers. Most retailers should be alert to the need to modernize to keep up with improvements in fixtures and equipment and to maintain a healthy store appearance.

■ Key Terms

Bellwether departments	Grid
Boutique	Model-stock approach
Contemplative goods	Salon selling
Departmentalization	Self-service fixtures
Feature locations	Space-productivity ratio
Free form	Store layout

■ Discussion Questions

1. Are downtown store windows less important than they used to be as a sales tool? Why? Do you think this is true of small-town stores?
2. Name some ways layout can be used to increase impulse buying?
3. What is a bellwether department? Would you expect a store's restaurant to be one? A store's luggage department?
4. If your space-productivity ratio is consistently better than that of similar stores, what might you conclude?
5. If your department's space-productivity ratio is not as good as that for similar departments in other stores, how might you explain?
6. What is the rationale for giving more counter and display space to the best-selling items? Is it likely that sales of poorer-selling items might be enhanced by giving them more space, while goods in most demand will sell anyway?
7. A grid layout is common for supermarkets, variety stores, and discount stores. Do you think a boutique or free-form layout could be an effective innovation for such stores? Why or why not?
8. Do you think space should be allocated to products on the basis of sales volume or profits? Is there a better way of allocating space?

■ Project

Visit several competing stores, such as variety stores, discount stores, supermarkets, or perhaps the same department in several department stores, and note what merchandise they are featuring. Then evaluate how effective their choices are. Perhaps you can develop recommendations for alternative feature items.

■ Exercises in Creativity

1. What ideas can you come up with for boutiques? Be as innovative as possible; even wild ideas are useful at this point. You may want to consider unique combinations of merchandise, and perhaps special types of customers to appeal to. You may also want to create some catchy names for your boutique ideas.

   Exchange and evaluate your ideas with others in your class. See if you can modify them to improve their salability.

2. Can you develop any ideas about the presentation of merchandise in windows that might help a large downtown store overcome the handicap of inconvenient purchasing?

■ Retailing in Action

1. Assume the role of buyer for a men's furnishing department in a medium-size department store. You are trying to convince top management that your department is a bellwether department. If you can sell this idea, your department will be given more space and display emphasis, and your advertising budget will be increased. How are you going to convince management that men's furnishings is indeed a bellwether department? What evidence or arguments would you use to support your contention?

2. Analyze the following departments and make constructive recommendations if needed. If you suggest changes, be as persuasive as possible.

	Selling Space in Square Feet	Yearly Sales	Average Sales per Square Foot
Luggage	800	$24,000	$30
Cosmetics	600	36,000	60
Men's furnishings	900	153,000	170
Hosiery	600	120,000	200
Total first floor	8,000	640,000	80

Cases for Part Two

THE SILVER QUILL—Planning a New Restaurant Venture

Joe Russo was facing a crisis with his first business venture, The Silver Quill. He had opened this short-order restaurant on one of the main arteries leading into downtown about five years before. For a while, Joe's friendliness and good food at reasonable prices attracted a sizable trade from downtown workers. Joe had even expanded his facilities several years after opening.

However, shortly after this expansion, sales began to decline. Joe attributed the decline to a number of fast-food restaurants, such as McDonald's, that had opened nearby. The new competitors had nowhere near the variety of food that Joe did. Still, their ultraquick service and low prices were cutting deeply into Joe's luncheon business, which had been the mainstay of his operation.

Joe recognized that his restaurant was at a critical point, and he was seeking new ways to revitalize the business. A move to another location seemed desirable, but there are the problems of building up a clientele all over again and the considerable new investment in facilities. However, Joe could think of no way to rejuvenate the faltering business in its present location. The alternative to moving was to accept continued decline and, eventually, dissolution of the business.

Then came an opportunity to relocate in a large, modern apartment complex being built near the center of the business district. Two buildings would contain some 1,100 luxury apartments renting at from $200 to $600 per month. They would appeal to young, single business and professional people, married couples without children, and well-to-do retirees. The new restaurant could be located in a shopping mall between the two 20-story buildings. Joe planned to continue using the name The Silver Quill.

Based on the number of residents, plus the noon business that he hoped to re-establish, Joe estimated that he should realize $300,000 in sales annually. He would have to sign a ten-year lease at a base rent of $900 a month for the first two years, and $1,000 a month after the first two years. Other expenses—for maintainence, utilities, and joint advertising of the mall—were expected to add $150 a month.

The proposed restaurant would require a considerable investment. Estimated costs for decorating, fixtures, and equipment came to $240,000. This seemed to be no problem, although interest charges would run $28,000 a year. The investment would depreciate at 10 percent per year. Joe calculated that he should be able to maintain a 60 percent margin on sales (that is, the cost of the food would be about 40 percent of what he sold it for). Variable expenses for the restaurant and kitchen should amount to 35 percent, which would mean that 25 percent of sales should be available for overhead and any profit.

One of the things that troubled Joe was whether he should change the motif and menu of the new Silver Quill from what it had been before. This part of downtown had none of the fast-food restaurants that had ruined him before; rather the competition around the new location was primarily fancy, expensive restaurants. He expected his major clientele would be the people living in the apartment complex. Would they be interested more in a short-order restaurant or in something fancier?

Questions

1. Compute a break-even point in dollar sales.
2. Based on Joe's estimate of sales, should he open the new restaurant?
3. Are there other factors that bear on this decision?
4. What retailing strategy would you have recommended to Joe at the time?
5. What do you think of his decision to use the same name for the proposed new restaurant?

SOUTHGATE SHOPPING CENTER—The Threat of New Competition[1]

Dale Schlesinger, manager of Southgate Shopping Center in southeast-suburban Cleveland, pondered the ominous presence of a major new competitor that had opened a year ago a bare eight-tenths of a mile away. The new competitor was the gigantic Randall Park Mall, billed as the largest shopping mall in the world. At the time, Randall had five major department stores for traffic generators (with a sixth planned to open later), and almost two hundred other stores—altogether some 2.2 million square feet, all under one roof. Sales were estimated "conservatively" at $200 million for the first year. In typical mall fashion, Randall is surrounded on all sides by ample parking, and because it is an enclosed mall, it sports an array of amenities, from fountains and benches to a miniature amphitheater for performances and entertainment of all kinds.

Southgate appeared to be vulnerable to Randall in several respects. First, it was old, almost twenty-five years old. Second, its growth had been relatively

[1] For two more detailed cases of Southgate's confrontation with the major new shopping center, see Robert F. Hartley and Donald W. Scotton "Southgate" and "Southgate B," cases 9-577-649 and 9-579-625, Intercollegiate Case Clearing House, Harvard University Graduate School of Business Administration.

haphazard. When it first opened in 1954, there were 40 stores. Over the ensuing decades, several expansions had brought it to some 140 stores and sales of $150 million a year. Third, Southgate is not enclosed for the all-weather comfort that marks most new shopping centers constructed in the last decade in northern locales. Furthermore, Southgate is not a mall. Rather, it is a series of strip centers: merely rows of stores sprawling over 200 acres in a rough U-shape. At the time of the Randall Park Mall construction, Southgate had three department stores: a small Penney store of 65,000 square feet, and a May Company and a Sears store, each having approximately 200,000 square feet. Such big stores are vital to the success of a shopping center, since they are generators. They often pull people from some distance, and they contribute greatly to the traffic flow in a center.

Unfortunately, Dale reflected, since Randall had opened, he had lost two of his generators. Penney's was not a serious loss since the store had sales of only $2 million. But Sears was a devastating loss. It took $35 million worth of business with it when it moved to Randall and, almost as bad, left a 200,000-square-foot store right in the center of Southgate visibly empty. Only the May Company stayed in Southgate, and there was continued fear that they also would leave. May was one of the five department stores that opened in Randall, which placed them in the unusual situation of having two 200,000-square-foot stores within a mile of each other.

The effect on Southgate's sales was dramatic. Volume slipped more than 25 percent, and a 6 to 10 percent inflation rate made the loss in per-unit sales considerably larger. Furthermore, Schlesinger knew that tenant morale was low. When one of the local TV stations talked to eight Southgate merchants, only one was positive about the future at Southgate.

Some observers suggested that the best course of action for Southgate would be to simply close down, tear down the existing buildings, and sell the entire site for apartment-house construction. But Schlesinger pointed out:

We have much lower rents—$2 to $8 versus $8 to $18 at Randall. This permits lower prices, or at least a much lower breakeven point for our tenants vis-a-vis those located at Randall.

We offer more ease and convenience of shopping for our customers—they can park right in front of the store—than is possible in a huge shopping center.

We have the steady draw of three supermarkets versus none at Randall.

Customer loyalty to the stores at Southgate built up over two decades of doing business in the same location has to be a decided plus.

We are in an interceptor location, positioned between the major source of customers for Southgate—those in the southern adjacent suburbs—and Randall.

Last, but not least, there is the possibility of "spillover" effect coming from customers satiated with the sheer size and complexity of shopping at Randall.

Still, Schlesinger had to admit that the vacant Sears store was a continuing eyesore. To date he had not been able to find a new tenant for so much space.

Questions

1. What prognosis can you give for Southgate at the above time?

2. What strategies would you recommend that Schlesinger and the owners of Southgate pursue?

3. What kind of tenant do you think Southgate should seek for the vacant Sears store? How successful do you think it might be in attracting such a tenant?

4. What type of store or shop do you think might find Southgate attractive? Why?

3

People Management

8 Organization and Structure of the Firm

Organization is necessary if the goals of any institution or group are to be accomplished. But some firms are better organized than others and, thus, better geared to accomplish their objectives.

Before we look at typical organizations of various types of retailers, let's quickly look at the essential ingredients in organization.

THE ESSENTIALS OF ORGANIZING

A retail store must identify activities that are similar and group them apart from unrelated activities. Then *responsibility* can be assigned to certain individuals. For example, merchandise buying should be separated from store maintenance, and in all but the smallest stores different individuals will be responsible for each. Various *lines of authority* should be designated so that every employee knows the superior-subordinate relationships: who is responsible to whom, what each job is, and who supervises whom. Finally, some *control* over the activities is necessary. Control means seeing that operating results coincide as closely as possible with what is expected and taking corrective action when they do not.[1]

In retail firms, activities can be organized according to the following categories:

1. Functions, such as buying, selling, advertising, and store operation
2. Product categories, such as women's wear, men's furnishings, and housewares
3. Geographic areas, such as northeast, midwest, south, or downtown and branch stores

Occasionally, a major retail firm may have an additional breakdown by certain customer types. These might be large-contract customers, motel and hotel operators, or office designers. Most retail firms find it necessary to have activities organized in a combination of ways. Figure 8.1 shows some ways of organizing retail activities.

Organizations need to be flexible and responsive to changing conditions. The desire to handle incoming stock fast to increase merchandise turnover and profitability may lead a store to reorganize stockrooms and receiving operations. As a retailer expands with branch stores, some changes in the traditional organizational structure are usually necessary.

Formal written organization charts are used by many large firms to define responsibility and lines of authority. While a new employee may find these organization charts useful in getting oriented, they fail to show informal relationships, which affect the smooth functioning of any organization.

Two firms seldom have exactly the same organizational pattern. The size of a firm, the type of operation, any special abilities or preferences of executives, and different merchandising emphases lead to somewhat

---

[1] For a more comprehensive treatment of business organization and management you may wish to refer to William H. Mewman, Charles E. Summer, and E. Kirby Warren, *The Principles of Management,* 2nd ed. (Englewood Cliffs, N.J.: Prentice-Hall, 1967); or Dalton E. McFarland, *Management Principles and Practices,* 4th ed. (New York: Macmillan, 1974).

FIGURE 8.1 WAYS TO ORGANIZE ACTIVITIES

1. By function:

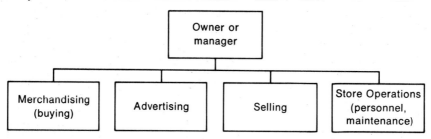

2. By products (combination functions and products):

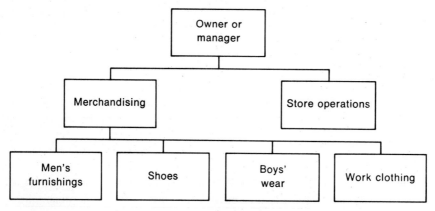

3. By geographic area (combination of functions and geography)

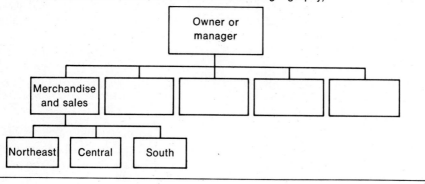

different approaches. But each of the following types of organization has certain characteristics:

Small stores
Department stores
Department stores with branches
Chain stores

SMALL-STORE ORGANIZATION

In the smallest store, the proprietor (perhaps with family members as part-time helpers) comprises the organization. All activities necessarily fall on the proprietor. As the store grows, one person can no longer handle all the activities. New employees are hired and assigned certain duties: selling, arranging stock, price-marking new merchandise, and bookkeeping.

As the firm becomes still larger, the owner will need to hire one or more managers to assist in planning and supervising. Some form of dual responsibility will result. Just as the chief executive of a country is ultimately responsible for everything that subordinates do, so the executive of a firm is responsible for the actions of the staff people.

As a small firm grows, *specialization* becomes possible. Instead of handling many activities, each person will be responsible for less but will develop expertise in certain areas.

Departmentalization

As a firm becomes larger, *departmentalization* is a natural organizational adjustment. The merchandise is divided into departments, which can be given separate attention and assigned to separate managers. A small men's store, as it grows in sales volume and number of employees, may find it desirable to departmentalize into men's clothing (suits, slacks, sport coats, topcoats), men's furnishings (shirts, underwear, hosiery, accessories), and men's shoes. The buying job for the whole store probably is too much for one person, and buying for the specific departments may be delegated. Departmentalization reaches its greatest extent in the huge department stores, such as Macy's in New York, Rich's in Atlanta, and J. L. Hudson in Detroit, which have two hundred and more selling departments each.

ADVANTAGES OF DEPARTMENTALIZATION   Departmentalization offers two major advantages: specialization and control. By having responsibility for one specific department, an employee can become a specialist. A better job of merchandising should result.

Control is needed if operations are to adhere as closely as possible to plans. It is easier to control the operations of a store if records and performance can be measured by functional or merchandise groupings. A department can be made a profit-center, with all applicable expenses and sales allocated to it. In this way, the performance of each department and its contribution to the overall performance of the store can be directly measured.

Performance can be compared with other departments and even with industry figures. Promotions and raises may depend on the relative contribution to profit. More than this, it is desirable to know which categories of merchandise are doing best and which are weak and should receive more attention.

HOW TO SET UP SELLING DEPARTMENTS   Some groupings of merchandise are customary and are expected by customers, such as the division of women's dresses and women's coats. But nontraditional classifications are being tested by some retailers with varying degrees of success. Table 8.1 shows various ways that departments might be set up.

A common problem when departmentalizing is deciding how far to go. A firm can divide too finely and develop employees so narrowly specialized that flexibility suffers. A retailer must ask questions before setting up a separate department: Is the volume becoming so large that more precise information and servicing are needed? Will customer needs be better served than under the present setup?

STAFF AND SUPPORTING DEPARTMENTS   As stores become larger, a number of *staff and supporting departments* become necessary. Examples are personnel, credit, sales promotion, unit control, comparison shopping, delivery, security, and so on. Most of these enable the selling departments to concentrate on their primary function. Some large retailers have merchandise-testing departments, which foster better buying and lead to more satisfied customers. Public relations and consumer relations are new departments in some stores. And certainly without a separate department to handle incoming freight, check it, mark it, and send it to the selling departments, a store could hardly function smoothly.

TABLE 8.1   BASES FOR DEPARTMENTALIZATION

Basis	Examples	Comments
Related merchandise	Piece goods, hosiery, lamps, shoes, appliances, living room furniture, meat	Logical, and the most common method
Type of equipment	In the supermarket, foods that require refrigeration are usually grouped together	Useful when highly specialized storage or display equipment must be used
Customer convenience	Gift department (items in this one department might range from small electrical appliances to pottery or tableware), ski shop, bath shop, cruise shop, bridal department	While merchandise is unrelated, the customer's reasons for purchasing are catered to
Customer groups	Budget shop, infants' clothing, junior miss, boys', and men's shops	Common method, based on customers' age, sex, and income
Innovative ideas	Unisex shops, his and hers, mod boutiques	Some of these can be classified under other headings, but they all represent efforts aimed at the nontraditional

Adjusting Organization to Increasing Size

As small firms become successful and grow substantially in size they must make the organizational adaptations necessary. No longer can one person, or even a few people, keep close track of all that is going on. No longer can all decisions be made by one person. Since there has to be delegation of authority and responsibility to others, capable people must be found who can take over important executive positions. And controls are needed to monitor performance and take corrective action before problems become serious. More than one firm has found that rapid growth outstripped its capability to adjust.

RETAILING ERRORS—*Organizational Failure with Rapid Growth: Korvette*

Eugene Ferkauf, the "Retailing Giant" we first encountered in Chapter 2, guided his Korvette into the largest discount chain. In the days of rapid growth, a group of thirty-eight men, almost all Brooklyn high school pals of Ferkauf, ran the chain. Called the open-shirt crowd, Ferkauf's management operated from a dingy old building on 46th Street in Manhattan, where Ferkauf presided at a beat-up desk in a corner of the board room.

As the chain grew to sales of $800 million, internal problems began to emerge. Ferkauf could not run forty stores through personal observation. He had failed to delegate responsibility and develop a strong management team; the organizational structure itself was ill-defined and morale fell; the firm lacked sophisticated controls. Ferkauf was also having a hard time lining up enough good management to run his stores outside New York City, which, being further away from headquarters, were subject to even less control.

Many stores were incurring heavy losses, particularly in the food and furniture departments, and the chain itself fell into the red. In 1966 Korvette was merged with Spartan Industries and Ferkauf was eased out of active management.

Sources: For more detail, see Lawrence A. Mayer, "How Confusion Caught Up with Korvette," *Fortune,* February 1966, pp. 153 ff.; "Korvettes Tries for a Little Chic," *Business Week,* May 12, 1973, pp. 124–125; Hartley, "Korvette—Indigestion from Growth," in *Marketing Mistakes* (Columbus, Ohio: Grid, 1976), pp. 31–44.

For Thought and Discussion When personal supervision by Ferkauf was no longer possible because of the steady expansion of stores, what might have been done to assure adequate supervision of stores?

DEPARTMENT STORE ORGANIZATION

Most department stores—until they expand into multiunit firms—are organized according to certain traditional functions. A four-functional structure was recommended by a management consultant some five decades ago. It is still the basis for department-store organization although, as would be expected, there are individual modifications. *The Mazur plan* proposed four functions or divisions:

Control, under the controller
Merchandising, under a merchandise manager
Publicity, under a publicity or promotion manager
Operations, under a store or operations manager[2]

Figure 8.2 shows a modern department store organized according to the Mazur functions.

Modifications of the Mazur Plan

The major modifications of the traditional organizational plan for department stores have been in two directions: (1) the personnel division is often given added emphasis by making it equal with the other four areas; (2) the publicity or promotion function is placed under the control of the merchandising function, which thereby assumes the greatest importance in the total organization.

There is a fundamental reason for the importance of merchandising in most retail organizations: it is the *sales generating* aspect of the business. All other functional areas merely help it perform this vital function. Without a successful merchandising operation, the firm will wither and die.

The Organization of the Merchandising Function

Many people entering retailing will be employed in the merchandising area. This part of retailing also typically provides the greatest career opportunities. As we have noted before, each merchandising department is a profit center, and above-average efforts by assistant buyers, buyers, and divisional merchandise managers can be quickly recognized. Figure 8.3 shows a typical organization plan of the merchandising function.

[2] Paul Mazur, *Principles of Organization Applied to Modern Retailing* (New York: Harper & Row, 1927).

FIGURE 8.2 FOUR-FUNCTIONAL DEPARTMENT-STORE ORGANIZATION

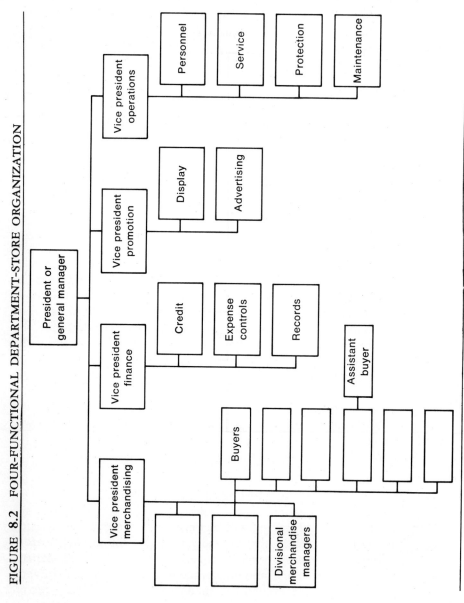

Source: Adapted from Paul Mazur, *Principles of Organization Applied to Modern Retailing*, New York: Harper & Row, 1927, Chapter 2.

FIGURE 8.3 THE ORGANIZATION OF THE MERCHANDISING FUNCTION

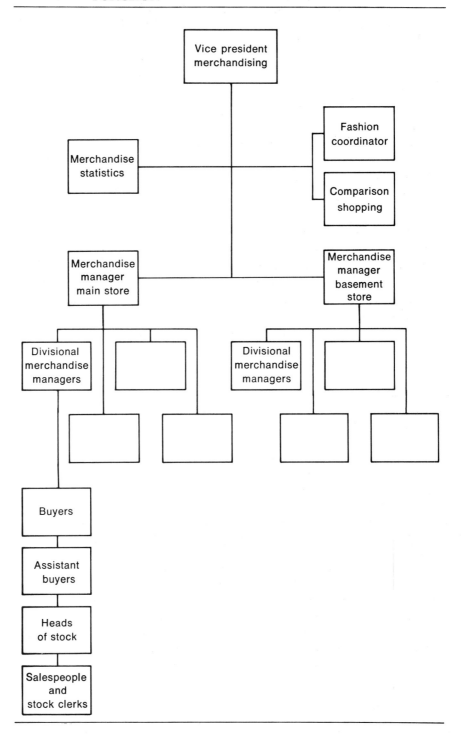

TABLE 8.2　THE MAJOR RESPONSIBILITIES OF DEPARTMENT
STORE DIVISIONS

Division	Responsibilities
Merchandising	Buying Selling Controlling stock
Publicity or Sales Promotion	Advertising Display Sales promotion events Public relations
Personnel	Employee selection Training Employee services Labor relations Executive development
Operating or Store Management	Store building and maintenance Store protection Operating activities—receiving, 　warehousing, shipping, delivery Workrooms, such as restaurants, 　bakeries, drapery workrooms, and 　laundries
Control	Accounting Expense planning and control Credit

Responsibilities of Major Store Divisions

Table 8.2 shows the common duties and responsibilities assigned to the
major divisions of a department store. There is disagreement today as
to whether the merchandising division should be responsible for *both*
buying and selling, and this will be discussed later in this chapter.

In this table the personnel function is shown as a separate division.
This reflects the increasing complexity of personnel activities and
problems. While some department stores, especially smaller ones, have
subordinated the publicity and promotion function under merchandising, the sheer scope of work in this area usually makes separation

FIGURE **8.**4 DEPENDENT-STORE ORGANIZATION OF A DEPARTMENT
STORE WITH BRANCHES

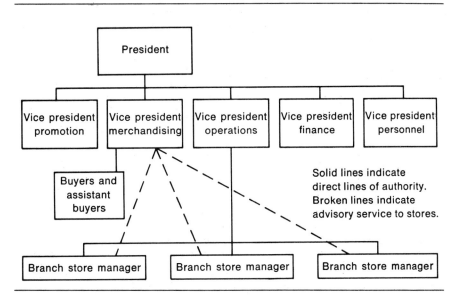

Note: This is simply a model, and may be modified. For example, Emporium-Capwell of Carter
Hawley Hale has a vice president of branch-store operations reporting to a general manager. All
branch managers then report to this vice president.

better. However, close cooperation and coordination should be maintained with the merchandising division.

MULTIUNIT DEPARTMENT STORE ORGANIZATION

Few department stores have been able to resist expanding to the
suburbs with additional units or branches. With the general decline of
downtown shopping areas in many cities, it can be fatal not to expand.
But branches pose some organizational problems, especially in regard
to the important merchandising function.

Figure 8.4 shows a typical organization chart for a department store
with several branches. However, as with most organization charts, it
does not give complete information about the coordination and communications relationships. For example, although the merchandising

function shows up on this chart as having only an advisory role with the branches, only a foolhardy store manager would contest the recommendations of a powerful buyer. Most department stores have found the best way to merchandise the branches is to have the parent-store buyers buy for the branch stores as well. Otherwise, these branches need their own full-time buyers, and this results in unnecessary expense and a lack of coordination among the stores.

At one time, buyers in most department stores acted almost as though they had their own stores. They were responsible for buying and pricing goods, and also for displaying, advertising, and selling them. Their success was measured by how well they translated all these activities into profits. The buyer would normally spend some time on the selling floor, supervising sales efforts, making display and merchandise-placement suggestions, and talking with customers to obtain their reactions. As branch stores were opened, buying occupied more time. The buyer then might delegate some responsibility to an assistant buyer. But eventually, some policy regarding the buying and selling activities had to be designed.

RETAIL CONTROVERSY—*Should Buying and Selling Be Separated?*

Whether to separate buying and selling responsibilities has become a major controversy, especially as department stores have expanded with more and more branches. Demands on parent-store buyers have increased as they have had to buy for branch stores also.

Arguments for Separation At first glance, there appear to be overwhelming reasons for separating the buying and selling activities:

1. These are really different jobs, and require different personalities and abilities.

2. A buyer must give less attention to the selling function, as stores increase buying demands.

3. Modern merchandise-control systems provide good feedback for buying, even when the buyer is no longer directly involved with selling.

4. Some merchandise is best grouped for selling purposes in ways that are not ideal for buying purposes. For example, most stores have ski shops today. Usually, these are serviced by at least two buyers: one for apparel

(perhaps even a buyer for women's and another for men's apparel), and a different one for the ski equipment itself.

Arguments against Separation   There are strong arguments on the other side. A major one is that the separation undermines the profit-center concept and dilutes responsibility for department profits. Who should be blamed for a poor sales and profit performance? The sales manager can find fault with the merchandise, while the buyer will cite halfhearted sales efforts. Another argument against separation maintains that the buyer should be in close contact with customers to assess their wants and buy judiciously. Furthermore, the person who buys the merchandise is best able to impart information about the merchandise to the sales force and generate maximum enthusiasm in their selling efforts. With tradition on the side of combining the buying and selling functions, you can see how difficult the decision to separate can be.

For Thought and Discussion   As an ambitious young assistant buyer, would you prefer to have buying and selling separated? Why or why not?

Increasingly today, buying and selling are being separated. But as a result, changes are being made in branch organizations.

Three patterns are used to organize branch stores relative to the parent store:

1. Dependent branches (also called satellite branches or brood hen– and chick organizations)
2. Independent branches (also called separate store plans)
3. Equal stores

Most department stores initially expanded with *dependent branches.* The parent store (usually downtown) operated the branch, the buyers allocated merchandise to it, the publicity director handled advertising for it, and the operations manager (or store superintendent) directly supervised it. This is the organization shown in Figure 8.4.

But as firms grew, deficiencies in the dependent-store arrangement often became overwhelming. Main-store buyers and operational executives were unable to give sufficient attention to all units as the number and size of branches increased. One solution was to treat all stores as *independent branches,* separate entities, with their own management and buying staffs. This provided flexibility and the best possi-

FIGURE 8.5 THE EQUAL STORES CONCEPT OF BRANCH-STORE
ORGANIZATION

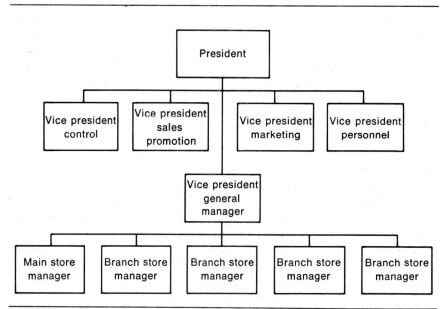

ble adjustment of merchandise and operating policies to local conditions. But it also required great duplication of effort. Furthermore, with each store buying independently, the big advantage of large-scale purchasing was lost, and quantity discounts and buying power were sacrificed.

These drawbacks were too much for most retailers. Accordingly, a further organizational adjustment was made. Major management functions, including buying, were centralized at a single headquarters, in the manner of chain stores. This was the *equal-stores* concept, and it made the downtown store equal (not superior) to the branch stores, as Figure 8.5 shows. Usually, the separation of selling responsibilities from buying accompanied this organizational change.

CHAIN-STORE ORGANIZATION

A chain is a group of stores with generally similar merchandise and operating techniques that is centrally owned and controlled. Chains can be very large, with hundreds and even thousands of stores under a single organization.

The organizational structures that were developed to permit such growth are the epitomes of flexibility. But also they permit close control of widespread operations. There are wide differences in chains, not only in size and number of stores, but also in modes of operation. There are general-merchandise chains, such as Penney and Sears, variety chains, and drug, food, discount, and specialty chains of every type. One would expect to find major differences among such diverse operations, but there are a number of elements common to all chains.

Common Characteristics

As more authority is centralized in the home office, the store manager becomes less important and is paid less. At one extreme—and this is most prevalent among discount-store chains, such as Zayre—the store manager "carries the keys" but actually makes few decisions concerning the store's operating and merchandising policies. On the other hand, chains like Sears and Penney traditionally have decentralized some of the buying and sales-promotion activities. The managers of these stores have considerable choice in selecting and emphasizing merchandise, although the range of offerings has initially been screened by the central buying office. Major department-store ownership groups, such as Allied Stores, Federated Stores, and Carter Hawley Hale Stores, have the greatest amount of decentralization. They give each store unit a large amount of independence and each store usually has its own buying and sales-promotion staff. Yet, as the following example shows, this does not diminish the pressure for better performance.

SUCCESSFUL RETAILING STRATEGY—Motivating Organizational Units Through Intrafirm Competition: Carter Hawley Hale Stores

Any chain can stimulate competition among its stores by publicizing operating results and the comparative standings of the various units, and pushing for better relative performance. The more operating independence the management of any particular store has, the more incentive there will be to outperform other stores of the chain.

This incentive is particularly evident with Carter Hawley Hale Stores, a rapidly expanding department-store ownership group that acquired Neiman-Marcus and Bergdorf-Goodman. Stanley Marcus, president of Neiman-Marcus, notes: "When you are an independent and buy yourself, it's easy to be satisfied with average performance. But when you are part of a diversified retailing operation and are confronted by the performance of your peers, your feeling becomes one of 'Golly, I can do as well as they,' and you do, too. Let's face it, you have to."

Sources: For more detail, see "Broadway-Hale's Elegant Growth Plan," *BusinessWeek,* April 15, 1972, p. 92; "Carter Hawley Hale, Carriage Trade Merchants," *BusinessWeek,* October 4, 1976, p. 90; Eleanor Carruth, "Carter Hawley Hale Acquires a Touch of Class," *Fortune,* December 1976, p. 176.

For Thought and Discussion How would you rate the effect of competition among the individual stores of Zayre, Safeway, Sears, and Carter Hawley Hale? Could such competition be destructive?

Chain organizations usually find it necessary to have more divisions than department stores. A real-estate division becomes important in purchasing new sites, building new stores, and disposing of old stores. A traffic and warehousing division may be needed to improve the merchandise handling. A representative chain organization is shown in Figure 8.6.

The far-flung units of most chains necessitate the development of comprehensive reports so that headquarters can be kept informed of operations and can maintain effective control. Field supervision is maintained by executives, each of whom is responsible for the performance of a group of stores. Stores may be divided into districts, regions, or zones.

Management Resources Needed

The rapid expansion of a chain is sometimes limited more by insufficient management resources than by a lack of funds for opening new stores. The importance of the personnel function in most chain organizations reflects this. A chain adding fifty or more stores a year puts heavy demands on a personnel department for the necessary store managers, assistant managers, and other personnel. Usually, these

FIGURE **8.6** GENERAL ORGANIZATION OF LARGE CHAINS

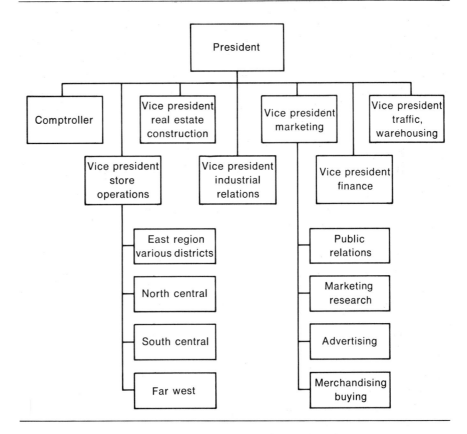

Note: Again, this is simply a model and is subject to many modifications. For example, there may well be additional vice presidents, such as a vice president of public relations, and a vice president of personnel. In very large chains, the executives in charge of various regions or geographical divisions may be vice presidents who report to a senior vice president.

executives receive their training within other stores of the chain from experienced store managers, with guidance furnished by the corporate personnel department. However, a lack of incentive for training subordinate managers may thwart expansion. We noted earlier in this chapter that a dearth of well-trained store-management people contributed to the problems of Korvette. On the other hand, in its early years the J. C. Penney Company grew many times as rapidly as Korvette and never exhausted its pool of well-trained, highly motivated managers.

SUCCESSFUL RETAILING STRATEGY—*Stimulating Management Development During a Time of Tremendous Growth: J. C. Penney Company*

Between 1912 and 1926—fourteen years—the J. C. Penney Company expanded from 34 stores to 747; in seven more years it grew to 1,466 stores, a growth rate bound to place the severest strains on management-development resources. But in these early years of the Penney Company each manager had an interest in finding the best possible people and giving them exceptional training.

Each store manager was given the chance to finance a one-third interest in a new store—in other words, to become a partner of the company—provided he had trained a new manager capable of managing the new link in the chain. For every person sent out as a well-trained store manager, the sponsoring manager was entitled to one third of the profits of the "student's" store. This made millionaires of many store managers in the early days of the Penney Company; it also served as a tremendous spur to competent training.

Decades ago this incentive was abandoned by the maturing Penney Company, but it had served its purpose of providing well-trained managers in the great numbers needed.

Sources: For more detail, see Norman Beasley, *Main Street Merchant* (New York: McGraw-Hill, 1948); and Hartley, "J. C. Penney Company—Unchanging Policies," in *Marketing Mistakes* (Columbus, Ohio: Grid Publishing, 1976), pp. 19–30.

For Thought and Discussion

1. What are some other, perhaps less drastic, incentives for store managers to develop trainees?
2. Compare and contrast the difficulties of Korvette with the organizational adaptation of the J. C. Penney Company.

Ownership Groups

Chains have more or less uniform stores; ownership groups do not. Many of the leading department stores that were once independent have merged into ownership groups such as Allied Stores Corporation, Carter Hawley Hale Stores, Federated Department Stores, Inc., and Associated Dry Goods Corporation. For the most part, the department stores retain their original names and have their own merchandising and operating policies. While certain objectives are established by corporate headquarters, the individual stores are permitted to operate quite independently, far more so than are the individual outlets of a chain organization.

CENTRALIZATION VERSUS DECENTRALIZATION

Whether to centralize most authority in headquarters or to delegate it to the individual stores is a common problem today. And it is not limited to big retailers with many units and branches. The small independent merchant often wants to add one or several stores, perhaps as new shopping centers tap other suburban areas, and wonders how much authority to delegate to the individual stores.

There is no agreement as to what is best. Department-store ownership groups seem to be moving in the direction of more centralization. But some major chains are decentralizing and upgrading the jobs of store managers and divisional executives.

Data-processing systems enable headquarters to receive information quickly. This provides an incentive for increasing centralization. However, many organizations have found that decentralization makes for a better caliber of management personnel. The manager or trainee who has freedom of action and the opportunity to use initiative tends to be more motivated, enthusiastic, and innovative; and the result is a more productive store. This may be a powerful argument for delegating as much authority as possible to the lower levels of the organization.

■ Summary

In this chapter, we have taken an overall look at retailing organizations, from small stores to department stores to chains. We have also considered some of the issues related to organization, such as whether buying and selling should be separated and the question of centralization versus decentralization. In the next several chapters, we will discuss "people problems" and supervisory relationships. A handsome organization chart, with all duties and relationships clearly defined, does not necessarily solve the personnel problems of the organization. Since retailing is heavily dependent on people (in contrast to much of manufacturing, where automated machinery dispenses with many workers), personnel departments and supervisors must meet many challenges.

■ **Key terms**

Control	Lines of authority
Departmentalization	The Mazur plan
Dependent branches	Responsibility
Equal stores	Specialization
Independent branches	Staff and supporting departments

■ **Discussion questions**

1. Why does one firm seldom have exactly the same organizational structure as another firm? Does this mean that one kind of structure is more effective than another?

2. What are the disadvantages of novel ways of departmentalizing selling departments?

3. Why do you think that organizational problems typically become the curse of rapid growth? That is, why does growth seem to come faster than organizational adjustment? Are there any remedies to this common situation?

4. What makes the merchandising function the most important in a retail firm? What do you think are the consequences of this?

5. Is it desirable for the buyer to spend time on the selling floor talking with customers and salespeople? Why or why not?

6. What disadvantages do you see in centralized buying?

7. What drawbacks do you see in having a weak store manager who is primarily limited to "carrying the keys," rather than one with authoritative, decentralized responsibility? Consider this from both the viewpoint of the firm and that of the store manager.

8. What are the organizational advantages in having a number of relatively autonomous stores in a given corporation? What disadvantages can you think of?

■ **Project**

Bring to class an organization chart of the firm for which you work; or devise a simple functional organization chart for a small firm or your own proposed business. What strengths and weaknesses do you see in the organization?

■ Exercise in Creativity

Assume that you are the owner of a small, expansion-minded retail dry-goods store. You are in a small town of about 5,000 people and see an opportunity to expand to other small towns, where competition from major chains is not particularly strong. How would you attract capable executives to your organization? What inducements would you offer? How would you screen applicants?

■ Retailing in Action

Which would you prefer to manage initially: a Zayre store, a Penney store, a department of a department store, or a branch outlet of a department-store ownership corporation? While you will want to consider the probable differences in salary, you should also look at the following factors: freedom of action, the years of experience needed, prestige, and advancement opportunities. Evaluate these and any other factors that seem important to you. Develop the pros and cons of each position from your own viewpoint and aspirations.

You may want to pursue this further, and talk to managers of these various types of operations.

9 Retail Personnel Management: Its Importance and Its Problems

The trend toward self-service and the elimination of salesclerks has been under way for several decades. Not only supermarkets and discount stores, but also hardware, drug, variety, and even some departments of department stores have turned to self-service. As we saw in Chapter 7, self-service gasoline stations are becoming a major method of retailing petroleum. In light of such a pronounced trend, one may question the importance of personnel management in retailing. Yet in

1960, 8,388,000 persons were engaged in retailing; by 1977 this figure had risen to 13,902,000.[1]

As retail firms expand, they require more employees of all kinds. We noted in the last chapter that some department stores are upgrading the personnel function to the same level in the organization as merchandising, operations, control, and publicity. The personnel function is more important than ever.

INCREASED EMPHASIS ON PERSONNEL MANAGEMENT

To a large extent, the increased attention given to personnel and labor relations reflects changes in our social and business environment. It is by no means unique to retailing. The growth of labor unions is one tangible indication of these changes. So is the growth of federal and state legislation dealing with wages and hours, social security, unemployment insurance, mandatory collective bargaining, and job discrimination. During the 1950s and 1960s labor was scarce, so many firms had to increase their efforts to find and keep qualified people.

Retailing has some unique characteristics that make personnel relations more important than in many nonretail industries.

LABOR INTENSITY *Labor intensity* occurs when a business does not lend itself to mechanization and the substitution of machines for employees. Retailing is one of the most labor-intensive types of business. Consequently, salaries are the largest single item of expense in a retail store. This is true even in self-service stores, since people are needed to receive, mark, and handle the merchandise, to replenish counters and shelves, to work at the checkout counters, to maintain stock records, and to perform many other tasks. And where clerk service is provided, the sales transaction takes about as much time now as it did a thousand years ago.

THE IMPORTANCE OF CUSTOMER GOOD WILL We live in an age of impersonality. The tendency during prosperous times has been to take the customer for granted. The phenomenon of consumerism reflects customer disillusionment with this treatment. A most important ingredient of *customer good will* is the customer's relations with the employees

---

[1] U.S. Department of Labor, Bureau of Labor Statistics, *Employment and Earnings,* February 1978, p. 57.

of a firm. This is not the domain of the salesclerk only; credit interviewers, delivery people, and switchboard operators contribute. If firms are to maintain good customer relations—if they are to have repeat business—the personal contacts between customers and employees are all-important. It is the responsibility of personnel management to motivate employees toward courtesy, friendliness, and interest in the needs of customers.

HIGH PERSONNEL TURNOVER AND DIFFICULTY IN ATTRACTING GOOD PEOPLE   *Personnel turnover* refers to the number of employees leaving a store's employment during the course of a year. This is usually designated as a percentage of the average work force. For example, a 25-percent turnover rate means that one out of four workers left in a year and had to be replaced with new people.

   For several decades, retailers have been plagued with high personnel turnover, 50 percent and higher for some stores. This adds greatly to the costs of hiring and training. It results in lowered productivity, reduced employee loyalty and morale, and consequently, greater customer dissatisfaction. High turnover and the inability to attract good and well-motivated people have led some retailers, in desperation, to self-service. Such retailers thought it better to have no salespeople or store employees in contact with customers, than to have rude, unknowledgeable, and uncaring clerks alienate customers. The need to recruit and train better employees is of vital concern to most retailers.

LARGE NUMBER OF PART-TIME EMPLOYEES   Retail business has many peaks and valleys of customer traffic and sales. The whole success of the year rests on the November and December sales volume. Various promotional events throughout the year also strain efforts to cope with peak customer traffic. But other times of the year and certain days of the week produce less traffic than average. Today, retail firms are finding it necessary to remain open for more hours than ever before. The long hours and erratic customer traffic force a retailer to use many part-time people. This may work well if part-time people are properly selected and trained; but part-time hiring places added strain on the personnel department, especially when seasonal employment is nearing a peak and marginal and inexperienced workers must be hired. Furthermore, close supervision is required if these employees are to be effective in their jobs.

NEED FOR A LARGE PROPORTION OF EXECUTIVES   Department stores require about one executive for every ten employees, and the requirements of other types of retailers are similar. Yet, high turnover also faces the management level. Personnel departments, as a consequence, are burdened in two ways: they must recruit eligibles for junior- and higher-level executive positions, and they must develop training programs and incentives to move employees to higher positions.

DIVERSITY OF RETAIL JOB REQUIREMENTS   As we noted in the first chapter, few businesses have the diversity of employment that retailing has. For example, selling expensive furniture or clothing is vastly different from selling candy and notions. But nonselling jobs present the widest diversity: stockroom personnel, store managers, industrial engineers, truck drivers, garage mechanics, doctors and nurses, accountants, architects, economists, heating engineers, people skilled in watch repair, in police work, and so on. Many of the demands placed on the personnel department are therefore far from routine.

FUNCTIONS OF THE PERSONNEL DIVISION

We will consider the activities of retail personnel management under the following headings:

Recruiting
Training
Maintaining satisfactory personnel performance
Management development

As a retail firm becomes larger, the personnel function becomes more important and requires specific programs and a specialized staff. However, personnel relations do not belong exclusively to the personnel department. No supervisor of a firm can escape employee relations. Each management person is involved in training, in motivating, in supervising, and in the development of good or bad employee relations and morale. The presence of a personnel department and specific personnel policies and guidelines does not excuse the department manager or the line supervisor from responsibility for human resources. (In the next chapter, we will take a closer look at the problems of supervision.)

Recruiting and Selecting

Recruiting employees, whether rank and file or management, is a lengthy and rather complex procedure. Several steps are involved: (1) sources of prospective employees must be found; (2) employees must be selected from the prospects available; and (3) new employees must be introduced to the store and to their jobs.

Before a personnel department can go out and effectively seek employees, it should analyze the number and types of vacancies and the specific requirements needed to fill those vacancies. Each job in an organization can be studied to determine the kind of work to be done, the method of doing it, and the particular employee characteristics required. The result of such an analysis is a *job description,* which defines the type of prospective employee to look for, the position's pay scale relative to other jobs in the organization, and the training and supervision needed for adequate performance. Since specific duties have been set down, the task of evaluating employee performance is also easier.

As an example of how a job description is useful in determining recruitment needs, let us assume that a selling position is open in a main-floor candy department. The major duties consist of weighing candy purchases and keeping the department clean and orderly. Such a position might require a person who is reasonably attractive, clean, pleasant with customers, and who has enough manual dexterity to rapidly weigh and package candy purchases. Since most of the selling is order taking and can be quickly learned, there is no need for an experienced salesperson. The pay scale would be rather low compared to other sales positions, and such a position would probably be filled with a young, inexperienced person. In contrast, the requirements for a sales position in a corset department, in men's suits, or in carpeting would require someone with different qualifications and experience.

Retailers today must heed many legal requirements affecting personnel. In recent years, the federal government has been very active in assuring that women and minority groups are properly represented in the work force. For example, the Age Discrimination and Employment Act of 1967 prohibits discrimination in the hiring of persons between the ages of forty and sixty-five. Title 7 of the Civil Rights Act of 1964 prohibits discrimination in hiring on the basis of race, national origin, sex, or religion.

A federal agency, the *Equal Employment Opportunity Commission (EEOC)* has jurisdiction over firms of twenty-five persons or more. The EEOC may intervene if a firm's percentage of minority employees differs substantially from the minority's percentage in the population of the community in which the firm is located. Furthermore, larger firms are required to prepare affirmative action plans showing how they intend to implement EEOC regulations. A number of states also have antidiscrimination requirements.

SOURCES OF PERSONNEL   The prestige department store usually has little difficulty finding qualified employees. Many job candidates seek out such a store. Others may be recommended by store employees. Such a fortunate store may even keep an availability file and draw candidates from it as vacancies occur.

Most retailers are not so fortunate and may have to use a variety of means to locate prospective employees: classified ads, window signs, and government and private employment agencies. High school, business school, and college placement offices may be other personnel sources. Distributive education training programs are offered by many local high school systems and are partly supported through federal grants. These courses usually include career development training for students who often work part-time in local stores. These programs are of value in pinpointing students who are interested in a retail career.

Many retailers have recruited executive trainees haphazardly. Some firms have been content to wait for applicants off the street, or for an occasional unsolicited application. Other retailers have made concerted efforts to recruit prospective management people from college campuses. In general, however, retailers have neglected to undertake programs to encourage college students to enter the retailing field.

THE SELECTION PROCESS   Selecting employees from available candidates is one of the more time-consuming activities of the personnel department. However, retailers are not always able to be very selective. The relatively low pay and low prestige of certain jobs make it impossible to screen prospects as carefully as might be desired. Such a situation partly accounts for poor service and for some surly and unknowledgeable salesclerks. Retailers who can be selective use interviews, skill and aptitude tests, and physical examinations, in addition to initial screening through application blanks and checking of references.

Interviews and tests tend to be notoriously poor predictors of employee success or tenure.[2] As we noted before, one of the personnel problems confronting many retailers has been the high turnover of employees. Many leave within a few months, and the costs of hiring and training replacements are a continual expense. There is evidence that certain employee characteristics, such as age, education, and marital status, may correlate with sales performance and longevity on the job.[3]

Care has to be taken to prevent any inadvertent discrimination in the selection procedure. We cannot go into the specific provisions and

[2] Some success has been reported, though, in using personality tests to identify high- and low-performing store managers for a specialty-goods chain. See J. P. Muczyk, T. H. Mattheiss, and Myron Gable, "Predicting Success of Store Managers," *Journal of Retailing* (Summer 1974), 43–49.

[3] For example, see Charles N. Weaver, "An Empirical Study to Aid in the Selection of Retail Salesclerks," *Journal of Retailing* (Fall 1969), 22–26; and Robert F. Hartley, "The Weighted Application Blank Can Improve Retail Employee Selection," *Journal of Retailing* (Spring 1970), 32–40.

guidelines of governmental regulations here. Do note, though, that caution must be exercised in using ability tests to measure eligibility. A firm must have specific evidence that such tests really can predict job performance and do not discriminate against minorities who have cultural backgrounds that impede ability to score well.[4] Also, arbitrary job requirements, such as age, sex, marital status, and the like, may be challenged unless, again, the employer can prove that such requirements affect job performance.

In many firms, the personnel department screens the candidates, and the line executive (perhaps a buyer or department manager) for whom the employee will be working conducts a final interview. Having these executives involved in the final hiring decision tends to make for a close employee-supervisor rapport.

INTRODUCING NEW EMPLOYEES TO THE JOB   The final step in recruiting new employees can be important in reducing labor turnover and increasing employee longevity. Introducing the new employee to the firm and the rest of the staff helps give a sense of belonging and hastens the work adjustment. The personnel department and a designated person from the area in which the new employee is to work should share responsibility for this introduction. Regardless of the size of the firm, the first few days of getting acquainted are so important for later job satisfaction that definite procedures should be developed for new-employee orientation.

Training

The objectives of training are to improve worker performance and morale, which should translate into a more efficient operation and better customer satisfaction. Many large firms have formal training programs with at least some *centralized training* conducted by the training department. Some on-the-job or *decentralized training* usually is also involved, but actual job supervisors are responsible for this. In smaller firms, training tends to be informal and decentralized; any questions, problems, and mistakes are taken care of on the job.

The larger the store, the more complicated the training program becomes. Larger size brings many different employees and widely differing jobs. Policies and procedures need to be prescribed in some detail and must be learned by new employees and, sometimes, re-

---

[4] For specific details, see *Guidelines on Employment Selection Procedures* (Equal Employment Opportunity Commission, August 1, 1970); and *Proposed Employment Testing and Other Selection Procedures* (Office of Federal Contract Compliance, April 15, 1971).

learned by older ones. Part-time workers and management trainees also add to the demands on a training department in a large store.

A challenging new idea, especially for the large retailer, is to extend the training function beyond well-screened and carefully selected employees and management.

RETAILING CHALLENGE—Expanding the Training Function

Training by retailers can be expanded, and given new reach and an enlarged perspective. In addition to training regular employees, it can be used to tackle some of our social problems. Employment training for minority workers, and consumer counseling warrant particular attention from concerned retailers.

Training Disadvantaged Minority Workers   Both the community and store can benefit from special programs to train disadvantaged members of minority groups for sales and other positions. These programs may require special tailoring to different standards and expectations. The following is from *Time* magazine:

Many of the hardcore [unemployed] are without the remotest idea of what is required of a worker. Quite a few have never learned to tell time or even read simple signs; they have no familiarity with such routine disciplines as getting up at the same hour every morning. Some are completely unable to cope and go back to the streets, never to return.

These very real difficulties have led some retailers to give up or to be satisfied with token efforts.

Consumer Counseling   Many consumers, especially younger ones and those from the ghetto, must buy as carefully and knowledgeably as possible if their limited purchasing power is to be used efficiently. But these very customers are the most naive and ignorant in the marketplace. A retailer's training department could perform a worthwhile public service, as well as contribute to good public and customer relations, by adding consumer counseling services. Such a program might include the following rules for good consumership:

1. Buy necessities first and luxuries last.
2. Try to get the best quality for the lowest price (the retailer is certainly in the best position to advise consumers on this).

3. Budget income and plan purchases.

4. Meet some needs through home production.

5. Take advantage of consumer benefits available to the poor.

Sources: "The Executive as Social Activist," *Time,* July 20, 1970, p. 64; Elliott B. Glicksman and Vera Massey Jones, "Consumer Legislation and the Ghetto," *Poverty and Human Resources Abstracts,* 4, No. 3 (May–June 1969), 50; and Louis G. Richards, "Consumer Practices of the Poor," *Poverty and Human Resources Abstracts,* 2, No. 6 (March-April, 1969), 131.

For Thought and Discussion

1. What difficulties do you foresee in implementing such a program?

2. Do you think such a consumer counseling program would be practical for the small retailer? Why or why not?

3. Do you think the problems of training disadvantaged minority workers can be overcome?

4. What suggestions would you have for coping with such problems?

Maintaining Satisfactory Personnel Performance

It is not enough to hire and train employees. An important personnel management function is to keep employee performance satisfactory. This is by no means solely a personnel department responsibility; an employee's immediate supervisors must certainly have major responsibility here. Still, the personnel department should set up and coordinate equitable policies and procedures. It will be involved in the following areas affecting employee performance:

Compensation

Evaluation of personnel

Promotion, transfer, demotion, and discharge of employees

Suitable working conditions

Various employee services, such as health services, recreational and educational activities, and insurance and credit plans

Handling employee complaints and union demands -

COMPENSATION   A major reason why people change jobs is to get more money. However, one should not presume that money is the only factor that motivates employees and creates job satisfaction. Numerous studies have found that steady work, opportunity for advancement, pleasant associates, good supervision, and desirable working conditions are listed by workers as even more important than pay. If an employee thinks there are flaws or inequities in the pay scale, a serious personnel problem can result. This is particularly true if the pay scale is lower than for similar jobs with similar firms (unless there are certain offsetting features, such as a higher-status store or more fringe benefits); or if fellow workers are seen as favored in pay scale or frequency of raises.

This suggests that a firm should periodically determine average pay scales in its community. Usually, such surveys are not difficult to make, since all employers have an interest in maintaining equitable pay scales. Furthermore, raises as well as salaries of new employees must be carefully planned so that they will be as fair as possible.

The firm interested in building employee good will by paying in proportion to responsibilities and difficulty of work will want to conduct *job evaluations.* Such evaluations carefully appraise the value of all jobs and the relationships among them. While considerable time and judgment are involved in developing job evaluations, the result can be more equitable wage rates, better-planned raises, and improved employee morale.

There are three basic methods of paying retail employees:

1. Straight salary
2. Straight commission
3. Some combination of salary and commission (or bonus)

A straight salary normally offers the greatest security and least incentive for salespeople; the straight commission is the other extreme, providing maximum incentive and minimum security. This is shown in the continuum, which also shows the combination plan as being a middle ground, a compromise between maximum and minimum security and incentive.

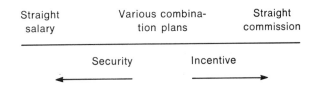

Besides offering maximum security, which tends to minimize personnel turnover, a straight salary plan helps management exercise better control over salespeople, who are not dependent on the volume of sales for their pay. Lower-pitched sales incentives are more likely to generate customer good will than a commission plan, which will stimulate high-pressure sales tactics. For nonselling jobs, such as those in offices or stockrooms, the difficulties in setting quotas or in finding a satisfactory basis for a commission makes the straight salary plan prevalent.

In order to attain some balance between incentive and security for salespeople, many types of *combination compensation plans* are used. A base salary and commission or bonus arrangement may be proportioned to total pay. Often such a plan involves some sort of quota arrangement in which there is a base salary, plus a commission on all sales in excess of a certain quota. Managerial personnel, such as buyers and store managers, are often paid a salary and have some bonus arrangement based on sales, or on the profitability of the department or store for which they are responsible. Such bonuses are often given as a reward for an increase over a previous year's sales or profits.

PERSONNEL EVALUATION   The worth of its individual employees and executives—how well each performs the job, and the potential of each for greater responsibilities—is important to any firm. This worth must be accurately assessed if compensation and pay increases are to reward the best producers. Accurate assessment is also important for promotions, which should be based on merit if a firm is to have good executives. And if a firm is to have a high-level work force, the poorly performing employees need to be identified. Perhaps a transfer or termination should be made. Often a low performance level can be improved by the greater mutual understanding that results from the evaluation process.

Ideally, the morale of the work force will be raised by periodic *performance evaluations* that include discussions between members of management and each employee being evaluated. For best results, we all need feedback on how we are doing and how we can improve. Better rapport and communication with superiors can clear up misunderstandings and make appreciation more obvious. In reality, the evaluation process frequently causes serious problems. It is difficult to evaluate personnel objectively. Morale is often temporarily injured. For example, such things as ability, loyalty, enthusiasm, and attitude toward the store are all difficult to define and measure, and different raters may differ in their evaluations of the same employee. Too often the discussion that follows the evaluation report fails to establish rapport between the superior and the employee, and the employee becomes resentful and argumentative. After all, none of us likes to be criticized.[5] But most personnel experts agree that these reports *should*

---

[5] For an article dealing with some of the issues of job evaluation from the employee's viewpoint, see Harold D. Janes, "Issues in Job Evaluation: The Union View," *Personnel Journal* (September 1972).

be discussed with the employee if his or her performance is to be improved.

Despite the possible disadvantages of periodic and systematic performance evaluations, they are desirable for most firms, especially large firms, where higher executives cannot know every employee personally. Where objective standards can be used, such as sales, selling cost, profitability, and ratio of errors, with opinions of more qualitative factors obtained from a number of persons, results can be worthwhile. While an employee's most immediate supervisor usually makes the evaluation, the personnel department is involved in establishing procedures, coordinating, and keeping central records.

Figure 9.1 shows a performance evaluation form used by a major general-merchandise chain for its salespeople and selling-department managers. Note that an attempt has been made to quantify the appraisal wherever possible, with sales, hourly production rating, and individual payroll costs calculated. On the other hand, many of the performance measures, such as "Recognizes and responds to customer need for help," and "Has friendly and courteous manner toward customer" are judgmental and not quantifiable. Figure 9.2 shows the second half of the performance evaluation form, which is applicable only to department managers. Again, some items are appraised objectively in quantifiable terms. Other items are evaluated only by the subjective judgment of a superior, for example, "Shows judgment in merchandise planning," and "Develops competent sales people."

PROMOTION, TRANSFER, DEMOTION, AND DISCHARGE In many firms, the movement of personnel, especially managerial people and trainees, is common. Most promotions involve a relocation, whether to a different department or a different store. But many changes or transfers are really lateral; that is, they do not increase responsibility, but they widen the person's breadth of experience and test his or her versatility. In the new job, an employee may bring ideas for improving operations that can come only from exposure to different situations and different management techniques. Some chain organizations, in particular, have a habit of transferring their management trainees often and with short notice to expose them to the strengths and weaknesses of a variety of managers.

But a manager-to-be who is moved too many times may become confused. Certainly the strain of a constantly uprooted family may affect a worker's effectiveness. There are limits to flexibility. Moving personnel to other stores and cities is a sizable expense for the company involved, and one that may not be readily justified by the value received. On the other hand, any employee may become stale if allowed

FIGURE 9.1 PERFORMANCE APPRAISAL FORM FOR SALESPEOPLE AND DEPARTMENT MANAGERS

PERFORMANCE REVIEW
SALESPEOPLE AND DEPARTMENT MANAGERS

Name_____

Department_____

Continuous
Service Date_____

Date of
Appraisal_____

POSITION CLASSIFICATION: ☐ Salesperson   ☐ *Department Manager

DUTIES	PERFORMANCE RESULTS	S−	S	S+
1. SELLING AND SALES PERFORMANCE Determines customer needs, sells-up, and refers customer to other store services. Maintains a high level of Sales Productivity Performance.	Succeeds in suggestion selling, multiple selling, and selling-up.			
	Knows and uses the Catalog effectively to satisfy customer's merchandise needs.			
	Maintains an aggressive enthusiastic selling attitude.			
	Willmark Shop Date_____ _____% Spring 19____ Fall 19____ Spring 19____ Fall 19____			
**Retail Sales	$ $ $ $			
**Hour Prod. Rating	$ $ $ $			
**Selling Payroll Cost	% % % %			
2. CUSTOMER SERVICE Gives prompt, efficient customer service.	Has friendly and courteous manner toward customer.			
	Recognizes and responds to customer need for help.			
	Inter-sells between departments as needed.			
	Promotes credit selling.			
	***Promptly refers customer to Plus Service cashier.			
3. MERCHANDISE PLANNING, PROMOTION AND STOCK KEEPING Maintains displays and merchandise to Company standards. Maintains good instock position. Keeps a balanced merchandise assortment.	Keeps stock straightened, clean and orderly.			
	Replaces signs and prices promptly.			
	Uses display properties to best advantage.			
	Counts stock accurately.			
	Exhibits good timing in suggesting merchandise to be promoted.			
	Reports best sellers quickly.			
	Stocks reflect knowledge of fast and slow moving merchandise.			
	Observes merchandise trends and suggests items to be stocked or discontinued.			
	Presents merchandise so as to invite self-selection.			
OVERALL APPRAISAL—Salesperson (Duties 1 through 3)				

This form to be used for *all* salespeople.

*Department Manager—See Standard Procedure Instructions.

**To be used for evaluating individuals where a record of personal sales, hourly productivity and selling cost is maintained.

***Only to be used in evaluating employees working in plus service areas.

29263-1

Refer to instructions in Retail Store Operations Manual, Chapter 2

FIGURE 9.2 PERFORMANCE APPRAISAL FORM FOR DEPARTMENT MANAGERS ONLY

PERFORMANCE REVIEW—RETAIL SALESPERSON AND DEPARTMENT MANAGER

DUTIES	PERFORMANCE RESULTS	APPRAISAL S−	S	S+
ADDITIONAL DUTIES FOR DEPARTMENT MANAGER				
4. MERCHANDISE CONDITION REPORT	Maintained Gross Profit % to Net Sales Dept.___, ___%; Dept.___, ___%; Dept.___, ___%; Dept.___, ___%			
	Year to Date B & X Liquidation Dept.___, ___%; Dept.___, ___%; Dept.___, ___%; Dept.___, ___%			
	Meets turnover objectives Dept.___ Budget___ Act.___; Dept.___ Budget___ Act.___; Dept.___ Budget___ Act.___; Dept.___ Budget___ Act.___.			
	DEPT./GROUP SALES VOLUME & SELLING PAYROLL COST 　　　　　　　Last Year　　This Year　　% Inc./(Dec.) Spring　　$_____　$_____　　___% Fall　　　$_____　$_____　　___% Year　　　$_____　$_____　　___% Selling Payroll Cost _____ % _____ %			
5. MERCHANDISING	Uses mark-down % in line with budget.			
	Shows judgment in merchandise planning.			
	Knows competitors prices, lines and grades of merchandise.			
	Percent of in-stock check. Dept.___, ___%; Dept.___, ___%; Dept.___, ___%; Dept.___, ___%			
	Percent of Inventory Recovery Dept.___, ___%; Dept.___, ___%; Dept.___, ___%; Dept.___, ___%			
	Maintains a satisfactory set of Basic List Records. (Schedule counts, correct counts, Scheduled reviews and judgment in specifying quantities.)			
	Inventory Management in Relation to Budget.			
	Displays and Housekeeping meet Company standards.			
	Handles reports promptly and accurately.			
6. SUPERVISION Develops a competent salesforce	Develops competent sales people.			
	Stimulates the sales performance of salespeople.			
OVERALL APPRAISAL—Department Manager (Duties 1 through 6)				

7. CHECK CURRENT STATUS OF THIS INDIVIDUAL

☐ Immediately Promotable—Give Position_____

　☐ Yes ☐ No—Available for Transfer

☐ Satisfactory—Continue on Present Position

☐ Unsatisfactory (☐ Put on Probation, Date of Next Review_____)

8. SUGGESTIONS FOR IMPROVEMENT

9. SALARY SUMMARY

Current Rate $_____

Date of Last Increase_____Type_____Amount $_____

Date Reviewed　　Appraiser Signature_____

_____　　Employee Signature_____

My overall performance appraisal has been discussed with me as of this date.

▲ STORE STAMP ▲

to remain too long in an unchallenging position. Most ambitious people welcome transfers—whether lateral or upward—because such moves indicate that someone is aware of them and systematically exposing them to fresh challenges and experiences.

Individual differences in ability, personality, and drive being what they are, demotions and terminations are part of any organization. Demotions present particular difficulties because of the resentment and the feeling of defeatism and frustration that they often engender. Termination frequently is a better remedy for personnel problems. However, it should generally be a last-recourse solution, after relocation attempts and adequate warning or probationary periods have been tried. Of course, there are situations where there is no alternative to immediate termination, such as cases of dishonesty or serious breaches of conduct. Often, the discharged employee, his friends, and his relatives remain hostile to the firm and spread unfavorable comments in the community.

Exit interviews are used by many firms when an employee is about to leave voluntarily or be terminated. These interviews may help relieve some of the employee's resentment by offering a sounding board. They can also furnish management with clues to certain working conditions or supervisory deficiencies that should be corrected.

WORKING CONDITIONS   In many ways, retail employees have better working conditions than their counterparts in industry. Since retail stores are designed with the comfort of customers in mind, air conditioning, carpeting, pleasant lighting, and attractive fixtures and displays are standard. Large stores have employee lounges and cafeterias. Most stores are located in desirable geographic areas and are close to other stores and activities. These working conditions are among the real pluses of a retailing career.

One of the negatives, however, is the long business hours.

RETAIL CONTROVERSY—How Many Hours to Remain Open?

A marked trend has developed for night and Sunday openings. Even major holidays, such as Memorial Day and Labor Day, are finding many stores open. Originally started by "hungry" discounters trying to compete against well-established major chains in the suburbs, the movement has rapidly spread to the big retailers. Some stores, especially supermarkets, have tested a 168-hour week (168 hours = 7 days × 24 hours a day). In other words, they never close.

Arguments for More Hours Open

More hours open provide more convenience to customers and increased sales. Customers want this; many prefer to shop with their families on Sundays and holidays.

Expenses do not rise in proportion to longer hours, since skeleton crews and low-cost part-time workers can be used.

To keep ahead or abreast of competition, stores have to stay open longer hours at night and on Sundays and holidays.

Arguments Against More Hours Open

Customers will shop during the hours a store is open; they do not demand unreasonable hours open for shopping.

Employees resent longer hours and Sunday and holiday openings; this resentment leads to more personnel turnover.

The heavy reliance on part-time workers necessitated by longer hours decreases operating efficiency and service to customers.

For Thought and Discussion Assume you are the chief executive of (1) a small grocery store, (2) a gasoline station, (3) a women's dress shop, and (4) a downtown department store. How would you assess the desirability of long hours open?

Naturally, the individual retail employee's working hours have not lengthened, even though stores remain open more hours; the forty-hour work week is fairly standard for retail workers in metropolitan areas. A *platoon schedule,* or system of shifts, has been devised by some stores. Two or even three shifts may be used: 9 A.M. to 5 P.M. and 5 P.M. to 9 P.M. Monday through Friday; and a third shift for weekends. The latter two shifts are staffed mostly with part-timers. The alternative is to juggle employees' hours daily, with a hodgepodge of different schedules. Of course, two or even three sets of supervisory executives in both selling and nonselling areas are needed in platooning. Some stores are paying their employees premiums for Sunday work.

On occasion, management people may voluntarily put in more hours, especially if they feel the need to check out certain problems or appraise customer response to promotions. Sometimes, top management arbitrarily decrees that buyers and other lower- and middle-level executives put in longer hours. This may happen at the peak Christmas season. It may also happen when there is a sales or profit decline.

EMPLOYEE SERVICES   Major retailers have been among the progressive firms in providing services for their employees. Vacations have become more liberal and now compare with those in other industries. Group life insurance, pension funds, group health allowances, and medical care are common. Most retailers (except the supermarket chains) offer their employees discounts on purchases made in the store; these discounts typically range from 10 to 20 percent off the regular selling price, and employee-discount purchases may come to over 4 percent of total store sales.

Even profit sharing for employees and executives is widespread, more so than in any other major industry group. J. C. Penney Company and Sears, Roebuck have long had employee participation in profit-sharing plans; Montgomery Ward adopted a general profit-sharing plan in 1963. While profit sharing by executives is not uncommon in many industries, its expansion to all employees—sales and sales-supporting people as well as management—is a credit to retailing. Such programs not only encourage employees to remain with their firm, they also incite efforts for greater sales and profits.

Personnel departments may be involved in overseeing a variety of recreational and educational activities, ranging from athletic events and all-store picnics to orchestras and dramatic groups. Some stores offer scholarships and work-study arrangements to encourage employees to continue their education.

HANDLING GRIEVANCES AND UNIONISM   The personnel department is the natural place to handle employee complaints and grievances dealing with working conditions, fellow workers, or employee-supervisor relations. Personnel's representatives can be objective in ironing out problems. Sometimes, a transfer to another department or branch store may be the best solution. But regardless of efforts to reduce friction or possibilities for complaint, some problems are bound to arise in any large organization. Definite *grievance procedures* should be established for handling such complaints promptly and effectively. For example, if an employee feels ill-treated by a supervisor, he or she should be able to register a complaint and be heard, preferably the same day, by an objective person. The supervisor's position may also need to be presented or clarified, and perhaps the problem can be resolved at that point. Otherwise, it may be wise to discuss other alternatives, such as a transfer. If possible, all parties should reach general agreement.

Channels and procedures for handling complaints should be well communicated to employees. Otherwise, resentments may fester and spread. If a store is unionized, minor problems may turn into serious disputes.

Retail labor unions are not widespread, even though some date back to the 1800s. In those days, retail workers had low pay and incredibly long hours. It was not uncommon for a clerk to work from sunrise to 9 P.M. every day except the Sabbath. Male clerks were given one evening a week off "for courting." It is not surprising that early union activity centered on seeking shorter hours, and such unions were called early-closing societies.

What is surprising is the small number of retail employees today who are unionized: less than a million out of over 13 million employed in retailing. Sales-supporting employee groups, such as truck drivers, warehouse workers, and elevator operators (of which few are left) have generally been more union prone. The largest retail clerk's union, the Retail Clerks International Association, has over 500,000 members; Amalgamated Meat Cutters and Butcher Workmen of North America has about 200,000 members in wholesale and retail food firms.

Despite strenuous union membership efforts, many retail workers

At the U.S. Open Tennis Championships at Forest Hills, New York, clothing workers distribute consumer boycott leaflets. The leaflets urge tennis buffs to avoid buying sporting goods manufactured by the AMF-Head Division. For the most part, retail employees have not been as organized and aggressive as workers for manufacturers have. Do you think this union protest and boycott is likely to be effective? (Courtesy of the AFL-CIO News)

are not union minded. This is due partly to the blue-collar image of most unions; retail workers consider themselves white collar. It also reflects the large number of part-time and seasonal workers employed in retailing, who feel that union membership would not be worthwhile. Furthermore, the short training period for many retail jobs makes it easy to hire replacements; therefore, a striking worker's job might be in jeopardy. In a unionized store, some employees may be given fast promotions to nonunion "junior-executive" status, thereby avoiding the union.[6]

Management Development

Large retailers find it necessary to make a strong commitment to management development to have executives ready to handle rapid growth. Opening a new store requires a large number of key people. Long store hours often necessitate platooning supervisors. Most retailers have found that their executive requirements, at least at the lower and middle levels, are best fulfilled by promotion from within. In such internal management development, the personnel department usually plays a major role; some large retailers have even organized an executive-training division under the personnel function.

AN EXECUTIVE-DEVELOPMENT PROGRAM   Firms vary in the composition of their *executive-development programs,* as would be expected. In general we find that most programs provide some degree of the following:

Continual monitoring of progress
Position rotation
Formal training or conference programs

Probably nothing would be more frustrating to any ambitious individual than to be placed in a particular slot and seemingly forgotten. Most large retailers, after a trainee has been selected for the executive-training program, are continually monitoring that trainee's progress. Performance reviews may be more frequent than for rank-and-file employees. Counseling is usually available. Other perquisites of the trainee are participation in management conferences, recognition

[6] For an indication that retail unionism may be strengthening, see "The Big New Retailing Union Eyes the Services," *Business Week,* March 5, 1979, pp. 73–74.

by top executives, and the status afforded by being on the executive payroll.

Many retailers rotate their trainees rather frequently to expose them to varied assignments, to many aspects of the operation, and to a variety of executives, who inevitably have different strengths and weaknesses, which the trainee can emulate or avoid as he or she develops skills. In addition to providing a better feel for the overall operation, rotation helps ascertain the particular strengths and interests of the candidate.

Chains also rotate their executives and trainees, sometimes quite frequently and on short notice. Usually the moves are more frequent in the early years when an employee is preparing for more important positions; later, moves usually accompany significant promotions.

Some formal training programs are often part of executive development. A wide range of subjects may be covered. Top executives of the firm may speak on their areas of expertise. For example, in the Executive Conference Program at Macy's, the vice president for control discusses the "Function of Divisional Control," and the vice president for merchandising discusses "Merchandising Policies." The abilities of junior- and even middle-management people may be developed by:

Seminars: small group discussions and problem solving

Brainstorming: an exercise to stimulate ideas and creativity

Role playing: assuming different roles in exercises to acquaint trainees with problems and attitudes in various parts of the organization

Sensitivity training: a human relations exercise that helps participants gain self-awareness of their behavior patterns and relations with other people, including superiors and subordinates

Case studies: evaluating problems and decision alternatives that have arisen in similar organizations

Special courses offered by universities

RETAIL CONTROVERSY—How Long Should the Executive-Training Program Be?

The lengths of formal training programs vary widely. Some programs continue for years; participants rotate through many different assignments and attend a variety of formal training sessions and conferences. While a lengthy program is a tangible indication of a firm's interest and investment in its junior executives, perhaps this can be carried too far. Some firms would argue that it is best, both for the trainees and the firm, to let trainees get their feet wet as soon as possible.

"Young people today want in on the action. They don't want to sit around for six months . . . ," says the chief financial officer of Jewel Companies, a $3.3 billion, Chicago-based, diversified supermarket chain. Industry observers rank Jewel as a leader in management-development programs. Jewel makes it a practice to recruit business school graduates and then move top performers quickly into executive posts, "to give new people responsibilities and challenges early in their careers." Jewel's highly decentralized management setup allows executives at all levels more freedom of action and more scope for their initiative. Rapid advancement and profit sharing are attractive lures to bright young talent.

Sources: "Jewel Lets Young Men Make Mistakes" from the January 17, 1970 issue of BusinessWeek, pp. 90–92; and "Jewel: A Merger with Skaggs to Master the 'Combo' Store" from the June 12, 1978 issue of BusinessWeek, pp. 154–156. © 1970, 1978 by McGraw-Hill, Inc. New York, NY 10020. All rights reserved.

For Thought and Discussion

1. How do you feel about the length of a training program? Why?
2. Can you think of arguments against the philosophy of Jewel?

PERSONNEL PROBLEMS

The importance of people in retailing can hardly be overemphasized. The face-to-face contact with the potential customer furthers customer satisfaction and store loyalty, or destroys it. Yet certain serious people problems confront many retailers:

High personnel turnover
Poorly motivated employees
Inability to acquire competent workers

Retailing is not considered a high-status industry. While this viewpoint is changing, especially with better-trained and more professional management people assuming control of many family-run businesses, the fact remains that many retail jobs require little skill or training, that they involve clerking, or moving merchandise, and not much else. Retail pay and retail hours have also been unattractive to many capable workers. The result, during several decades when the supply of labor was less than the demand, was that retailers often had to be content with marginal workers who were less dedicated to their jobs than might be desired.

This situation causes a whole series of problems. We have noted retailing's high labor turnover. A lack of job interest generates excessive absenteeism, a major headache for supervisors who must cope with providing adequate customer service, stockkeeping and stock counting needs, and so on while the workforce is inadequate. Poor morale, excessive errors and omissions—all the things that customers complain about—thrive in an unenthusiastic work force.

Where Does the Blame Lie?

Does the blame for this situation lie with the personnel department? Does it lie with top management or first-level supervisors? At least in some stores, the answer may be with all of these.

Top retail executives traditionally have equated success with shrewdness and hard work more than with education and innovative thinking. And they have been reluctant to pay for the caliber of personnel that other industries have long wooed. Retailing has typically lagged behind other industries in the use of research, scientific controls and automation, and the latest analytical techniques and controls for management. Decisions have been made by intuition and hunch, or "as we have always done it."

Supervisors are often poorly motivated to train and encourage their employees. In many departments, the emphasis is strictly on improving sales volume, and this leaves little time for employee development. Perhaps this is more evident among small retailers and smaller units of chains, where some managers are particularly inept in human relations and in developing their subordinates for better jobs.

And the personnel department? It is sometimes little more than a keeper of personnel records and a crude screener of off-the-street applicants. Many personnel departments exercise little creativity in developing better techniques for selecting employees, devising better training methods, and stimulating executives toward better supervisory techniques.

The Challenge of Personnel Management

Customers today demand service and are quick to express their displeasure and switch their business when service is poor. At the same time, workers are increasingly discontented and alienated from their work.

This is the challenge facing personnel management: how to make work more stimulating, more interesting, more "enriching."[7]

Our economy, which once had a shortage of labor is developing labor surpluses, at least in some parts of the country and in some occupations. This means that, in the coming years, retailers should have more able workers to draw from to meet their expanding needs. There may be a new chance to acquire the able and motivated employees needed for successful retail operations and better customer service. But good supervision, which is primarily the responsibility of line executives, from assistant buyers to store managers, will always be important in personnel management.

■ Summary

In this chapter, we examined personnel relations, mainly from the point of view of top management and the personnel department. Recruiting and training new employees are important personnel department functions. Satisfactory employee performance depends on a number of matters that involve the personnel department, such as compensation and its comparability to that offered by similar employers in the community, working conditions, and the fairness of employee performance evaluations. But the appropriateness of employee selection and training also bears on job performance; and so does the caliber of first-line supervision. Larger retailers are having to direct more time and resources to management development if they are to have executives capable of handling rapid growth. However, high personnel turnover and poorly motivated employees continue to plague many retailers. In the next chapter, we will look at personnel relations from the perspective of the first-line supervisor.

■ Key Terms

Centralized training	Grievance procedure
Combination compensation plan	Job description
Customer good will	Job evaluation
Decentralized training	Labor intensity
Equal Employment Opportunity Commission (EEOC)	Performance evaluation
Executive-development programs	Personnel turnover
Exit interviews	Platoon schedule

[7] For a discussion of the need for "job enrichment," and initial steps being taken in this direction, see Michael Putney, "Work & Enjoy It, Inc.," *The National Observer,* March 17, 1973, pp. 1, 16.

■ **Discussion Questions**

1. What does a 20-percent personnel-turnover rate mean? Which is generally the worst: a 20-percent turnover or a 50-percent turnover?
2. Why does retailing usually need a larger proportion of executives, such as one executive for every ten employees, than manufacturing does?
3. Why is a job description important?
4. It has been found in a number of studies that the level of compensation on a job is less important than other factors, such as pleasant associates and good working conditions. Under what conditions would you expect such findings to be valid?
5. What are the disadvantages of personnel evaluations? What can be done to minimize these drawbacks?
6. Why do you think labor unions for retail employees have been relatively unimportant, at least as compared with manufacturing? Is this likely to change?
7. What are the advantages of job rotation for the trainee or executive? Are there disadvantages?
8. How would you evaluate the effectiveness of a personnel department and its policies?

■ **Project**

Determine the strength of retail unions in your community. This may entail talking to union representatives. Ascertain the size and importance of unions that cover retail employees. Also, ask what benefits they offer retail employees. Contact one or several members of retail management and find out their perception of unionization in their stores. Finally, develop an objective analysis of the pros and cons of union activity in your community, from the standpoint of: (1) retail management, (2) employees, and (3) customers.

■ **Exercise in Creativity**

As the newly transferred manager of a discount store, you find that the store has experienced difficulty in recruiting able and conscientious employees. How would you endeavor to attract more capable job applicants?

■ Retailing in Action

As a newly appointed store manager, you find that the personnel-turnover rate for your store for the past several years has been 70 percent. How would you attempt to reduce this rate? What would your effectiveness depend on? Would you want to eliminate personnel turn-over completely?

10 Supervising the Retail Worker

Success in moving up the ranks of management in any organization is directly related to how much you can get done *through people.*

Supervision is a vital part of the people-management function in a firm. For the junior executive it can be a heady experience, and one that comes quickly in many retail jobs. But supervision is somewhat more complex than it may seem to the casual observer. One must recognize certain principles of human relations and motivation. More than this, good supervisors find that the variety of problems they encounter can be a learning experience. Supervision involves people, and people, as we know, are rather complex.

The perspective taken in this chapter will be that of a junior executive, the first-line supervisor in the lower ranks of management; that is, the selling-department manager, assistant buyer, or assistant store manager. To make this perspective more real, this chapter will present several role-playing situations.

CHARACTERISTICS OF RETAIL WORKERS

The work force in most departments of a store, whether selling or nonselling, will have the following characteristics:

Preponderance of women

Many young people, some on their first job

Large proportion of part-time workers

Many who consider the job a temporary occupation (For many students and young people, expectations are not to remain in retailing but to go to school, go into military service, get married, and so on. For many older women, the job in retailing is a temporary means of supplementing family income strained by college costs or other expenses.)

In some ways, these characteristics make supervision difficult, or at least different from the supervision of more career-oriented workers. Initial supervisory experiences are both frustrating and rewarding. And they can pave the way for greater challenges.

As many as two-thirds of total employees in department stores may be women; so it may be necessary to give special consideration to working conditions, such as physical duties, physical facilities, and hours worked. Young part-time employees will need close supervision, detailed explanations and instructions, and constant follow-up, to assure that they understand directions correctly and that they do not become careless or forgetful. Many of these employees consider the job temporary; this and a low wage rate make it more difficult for the supervisor to motivate them. Unless the work force is relatively experienced or strongly motivated, the supervisor may need to devote considerable attention to planning assignments each day; the alternative will be people wasting time by missing tasks that need to be done.

INGREDIENTS OF SUPERVISION

Supervision refers to the day-to-day relations between supervisor and immediate subordinates. *Effective supervision* may be defined as providing a job environment that encourages a high level of goal-directed accomplishment. The following elements are involved in supervision:

Planning: making work assignments

Directing: issuing instructions

Motivating: stimulating good performance

Following up: checking to see that instructions are followed and that performance is satisfactory

These elements of supervision are closely related, and they touch on the complexities of human relations and management theory. For example, training and directing are almost inseparable, since an employee who has not been adequately trained can hardly be expected to carry out instructions. The manner of directing is closely associated with problems of motivation. And permeating all is the subtle skill called leadership, which is complex and not easily defined. But for our purposes, it is enough to recognize that supervisory and leadership skills can be learned.

Planning Work Assignments

Before a work group can possibly accomplish a high level of productivity, there must be some *planning:* What tasks need to be performed today? this week? Which employees are best able to perform these particular jobs, either because of their experience and ability or because they are not tied up with other tasks?

Planning means deciding in advance what is to be done. The opposite of planning is sometimes called fire-fighting, which suggests that manager and organization are whipped from one problem to another and can do no more than make urgent—and sometimes too hasty—decisions and actions.

In a junior executive's first supervisory position, the opportunity to develop planning skills will arise. Later in this chapter, we will see that sometimes planning can best be done in consultation with subordinates. Their participation may stimulate cooperation, motivation, and fruitful ideas.

In retailing, the need to keep people productive by carefully planning work assignments is often greater than in other fields. The work flow is intermittent, since customer traffic builds up during certain hours of the day and on certain days of the week and is at a minimum during other periods. Yet enough employees must be present to handle the peaks of customer traffic. If they have not been given sufficient work for slack periods, then overall productivity will suffer. The result may be that, because of other pressing tasks, not all the personnel of a selling department are available to handle peak customer traffic and some sales may be lost. Or else important nonselling tasks, such as maintaining stock records, replenishing stock, making needed markdowns, or other housekeeping and merchandising assignments may have to be delayed. When work assignments have been carefully made, the supervisor may escape an embarrassing situation like the one that follows.

ROLE PLAY—Supervisory Dilemma: Lack of Adequate Work Assignments

Assume the role of a newly promoted assistant buyer for the men's furnishings department of a large department store.

You are busily writing a fill-in order in the departmental buying office. You had intended to do this earlier in the day, but a flurry of customers over the lunch hours, when the department was short-staffed, had required you to be on the sales floor. Now the clerks are all back from lunch and customer traffic has lessened.

Suddenly the divisional merchandise manager looks in and says to you: "You'd better get out on the floor right away! Your people are standing around visiting with each other. Can't you find something for them to do? A single cannon ball would get them all."

For Thought and Discussion

1. Can you really be blamed for the actions of sales clerks when you are busy with other important duties and cannot be present to supervise them personally?
2. How successful do you think you could be in preventing this situation from occurring again?
3. Assuming that you have six sales clerks in the department after the lunch hour, what specific work assignments might you prescribe to increase their productivity during slack periods? Are there any alternatives you might consider to keep this situation from happening again?

Directing

Directing is issuing instructions to subordinates, or otherwise indicating what they should do. Effective communication is a key element. For communication to be effective, the transfer of information or instructions by the sender (the supervisor) has to be clearly understood by the receiver (the subordinate). There is no effective communication unless the meaning perceived by the receiver is the same as that intended by the sender.

Face-to-face supervision, which usually involves oral communication, is more characteristic of the typical retail situation than is long-range supervision, which usually relies on written communication. Generally, oral communication is superior to written communication because it permits two-way communication: the receiver can ask questions on any points that are unclear, so instructions can be further explained or clarified as needed.

Yet, certain barriers hamper even oral communication. They can lead to misunderstandings and frictions that distort the perception of messages between individuals and forestall effective communication.

BARRIERS TO COMMUNICATION   One of the more common barriers to effective communication is that words themselves often convey different meanings to different people, especially to people on different levels in an organization. Take, for example, the words *prompt, reasonable, conscientious,* and *usually;* perceptions of the degree of action suggested by such words may differ widely. A superior may also use language that the employee finds unfamiliar and hard to understand.

Barriers can arise from the different attitudes of people at different levels in the organization. For example, an employee may not view exhortations for greater productivity in the same way that a supervisor or higher-level executive does. Prejudices, deep-rooted personal feelings, complacency, and indifference all impede accurate interpretation of a supervisor's message.

Supervisors should be aware of the possible barriers to good communication and be prepared to minimize or overcome them. A good instruction has certain characteristics that will tend to minimize communications problems.

1.   An instruction should be clear.   The need for clarity is a matter of common sense, yet it is often violated: while an instruction may be clear to the supervisor issuing it, it is not always clear to the person receiving it. Especially with young and relatively untrained employees, clarity of instruction is most important. If need be, the supervisor should have the employee write the order down or repeat it to demonstrate comprehension.

2.   An instruction should be complete.   Telling an employee to change the front display is vague. It does not indicate the purpose of the change, what should replace the present display, or what particular extra touches are desired. A complete order should leave no question in the mind of the person receiving it about what should be done. Usually an instruction should also indicate when a task should be completed. When many tasks need doing, an indication of priority—which task should be done first—is desirable.

3. An instruction should be reasonable.   A supervisor must consider whether the person receiving the instruction has the necessary experience and ability to carry it out satisfactorily. For example, asking a new part-time clerk to change a display might be unreasonable and might result in a bungled or unfinished job. Furthermore, in issuing an instruction the supervisor should consider store rules, equipment, and other aspects of the operating situation that might influence the employee's ability to comply with reasonable effort.

EXPLAINING WHY   Many good supervisors explain why a particular order is being given. This is good for morale because it gives the subordinate a little more sense of personal importance. He or she may be able to carry out the instruction better since its relation to wider activity is clear. Especially when the subordinate can exercise some initiative in carrying out the order, understanding why it was given may be important in the interpretation. For example, the instruction to change the front display may be made more effective when the reason for it is given: "This new shipment of blouses is being advertised in tonight's paper, so we should give them a good display, with a mannequin and an 'It's New!' sign." Such an explanation will make it easier for the subordinate to implement the instruction at the same time that it offers the subordinate an opportunity to participate in planning the display.

Participative Directing Versus Autocratic Directing

Directing can have two extremes. In *participative directing,* the supervisor consults the people responsible for executing a task about its workability and better ways of accomplishing the same results. In other words, the subordinates participate in the decision. For example, the buyer may call his assistant buyer and senior salespeople together, bringing to their attention a slow-selling category of goods. He may then ask for suggestions for increasing sales or getting rid of the goods. Out of this discussion may come recommendations for promoting the goods through suggestive selling, an improved display, a price reduction, or a change in counter location. Some of these may be ideas the buyer had not thought of.

Autocratic directing is simply issuing orders without any input from subordinates. For example, the buyer in the above situation might have a departmental meeting and tell the salespeople: "These bedspreads are not selling. We will mark them down 25 percent, and then I want everyone here to make a real effort to sell one bedspread a day until they're all gone."

BENEFITS OF PARTICIPATIVE DIRECTING   One benefit of employee participation is obvious: greater cooperation and enthusiasm for work. A person will work a lot harder for a plan to which he or she has contributed. Sometimes employees can point out practical difficulties in a plan and suggest alterations. An innovative idea may evolve. The work environment becomes harmonious; the executive can be more a coordinator of ideas than a boss. Such an environment tends to be conducive to the personal development of subordinates. They begin to generate ideas and develop judgment, and they are motivated to seek more responsibilities. This is especially desirable for management development: a trainee who is exposed to participation will learn more quickly than one who is ordered about autocratically.

DANGERS OF PARTICIPATIVE DIRECTING   Participation should not always be invited, even if the executive prefers this management technique. Consulting with subordinates is often impractical, especially about little things or when action has to be taken quickly. The caliber of the work force may weigh against inviting participation, or if most of the employees are new and untrained, if they lack interest, or if they are not very competent. An employee participating in a plan may feel free to change it later, without consulting the supervisor. Furthermore, there is some possibility that the instructions finally coming out of extended group participation will be fuzzy, rather than complete and clear.

Most of these dangers can be avoided or minimized if the supervisor is careful about inviting employee participation. The young supervisor can look for opportunities to use this management technique and to experiment with it. It can be used with one subordinate or with a whole group, depending on the situation.

The matrix in Figure 10.1 depicts the two major factors that should bear on the amount of participation invited by a supervisor: the caliber of the employees involved, and the deliberation possible, or the urgency of the particular decision being considered. The higher the caliber of subordinates, the more effective participation may be; the more urgent the decision, the less time will be available for participative discussion and consensus.

FIGURE 10.1 MATRIX OF PARTICIPATIVE POSSIBILITIES

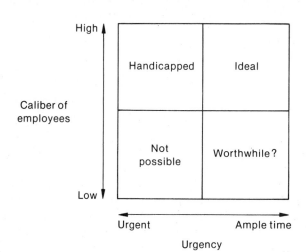

Motivating

Motivation refers to how strongly an individual wants to do a job well. This is a murky area of human relations and supervision. It varies greatly with individuals. Some people may be motivated with little or no outside stimulus: they are "self-starters." Other persons may be motivated by certain job-related factors, such as compensation, working conditions, an understanding supervisor, status, or even harsh criticism.

A supervisor should be keenly interested in motivating employees, since their efforts affect the productivity of the department or store very much. Different supervisory techniques may be called for with different employees. One employee might perform best under the critical eye of the boss, while another might resent close supervision or be so upset by it that efficiency would suffer.

Usually, a manager has limited influence on individual motivations; but employee dissatisfaction or negativism can be corrected. For example, a supervisor may recognize that a different compensation plan— one offering more potential income to salespeople through commissions—would act as a strong motivator. Yet store policies may prevent any change in the method of compensation. However, perhaps working conditions could be improved, even if only by adding an extra table for wrapping or an improved tape dispenser.

In other areas of the job environment the supervisor has more control and can stimulate employees to greater efforts.

BUILDING EMPLOYEE SELF-ESTEEM   As we noted, permitting subordinates to participate in some planning and decisions can be an effective motivator. Many other little things can be done to make the work environment more attractive by enhancing a worker's self-esteem. For example, an executive can contribute to an individual's stature in the eyes of associates. Public recognition of good accomplishments and explanations to other people of the importance of a person's job are two instances. A supervisor can motivate at least some workers by counseling and encouraging them to take on new, challenging responsibilities. Some people are eager to take on more responsibilities to prove themselves. The supervisor who is quick to delegate new tasks and responsibilities to such people is not only advancing their training, but also enhancing their self-esteem and making the supervisory job easier at the same time.

PROVIDING SECURITY   We are not talking here about old age benefits, but about building a work environment in which uncertainty is reduced. Uncertainty breeds feelings of insecurity. Yet, change is inevitable today—change in executives, in methods of operation, and in many other features of the work situation. All sorts of rumors and uneasiness are spread in many organizations by the grapevine, or informal communication channels. The supervisor can remove most of this source of insecurity by sharing all information with subordinates. This means telling them as far in advance as possible about any changes that will affect them. An even more positive approach is to share information about current problems and future plans with subordinates, even when these do not directly affect them. Such information puts them in the comfortable position of knowing what to expect and why. Two-way personal communication not only builds morale, but may also give the supervisor a better grasp of a situation through feedback from employees.

JUST AND EMPATHETIC SUPERVISION   *Empathy* is putting oneself in another person's position to see and feel from that person's viewpoint his or her feelings about the job, hopes and aspirations, and worries and problems. Just supervision suggests consistency and fairness. These ingredients in effective supervision can have a powerful effect on the loyalty of employees and the motivation they bring to their jobs.

EFFECTIVE SUPERVISORY ACTIONS—Supporting Subordinates

Supervisors should support their people, should represent their needs outside the department, and should back them up. This might mean vigorously seeking every salary increase an employee deserves, pushing for better working conditions, negotiating frictions with other departments. Able trainees should be pointed out to superiors and their promotability emphasized. The supervisor should be willing to take the blame for subordinates' mistakes (rather than passing the buck); after all, the supervisor is responsible for what happens in his or her area, and sufficient training or follow-up might have prevented the mistake.

For Thought and Discussion

1. Sometimes a supervisor won't want to accept responsibility for the carelessness or ineptness of certain subordinates. "I cannot be everywhere at once," such a supervisor may complain. How would you answer this assistant manager of yours?
2. "I do not want to lose my top producer. Therefore, I'm not going to recommend her promotion." Evaluate this statement.

A feeling that the boss plays favorites can undermine motivation and harmony. A common complaint is, "He (some other employee) gets all the soft assignments." It is not always easy to determine just what is fair. Equal treatment is not really the answer, since employees differ in length of service, abilities, age, and strength. Fairness may actually require giving special treatment to those employees with long service or poor health.

INCENTIVE ACTIVITIES   Many types of *incentives* have proven useful in motivating employees, especially those in the sales force. Some firms use sales contests, meetings, and special awards and recognition. But even nonselling employees can be motivated by specially designed incentive programs.

Contests   Essentially competitions with rewards given to the winning participants, contests are most appropriately used for a limited time to accomplish one or a few specific, short-run objectives. Money may be awarded, but other kinds of awards, such as a day off, or a trip, can be just as effective.

An important ingredient in contest planning is the objective: What is the contest's purpose to be? Some objectives might be to generate more sales, to build better displays, to promote special items (sometimes this can be before-season goods, such as a July Blanket Event), to introduce a new product or line, or perhaps to clear out slow-moving goods? These, of course, are selling objectives. Nonselling objectives might be a higher ratio of goods processed to labor hours, faster wrapping time at the gift-wrapping department, fewer errors in processing customer accounts.

The theme, rules, length, and prizes of the contest need to be determined. Above all a contest should generate excitement. If it does not, the effort is probably wasted. Excitement can come in many ways. If supervisors are enthusiastic, this tends to be contagious. Constant feedback and exhortations also help. For example, one store, in a July Blanket Event, organized its employees into teams. A loud bell was rung every time a blanket was sold, and "thermometers" were displayed showing how the various teams were doing in their selling efforts.

While the bell ringing might have disturbed customers, it certainly made the contest attract attention. The variety of possibilities for contests is limited only by the imagination of the supervisor and subordinates. But several dangers should be noted.

The first applies mainly to sales contests. Overselling and high-pressure tactics may antagonize customers. Aggressive selling efforts during a contest may result in less than normal business after it ends, perhaps because of a psychological letdown or overstocking customers in order to get contest credit. The latter is known as "borrowed business"; that is, it is borrowed from future sales.

The second danger is inherent in any contest: not everyone can win. While the winner's morale may be boosted, losers may feel less motivated than before the contest. In planning a contest, efforts should be made to assure that all participants have a reasonably good chance of winning a prize. If the same persons win repeatedly, you can see that the requirements need to be changed or the contest idea itself discarded.

Contests should never be substituted for good compensation plans or adequate working conditions. But when they add a little extra "pizzazz" to the work environment, they can be an effective motivational device.

Meetings Many stores and departments have periodic meetings for their employees. Meetings can inform employees about new policies or new merchandise; they can be used to correct certain deficiencies, such as carelessness in handling charge sales; and they can generate fresh enthusiasm. At the very least, all meetings should provide better communication and thereby increase job involvement.

Too often, meetings are routine, uninteresting, uninspiring. Some executives conduct more stimulating meetings than others (just as some professors conduct more stimulating classes). But many managers do not fully recognize the possibilities for using meetings for training, motivating, and even inspiring employees.

Planning is important for effective meetings. They should be designed to accomplish one or more specific purposes. Managers should think carefully about when to hold meetings, rather than simply following custom. Many stores have habitual Saturday meetings before opening whether there is anything worth communicating or not. If possible, meetings should include programs that involve participation of employees and, occasionally, even outside participants.

Recognition This is such an easy way to motivate employees: simply give them formal and public recognition when they are doing a good job. Recognizing a job well done builds an employee's self-esteem and is a good supervisory approach. For nonretail salespeople formal recognition is rather widely practiced. For example, some firms have "sales achievement clubs" that award certificates and publish names on a special roster. Newspapers and magazines often publish the names and pictures of insurance companies' "million dollar club" members, those agents who have sold a million dollars' worth of insurance. Some realtors also give such public recognition to their outstanding agents. But retailers have not generally used this method of motivation. The following are a few possibilities for giving formal recognition to outstanding retail employees, both selling and nonselling:

Publishing articles with pictures of top performers in the store's house organ

A personal letter from the store's general manager or merchandise manager

Inscription of names on prominently displayed plaques

Special congratulatory parties, or recognition during a Christmas program or other party

Recognition can take many forms, some material, such as medals and certificates, others intangible, such as a personal greeting from a top executive. The costs of such recognition are slight, while the benefits in stimulating employees can be significant.

Following up

Unless a supervisor checks up on the way instructions are being followed, the end result may be different from what was expected; both the manager and the employee may be embarrassed, or worse. *Following up* simply means checking to assure that everything is proceeding well and on schedule, and that no problems are unresolved. It is a naive supervisor who issues instructions to an untried employee and makes the assumption that, without some checking, everything will be done as ordered.

Follow-up need not be a negative reflection on the employee. Sometimes instructions are misunderstood or misinterpreted. Often the priorities of an order are not made clear, so that a particular assignment is put aside until later. For the new or relatively untrained employee, some follow-up and consequent support or assistance may be indispensable to the successful accomplishment of the assignment. Furthermore, the wise supervisor who trains employees to ask questions if they do not understand an instruction can prevent much wasted effort.

HOW CLOSELY TO SUPERVISE?   Close supervision implies constant follow-up. The manager continually observes and makes suggestions to the worker. Various derogatory phrases describe such close supervision: "back-seat driver," "nit picking," "always needling." Yet, with some employees and some situations, close supervision is necessary. At other times such close follow-up is not in the best interests of a smooth-running organization.

Closeness of supervision or constancy of follow-up may be depicted as shown in Table 10.1. Generally, most supervision falls somewhere between the extremes described; otherwise, either worker frustration or anarchy would reign in many organizations.

It is well to note, however, that different conditions (worker charac-

TABLE 10.1   FACTORS AFFECTING CLOSENESS OF SUPERVISION

	Degree of Supervision	
	Minimum Supervision (no follow-up)	Maximum Supervision (constant follow-up)
May be described as	Hands off	Always needling
Best used when		
Workers are	Experienced and reliable	New; untrained; or poorly motivated
Situation is	Familiar; relatively routine; of moderate importance	Unfamiliar; the stakes are high

teristics or the nature of the situation) affect the closeness of supervision required to do an effective job. The good manager will vary the follow-up, and tailor it to the situation and the worker. During a training period close supervision is normally expected. But for an experienced worker such close supervision would probably be insulting. A particular job that involves high stakes generally requires constant follow-up, even with experienced subordinates. Sometimes the high stakes may be a junior executive's worth as perceived by higher management.

ROLE PLAY—Supervisory Dilemma: Closeness of Supervision

Assume the role of assistant buyer for the bedding department of a medium-sized department store. Your experience qualifies you for promotion either to assistant buyer of a major department or to buyer of a small department.

The scene is early afternoon. You are supervising the finishing stages of a display for a new line of bedspreads. The general-merchandise manager has the habit of strolling through the store on his way to and from lunch. On this occasion he approaches you with rather a quizzical look and asks you why the stock of sheets displayed on a main-aisle counter is so low.

For Thought and Discussion

1. How would you answer this question?
2. What action would you take at this point?

NEED TO RESCIND INSTRUCTIONS   In the process of following up an order, the manager sometimes finds that its execution is no longer necessary, or even desirable. Perhaps some other action deserves higher priority. Or perhaps the order was a mistake. Therefore, the original order needs to be rescinded or countermanded. And here it is best to explain why.

The junior executive, and even the senior one, may be reluctant to admit a mistake. Admission may be seen as an embarrassing loss of face. Thus the temptation is to not rescind the order, but also to not follow up to see that it is done. Such inconsistent follow-up tends to undermine future orders. And the supervisor is more likely to inspire confidence by admitting a mistake, just like everyone else.

PROBLEMS IN SUPERVISING

Problems encountered in supervising can be broadly placed into two major categories: (1) handling grievances, and (2) disciplining. Both can be solved in a positive manner that may even strengthen harmony and morale. On the other hand, ignoring or clumsily handling these problems can easily lead to more serious ones. If the firm is unionized, the result may even be a walkout.

Grievances

Grievances usually are minor. Yet if they are not handled carefully—and promptly—they can fester and become serious. A rough corner of a counter that snags stockings, a small error in tabulating time-clock hours, frequently running out of paper towels in employee restrooms, lost telephone messages—these are examples of minor grievances that can easily be corrected. *But they require some supervisory attention if they are to be corrected.*

Another category of grievances involves relations among fellow workers. The retail selling situation often stimulates petty bickering, jealousy, and sometimes more serious hostilities. This is especially true if an incentive commission or bonus arrangement is used to reward higher sales production. Certain complaints are common.

ROLE PLAY—Supervisory Problem: Handling Employee Gripes

Assume the role of assistant department manager for a dress department. You have recently been promoted to this job from a trainee position in the hosiery department.

It took only a few days for you to be confronted with the following complaints:

"_____ is always grabbing the best sales prospects."

"_____ refuses to handle exchanges or refunds, but always waits for someone else to do it."

"_____ stole my customer when she came back, after I had spent a half an hour with her."

"_____ doesn't do her share of housecleaning and stock work."

For Thought and Discussion

1. What would you do at this point?
2. How could you maintain more equitable employee relations?

Sometimes such complaints have little foundation, but they may be legitimate, and supervisory action then needs to be taken. If hostility cannot be soothed, rescheduling hours, or transfers to separate departments may be the only satisfactory solutions. But some action, or at least further investigation, usually is required.

A set of rules for handling human relations problems follows:

1. Get the facts.
2. Weigh the validity of the grievance, as well as the seriousness of it, and any extenuating circumstances.
3. Take action to correct or ameliorate the situation.
4. Follow up to assure that the problem has been corrected in the way most satisfactory for the organization.

As mentioned earlier in this chapter, the manager should be careful not to play favorites. Some employees suspect favoritism even when it does not exist. As a rule, workers at the same level and with approximately the same length of service should be treated similarly. But a senior employee can be given some preferential treatment, such as first choice of working hours, vacation time, lunch periods, and the like.

Some grievances are major. These often involve a subordinate's feeling that he or she has been mistreated, especially by the boss. When there is a simple misunderstanding, a quiet talk may soothe the situation. But sometimes things cannot be so easily settled; perhaps there was disciplinary action that the worker considered unfair or unwarranted.

With unions, a formal grievance procedure usually exists. In firms with no such formal procedure, an employee should be able to bypass the immediate boss and appeal to a personnel department representative. Sometimes managers abuse their power or see a problem from too close a perspective. The supervisor should not resent such an appealed grievance, but rather should recognize that he or she might be wrong. Morale is less likely to suffer if a supervisor is clearly anxious to arrive at a fair settlement.

Disciplining

Disciplining is one of the more unpleasant aspects of a supervisor's job. Carelessness, insubordination, lack of cooperation, disregard of instructions, and out-and-out theft all require action by the manager. Not disciplining an employee when the standard of performance or behavior falls below an acceptable level encourages a poor attitude not only on the part of the offending employee, but also from employees who see one of their colleagues getting away with something. A general deterioration of productivity can result.

The other extreme is also bad. Discipline can be too severe. It can be administered harshly without consideration of circumstances, although it is doubtful that many workers today would tolerate such a situation. Sometimes, however, an executive who is dependent on a superior for promotion may be forced to accept less-than-desirable treatment.

Reprimands, demotions, temporary layoffs, withheld promotions or raises, poor evaluation reports, and outright discharges are penalties that can be imposed. *Discipline* can vary from the minor—a quiet reprimand—to the most drastic—disrupting a subordinate's career advancement by a poor evaluation report, vetoing a promotion, or even firing.

Two conditions of good discipline should be noted. First, it should *not* be used as punishment. Less than optimal behavior on the job is not reason for punishing. Second, the purpose of disciplinary action should be solely to improve future behavior. This future behavior, however, may not be limited solely to the employee being disciplined. The rest of the work force will be influenced by the promptness and type of disciplinary action imposed on one of its members. Sometimes it is desirable to work with the personnel department on a recurring discipline problem, such as excessive absenteeism or tardiness. Personnel has the time and resources for getting to the root of such problems, while the department manager may not.

GUIDES FOR DISCIPLINING   Several general principles for effective disciplining are rather obvious, though not always practiced. These principles simply bring to the situation some good human relations practices.

1. Disciplining should be done in private.   This applies whether a simple reprimand is to be given or more drastic action is to be taken. Privacy not only saves the subordinate from acute embarrassment, but also gives him or her the opportunity to defend the conduct in question. There may be reasons that excuse the employee's actions. Yet this principle of good supervision is often violated. When a salesclerk or other employee is reprimanded in the presence of a customer, the effect on morale will obviously be detrimental.

2. Misconduct should receive prompt, objective attention.   Action should be taken when facts are fresh in mind. To wait until details are half forgotten destroys the effectiveness of discipline and may result in undue resentment. For example, if an employee frequently takes too long a rest break, the reprimand should come shortly after an occurrence of this, and not some time later, perhaps in conjunction with discipline for another type of misconduct. A caution should be noted here, however. Discipline should be objective. A supervisor should not act when angry or emotionally upset. It may be necessary to delay until everyone has had time to cool down. Perhaps additional facts need to be gathered in order to make a wise disciplinary decision.

3. Warn before acting.   Except in cases of serious misconduct, such as dishonesty or rudeness to customers and fellow workers, an employee should not be reprimanded for something he or she did not realize was wrong or did not understand the importance of. This suggests that a person should be formally warned for a first offense and disciplined only if the action is repeated. It also suggests that the manager has some responsibility to keep subordinates informed of certain rules for which disciplinary action may be taken. For example, many stores have a regulation against employees having personal packages and handbags under the counter (because of possible theft). Certainly any discipline toward a new employee who was unaware of this regulation would be unjust.

4. Disciplining should be consistent and fair.   Nothing is more destructive of morale than for one member of the group to be allowed to get away with something for which others are punished. A common example is the time allowed for lunch. If some employees are allowed to abuse this by staying longer than the prescribed time, then consistency is lost. However, discipline should not be harsh and unbending. Sometimes exceptions have to be made and rules bent a little. The inexperienced worker may deserve a different action than the experienced. Special problems at home may force one employee to arrive late sometimes, and disciplinary consistency may have to be sacrificed. To avoid having such exceptions interpreted as favoritism, the reasons for any exceptions should be made known.

■ Summary

People management is part of the function of every manager. Sometimes, for instance when confronted with seemingly more-vital and less-routine merchandising decisions, the retail executive may take for granted day-to-day people management. Yet supervisory skills are an important part of a manager's effectiveness.

For lower-level executives, people management concerns rank and file employees. As a person progresses up the executive ladder, supervision of other executives replaces this. But the same principles of planning, directing, motivating, following up, and disciplining still apply. And success at all levels depends on working through people to achieve desired objectives.

■ Key Terms

Autocratic directing	Grievances
Directing	Incentives
Discipline	Motivation
Empathy	Participative directing
Following up	Planning

■ Discussion Questions

1. Why is planning work assignments so important in retailing?
2. "I do not have time to explain *why* something should be done. My time is too valuable for this, and my workers wouldn't understand anyway." Comment on this statement.
3. What might you do to better assure that your orders are understood?
4. When would you follow up on your orders and instructions?
5. As the manager of a medium-sized Penney store, would you use autocratic or participative directing upon learning that the zone manager would be visiting your store tomorrow? Why?
6. As the new buyer of a women's sportswear department, you have a chance to buy a line of matching ensembles (slacks, shorts, and tops) at close-out prices for immediate delivery. Would you favor autocratic or participative decision making? Why?

■ Project

Look up several books on supervision, *or* talk to several managers, and see how many principles of supervision you can find. Critically evaluate these principles and give reasons why you think any of them may be flawed.

■ **Exercise in Creativity**

You believe that the morale and enthusiasm of your salesforce, and
consequently sales, would be improved by a sales contest. What are
some ideas for such a contest that might be both practical and effective?

■ **Retailing in Action: Role Plays**

1. As a new department manager you observe that most of your
   younger part-time salespeople are vigorous gum chewers. You feel
   this is annoying to customers. Would you take any action to prevent
   or minimize this? If so, how would you do it without creating
   employee ill will?

2. As the assistant manager of a variety store, you learn from several
   employees and even a customer that one of your young salespeople
   has noticeable body odor. How would you handle this situation?
   Would your approach to the problem be different if the employee
   were a long-time employee of the store?

3. You have heard rumors that some of your employees are talking
   with other employees about starting a union. How would you react
   to this? Would you attempt to do anything to stop such efforts?

4. As a department manager you have been ordered by your superiors
   to increase the productivity of your salesforce. This may mean that
   some salesclerks will either have to be laid off or have their hours
   reduced. Of course, if sales could be increased, productivity would
   also be increased. You have called a meeting for Saturday morning
   before the store opens to inform your people of this. How would
   you handle the situation? What would you say?

Cases for Part Three

STACEY GOMEZ—Problems with Subordinates

Stacey Gomez had graduated from a small liberal arts college with a degree in economics. She had, though, taken as many retailing courses as were offered, since retailing had always intrigued her and she knew for certain that opportunities for women in retailing were perhaps better than in any other field of business. After graduating, she had no difficulty being accepted to the executive-training program of a major department store in a West Coast city. And she had progressed quite satisfactorily, she thought: she had been promoted to head of stock after several weeks and then, just last week, to assistant buyer. But that had brought out a problem that was giving her real difficulty and undermining her self-confidence.

She had been transferred into the women's sportswear department—a large, important department, to be sure. The trouble was that the salesladies had all been with the store for years, and were almost contemptuous of a new, young assistant buyer. Only yesterday, Stacey reflected, she had been ordered by Mrs. Robinsky, the buyer, to have a certain display changed.

"Sara, would you change this display to those new College Town dresses that we've just received, as soon as you can?" Stacey had courteously asked one of the senior salesladies.

The response shook her, to say the least: "Dearie, I'm here to sell—and I'm very good at it. I'm not going to sacrifice my commission by working on a display."

"But . . . Mrs. Robinsky wants it done as soon as possible," Stacey had stammered.

"Then you'll have to do it yourself," Sara challenged. "I'm not going to do it . . . unless Mrs. Robinsky specifically directs me too."

Stacey heard herself responding, "This is an order!" as the older saleslady stalked defiantly away.

Questions

1. How should Stacey have handled this situation?
2. Does this example reflect negatively on her leadership and managerial ability?

JIM RENFREW—*How Can We Improve the Caliber of Our Employees?*

"Something must be done about improving the caliber of our employees," Jim Renfrew, merchandise manager for DuPrew's, a discount chain of some twenty stores in the Southeast, was complaining to Jessica Reinhard, the personnel director.

"We've had problems recruiting high-level people," Jessica admitted. "It seems that not very many people want to work for a discount store, especially one that is local in scope and doesn't have a national reputation like K mart or Woolco."

"Is our pay scale out of line with that of other retailers?"

"That of our regular employees is fully as high as that of other stores in the respective communities; sometimes we've even gone a little higher. As you know, our store managers don't have the authority or responsibility that some other chains give to theirs, as we have a high degree of centralization at headquarters here. Consequently, we haven't been paying our store managers nearly as much as, say, K mart. On the other hand, our managers don't have to wait seven to ten years before getting a store to manage. Are you concerned with the caliber of our managers, too?"

Jim shuffled some papers on his desk and pulled one out. He pushed it across to Jessica. "Look at these data, Jessica, regarding some of the latest store inspections by headquarters' execs. Our managers have little to do but supervise their employees so as to run a clean and orderly store. Yet more than half of these inspections report stores being dirty, bins and displays empty or else so jumbled that customers couldn't find anything even if they tried, merchandise off sale that's languishing in the stockroom—all in all, we're seeing lousy managing. Sure, some of the fault lies with the employees, but our managers seem to be even more culpable for letting them get away with it."

In spite of himself, Jim heard his voice rising. He took a deep breath. "Jessica, I don't know what to do about the situation. I hope maybe you can come up with some ideas. How can we improve the caliber of both our regular employees and our managerial personnel? There must be some way we can overcome the handicap of a poor image when it comes to recruiting people."

"One solution that comes to mind, Jim," Jessica said quietly, "is simply to raise our wages, for both management and nonmanagement people."

Jim sighed. "I don't think we can consider that—not at this time, at least—without driving our profit picture completely out of line."

"Well, then," Jessica pursued, "I think the problem boils down, first, to how to recruit better people—and to do this we need to make our company appear to be a better place to work than it presently seems to most people—and, second, to how to better motivate our present employees and managers."

"That sounds like a good analysis, Jessica. I think you're on the right track.

Could you do some more analysis—maybe get together with some of your people and perhaps some of our better management people, as well—and come up with some creative solutions for these twin problems? And the situation is rather urgent. Could you present these recommendations to me within ten days?"

Questions

1. What recommendations do you have for attacking these identified twin problems? Be as specific and also as creative as possible.
2. Do you think Jessica has correctly identified the problems, or are there others that, perhaps, she overlooked?
3. Do you really think it is possible for a discount chain to attract as high a level of management and nonmanagement people as a prestige department store? If not, what are the probable consequences?

4

Merchandise Management

11 Assortment Planning

There has long been a saying that to be a successful merchandiser one must have *the five rights:*

Have the right merchandise.
Have it in the right place.
Have it at the right time.
Have it in the right quantity.
Have it at the right price.

Of course, such a guide is too simple to be of much help in merchandise planning. It is well and good to maintain that we need the right merchandise and so forth, but when it comes to translating this goal into practical reality, the task becomes more difficult. Who is to say what is the right merchandise, what is the best price, or what is the optimal quantity, especially in advance of the season, before customer demand can be tested? At best, such a "formula" represents part of the challenge of merchandising and retailing: it offers a goal to seek, but a goal not likely to be achieved, except by accident and luck. However, we can examine ways to try to improve our efforts. And in this chapter, we will consider how to seek the right merchandise.

THE TARGET MARKET

In Chapter 5, it was noted that a retailer should consider who the desired customers are—the target market for the store's efforts. Merchandising, promotional, and other policies should then be geared to wooing this target market. Furthermore, these policies should be compatible with the image a firm is attempting to create.

Merchandise quality and prices are vital ingredients in appealing to a particular category of customer. Sometimes merchandise is chosen without regard to a unifying image. Such hit-and-miss merchandising may result in tying up funds in slow-moving goods with no customer appeal.

Retailing errors in efforts to attract target customers frequently come about from a lack of consistency in merchandise planning among the various departments and merchandise categories. For example, high-priced, famous-brand men's shirts would be wrong for a store attempting to attract a working-class clientele by emphasizing lowest prices. Admittedly, consumers themselves may show inconsistency in shopping behavior: the wealthy suburbanite quibbles over the price of men's underwear; or the blue-collar laborer insists on the highest-quality fishing gear. But for best results, merchandise should be consistent in quality and price levels throughout the store. And assortments should be carefully planned with this in mind.

RETAILING STRATEGY—*Trading Up*

Some major retailers have begun to take fresh looks at their merchandising policies, store images, and target customers. Some have decided to change their traditional appeals, which were primarily to economy-minded and, thus, often lower-income consumers.

Several major stores have adopted the policy called *trading up*. Macy's found itself squeezed by no-frills discounters on the one hand, and fashion-oriented retailers like Federated, Bloomingdale's, and Abraham and Straus units on the other hand; Macy's overhauled its merchandising and buying practices to become more of a medium-price fashion store. Filene's in Boston did likewise; the downtown store received a massive facelift to brighten and modernize its dour appearance, and suburban expansion also emphasized a changed format. The May Company, a giant St. Louis–based department-store chain, has also been steadily upgrading the more profitable, so-called discretionary merchandise: fashion accessories, ready-to-wear, men's and boy's wear, and home furnishings.

And now the J. C. Penney Company, the nation's third largest retailer with 1977 sales of $9 billion, has joined the trading-up crowd. With a multimillion-dollar budget for remodeling and a massive increase in advertising, Penney is attempting to make a complete break with its image as a private-label seller of mostly soft goods to price-conscious customers. It wants to transform itself into a chain of moderate-price department stores with an emphasis on brand-name goods, and especially higher-fashion women's apparel. Penney is betting that it can successfully trade up both its image and its prices.

Penney is also gambling that it will be more successful in doing this than Sears was. Sears attempted to upgrade its image—and its profit margins—in 1974–1975, only to see earnings tumble 28 percent as its traditional, price-conscious customers became disillusioned by the emphasis on higher prices. Sears soon abandoned its attempt to trade up.

Comments   Trading up, as seen from these examples, has involved three major focuses: (1) greater emphasis on fashion merchandising; (2) carrying higher-price items in nonfashion departments; and (3) rejuvenating physical facilities. These are not easy or inexpensive changes to make; they involve costly expenditures and major organizational changes. But some retailers have deemed this to be necessary.

Sources: For more information on Penney's policy changes, see "J. C. Penney's Fashion Gamble," *Business Week,* January 16, 1978, pp. 66–74. For more detail on Sears' retreat back to traditional policies, see "At the Top of the Tower," *Time,* November 21, 1977, p. 80.

For Thought and Discussion

1. Do these stores have to abandon their lower-income clientele to make these changes? How could they keep these customers?

2. Do you think such drastic changes in retailing strategy are wise in a time of inflation and diminishing purchasing power?

ANALYZING DEMAND

Retailers are purchasing agents for their customers. The goods they buy for resale reflect their judgment of what their customers will be most interested in. Such judgment about the market may come from hunch and intuition, perhaps as the result of long experience. But generally, a more systematic and objective study of market (customer) demand is desirable. This is true even for the veteran merchant who has developed almost an instinct for what will sell. Conditions change, and old preferences may be those of an ever-smaller segment of the potential market.

Certain sources of market information are available to all retailers. While these must be translated into practical merchandise requirements, they can at least guide the buyer in planning assortments.

Internal Sources of Market and Merchandise Information

A merchant who wishes to keep attuned to the target market and its changing preferences can find a number of sensors or feedback devices. The major internal, or store, sources available to any retailer may be categorized as follows:

Past sales
Want slips and books
Comparison shopping
Customer panels
Miscellaneous

We will discuss each of these in more detail. It is well to note that the merchandiser must make some conscious effort to develop each as an information source.

PAST SALES   Past sales of various items and categories of goods can serve as the single most important source of market information. Past sales provide evidence of what sizes, styles, and colors of goods are meeting with customer acceptance. This information is especially valuable for *staple goods,* those necessities that are little affected by changes in style preferences (examples of staple goods are men's underwear, thread, hardware items, and many food products). *Fashion goods,* on the other hand, have some style distinctiveness that customers see as relatively important; since this is a fleeting thing, especially for many styles of clothing, past sales may not serve as an accurate gauge of future demand.

For past sales data to be usable, it must be maintained according to a fairly detailed breakdown. For example, if a firm is trying to ascertain the probable market for thread, it must know more than how many total spools of thread were ordered and sold in preceding periods. It must know how much of each of the various colors and gauges was sold.

For fashion goods, repeat sales are less likely. But within certain merchandise classifications, there may be some indication of probable total demand in the next selling period. For example, styles of women's blouses may vary considerably from one season to another, but past sales data may help in planning by price lines, sizes, and perhaps by tailored, sporty, and dressy styles.

Some retailers conduct what is known as a *style-out* for the merchandise categories that are influenced by changing customer demand and style popularity. In a style-out, the merchandiser compares goods currently selling well and ascertains customer-attracting features.

ROLE PLAY—A Style-out

Assume the role of assistant buyer for a blouse department. You have been asked to participate in an interdepartmental style-out. The time is late winter. The objective is to analyze early trends so as to have better buying information for major spring purchases.

You pull the sales records of the early sample shipments that have been received. Then you examine the goods themselves. You notice that some of the better-selling numbers are rather loose fitting with a belted back. You also notice that the color lemon accounts for more early sales than other colors; in fact, the stock of lemon blouses is now broken in size.

You present this information at the style-out. Several other buyers and assistants have rather similar findings. The assistant buyer of junior dresses in particular has corroborating information: in her department belted backs and lemon colors are leading the way in early sales.

For Thought and Discussion

1. Would you be willing to make buying commitments for major spring purchases based on such early information?
2. What risks do you see in doing so?
3. Are there any risks in waiting for more demand information?
4. What other sources might contribute to your decision?

WANT SLIPS *Want slips* may be used in keeping abreast of changing customer wants and also of deficiencies or out-of-stocks in present offerings. A want slip is simply a systematic recording by salespeople of customer requests for merchandise that the department is unable to supply. A want slip can be as simple as a blank sheet of paper filled out with pertinent information about the product requested, or it can be a more complex form. If want slips are to be effective, salespeople must be motivated to fill them out and forward them to the executives who can act on the information, usually the buyers and merchandise managers. Want slips can be a valuable source of market feedback, or they can be worthless. Effectiveness depends on how well department executives encourage and follow up on their use by salespeople.

COMPARISON SHOPPING The successful merchant at any level in an organization is usually a keen student of what other stores are doing. New merchandise and its observed customer acceptance are noted with particular interest.

Large stores may have separate staff departments that continuously monitor competing stores and forward their findings to various executives. These departments may be called *comparison-shopping* or service-shopping departments. Their function is to systematically provide data that might be only sporadically gained otherwise. In addition, they usually investigate customer complaints regarding service, merchandise, and prices of the store in relation to its competitors.

CUSTOMER PANELS Large retailers sometimes use *customer panels* or advisory committees to gain input about new product decisions or emerging style preferences. These panels are small groups of consumers who may represent a cross section of the store's customers or of those interested in the particular merchandise categories under consideration. College advisory boards and teen-age boards have been employed. Members not only offer opinions on goods with selling potential among their peers, but also may do sales promotion work at their schools.

MISCELLANEOUS Less formal sources of information are talking with customers, observing what displays and merchandise seem to interest them, and encouraging salespeople to relay customer comments. Traditionally, many retailers insist that management people—from buyers to presidents—spend some time on the sales floor observing, talking with customers, and even selling. As firms have become larger, and as buyers have been given responsibility for providing for branch stores in addition to the main store, such face-to-face contact with customers has often been abandoned.

External Sources of Market and Merchandise Information

In addition to internal sources for market information, a broader perspective can be gained from external sources, such as the following:

Vendors
Trade publications
Noncompeting stores
Resident buying offices
Miscellaneous

External sources are particularly helpful for making decisions on fashion merchandise. Formerly, styles achieved popularity in New York City or on the West Coast and took months, or even years to spread through the rest of the country. Now, the mass media rapidly disseminates new styles and modes of living. The alert merchant must keep abreast of happenings in other stores and other parts of the country.

VENDORS Sales representatives and suppliers can provide helpful knowledge about what styles and colors are selling best. Relying on the information and advice of vendors may be viewed as dangerous by some retail buyers. They reason that vendors are interested in serving their own needs first. A vendor who has heavy slow-selling stock may be tempted to try to push it off on an unsuspecting buyer. But retailer-supplier relationships thrive on repeat business, and repeat business is built up on mutual trust. It is a shortsighted vendor indeed who would jeopardize a good relationship by supplying misleading information.

TRADE PUBLICATIONS There are numerous trade journals for almost any product line or type of business a retailer may be in. Information on new products and styles, examples of successful operations, current developments, and general price and supply conditions are among many relevant topics discussed in these publications. Some of the well-known retailing publications are:

American Druggist	*Daily News Record* (men's wear)
Chain Store Age	*Discount Merchandiser*

Department Store Management
Drug Topics
Footwear News
Hardware Age
Hardware Retailer
Home Furnishings Daily
Jewelers' Circular
Men's Wear

Merchandising Week
    (electrical appliances)
Modern Retailer
    (discount stores)
Progressive Grocer
Stores
Supermarket News
Women's Wear Daily

Observing the styles and advertising in such consumer magazines as *Vogue, Mademoiselle, Seventeen,* and *Good Housekeeping* can also be helpful in assessing emerging trends. Even *Family Circle* and *Women's Day,* sold almost entirely in supermarkets, should not be disregarded.

NONCOMPETING STORES   Stores in a chain or members of a trade association or buying group often relay experiences with new merchandise and styles to other stores. Certain retailers tend to be style leaders; this is particularly true in New York City, where ideas and styles are often introduced first. Many ideas about products and styles, displays, and operating methods can be gained by visiting other stores, perhaps while on buying trips or attending trade shows and conventions.

RESIDENT BUYING OFFICES   Most of the country's department and specialty stores use *resident buying offices* as a major source of merchandise information. These offices are located in the major wholesale markets; most, of course, are in New York City, since this is the center of the garment industry and many other merchandise categories. Resident buying offices are able to check the pulse of the market and keep abreast of new products and styles being introduced and new sources of merchandise. They serve as a vital communication center for their far-flung retail store affiliates. Also, they perform a necessary screening function for retail buyers coming to market. We will discuss resident offices in more detail in the next chapter.

MISCELLANEOUS   Trade or merchandise shows for certain categories of goods, such as toys, hardware, sporting goods, and furniture, have traditionally been used to introduce new products. The buyer's job of comparing and selecting is made easier by having the newest offerings of many manufacturers displayed in one place at the same time. Catalogs and price lists are used, especially by smaller retailers, in making part or all of their merchandise commitments. Individual units of chain organizations may make their selection from merchandise samples, or from trial shipments authorized by the central buying office.

MERCHANDISE ASSORTMENT PLANNING

We discussed merchandise breadth and depth in considerable detail in Chapter 5. Let's briefly review this discussion, since the overall decision regarding these two contrasting alternatives vitally affects merchandise assortment planning.

Breadth and Depth of Merchandise Offerings

A department or a store may decide to offer broad assortments, or it may choose instead to feature depth. Rarely can a store maximize both breadth and depth; some compromise will usually have to be worked out. Otherwise the investment in inventory and the resulting lowered turnover of goods will wreak havoc with profits. (Chapter 14 discusses the importance of merchandise turnover.)

Merchandise breadth refers to the number of different categories or classifications of products a store may carry. Thus a discount store offers a wide assortment of goods, ranging from clothing to auto accessories. A specialty store provides a narrow assortment, perhaps only shoes or even women's shoes.

Depth refers to the number of offerings—brands, styles, sizes, and prices—within a particular product category. One store may offer greater depth in women's sportswear than most other stores do. In it a customer is able to choose from the largest assortment and has more chance of finding the particular item that meets her special needs.

Occasionally a retailer will shun a definite merchandise assortment policy and practice what might be termed a *flexible assortment approach* guided by special sales, distress goods available, and other opportunities for expedient purchases. John's Bargain Stores have long practiced a flexible assortment policy. A chain of discount stores catering to low-income groups, John's carries no basic inventory. Instead, its buyers are constantly seeking out-of-season, closed-out, and discontinued items. Surplus stocks of well-known brands are sometimes offered; and some goods cannot be identified by brand.[1]

---

[1] For more information on John's Bargain Stores, especially during the period when they were rapidly expanding, see Frank Schlesinger, "John's Bargain Stores," *The New York Retailer* (April 1963), 10–19.

Stock Balance

Stock balance means having an assortment of goods that is reasonably attractive to customers. This is what retailing is all about. A good balance of goods should be maintained for each merchandise classification, such as men's sport shirts. Likewise, a department and an entire store need to strive for a good overall balance. Merchandising success, and executive promotions, are often measured by the results of these efforts.

A well-balanced stock contains the following ingredients:

1. A variety of "wanted" goods adequate to meet most demands of the store's customers[2]
2. A quantity of each item adequate to minimize outs and lost sales
3. An appropriately restrained inventory investment

There is a limit to how much money can be invested in merchandise if a department and a store are to be profitable. A compromise usually has to be arrived at, with somewhat less than the desired variety and quantity of goods finally approved. Figure 11.1 graphically illustrates this balancing act. Maintaining the balanced stock poses an interesting set of managerial problems.

Keep in mind that sales of many items take place sporadically, seasonal factors may act to curb demand or increase it, delivery time from the manufacturer may require weeks and even months. And almost every item has a different rate of sale. A good balance can erode quickly and be difficult to regain. Inevitably, not all items will sell equally well; some will even turn out to be duds. Unless constant efforts (perhaps even drastic price reductions) are directed to selling the various items in the inventory, stock balance will suffer. Too much money tied up in slow-selling and marginal goods will stymie the buying of other new and needed goods.

Every assortment has some items that are bestsellers or are so basic as to have continual customer demand. Constant attention should assure that these are never out, that no sales are lost because of being temporarily out-of-stock. Some stores have even drawn up lists of such items—*never-out lists*—and woe to the assistant buyer or department manager guilty of carelessness here!

To assure that items with steady demand are more likely to be

---

[2] To be completely specific, the term *variety* refers to the number of *different items* that the department or store carries; the term *item* refers to a particular article of merchandise that is different from other articles of merchandise. Therefore, each style, each color, and each size of each brand carried represents a different item.

FIGURE 11.1 THE BALANCING ACT BETWEEN THE VARIETY AND
DEPTH OF STOCK DESIRED AND THE FUNDS AVAILABLE
FOR INVESTMENT

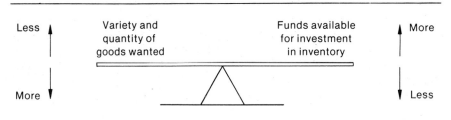

maintained in stock, stock lists are used: *basic-stock lists* for staple and
regularly stocked items, and *model-stock lists* for shopping goods and
fashion items. A never-out list may be used for certain key items. These
tools in assortment planning will be described in more detail in the last
section of this chapter.

Merchandise Emphasis

In planning the overall merchandise assortment, the merchandiser
should formulate a policy for the role that special promotion merchandise will play. Suppliers may offer various opportunities for special
goods involving discontinued numbers, overruns, or specially tailored
offerings that utilize a supplier's unused production capacity.
Sometimes, when a supplier or a retailer is in financial difficulty, bankrupt or *distress merchandise* is sold at deep mark downs from regular
prices to achieve rapid disposal. Such goods can be resold by the
retailer at attractive prices and give a store the ingredients of special
price promotions and traffic stimulators.

   As you would expect, it is often difficult for the buyer to pass up such
attractive offerings, which are one-time opportunities. But somehow
there are always other bargains. For some stores, like John's Bargain
Stores and certain basement operations of department stores, the major
merchandising efforts are geared to finding special deals. Other stores
find that such opportunities should be grasped in moderation. While
close-outs and other special-situation goods offered at attractive prices
may stimulate sales, they can jeopardize regular merchandise assortments and also the reputation of a store. Regular merchandise tends to
suffer when much effort and investment go into special sale items. A
store may gain a reputation as a promotional store, with the result that

customers are reluctant to buy regular merchandise not on sale. Furthermore, the tag ends of numerous special buys are difficult to get rid of and tie up investment that often could be put to better use.

Seasonal goods present merchandising challenges and pose some dangers. Many have very short sales lives, as do Halloween toys and Valentine candy. While seasonal goods can generate extra business, the buyer must be careful that various goods, which are fit only for a limited selling season, are not overstocked. This can happen if demand estimates are unrealistic. The result is that money is tied up in inventory for at least a year and the opportunity to buy more salable goods is denied.

For many merchants, especially beginning ones, the excitement of finding special purchases and maximizing sales opportunities takes attention away from regular merchandise, the day-to-day staples. Such practice is most misguided. Relegating regular merchandise to second place eventually drives customers to competitors. Keep in mind that the customer lost because of a temporary out or limited selection of basic merchandise may never return.

Other Assortment Considerations

PRICE LINING *Price lining* is widely used by retailers because it offers particular advantages, both from the customer's viewpoint and from the retailer's. Only a few price levels are used for any given category of merchandise, and all items are marked at one of these established pricing points. For example, men's sport shirts may all be priced at one of three prices, $5.95, $8.95, or $12.95, regardless of small differences in costs.

In this example three price lines, a low range, a middle range, and a high range, are offered. Presumably most customers will be able to satisfy themselves at one of these price points. The customer interested in higher quality or a more distinctive flair would be lost; similarly, the customer interested in low-end and bargain goods would probably look elsewhere. But the large middle-of-the-road group of customers presumably would be attracted.

The main advantage of price lining, both for clerks and customers, is that it minimizes confusion and makes selling and shopping easier. You can imagine the situation if a dozen different prices were offered, reflecting that many differences in costs. Not only would display and stocking of so many price groups become difficult, but customers would also be confused by apparent small price differences of no real consequence. Buying and stock control are also simplified by price lining, since only those suppliers who offer goods that fit in with the designated price lines need be considered.

But, in the above example, what about a customer who wants a $7 shirt and can find only a $5.95 and an $8.95 group to choose from? There is always the risk that the price lines offered may not be satisfactory to some customers. Price lining also presents problems when wholesale prices are changing, as during inflation. Eventually, as costs rise (or as quality at the prescribed price lessens), a retailer is forced to raise his price lines or face decreasing profits. When this first occurs customers may resent the jump in prices. Price lining also presents difficulties with markdown goods: pricing at the next lowest price line may represent too severe a reduction, and reduced-price goods may not stand out when placed with regular markup goods in the lower price line.

SIZE, COLOR, AND STYLE ASSORTMENT   Just as a firm finds it desirable to limit the number of prices for each category of goods to make shopping and stockkeeping less confusing, so it should limit the variety of sizes, colors, and styles. With many product categories, most sales come from only a few sizes; the same is generally true with colors and styles. For example, in men's shoes there are more than two hundred different sizes of lengths and widths; yet forty-five sizes account for 85 percent of men's shoe sales.[3]

The natural question at this point is: How many sizes, styles, and so on, should a retailer attempt to carry? Few stores can stock all sizes, styles, and colors in a given category of goods. The great growth of discount firms was achieved by carrying only the best-selling colors and sizes. Other retailers have since followed this merchandising approach and have also been reluctant to stock anything but the most popular items. As a result, the customer who has an unusual size or who wants a more distinctive color or style often finds shopping frustrating.

Some compromise is needed between carrying only a very basic merchandise assortment, and offering the most complete variety possible. For example, stocking larger or smaller sizes than those most in demand may require a heavier inventory, but additional customers may be won for the store and these may be more loyal than average customers. Some retailers have achieved outstanding success by catering to outsize consumers: Lane Bryant, described in an earlier chapter, built up a business of more than $300 million by doing so.

[3] From *Establishing and Operating a Retail Shoe Business,* U.S. Dept. of Commerce, Small Business Series No. 34 (Washington, D.C.: U.S. Government Printing Office).

DECISIONS ON NEW PRODUCT LINES

Retailers face continual pressure to add new products and product lines, and even entire new departments, to their merchandise composition. Our marketing environment is such that each producer strives to bring to the market new and different items in the hope of gaining a brief competitive advantage. Producers often use heavy advertising and mass sampling of new products to consumers to try to force space for the new items on retailers' shelves. Because of the proliferation of new products, the average supermarket now carries 7,000 items, while a drugstore will carry up to 12,000. A discount store may have 40,000 different items.

The constant influx of new products presents problems for retailers. New products to be added to existing product lines should be screened, and certain selection standards should be developed. Products presently carried need to be cleared out as sales potential slackens, unless there are sound reasons for their continued stocking. With many new products becoming available, it is virtually impossible for any one retailer to stock them all. Some products will undoubtedly prove to be duds, and only a few will win strong customer approval. At the same time, unless older products are continually monitored and put into clearance when sales taper off, there will be no display or counter space, and no money available, to stock the new.

Criteria for Selecting New Products

In making the decision to add a new product, or the bigger decision to add a new product line or even a new department, a retailer has to make a judgment: Will the addition contribute to sales and profits at least as much as other merchandise investments? Often such a decision is based on hunch, or intuition, or blind optimism. Adding a new product may not present much risk for the retailer; he can usually test it out with a sample order before investing much money. But adding a new product line or an entirely new department involves considerable investment as well as managerial time for planning and setting up. An incorrect decision can be costly, and hunch and blind optimism may be poor guides for decision making.

Decisions on new products are easier if certain criteria are established that the prospective product or product line must meet. While the retailer still has to judge how well the criteria are met, he is forced to make a systematic evaluation. And a good merchandise assortment is more likely to grow with careful planning than with haphazard acquisition.

Specific criteria will vary to some extent with different firms and different managerial priorities. The following at least should be considered:

Compatibility: with available selling and stockroom space; with available selling resources; and with store image
Profitability: estimated near-term profitability and estimated growth potential
Traffic generation

Each of these criteria for selecting new products is important enough to deserve further discussion.

COMPATIBILITY   Many retailers have limited space, both on the selling floor and in the stockroom. As products become more numerous, demands on space increase. An attractive buy may have to be turned down simply because adequate space is not available. For example, lawn and garden supplies have shown great growth in recent years; but the space requirements of such bulky goods prevent many retailers from taking advantage of these opportunities.

A self-service store may find itself unable to handle watches, higher-priced jewelry, cameras, major appliances, and better dresses, because these require knowledgeable salespeople. Some discount stores have attempted to solve this problem by having such departments served by clerks or having a bell that customers can ring to summon help. However, unless there is sufficient customer traffic, the selling expenses of such manned departments may be prohibitive. A compromise usually has to be made between customer service and a limited sales staff. The result often is that, without the adequate information that could be provided by knowledgeable salespeople, the full sales potential of such incompatible products is never realized.

A new product candidate should also be evaluated for its compatibility with the desired store image. While a wide range of products will fall within the desired range, exceptions can occur. For example, some discount stores in an effort to upgrade their image have refused to handle seconds, imperfects, or distress merchandise. A reputable retailer who fails to keep an eye on product acquisitions may be shocked to find that pornographic magazines and paperbacks have gotten into the stock (or that a leased newsstand on the premises has some questionable literature) and be suddenly confronted by indignant customers. A store seeking a prestige or fashion image must beware of overusing sale and special-purchase merchandise, since this may give it a reputation as a promotional store, a reputation not entirely compatible with an image of prestige and high fashion. Merchandise should be neither above nor below the desired store image.

PROFITABILITY The retailer should carefully judge the expected near-term and longer range profitability of a prospective new product. Several things enter into this estimate of profitability. *Gross margin,* which is the difference between the cost of goods and the expected selling price, gives a measure of profitability per unit sold. The temptation is to stock the brand or particular item that offers the highest gross margin (or more correctly, the highest initial markup percentage). For example, suppose you were to decide whether to stock Brand A or Brand B:

	Brand A	Brand B
Expected selling price (retail)	$5.00	$5.00
Cost	2.50	3.00
Gross margin	$2.50	$2.00
Gross margin as a percent of retail price (the markup percentage)	50%	40%

One would be inclined here to stock Brand A, which carries the higher per-unit profit. However, assuming that there are no significant differences otherwise, two other factors should enter into the decision: expected sales, and the investment needed for initial stocking.

RETAILING TOOL—*Analysis for Choosing the More Profitable Product to Stock*

Continuing with the question of whether to stock Brand A or Brand B, compare estimated sales of the two brands with their gross margins.

Analysis 1 Expected sales related to total gross margin:

	Brand A	Brand B
Estimated sales (units)	200	300
Gross margin	$2.50	$2.00
Total gross margin dollars:		
$2.50 × 200 = $500		
$2.00 × 300 =		$600

In this example, then, assuming that estimates of sales are reasonably accurate, Brand B would be the better product choice, despite its lower gross-margin percentage. However, if it is anticipated that there are differences in inventory needed for the two product candidates, then an additional analysis should be made.

Analysis 2   Inventory investment required for adequate stock:

	Brand A	Brand B
Expected monthly sales (units)	200	300
Cost per unit	$2.50	$3.00
Inventory required to maintain assortment and minimize outs and lost sales (units)	400	800

Average investment required:

$2.50 × 400 = $1,000

$3.00 × 800 = $2,400

Gross margin return on investment (total gross margin as percent of average investment):

$$\frac{500}{1,000} = 50\%$$

$$\frac{600}{2,400} = \qquad 25\%$$

As you can see when the analysis is carried further, Brand A is clearly the best choice in this case. Brand A requires much less investment in inventory and the percentage of the *gross-margin on investment* is twice as high.

Several things can account for the higher inventory required for Brand B. The manufacturer may be located farther away, or be small, so that delivery is slow or uncertain; uncertain availability would require a larger back-up stock to guard against lost sales. Furthermore, a larger assortment of Brand B might be needed to provide the necessary colors, sizes, materials, and patterns.

For Further Analysis   If the inventory requirements were 500 for Brand B and still 400 for Brand A, which would then be the more profitable to stock?

Expected growth should be taken into account. Sometimes merchandise must be stocked and displayed for some time before sales become worthwhile. For example, most retailers expand their stocks and counter and display space for such seasonal goods as Christmas cards, ornaments, toys, and so on long before sales warrant this. They feel that the notability so gained helps when consumers are ready to buy.

TRAFFIC GENERATION   The amount of customer traffic that a new product or department is likely to draw can sometimes be a major consideration, more important, even, than profitability. Of course, some product lines both attract extra traffic and produce good profits; but this is exceptional. More likely, traffic generators represent good bargains to customers or else are competitively priced basic needs. Many retail stores, especially in farming and industrial areas, carry a rather extensive assortment of work clothing: overalls, coveralls, work uniforms, and the like. These items carry some of the lowest markups found in retailing. But the store that carries adequate stocks not only provides a service to many of its customers, but may also find that the customers who come into the store for work clothing buy other things as well.

So important is traffic generation that some retailers habitually run specials that carry minimum markups; sometimes such goods may even be "loss leaders," offered below cost in order to draw more customers. Supermarkets, in their weekend ads, characteristically use leaders, assuming that the customers attracted will stay around and buy all their grocery needs.

Many retailers practice scrambled merchandising (discussed in Chapter 2). They stock various goods that have a high sales volume and good profitability but are unrelated to the major product lines of the store. A supermarket having such nonfood items as hosiery, notions, toys, and gadgets is stocking goods that sell well in heavy traffic.

Experimentation for New Product Decisions

No retailer can afford to stand pat with only his present and proven items of merchandise. New products and styles are constantly flooding the market. Some may not represent much improvement over the old, but new products continue to attract consumers. And competitors will assuredly promote their new offerings. But not all new products are successful. It is estimated that four of five new products fail and are soon dropped by their manufacturers. What are the risks a retailer faces when stocking new products, and how can the retail buyer minimize these risks?

Usually a retailer's risk of new-product failure is far less than that of the manufacturer, who may incur such awesome losses as $100 million (as DuPont reportedly did in discontinuing Corfam). The retailer's risk, while less, may still involve the following:

1. The tying up of space (both selling and nonselling) that could be used for better-selling items
2. Markdowns required to eventually clear out the poor sellers, perhaps at cost or even below

To minimize these risks, the retailer often samples, or tests, new product offerings. A small quantity will be purchased, perhaps placed in a high-traffic location, maybe given a small advertisement, and the sales response will be carefully noted. Sometimes even a half day of selling will provide enough information for a much larger order to be placed for the promising new item. Stores affiliated with buying groups may compare sales results. Many chains have certain stores in which they customarily test new products before making the decision to disseminate them throughout the chain.

There are times, however, when experimenting with small quantities before making larger commitments may mean that the opportunity to feature the new item is lost. This is a special danger with seasonal and fashion goods. Many manufacturers of such goods are small and can make only a limited quantity, which can be quickly spoken for by a few large retailers. An order placed after a reasonable testing period may not be filled; even when additional orders can be honored, the delay in shipping may bring the reorder to the store past the prime selling period.

RETAILING STRATEGY—*Handling Risks of New Fashion Merchandising*

To avoid the possibilities of delayed reorders or inability to get reorders on fast-moving fashion goods, experimentation may have to be more limited than is really desirable. This forces the buyer to accept more risk and place a larger initial order. Sometimes a buyer may have to rely on a gut feeling and take a chance without any testing. In other words, a compromise may have to be reached between two kinds of risks: the risk of having too much of a poorly selling product, and the risk of not having enough of a hot item. Such are the challenges of merchandising.

May Company and Fashion Risks   "We've really encouraged our merchandising specialists to stick their necks out," says Stanley Goodman, chairman of the May Company. "We can't match Sears in buying clout, but if we can move faster in spotting trends, we'll do better." May buyers, for instance, were quick to spot the bow-tie boomlet, and many May stores featured twice the number of bow ties that their major competitors stocked. May stores were also among the first to pounce on old wicker furniture, antique bottles, and other nostalgia items. "One of our California people was convinced that a replica of the old Philco radio, shaped like a Gothic window, might do well," says Goodman. "We convinced Philco to make 1,000 of them, and they sold out at $150 each."

Hudson's and Fashion Risks   A faltering Hudson's in Detroit found its high-margin softgoods business in particularly bad shape. Part of the blame rested on a reluctance to take markdowns on poor-selling goods in order to free funds for up-to-date fashions. Furthermore, many buyers were "inclined to play it safe": they often wasted time testing a wide assortment of styles. Then when an item suddenly took off, they were caught with a short supply and too little time to get prompt delivery on reorders.

Now under new management, buyers are told they must spot trends sooner, and gain greater flexibility by buying fewer lines in depth. "In fashion buying, we want self-confidence, conviction, taste, and a lot of courage."

Sources: "The May Co. Moves into Catalogue Stores," from the August 4, 1973 issue of BusinessWeek, p. 48; and "A Swinging Merchant Goes for Growth," from the November 18, 1972 issue of BusinessWeek, pp. 60–61. © 1973, 1972 by McGraw-Hill, Inc., New York, NY 10020. All rights reserved.

For Thought and Discussion

1. The fashion merchandising policies of May and Hudson's seem to be about the same: "develop an instinct for what will sell and have the courage of your convictions." Does this mean that in fashion merchandising there is no room for objective, systematic analysis and decision-making?
2. How is the beginning buyer to develop the skill and "instinct" needed for such apparently risky decisions?

DROPPING ITEMS

As more products are added to the assortment (for example, a typical supermarket will add 800 new items every year), there comes a limit to how many different products can be stocked with the available space and investment money. Decisions have to be made to drop some items from the assortment.

Sometimes the manufacturer makes the decision to drop a product by discontinuing production. More often, the retailer must decide how many brands, prices, and styles he can continue to offer.

Product Mistakes of Retailers

Merchandising mistakes are more common with small retailers than with large ones. There is a natural reluctance to admit mistakes, accept the losses thereof, and reinvest funds in more promising goods. (Even the buyers of Hudson's were guilty of this reluctance.) Items may be found in some inventories that are two, three, and even more years old, and are still occupying space and investment money that could be better utilized.

Retailers, and especially small independents, also have a tendency to stock too many similar items and brands. Many goods really are substitutes for one another; one brand customers will generally buy interchangeably with another brand. Consequently there is no need to stock two or more such similar brands. An inventory can be streamlined without sacrificing sales.

All retailers need to evaluate the salability of their merchandise mix systematically and get rid of the poor performers. Too often, this is done sporadically and with haste when a serious overstock has developed. It is better to weed out poorly performing products regularly. There is less trauma. Investment money is not tied up for so long. Small initial markdowns are less painful than drastic ones made almost too late.

Criteria for Product Elimination Decisions

Any systematic evaluation of which products to eliminate should employ certain criteria:

1. Declining sales, relative to former periods
2. Little or no contribution to the sales of other products

3. Availability of good-selling items that can be substituted for the product in question
4. Failure of changes in merchandising efforts to improve the situation appreciably

While some judgment is needed in appraising products according to these criteria, at least there is a basis for systematic evaluation. An item that meets these four criteria should probably be dropped. But certainly the possibility of changing the price, the display, or some other aspect of merchandising, should be considered before a product is arbitrarily eliminated. Still, the tendency is to hold on to products long after their potential has diminished.

For certain goods of limited demand life, such as fashion goods, fad items, and seasonal merchandise, elimination decisions become extremely important. For fad and fashion goods, demand can erode very rapidly and completely: a fad or a fashion beyond its time can scarcely be sold at any price. For seasonal goods, elimination decisions, while urgent, are not necessarily as crucial. Such goods can always be carried over and put out for sale a year hence, although, of course, this ties up investment dollars that might better be spent for current, more salable goods. It is essential to monitor sales of limited-demand goods very closely to avoid accumulating heavy stocks of goods whose demand is rapidly drying up. Reorders of fashion goods, fad items, and seasonal merchandise should be reviewed very carefully so that replenishment stock does not arrive near the end of the selling period. This type of merchandising presents some of the greatest challenges for retailers; at the same time, the rewards for those who can assess the nuances of the marketplace can be substantial.

How to Eliminate Products

Tag ends, which are the leftover broken sizes and colors of discontinued numbers and styles, often present a frustrating situation. Drastic markdowns are usually needed; space, salesperson time and effort, and some advertising all may be necessary. Sometimes the situation can be extreme. It is not unusual for beginning buyers to invest too heavily in the fringe sizes and colors. Clearance counters are usually full of size 14 and 17 men's sport and dress shirts and the smallest and largest sizes of women's dresses and sweaters. Similarly, the clearance tables of shoe departments show a preponderance of the extreme sizes. Even drastic markdowns may hardly sell fringe sizes, since so few people can actually wear such sizes.

Some sort of clearance or periodic sales effort is needed if items are actually to be eliminated. Some stores have established a successful practice of Saturday "Early-Bird Specials," with tag ends from various departments greatly reduced and given prominent locations. Many stores have a month-end clearance; most stores have end-of-season clearances. These can be healthy stimuli to sales and customer traffic, while at the same time they prune stocks. An extreme example of inefficiency is the retailer who eventually relegates old goods to the dim recesses of the stockroom, rather than taking markdowns. They may be forgotten, but they still tie up investment.

TOOLS IN ASSORTMENT PLANNING AND MAINTAINING

To achieve and maintain an adequate and balanced stock some systematic listing of merchandise requirements must be kept. The more specific such a listing can be, the more useful it is.

Small merchants have a tendency to buy by "feel" rather than by systematic planning; the results may be unbalanced stocks, higher-than-needed inventory, and lost sales of fast-selling items. On the other hand, many large retailers have refined and developed stock lists to a fine detail. The chains, in particular, have done this and even use such lists to assess the performance of individual stores in the chain.

For example, a major variety chain requires its district managers (who are in charge of fifteen to twenty stores) to periodically check each store's stock assortment and ratio of out-of-stocks. A detailed checklist gives each item a numerical weight according to its importance and salability. A final overall rating of the store is made by adding the points of the items in stock and calculating the total as a percentage of the total possible points. A 95 percent in-stock situation is sought. Such a detailed check may take several days. Results are submitted to central headquarters, and comparative standings of the stores are publicized. Demotions have been known to occur if a store received several ratings under 90 percent, and promotions come rather quickly to the better merchants.

As noted earlier in this chapter, three types of assortment lists may be used:

1. Basic-stock list—for staples and continuously maintained items
2. Model-stock list—for certain shopping-type goods and fashions
3. Never-out list—for key items and best sellers

Basic-Stock List

A basic-stock list can be developed for those items that have stability in sales or have a seasonal or other variation in sales that is fairly predictable. This includes many items. Almost every department, no matter how fashion oriented it may be, has some items of a staple nature. In many departments, such as stationery, notions, hosiery, housewares, hardware, sporting goods, candy, toilet goods, and domestics and linens, staples account for most of the total sales.

With staple goods the basic-stock list can be quite specific. Items may be identified by color, size, price, brand, and other characteristics. Various items in the stock may be rated according to their relative importance. Thus, a man's 15-33 white shirt would carry a higher rating than a 17½-35 polka-dot shirt. A simple way to give such a relative rating is to assign points to each item, with more points indicating greater importance in the merchandise assortment.

IMPORTANCE OF MAINTAINING STAPLES Since staple items sell day-by-day in steady, if unspectacular, amounts, the merchant is tempted to pay little attention to them. The white muslin pillowcase in a domestics department is unglamorous compared to a brilliant new pattern in sheets; and few items in any department can be less pretentious than a spool of #50 white thread in a notions department. Special purchases, sales, new items, interesting styles, and the like tend to get the attention and enthusiasm. Sometimes, so much money is committed to such goods that none is left for the recurring order needs for staple goods.

RETAILING ERRORS—Lost Staple Sales That Send Customers Away

To minimize the importance of staple goods is a serious error. Out-of-stocks here not only represent lost sales, they also force customers to go to competitors to satisfy their needs, since many staple items do not have ready substitutes. Sending a customer away may have the following undesirable consequences:

The store may lose customer good will, because of the extra shopping effort required.

A customer may perceive the store as inefficient and poorly merchandised, and decide to shift business permanently.

A customer may decide to satisfy other buying needs in the competing store where the staple item is available.

For Thought and Discussion   If you were a buyer, would you be inclined to delegate maintaining staple goods to your assistant buyer? Why or why not?

Sometimes a buyer commits all resources to a special or opportunistic purchase and has none left for the monthly order of staples. The merchandise manager may also make a mistake when the buyer's monthly open-to-buy is used up, by refusing to approve further orders regardless of content.

Model-Stock List

A model-stock list may be used for many types of goods for which substitutes are readily accepted by the customer. Jewelry, men's neckties, handbags, women's apparel, furniture, pictures, and curtains and drapes are among those items that customers shop for without the same specific demand as for staple goods. For example, the woman shopping for a dress may have a requirement in mind (such as long sleeves, or black), but the particular decision will be made after she sees what styles are available and pleasing to her.

For certain fashion goods, styles and preferences change rapidly; identical goods often cannot be reordered, and past history on style popularity will be useless. Consequently, a stock list for such goods cannot be nearly as specific as the basic list for staples. Usually, there will be a lack of style numbers. However, it is still possible to plan and assess assortments by such categories as the following:

Price lines
Size distribution
Materials
Colors (sometimes)
Certain categories of style, such as long sleeves, high neck, modern,
    colonial, plain, fancy

In recent years, the use of the computer and computer printouts has greatly improved stock control by providing data on sales and stock conditions in the various categories deemed important.

Never-out List

Some buyers have gone a step beyond basic- and model-stock lists and systematically identified their key items and best sellers. Special controls may be established to assure that such items of greatest customer demand will never be out of stock. Some of these never-outs may be the best-selling staples; others may be seasonal items; some may be best sellers newly identified by the experiences of other stores in the chain or buying group.

In a chain, the various assortment lists are usually designated by headquarters buyers. In a department store, such listings may be closely controlled by merchandising executives, or they may be used more loosely by departmental buyers without any supervision or control by higher executives. Small stores often develop and use assortment lists haphazardly. If sales and demand are to be fully tapped while stock balance is kept lean, the importance of such tools for assortment planning and maintaining cannot be overemphasized. But they need to be carefully developed, constantly used, and periodically reviewed and adjusted.

■ Summary

The first step in planning a merchandise assortment is analyzing demand. A number of sources, both internal to the firm and external, can help with this. However, even with the help of these sources, analysis by no means eliminates all risks, especially in buying fashion goods. A buyer should constantly seek to have a well-balanced stock within the constraint of the funds available for investment in inventory. Effective decisions on new products and new product lines are facilitated by certain criteria for assessing prospective products, such as their compatibility, profitability, and traffic generation. Invariably, the buyer will have to make decisions on dropping certain items and how best to get rid of them. Important tools in achieving an adequate and balanced stock are the basic-stock list, the model-stock list, and the never-out list. With the assortment planning taken care of, a merchandiser's attention must focus on the actual buying environment. This we will examine in the next chapter.

■ Key Terms

Basic-stock lists	Distress merchandise
Comparison shopping	Fashion goods
Customer panels	The five rights

Flexible assortment approach   Seasonal goods
Gross margin   Staple goods
Gross margin on investment   Stock balance
Model-stock lists   Style-out
Never-out lists   Tag ends
Price lining   Trading up
Resident buying offices   Want slips

■ **Discussion Questions**

1. Compare and contrast the importance of past sales records for staple goods and for fashion goods.
2. How would you go about motivating your salespeople to make out want slips? Do you see any dangers in relying on want-slip information in making your buying decisions?
3. What are the advantages of using customer panels for merchandise information? Are there any disadvantages?
4. Evaluate the usefulness of vendors as sources of market information.
5. Some major retailers (including Sears) offer three price lines for many categories of goods (good, better, best). Evaluate this assortment strategy for both the large and the small firm.
6. A major dilemma frequently faces the buyer of fashion goods. If he or she attempts to test demand by sampling new styles, reorders may be difficult to get or be dangerously delayed. On the other hand, plunging in early in the season may result in heavy unsalable stocks. Can you resolve this dilemma? What would you recommend?
7. What is the difference between a basic-stock list and a never-out list? How would you develop a never-out list?
8. Evaluate the pros and cons of expanding stocks of seasonal goods, such as Christmas cards, ornaments, and toys, long in advance of the selling season.
9. Do you think there is enough potential for a store selling distress and odd-lot goods in your locality? Who might be the customers? the competitors?

■ **Project**

Select a category of merchandise (for example, men's shirts, ready-made drapery, blouses, dresses, or hosiery) and "shop" several large stores (either department stores or chains such as Sears and Penney) and several small independent stores. Note and evaluate the price lines carried in the category by each store. For example, are there too many or too few price lines? Are the gaps between prices too great?

■ Exercise in Creativity

Your store has had a history of missing the best-selling styles in swimwear and summer sportswear fashions. What recommendations would you make for trying to overcome this problem and be more "on top" of current fashion trends?

■ Retailing in Action: Role Play

Discount stores have been most effective in discounting appliances. Consequently, some department stores have found that to remain competitive in price with discounters their appliance departments have to operate at too low a gross margin to remain profitable. As a result, some have dropped appliances.

You are the merchandise manager of a department store facing such a situation. What would your decision be? (You should look at any possible alternatives to dropping the department as well as the pros and cons of doing so.)

■ Retail Math

To fill a void in your stock assortment, you want to buy a brand of light fixtures that you can retail for $50 (actually $49.95). You think you can sell 20 units a month at this price. Your choice of brand has narrowed to three possibilities: Brand A costs $27; B, $28.50; and C, $31. After querying your salespeople and your assistant buyer, you estimate that Brands A and B are equally salable, but Brand C is particularly attractive and might sell an additional 25 percent more at the $50 price. Delivery times are 45 days for A, 21 days for B, and 30 days for Brand C. For an adequate stock, you believe you will need to maintain a three-months' supply of Brand A (which at estimated sales of 20 units would be 60), one month of B, and two months of C. These differences are due to the varied delivery times. Which brand would you buy, based on return on investment?

12 Introduction to Buying

Roberta Pinelli is a buyer for an eighteen-store women's apparel chain in Georgia and the Carolinas. On a two-week buying trip to New York City, she may spend several hundred thousand dollars on dresses and slacks outfits. The buyer of women's wear must choose from hundreds of different designs and fabrics. To add to the difficulty, "We're picking clothes eight months in advance," Ms. Pinelli says. "There's no way to really know what will sell well." While she is usually able to make her selections from model garments, sometimes she will have to base her judgment on small swatches of cloth. She will visit many different garment makers in the process.

Once Ms. Pinelli makes her decision, there is almost no haggling over prices. But there is bargaining with the manufacturers over advertising allowances, and she uses her buying muscle to get as much advertising money as possible. She hopes, for example, that manufacturers will pay for almost half of the fifty or so full-page ads, costing around $300,000 total, that she expects to place in newspapers. A buyer of Ms. Pinelli's purchasing power can also command certain extras from manufacturers, including early delivery dates and special alterations. If she chooses—and she usually does—she can even partake of considerable entertainment while on the road.

DETERMINING WHAT TO PURCHASE

In the last chapter we noted the tools used in assortment planning, particularly the basic-stock list used for staple goods and the model-stock list for fashion goods. Staple and fashion goods require different tools and techniques for assortment planning, and the quantity to be purchased is determined somewhat differently also.

These differences in buying techniques often present difficulties to a newly transferred buyer. The successful buyer of a predominantly staple-goods department, such as notions or housewares, probably built success on careful recordkeeping and scheduled buying dates for various categories of goods. In a fashion-goods department, demand estimates are more uncertain, salability of many items is short lived, timing is all important, risks are greater, and some chances have to be taken on new or unproven items if sales are to be maximized. It is equally difficult to move from fashion goods to staple goods, since fashion buyers tend to be less wedded to details, perhaps less devoted to a scrupulous reorder schedule, and they may find merchandise outs increasing as a result.

Buying Staple Merchandise

Most staple goods, with some seasonal variations for certain categories, can be bought automatically once certain decisions or judgments have been made. After the items in the assortments have been determined, adequate stocks should be planned to minimize outs, while keeping inventory investment within planned minimal figures. How much to purchase at any one time depends on:

1. Estimated sales for the next period of time
2. Quantity of goods presently on hand and on order
3. Desired stock at the end of the period

Where there is little or no seasonal variation in sales of particular items and categories, immediate past sales (and any upward or downward trend from earlier periods) should be a good guide for estimating sales. For new merchandise, or for a new buyer coming into a department with poor merchandise records, the job of estimating is more difficult, and a temporary overstock or out condition may result before adjustments can be made.

The temptation is to operate with minimum stocks (hand-to-mouth buying), thereby reducing investment or else freeing money to broaden assortments and add other lines. But there can be problems: an unexpectedly large sale or slow delivery can cause temporary outs of some merchandise. On the other hand, a larger quantity than needed may come from careless buying or from the desire to take advantage of a quantity discount.

The quantity of goods on hand can sometimes be ascertained by stock records. More likely, a stock count has to be made immediately prior to ordering, so as to have up-to-date information. Where the buying process has been systematized, a stock-counting schedule for the various merchandise classifications will be rigidly adhered to. But it is not always that simple: the buyer or trainee may find that absenteeism, a special sales event, or any number of other occurrences interfere with the counting of stocks on schedule. And where a store maintains a lean stock situation, a delay of even a few days in getting on-hand figures may result in an out-of-stock situation a few weeks later.

Where sales are uniform, the desired stock at the end of the period will be the same as the beginning stock. With some seasonality present, or where sales are trending upward or downward, there will be a difference, and reorders will either exceed sales for the period (if the sales trend is upward) or be less (if sales are declining).

RETAILING TOOL—Staple-Stock Replenishment

Formula:

    Quantity to buy = Estimated sales + Desired stock end of month
                  (EOM) − Goods on hand and on order

Example with seasonal goods:

    Golf balls in a sporting goods department are staple goods, but have strong seasonal sales. The following figures face the buyer of a medium-size department:

      Estimated sales: "X" brand golf balls
      March–April   24 dozen

May	30 dozen		
June	56 dozen		
		Goods on hand, March 1	5 dozen
		Goods on order March 1	16 dozen
		Desired stock, April 30	30 dozen

Problem: Place April requirements now (March 1).

Solution: Substituting the above figures in the formula, we have

24 dozen + 30 dozen − 21 dozen = 33 dozen to buy March 1

For Further Analysis

1. What would May requirements be, assuming that desired stock at the end of May is 56 dozen?
2. If there are 20 dozen on hand March 1, how many golf balls should be bought for April, assuming the other figures are the same?

In the preceding example reorders in the spring will exceed sales, since expected sales are rapidly trending upward. We want to maintain a one-month supply of golf balls. Consequently the desired stock at the end of each month will be the estimated sales for the next month.

Buying Fashion Goods

Buying fashion goods is more of an art. The season or selling period is definitely limited: possibly only a few months of peak sales, then such a slackening of demand that drastic markdowns will be necessary to get rid of any goods remaining. As noted in the last chapter, past history of particular styles is often not of much help, since customer acceptance may completely change. However, certain past-history information about fashion items is of significant aid to the buyer. While the popularity of a new style at the beginning of the season may be unknown, the buyer can apportion purchases by sizes and price ranges with reasonable confidence, guided by previous years' records of sales. Initial orders of new items may have to be placed with little or no sales information; yet, because of the short selling season and the crescendo of demand for a popular style, reorders may be difficult to obtain as quickly as needed.

A somewhat similar replenishment formula can be used as in buying staple goods, except that it employs classification analysis (rather than item analysis), and the duration of the season must be most carefully considered when reordering.

EXAMPLE OF FASHION-GOODS REPLENISHMENT Women's sportswear in most parts of the United States (the situation is different in
the southern and western states) peaks in May and June; by July 4
most stores begin to run clearance sales on such goods. This merchandise is purchased some months in advance, after viewing sample lines
usually shown by manufacturers in the winter. A store has stock records
to show quantity and price lines sold during the previous year, and this
information serves as a useful guide for expectations for the coming
season.

RETAILING TOOL—Reordering Fashion Goods

Formula:

Amount to purchase for peak season selling = Estimated sales (during
peak season) + Desired stock (at end of peak season) − Goods on hand
and on order

Example:

In placing reorders for $12.95 women's Jamaica-length shorts, one
buyer faced these figures as of April 1:

Previous year's sales	March	20 units
	April	70
	May	280
	June	400
	July	250 (mostly on markdowns)

The buyer estimates a 20 percent increase in sales for this year.

Goods on hand, April 1:   180 units
Goods on order, April 1:   120 units
Desired stock, June 30:   0 (sales in July can be closeouts and
                                   special purchases)

Problem: Plan $12.95 Jamaica-length shorts commitments for the spring and
summer selling season.

Solution: Estimated sales for April, May, and June:

= (70 + 280 + 400) + (20 percent increase)
= 750 + 150
= 900 units

Now substituting in the above formula, we have

900 + 0 − 300 = 600 units needed for peak selling season

The buyer may want to place all of these orders at this time, April 1, provided she has enough selling experience with the new styles or enough confidence; this should assure delivery during the coming peak demand. However, the 600 units could be ordered with staggered delivery dates, such as 300 for May 1, and 300 for June 1 delivery.

For Further Analysis

1. In the above example, if the July sales were to come from stock, rather than from closeouts and special purchases, how many units should be purchased?

2. Has our buyer made a mistake in not considering possible August sales? Why or why not?

FADS   A *fad item* represents the extreme of popular acceptance. Virtually impossible to predict, the fad may rise to dizzy heights of popularity, and fall from grace even faster. Figure 12.1 depicts the life cycle (the duration of customer demand) of typical staple, fashion, and fad items.

Fads may occur in many lines of merchandise, not just clothing. For example, records, jewelry, shoes, even sunglasses may have their fads. Toys have witnessed some of the more extreme fads. Some years ago, hula hoops soared to fantastic popularity, largely on the basis of a demonstration on a popular TV program. It was virtually impossible for manufacturers to produce them fast enough and for merchants to keep them in stock—until the end came.

FIGURE 12.1 TYPICAL LIFE CYCLES OF STAPLE, FASHION, AND FAD ITEMS

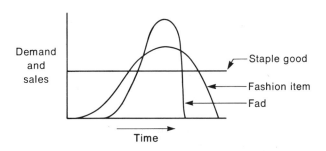

One Kresge manager, in a frantic effort to keep up with demand, ordered a semi-truck load of hula hoops. These arrived just as the demand lessened. A week later hula hoops could not be sold at any price. Fortunately for this store manager, he was transferred a few months later to a bigger store. His successor discovered to his horror a stockroom full of hula hoops. He spent the next several years giving them away.

As you can imagine, the rewards of good timing for fad items can be great: sales can skyrocket far beyond normal expectations. But the last buy, based on heady enthusiasm, may be late and overoptimistic. Stock records and past sales information are of little help in making such quantity-to-purchase decisions.

SPECIAL BUYING SITUATIONS

In addition to regular buying of staples and fashion goods, usually according to basic-stock lists and model-stock plans, a buyer is confronted with other buying situations or opportunities. Sometimes these can be anticipated and planned in advance, as for special annual sales events, such as anniversary sales and white goods promotions, or for end-of-season closeouts. Other situations may arise as opportunities, as when a manufacturer or supplier has a lot of goods that must be disposed of at a sacrifice, because of financial pressures or demand miscalculations. The retail buyer who has open-to-buy money left after meeting regular requirements may be able to use such opportunities to good advantage.

Other irregular buying situations may come with new and untried goods that a supplier is eager to place in a store and will make certain concessions for. The supplier may offer goods on *consignment,* which means that title and ownership (and therefore investment in inventory) do not pass to the retailer until the goods are sold.

Special orders for customers who want odd sizes or items not normally stocked can be an extra source of business for the department willing to devote the extra effort. In some departments, more items are sold by sample than from inventory, necessitating many special orders. This is prevalent with bulky products of high unit value, such as furniture.

A buyer of a large retail firm or buying group may do some *specification buying.* Knowing the customers' requirements and wants better than a more distant manufacturer can, such a buyer may specify certain features, quality, and prices, and then search for vendors willing and able to supply goods with such specifications. Sometimes a buyer with imagination may "create" a novelty with good sales potential, such as the replica of the old Philco radio described in the last chapter.

Many retailers' private brands reflect specification buying. Some retailers' brands have such high quality and dependability that they are widely accepted by consumers, for example, the private brands of Sears and Penney. Often, specification buying results not only in more attractive features and quality from the consumers' viewpoint, but also in lower prices than comparable nationally advertised brands'.

Here are some of the advantages and disadvantages of certain special buying situations.

Promotional Purchases

SPECIAL SALE AND PROMOTION GOODS   Major sales events usually require special purchases. The emphasis on sales varies greatly from store to store. Highly promotional stores may force their buyers to continually search for manufacturers' closeouts and other price concessions and buying opportunities.
Disadvantages: Merchandise purchased for promotional purposes does not always yield an overall sales gain, since such goods may curtail the sale of regular-priced items. Odd lots of such nonregular goods may be difficult to dispose of completely, may not fit in with regular assortments, and, therefore, may lead to overstocks with no money left for regular goods.

JOB LOTS AND DISTRESS MERCHANDISE   Job lots and distress merchandise are a type of promotional purchase usually offered by manufacturers toward the end of the season. They generally are goods left over in broken or incomplete sizes, colors, and styles. Some merchants are attracted to the very low price that makes such odds and ends candidates for quick sale and generators of traffic.
Disadvantages: Even more than most other sale goods, job lots and distress merchandise may clutter an inventory and be difficult to sell out; at the extreme, they can tie up investment money that ought to be spent on regular goods to avoid outs.

New-Product Placement Incentives

CONSIGNMENT GOODS   When a vendor is having difficulty placing merchandise with retailers, perhaps because it is new and unknown or because many similar goods are already on the market, the vendor may offer a retailer the inducement of not paying (and tying up investment dollars) until the goods are actually sold. Since the supplier owns the goods until they are sold to customers, the supplier assumes the loss if the goods are unsalable.

Disadvantages: While consignment buying would seem to be attractive from the retailer's viewpoint, it is generally resorted to with marginal goods from weak vendors. Selling effort and space may be wasted if such goods have little customer appeal; a store's reputation may suffer if they are of poor quality; and time may have to be spent counting unsold items and returned goods and arranging to have them shipped back to the manufacturer.

GUARANTEED SALES   Also called memorandum terms, *guaranteed sales* are similar to consignment arrangements in that anything unsold or selling too slowly in the opinion of the retailer can be returned to the vendor. The difference is that the retailer *does* take title or ownership when the goods are placed in stock, thereby committing funds for inventory and assuming such risks as fire and flood damage.

Disadvantages: Products sold under guaranteed sales often have disadvantages similar to those of goods sold on consignment. Strong vendors with brands and products already in substantial consumer demand will hardly resort to such concessions to persuade retailers to stock their products.

Special Buying Situations for Regular Merchandise

SPECIAL ORDERS   Some departments with merchandise having high unit value and many style, fabric, and color combinations, such as furniture, do much of their buying through special orders. For other departments, willingness to special order greatly increases the assortment offered the patient customer and can generate extra business, as well as customer good will.

Disadvantages: Some buyers are reluctant to encourage special orders unless the customer virtually insists on it. The staff time required to process such orders and the extra handling-and-transportation charge from the vendor make profits doubtful. As well, special orders may be the source of numerous complaints and follow-up efforts.

SPECIFICATION BUYING   Usually only large retailers buy by specification, those who have the market clout to motivate manufacturers to allocate part of their production runs to special product, packaging, and brand demands. The private brands of the large retailers reflect specification buying. Some of these retailer brands are of better quality than national manufacturers' and bear out the ability of these large buyers to assess the wants of their customers. Furthermore, such goods can often carry a lower price tag than similar nationally branded merchandise. Where such brands and specification merchandise can be well established with customers (as at Sears and many other large retailers), customer loyalty is more assured, since the particular brand is only available at that retail firm.

Disadvantages: For a big retailer, the advantages of specification buying usually far outweigh the disadvantages. However, if a buyer miscalculates or is not sufficiently knowledgeable, a poorly performing product carrying the retailer's own brand name can be a most negative result. Not all buyers are willing to assume such risks nor the extra effort involved in taking over some of the manufacturer's product development workload. For small retailers unable to take on large quantity commitments, specification buying usually is not feasible.

TERMS OF SALE

The culmination of the purchase transaction involves the terms of sale. Sometimes these are rather rigidly set by the vendor or by the customs of the particular trade or industry. In other instances, especially if the retailer is big and represents a large present or potential sale, considerable haggling may take place over prices and terms. We will consider here discounts, datings, and miscellaneous other terms of sale.

Discounts

A *discount* is any reduction from the listed price that is allowed the retailer. The retailer should be familiar with the following discounts:

Quantity discounts
Trade discounts
Cash discounts
Seasonal discounts
Advertising allowances

Some of these discounts can be offered in ways that make them illegal under the provisions of the Robinson-Patman Act, which prohibits "discriminating" or charging different prices for "like" purchases to different wholesale or retail customers. While the Act is directed primarily at manufacturers, the buyer or retailer can also be found guilty if he "knowingly" benefits from the price discrimination.

QUANTITY DISCOUNTS   It is natural for buyers of large retailers to bargain hard, to fight for the best price they can get, the biggest discount, free goods, or other price concessions. As we saw at the beginning of this chapter, Roberta Pinelli prefers to use her buying muscle to get as much advertising money as possible. When discounts and other concessions can be justified by economies resulting from large orders (perhaps savings from longer production runs, lowered selling costs, and lower billing and collecting expenses) then legality is less likely to be questioned. Sometimes discounts are pursued too hard and may lead to possible violations of Robinson-Patman. Cumulative quantity discounts,[1] in particular, are of questionable legality: the "cost-savings" justifications may be fictitious, because many small orders (with their higher handling costs) can be accumulated for the quantity discount. Noncumulative quantity discounts are based on the single order and are less questionable.

TRADE DISCOUNTS   Trade or functional discounts are frequently given to different members of a channel of distribution according to the functions they perform in their channel positions. For example, a full-service wholesaler may be offered a 30 percent discount by a manufacturer, while the retailer is only given a 15 percent discount. The justification is that the wholesaler performs more services for the manufacturer, particularly in reaching smaller retailers, and assumes some distribution costs that otherwise would have to be borne by the producer.

CASH DISCOUNTS   Cash discounts are reductions from the billed price and are given by vendors in return for prompt payment. A typical cash-discount offer is 2/10, net 30, which means that the buyer may deduct 2 percent from the invoice price if he or she pays within 10 days, while the net invoice payment is due within 30 days from the invoice date. A retailer should try if at all possible, even if it means borrowing money, to take advantage of such cash discounts. Two percent is a sizable price reduction for paying early; in some lines of merchandise, such as apparel, the discount may even be 7–8 percent.

---

[1] A cumulative quantity discount applies not to a particular order, but to the total accumulated orders over a period of time, usually a year.

SEASONAL DISCOUNTS   For many seasonal goods, such as toys, swimwear, and paint, seasonal discounts are offered to induce retailers to purchase in advance of the peak selling season. Advance purchases enable the manufacturer to lessen the extreme peaks and valleys of seasonal business. While the retailer may gain attractive price reductions by ordering early, the decision should be weighed against the availability of inventory investment funds and stockroom space. As well, the retailer should consider the possibility that lower wholesale prices may be offered before the goods can be sold.

ADVERTISING ALLOWANCES   Manufacturers frequently offer retailers special allowances for advertising their particular brands in local newspapers. Besides expecting that retailers will more aggressively feature such advertised items in their stores, manufacturers also benefit indirectly from lower local advertising rates. Most often, these advertising subsidies are in the form of co-op payments, with the retailer paying part of the cost of a particular ad featuring a manufacturer's products and name, and the manufacturer paying the other part.

While advertising allowances can be attractive to retailers and ease some of their promotional burden, care must be taken that the products have sufficient sales potential to be worth advertising at the time. The retailer must spend some money, usually at least half, on such ads. As Roberta Pinelli says concerning the bargaining process to get some advertising allotments, "You're stupid to take something just because you can get advertising on it."

Future Dating

Future dating is commonly used to encourage retailers to buy in advance of a season or before they have adequate funds available to invest in inventory. A typical example of future dating is 2/10, 60 days extra, which means that the buyer has 60 days before the ordinary dating of 2/10, net 30 begins, or a total of 70 days to obtain the 2 percent cash discount and 90 days for the net 30. EOM (end of month) dating is common. For example, an early June purchase may specify 2/10 EOM, which means that the 2 percent cash discount may be taken through July 10, or 10 days after the end of the month. It is common billing practice to consider invoices dated the 25th of the month or later as carrying over to the next month. With some early purchases of seasonal goods, such as toys, an invoice for an order in June may be dated "as of October 1," with the terms figured from that date. ROG (receipt of goods) dating or AOG (arrival of goods) dating is commonly used on the West Coast, where stores are located great distances from the vendors' shipping points, so that merchandise may arrive well after the invoice. The date of the cash discount and terms then begins when the goods are received.

ANTICIPATION   Sometimes retailers pay their bills before the due dates and take an extra discount, which is called *anticipation.* For example, a 2/10, 60 extra invoice might be paid in 20 days, which is 50 days prior to expiration of the cash discount period. The retailer then would deduct both the 2 percent cash discount and perhaps 9 percent interest for 50 days as the anticipation. On $10,000, this would amount to $125:

$$.09 \times \frac{50}{360} \times \$10,000 = \$125$$

Of course, such an extra discount is deducted after the original cash discount is figured. Where allowed by the manufacturer, the retailer receives a good return for anticipation, while the vendor gains immediate funds.

LOADING   *Loading* is practiced by a few retailers. Under this policy, selling departments are charged any differences between a cash-discount rate demanded by management and that actually received from vendors. Usually such an arbitrary discount rate is set higher than what is normally received. For example, 6 percent may be established as the cash discount that all buyers must attain. If a buyer is able to get only 2 percent from a particular vendor, then these purchases are charged or loaded with the extra 4 percent. The rationale for loading is to motivate the buyer to drive harder bargains. But the result often is that purchase costs are inflated, and this tends to bring higher selling prices than there would be without such loading. The buyer in this situation must be careful not to price out of line with competition.

Perhaps the ultimate in loading was the infamous 599 account of Sears. This was an internal kitty built up by Sears buyers, who deliberately overcharged Sears stores for their purchases. More than $1 billion a year was going into the kitty, and the money was made available for many purposes ranging from national advertising to coverage of markdowns. The following example shows the impact of such loading:

Take a small appliance that costs Sears $10. At a loaded cost of $11, the results would be as follows, given a target markup of double the cost price (this is a keystone markup, described in the next chapter):

True cost	$10	Loaded cost	$11
Markup	$10	Markup	$11
Retail	$20	Retail	$22

If 100,000 items are sold, then $100,000 goes into the kitty from this one item.

Such a kitty furnishing extra advertising funds and a cushion to compensate for markdowns was contagiously intriguing; but it finally got seriously out of hand. Too many buyers inflated purchase costs so that they could contribute to this burgeoning kitty. As a result, Sears' prices in many areas were pushed above competitors', and sales suffered. Effective February 1, 1979, the company put an end to the 599 account.[2]

Miscellaneous Negotiable Terms

Other items may be negotiable in the purchase situation, such as shipping terms, exclusiveness of goods, price guarantees, and dealer aids.

Transportation charges are a major addition to the cost of goods. Usually, prices are quoted *f.o.b.* (free on board) factory; this means that the retailer pays transportation charges from the vendor's delivery platform. Occasionally, the shipping point might be negotiated, with the buyer seeking f.o.b. store (the vendor paying all transportation to the retailer's premises), but seldom achieving it. The buyer should specify shipping instructions on the order form. "Cheapest" may be designated in order to hold transportation costs to a minimum; occasionally "fastest" may need to be specified to prevent or minimize merchandise out-of-stocks.

It is usually to the retailer's advantage to have the "exclusive right" to handle a certain brand of goods within a given area. This eliminates direct price competition, since no nearby retailer will have these particular goods and be able to undersell. Even where competing stores handle some items of the same brand, the retailer may be able to negotiate temporary exclusive distribution of a certain new style.

When buying seasonal goods some months in advance of the main selling season, a buyer wants assurance that any price reductions after

---

[2] For more detail on Sears' loading problems and their effect on sales, see "Sears, Facing an Array of Nagging Problems, Moves to Reorganize," *Wall Street Journal,* December 27, 1978, pp. 1 and 21; and "Sears' Strategic About-Face," *Business Week,* January 8, 1979, pp. 80–83.

the order is placed will not cause an inventory loss. (While price rises are more frequent, prices do go down sometimes.) Usually vendors are eager for these advance orders and can be persuaded to offer price guarantees, so that the retailer would be refunded the difference between the price at which he placed the order and any lower one that develops before the peak season.

Manufacturers may provide dealer aids, usually in the form of point-of-purchase window or counter display materials, that may help in the sale of their products. Such materials are often furnished free and without any encouragement from the retailer; and many are as quickly thrown away by stores. Sometimes, though, a particular rack, turntable, or manikin may seem so attractive to a retailer that he or she may pressure the manufacturer to give or loan it to the store.

SOURCES OF MERCHANDISE

The retailer may obtain goods from the following sources:

1. The manufacturer's showroom or factory
2. Resident buying offices
3. Manufacturers' salespeople and representatives
4. Catalogs or price lists
5. Local wholesalers

People commonly think of a buyer as a man or woman who frequently makes buying trips to New York City, or perhaps to foreign markets. While domestic buying is not centered entirely in New York City (for example, furniture manufacturers are concentrated in Virginia and the Carolinas), New York is the focal point for most women's and men's apparel manufacturers, jewelry, lingerie, piece goods, and many other product categories. For certain types of merchandise, special trade shows are held annually at places like the Merchandise Mart in Chicago and showrooms in Atlantic City, New Jersey. The concentration of many manufacturers' offerings at such showrooms, and the concentration of most product categories within a small area of showrooms in New York City simplifies the buyer's job and enables him or her to compare styles, prices, and qualities among many sources of supply.

Many retailers maintain an affiliation with a resident buying office, usually located in the New York market. Resident buyers near the

Two buyers examine goods at a trade-show booth. A trade show allows buyers to view a variety of manufacturers' products. Being able to examine many offerings together under one roof reduces the time buyers must spend searching for new and different goods. (Erich Hartmann/Magnum)

market centers can keep in close touch with showrooms and factories and with the newest offerings and market communications, and can offer expert advice to the home-store buyers. Later in this chapter we will examine the role and services offered by resident buying offices in more detail.

While buyers for large stores frequently travel to New York and elsewhere, small retailers may find such buying expeditions to be prohibitively expensive. Several alternatives are available. While these do not provide the market "feel" gained from frequently visiting the major markets, they still are adequate and practical. Larger manufacturers have salespeople call on retailers with samples and market information. Other manufacturers, especially small ones, employ *manufacturers' representatives*. These are independent businesspeople who handle the products of several manufacturers (who are usually noncompeting) and receive a straight commission on everything they sell. By such contacts the small retailers can make reasonable merchandise choices, although the range is more limited.

TABLE 12.1   U.S. WHOLESALE TRADE, 1939–1972

	1939	1954	1967	1972
Number of wholesale establishments	190,000	250,000	311,464	370,000
Wholesale trade (billions)	$53.8	$234.0	$459.5	$695.2

Source: U.S. Census of Business, Wholesale Trade, for respective years, U.S. Summary.

Catalogs and price lists are an important source of goods for many retailers. Even the large ones rely on these for repeat purchases, especially of staple goods, since there is no need to evaluate the quality and salability of such goods each time. For bulky items, such as furniture and hardware, a catalog may be the only practical way to show the merchandise, and it is superior to a buyer's personal observation, since specifications and nonobvious features can be described.

Buying through local wholesalers offers particular advantages. Otherwise, wholesale trade would not have grown in the last thirty years, as shown in Table 12.1, during the very time when retailers were getting larger and pressing for the lowest possible prices to meet discount store competition.

Small retailers often have no reasonable alternative to buying from wholesalers, who can handle their small orders and provide almost immediate delivery. Wholesalers may also give both credit and some merchandising guidance that greatly benefit the small store. Almost all buying for drugstores and food stores is done through local wholesalers specializing in filling the orders of such customers. Since wholesalers serve a number of customers, they can buy in larger quantities at more economical prices and better shipping terms than individual retailers can. Consequently, the prices they charge their customers may not be much more than the customers would pay if they went directly to the manufacturer.

Even large retailers who can buy at advantageous prices from manufacturers may find the local wholesaler an attractive supply source, at least for some goods and some occasions. Because the wholesaler has local stocks of goods for immediate delivery, the large retailer can buy hand-to-mouth. The extra price paid through the wholesaler may be more than offset by the lower investment in inventory. At the very least, large buyers may look upon wholesalers as alternative sources of goods who can minimize out-of-stocks and lost sales. The difference in delivery time between a wholesaler and a manufacturer can be a month and more.

Rack jobbers are a special type of full-service wholesaler. They have come into prominence as many retailers have attempted to cut costs by adopting self-service and hiring fewer employees. Particularly in the discount and supermarket field, rack jobbers have taken over the task of stockkeeping and order taking for such nonfood products as notions, stationery, housewares, and hosiery; sometimes rack jobbers even supply their own display racks; all the retailer has to do is provide the space. The retailer is thereby relieved of the expense and tedium of maintaining adequate stocks of such goods, which come in many different sizes, colors, and styles and have relatively low unit values. Somewhat like rack jobbers, who handle nonperishable items, are truck wholesalers, also called *wagon jobbers,* who handle perishable items such as candy, cheese, and bakery products. They provide fast and frequent deliveries to stores and sometimes also to restaurants and hotels.

Occasionally a manufacturer takes over the role of rack jobber, providing direct store delivery and maintaining stocks and displays:

Hanes Corp., the manufacturer of L'eggs pantyhose, has had phenomenal success in marketing through supermarkets: "All we asked was $2\frac{1}{2}$ sq. ft. of their store." Each store averages $1,300 a year profit from a single "L'eggs" display, and there are no service costs since route girls do all the re-stocking and cleaning.[3]

SUPPLIER RELATIONS

A retailer will experience different degrees of satisfaction with resources (suppliers). Some will be reliable, others will not; some helpful and cooperative, others disdainful and rigid; some will have better and more consistent quality than others.

Concentration Versus Dispersion

The supplier/retailer relationship functions most smoothly when each is important to the other. This accounts for the powerful position of a

[3] "Our L'eggs Fit Your Legs," from the March 25, 1972 issue of BusinessWeek, pp. 96–100. © 1972 by McGraw-Hill, Inc., New York, NY 10020.

large retailer: the volume of business is such that its loss would be keenly felt by a supplier. The small retailer can never loom as important, although close ties with a local wholesaler may cement a not-unimportant relationship.[4]

A large retailer's importance to suppliers may be dissipated by dividing up the business among many. It might appear that dispersing a firm's business among many different vendors brings the greatest possible variety of offerings to customers and makes for the most active competition among suppliers. But usually the disadvantages outweigh the advantages. Once a firm is well established and has had experience with different vendors, there are great advantages, such as the following, in concentrating buying efforts with a few top-notch ones:

1. The retailer becomes important to the supplier, and vice versa. The rapport and cooperation thus gained may become manifest in many ways, from priority with new merchandise and order filling, to prompt cooperative attention to damaged merchandise. In a good relationship, a vendor may even help out a buyer who has made a bad or ill-timed purchase by arranging to take back the goods or have them transferred to another customer. The vendor may also accumulate special lots for sale events and other store promotions.
2. Costs can be reduced. Less search time is required of the buyer. Ordering and processing of goods are easier when fewer invoices and fewer shipments are involved. The store can maintain more continuity of stock records. Salespeople can be more knowledgeable about the performance and assortment of goods.

Rating Suppliers

A policy of concentrating purchases would be a disaster unless good, reliable suppliers are selected. Most buyers have to do some screening of the many supplier representatives and their offerings. Accordingly, some sort of vendor or supplier rating system can be a distinct advantage. This may be rather subjective and consist only of a few incidents of good or poor service that stand out in the buyer's mind. A systematic and more objective rating system is desirable.

---

[4] For some guides in becoming a "preferred customer" important to a supplier, see Alan J. Brokaw and Charles N. Davidson, "Positioning a Company as a Preferred Customer," *Journal of Purchasing and Materials Management* (Spring 1978), 9–11.

RETAILING TOOL—*Rating Suppliers*

Just as an employee can and should be rated according to various categories of performance, so can suppliers be rated according to their strengths and weaknesses. They may be rated according to the following factors:

	Worst	*Best*
Average delivery time		
Proportion of damaged merchandise		
Number of customer complaints		
Percentage of markdowns to total purchases		
Price of goods relative to quality		
Cooperation on sales, adjustments, special orders, and so on		

Some of these factors might be considered more important than others and the buyer might wish to weight these more heavily.

How do we assess these factors for each vendor? This can be done rather precisely for some of the factors. For example, by reviewing merchandise records, the time between order date and receipt date of merchandise can be quickly tabulated. Markdown data are usually quite complete, and a tabulation of markdowns by vendors is easily made. Records of returned goods and other damaged items are maintained in most stores, and vendor information can be quickly compiled. The matter of customer complaints may require an additional journal in the department and insistence that salespeople be conscientious in recording. The buyer and staff may have to make an evaluation as to how various vendors compare in the prices and qualities of their goods and in cooperation.

For Thought and Discussion

1. Can you think of any other factors on which it might be desirable to rate suppliers?
2. If you were asked to assign weights according to the relative importance of these factors, how would you weight them? Why?
3. Do you think that "customer complaints" is a good rating factor? Do you see any limitations to it as a measure?

Such a rating system may be developed and used by an individual buyer in order to do a better buying job in a department. In other stores, the initiative may rest with a divisional merchandise manager, or even with the general merchandise manager, to insist on its use in all departments. Certainly with such guidance, a supplier who shows up poorly compared to other suppliers would have to offer special assurances of better performance to expect much of that store's business. Weaker-performing vendors might thereby be prodded to better efforts.

An analysis made by one store of markups by suppliers or vendors in its housewares department is shown in the retailing tool that follows. Markups will be discussed in detail in Chapter 13, but for our purposes

RETAILING TOOL—Analysis of Markup by Vendor

Vendor code	Mark up by	Cost	Freight	Del. cost	Retail	MU% w/o Frt.	MU% inc. Frt.
105	Amer. Thermos	69	5	74	110	37.27*	32.73*
106	Wearever Alum.	1408	29	1437	2460	42.76	41.59
107	Mirror Alum.	191	6	197	345	44.64	42.90
134	Amer. Casserole	83	4	87	160	48.12	45.62
136	Ade-o-matic	10			15	33.33*	
1518	Dscrow	254			423	39.95	
1601	Puritan Fireplace	179	16	195	360	50.28	45.83
1602	Pantry Queen	105	11	116	176	40.34	34.09*
1603	Paper Arts	73			123	40.65	
1604	Proctor Ele.	1486			2445	39.22	
2208	Victory lite	119	6	125	246	51.63	49.19
2300	Wilbur Step	45.6	16	472	737	38.13*	35.96*
2301	Wagner Mfg.	81			137	40.88	
2304	West Bend Alum.	371	17	388	641	42.12	39.47
2307	Wooster Rubber	2827			4624	38.86	

Goal 38.7%   * Below Goal

Comments   The asterisk indicates those vendors whose goods were below the planned markup goal of 38.7 percent. Note the importance of considering the freight charges along with the cost of goods in order to come up with a markup percentage *including* freight. For example, as you can see in the above analysis, the markup percentage for Pantry Queen was well above the markup-percentage goal, but *not* when freight costs were added. This significant cost which includes freight is called the *delivered* or *landed cost*.

For Thought and Discussion

1. What rationale would you present to your merchandise manager for continuing to do business with vendors whose goods are well below the planned markup goal?
2. What strategies would you propose to increase your overall departmental markup?

now we can define the markup percentage as the difference between what goods sell for at retail and what they cost the merchant. Therefore, the higher the markup percentage, the more desirable the goods are for the retailer, provided that demand is similar to that for alternative goods. If a higher-markup item has more limited demand, on the other hand, a lower-priced, lower-markup item may be more advantageous to stock.

RESIDENT BUYING OFFICES

Because resident buying offices are located in the major markets, affiliation with one reduces the need for the many costly trips to market otherwise necessary to keep abreast of current offerings. While a retailer does not have to join a resident office in order to compete effectively, the advantages in doing so have led to a number of different offices developed to serve all sizes of retailers. Particularly in women's and children's apparel, these offices are widely used; they are also important in men's wear, home furnishings, jewelry, and certain other lines.

A major advantage of affiliation with a resident buying office is the market feedback provided. Information is readily available to clients about goods available, best sources of supply, fashion trends, prices, and hot items. A resident office may place orders upon request, check on deliveries, and handle adjustments. When the buyer makes a trip to market, the resident office assists in making the best use of the buyer's time. The office will arrange showings, screen vendors, accompany the buyer on visits to vendors (thereby providing some expert judgment in addition to the buyer's own), and furnish office space and stenographic aid in the resident office. These offices may act as clearinghouses for market feedback from all the stores served. For those retailers interested in imported goods, many buying offices have branches in foreign countries.

There are three basic kinds of resident offices: store owned, chain owned, and independent. Most store-owned buying offices are owned by a number of noncompeting stores, with expenses shared by all members of the group. One of the best known is AMC (Associated Merchandising Corporation), to which belong such major stores as Dayton-Hudson, Rich's, Abraham and Straus, Bloomingdale's, Bullock's, Emporium, and Capwell. Not only is information shared with all members of the group, but private brands are also developed for the member firms.

Chain-owned buying offices resemble store-owned ones, except that the common ownership of the chain outlets gives these buying offices more power. Central buying and forced adoptions of new merchandise are common. Allied Purchasing Corporation and Associated Dry Goods Corporation are examples of such chain or syndicate buying offices.

Smaller retailers necessarily must seek affiliation with independent offices if they are to have in-market representation. These are privately owned offices to which members pay a fee, perhaps based on annual sales or on services rendered. Some of the better-known independent offices are Atlas Buying Corporation and Independent Retailers Syndicate. A special type of resident buyer is the *merchandise broker,* who serves smaller retailers unable to afford the minimum cost of the regular independent buying offices. The merchandise broker receives remuneration from the manufacturer, often a 3 percent commission on all orders placed with the affiliated vendors.

FOREIGN PURCHASING

Increasingly, retailers are finding it desirable to offer their affluent customers foreign goods: Belgian laces, Danish furniture, Swiss wood carvings, Irish linens, even cricket cages and carved elephants from Kenya. Such imported goods give prestige to a store and impart a cosmopolitan image; more than this, however, imported goods tend to command high markups and yield high per-unit profits. Even supermarkets are testing foreign goods.

Foreign merchandise is obtained through the following sources:

1. Trips overseas by store buyers
2. Import wholesalers
3. Commissionaires or foreign resident offices

Large retailers periodically send certain buyers to visit foreign markets. But this is expensive, and it requires careful planning if the buyer's time is to be spent usefully.

Import wholesalers located in this country are middlemen who carry samples of foreign merchandise and may approach retailers with salespeople and/or catalogs. For smaller retailers this is the most practical source of foreign-made goods, even though the cost is higher than for direct purchase.

Resident buying offices, either foreign owned or American affiliates, assist buyers in the same way that resident buying offices do in this country. The complexities involved in doing business in foreign countries makes their services all the more essential and usually results in somewhat higher fees. For example, the independent (without American affiliation) commissionaires usually charge approximately 7 percent of the foreign cost of purchases they assist in making.

■ Summary

In this chapter we looked at some of the decisions facing the buyer seeking goods and negotiating for them. Buying staple goods is considerably different than buying fashion goods. Fad items present the highest risks. Special buying situations can be advantageous but, on the other hand, may tie up funds in slow-moving merchandise. A buyer must attempt to achieve the best terms of sale possible, since these can materially increase profit prospects. A number of sources are available for placing orders. The buyer needs to assess how well the alternative sources meet his or her needs. Supplier relationships can be extremely important in providing stability and a mutually advantageous environment for the purchase transaction. However, it is best to rate suppliers systematically to identify those who are not performing satisfactorily. In the next chapter we will turn our attention to pricing the goods bought from the various suppliers. We will consider both the philosophy and the mathematics of retail pricing.

■ **Key Terms**

Advertising allowances   Loading
Anticipation   Manufacturers' representatives
Consignment   Merchandise broker
Delivered or landed cost   Private brands
Discount   Rack jobbers
Fad items   Special orders
f.o.b.   Specification buying
Future dating   Wagon jobbers
Guaranteed sales

■ **Discussion Questions**

1. Differentiate between a seasonal discount and a trade discount. Which is more likely to have disadvantages from the retailer's viewpoint?
2. Evaluate the practice of loading from the viewpoint of the store and also of the buyer.
3. What is desirable about having exclusive rights to particular goods?
4. Would you expect a rack jobber to perform services for you with little or no supervision? Why or why not?
5. As the owner of a small men's store, what would be your policy regarding special orders? Why? Would it be any different if you were the buyer for a large men's department?
6. What is the difference between classification analysis and staple-goods analysis?
7. How should you reorder fad items? What data would you base your decision on?
8. Why isn't specification buying more widely used by retailers?

■ **Project**

Talk to a local wholesaler and find out what are seen as inducements for large retailers to do business with the wholesaler's firm. What are the inducements for small retailers? Then talk to a buyer of a department or specialty store and obtain that person's ideas about doing business with local wholesalers.

■ Exercise in Creativity

You are the buyer for a medium-size department store with four branches. You are aware that nostalgia is a theme that seems to be growing in popularity. Accordingly, you have persuaded a manufacturer to produce, according to your specifications, an old-style spinning wheel for sale as a conversation piece. How would you go about promoting the spinning wheel and attempting to make it a fad item. Be as creative as you can. But also try to be specific and practical.

■ Retailing in Action: Role Plays

1. You are the buyer of window air conditioners. Last year your sales were as follows:

April	9 units
May	17
June	60
July	70
August	20

   The date is June 15. You have 70 air conditioners in stock. Because it has been a cool season so far, your sales from April 1 to June 15 have totaled only 30 units. You have to decide now how many (if any) air conditioners you will buy for the rest of the season, as delivery will take 3–4 weeks.

   What would you do? Defend your decision to your merchandise manager.

2. You have been hired to manage a women's dress shop which last year had a volume of $120,000. After becoming familiar with the stock and the merchandise records, you find that dresses are being bought from twenty-five different vendors. The owner (who has been doing the buying, but wants you to take over) tells you that this makes it possible to stock a greater variety of dresses.

   What, if anything, would you suggest for selecting vendors?

■ Retail Math

1. Calculate the quantity-to-buy of a certain price of ski jacket. The relevant figures follow:

> Estimated sales, October, November, December   300 units
> Desired stock, December 31   0
> Goods on hand and on order, October 1   120
> Quantity to buy, October 1?

Since the desired stock is planned as 0 at the end of December, where is January and February ski-jacket business to come from?

2. A buyer orders 60 dozen women's blouses at $82 a dozen, with terms of 3/10, net 60. The invoice is dated March 3, and is paid May 1. Failure to obtain the discount is equivalent to paying what annual rate of interest using 360 days as a year?

3. A manufacturer offers terms of either 3/10, net 30 or 2/10, 60 extra. Either set of terms may be chosen, and anticipation is allowed at the rate of 10 percent with either. If a retail firm is prepared to pay the invoice within 5 days of its date, which set of terms should it choose?

13 Price Setting and Adjusting

A store's prices help determine its image and the customers it attracts. The price level in relation to other retailers' price levels—the *price differential*—contributes to the store's reputation. A major ingredient in a consumer's perception of quality is prices: high prices produce an aura of prestige and exclusiveness; low prices, when vigorously promoted, can create an image of bargains (even though these "bargains" may not all be such great values).

USING PRICE AS A COMPETITIVE TOOL

A major drawback to using price as an aggressive form of competition is that competitors can easily match price cuts. At least, this is true in the short term; in the longer term the smaller and less financially able stores may be driven out of business. The firm that uses price cutting as a major offensive weapon may find its profits severely hurt, without any appreciable permanent gains. Consider the following example:

RETAILING STRATEGIES—*Price Cutting at A&P*

In May 1972, with a flourish of advertising, A&P began converting its 4,200 stores to fit the slogan "Where Economy Originates," or WEO for short. A sort of superduper-discount-stores image was the aim. Prices were lowered on 90 percent of the merchandise, and signs galore proclaimed this. As A&P's chairman, William Kane said, "I want to get us back to good, sound, basic fundamentals. This company was built on quality foods sold at low prices."

The reason behind A&P's aggressive price cutting was that it had lost its number one sales position in the industry to Safeway the previous year. Kane thought it was necessary to shake the giant from its lethargy. And A&P's competitors shuddered. Vicious price wars developed that destroyed the profits of the whole supermarket industry in 1972. A&P, however, may have suffered the most. While it regained its sales lead from Safeway Stores, the net loss for the year 1972 was $51.3 million, the worst in the company's recent history, and it was forced to omit a dividend for the first time since 1925.

By the middle of 1973, A&P was toning down its WEO advertising. It was also quietly raising prices, hoping to get earnings back into the black and also hoping that the discount image it tried so hard to create would still remain and be an advantage.

But the years after 1973 were not good for A&P. It slipped further to third in the industry, now also behind Kroger. With the failure of the WEO campaign, new management moved to trim the number of losing stores, and by 1979 total stores had been reduced to 1,800. A self-critical advertising campaign promised "to put price and pride together again." But the company continued to either lose money or barely make a profit. Then in January 1979, one of West Germany's largest food retailers unexpectedly made a friendly offer to the four principal holders of A&P stock for their 42 percent controlling interest. The offer was about $7.50 a share, slightly over the market price, but far below the $39 a share that the stock had commanded eleven years before.

Sources: For more detail, see "A&P's Ploy: Cutting Prices to Turn a Profit," *Business Week,* May 20, 1972; Robert F. Hartley, *Marketing Mistakes* (Columbus, Ohio: Grid Publishing, 1976), pp. 97–110; "The Price of Grandma's Pride," *Time,* January 29, 1979, p. 45.

For Thought and Discussion

1. What other alternatives might A&P's management have tried, when confronted with a waning competitive position?
2. Do you think token price cuts on a few hundred items, rather than several thousand, would have been just as effective without being such a drain on profits? Why or why not?

Most retailers use price at some time as a promotional device to attract customers. A survey will show that the majority of newspaper ads emphasize special prices and sales.

Prices have strong competitive overtones. The price differentials that retailers seek depend to a considerable extent on their estimation of their competitors. If a retailer thinks the firm's position is strong, because of size, assortment, or a solidly attractive image, then there is less concern with matching the prices of competitors. However, not many stores can entirely disregard competition in their pricing decisions, or their business may quietly erode. But what about the other extreme of refusing to be undersold? This may be more drastic than necessary and may assume more price consciousness on the part of consumers than really exists. As we noted in Chapter 5, there is considerable evidence that some consumers view convenience, merchandise quality and assortment, and friendliness of clerks as more important than price.

Undoubtedly, the importance of price varies from person to person. The poor, the very consumers who should be most price conscious, are most naive or apathetic when it comes to shopping for the best values. This is less true of many middle-class consumers and those on fixed incomes. Price is especially important to growing suburban families of limited income and burgeoning wants, to whom the discount stores have an overwhelming appeal.

THE PRICE-QUALITY IMAGE AND PRICING ABUSES

In this section, let us jump from the role of retailers selling to consumers to the role of consumers themselves. This should not be hard to do, since we are all consumers. As retailers, it is well not to lose our empathy for the consumers we are supposed to serve.

With today's complex products and hidden ingredients, consumers have difficulty in assessing the quality of products. Often, even experience with similar products in the past cannot be relied upon because of the frequent introduction of new models.

The most common index of quality is the price of the product: the higher the price, the higher the quality. Yet this has led to abuses.

A retailer bought an assortment of women's blouses costing $4.80 each. He planned to sell them at $8.95, which would give him a comfortable 46 percent markup. Upon examining them, he picked out 4 dozen that he priced at $12.95. When asked the difference, he replied, "the price."

A survey by a Senate subcommittee found that a supermarket chain was selling its own brand of aspirin at 100 tablets for 19¢. This compared with 73¢ for Bayer aspirin, $1.17 for Anacin, and $1.19 for Excedrin. The testimony before the subcommittee revealed that the higher price brands "have no real advantage over an equivalent dose of regular aspirin." What is the difference? Only the price.[1]

For a retailer, the temptation to take advantage of this price-quality perception may seem most attractive. But there are inherent dangers:

1. Both state consumer agencies and the Federal Trade Commission are taking keener looks at any practices that may verge on being deceptive.
2. The long-term development of customer good will and repeat business may be jeopardized by short-sighted practices aimed at giving less than honest values.

The fact remains that the price-quality image leaves consumers vulnerable to deceptive practices. We will now discuss some of the more common pricing abuses indulged in by some retailers.

Comparative prices are frequent, especially in conjunction with sales. An item may be featured as "$7.77, regularly $14.95." It may so appear in newspaper advertisements, on display signs, and the salesperson may announce it to the interested customer. Of course, the objective is to make the item appear to be an exceptional buy.

Comparative prices may be truthful: the item may once have sold for such a price. But sometimes there are mild or even extreme exaggerations called *fictitious comparisons*. Large retailers who are more in the public eye than small ones may have to justify their comparative prices. But the government is unable to police all price comparisons. Exaggerated and deceptive fictitious price comparisons still persist.

Bait and switch, which we discussed in Chapter 4, is a common

---

[1] "Nothing, Says FDA, Beats Aspirin," *Washington Post*, June 23, 1971, p. C4. © the Washington Post.

merchandising practice. At the extreme, it is deceptive and abusive. The abuse is most prevalent in ghetto stores: an appliance or a set of furniture may be advertised at an unreasonably low price, the objective being to entice customers into the store. But when they attempt to purchase the "sale" item they find it, in the parlance of retailing, nailed to the floor. In other words, it is not available; the only piece at that price may be broken, shopworn, have missing parts, or carry a "sold" tag. The customer is then traded up to a more expensive and more profitable product.

But this is the extreme. It is commonplace for reputable retailers to advertise their most attractively priced items and then attempt to sell a customer something else. Some retailers even offer items below cost (so-called loss leaders) to generate customer traffic, expecting that regular-priced items will be bought as well. Some weekly grocery ads are of this type. The difference between such bait and switch advertising and the deceptive kind is that the sale item is available; customers can buy it if they so desire (and some, indeed, may buy nothing else but loss leaders).

False sales and supposed giveaways also result in customer confusion. The sign "Sale!" can be affixed to any item or display to give the impression of an unusual price advantage. Other signs frequently encountered—and not always legitimate—include "1¢ Sale," "Free," "Buy One, Get One at Half Price," "2 for 1 Sale," and the like. Even when the item is offered at a lower than usual price, the value may be far less than that indicated by "Free," and "1¢ Sale." In these cases, the price of the article that must be fully paid for to get the bargain may be increased.

Consumers have long been confused by an inability to gauge the best buy because of odd and multiple prices, and containers that are not uniform. Much of this is not the fault of retailers: the blame for confusing packaging and price smoke-screening lies with manufacturers. But some responsive retailers are now unit pricing. In addition to the regular price placed on the package or container, they are also posting prices by the ounce, pound, or other standard measure. This enables the customer to better determine the best buy among competing brands, as well as among the different sizes of the same brand.

MARKUP CALCULATIONS

Markup is simply the difference between what goods are sold for and what they cost the merchant: Selling Price − Cost = Markup. For a department and a store, the overall markup of all products must be sufficient to cover all expenses and provide some profit. While markup is important in actual dollars contributed toward store expenses and profits, the *markup percentage* is more useful to merchandisers in their day-to-day decisions.

Markup Percentage

It has become common practice to calculate the markup percentage on the retail- or selling-price base. The simple formula is

$$\text{Markup percentage on retail} = \frac{\$ \text{ Markup}}{\$ \text{ Selling price}}$$

For example, if a man's shirt costs $6, and is sold for $9, the dollar markup is $3. The markup percentage on retail is

$$\frac{\$3}{\$9} = 33 \text{ percent, based on retail}$$

The markup percentage can also be based on cost. In the preceding example, if the cost base is used, then the markup percentage is

$$\text{Markup percentage on cost} = \frac{\$ \text{ Markup}}{\$ \text{ Cost}} = \frac{\$3}{\$6} = 50 \text{ percent,} \atop \text{based on cost}$$

It can be seen from this that markup on retail must always be a lower percentage figure than the equivalent markup on cost. Also, markup on retail can never reach 100 percent, while on the cost base it can easily exceed this. The following shows some equivalent cost and retail markup percentages:

Percent markup on cost	= *Percent markup on retail*
25.0	20.0
33.3	25.0
50.0	33.3
66.7	40.0
100.0	50.0
200.0	66.7
300.0	75.0

There are several reasons for the popularity of the retail base in calculating markup percentages. First, it does not appear as large to any casual observer, and, in the interest of public relations, the more modest profit figure is to be desired. But there are other strong advantages. Such information is much more easily available than cost information and, therefore, both the calculation of estimated profits and the taking of inventory are simplified. The alternative would be to code the cost figures on each item of merchandise, a cumbersome procedure at best. Since most operating expenses are stated as a percent of sales, it is reasonable to base markup on selling price as well. For example, if markup were expressed as 50 percent of the cost of purchases, and expenses as 33 percent of sales, it would not be readily apparent whether a profit was being made. (In this case a profit would not be made.) Furthermore, since most retailers calculate markup based on retail, various operating statistics of noncompeting and affiliated stores can be compared.[2]

Applying the Markup Percentage of Retail

The simple formula, Retail = Cost + Markup or (R = C + M), always permits any one figure to be derived when the other two are known. However, when markup percentages are to be used (rather than dollar figures), then several modifications of the basic formula are more useful.

RETAILING TOOL—*Applying Markup Calculations to Pricing*

Several of the more common practical applications the buyer encounters are as follows:

1. Determining what selling price will yield a desired markup percentage when the cost is known:

   Problem: A women's dress buyer finds an attractive group of dresses priced by the manufacturer at $12 each. She would like to obtain as close to a 40-percent markup (on retail) as possible. What price would she have to sell these dresses for?

   Solution: The recommended formula is

---

[2] Some retailers, mostly small ones, still use the cost basis. However, since the retail base is far more widely used, we will consider only its computations here. For more detail about either the cost base or the retail base computations, see Ralph D. Shipp, Jr., *Retail Merchandising—Principles and Applications* (Boston: Houghton Mifflin Company, 1976), Chapter 3.

$$R = \frac{C}{100 \text{ percent} - MU \text{ percent}}$$

$$R = \frac{\$12}{1.00 - .40} = \$20$$

In the actual situation, the buyer would probably sell the dresses for $19.95.

2. Determining what cost will yield a desired markup percentage at a particular selling price:

Problem: A linen and bedding department buyer is budgeted for an overall 38-percent departmental gross margin (markup). He needs to buy bath towels to retail for $4.98. What is the minimum cost he should seek?

Solution: The above formula when solving for C becomes

$$C = R \times (100 \text{ percent} - MU \text{ percent})$$
$$= \$4.98 \times (1.00 - .38)$$
$$= \$3.09 \text{ each, or about } \$37 \text{ a dozen}$$

For Further Analysis   If an item costs $18.00 a dozen and, to be competitive, you must sell it for no more than $1.98, what is your markup percentage? If your planned departmental markup is 40%, what are your alternatives? Evaluate them.

AIDS TO CALCULATION   The frequency with which the buyer must make such calculations, especially when visiting the market to purchase goods, has led to the use of special slide rules and buyer's wheels. Figure 13.1 shows the slide rule type. Cost figures are located along the top of this device, and by lining up the correct per-unit or per-dozen

FIGURE 13.1 SLIDE RULE TYPE OF MARKUP INDICATOR

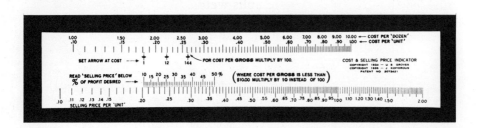

arrow of the middle section, the percent profit on selling price (markup on retail) can be seen at various selling prices at the bottom. For example, if an item is quoted at $4.00 per unit, one would set the unit arrow at $4.00 and look at the bottom to see that a 40-percent profit would require a selling price of approximately $6.75.

THE KEYSTONE MARKUP   A rather common method of arriving at the selling price—and one that requires no special slide rule or buyer's wheel—is simply to double the cost of an item. Accordingly, if a blouse costs a retailer $9.95, it could be retailed at $19.90 (or more likely, $19.95). This is known as a *keystone markup,* and is common in apparel, accessories, shoes, and cosmetics departments. Doubling the cost, of course, gives a 50 percent markup, which seems high. It can be justified when risks are considerable (as they frequently are with fashion goods), and when the comparability of competing goods is difficult for customers to assess. However, while the keystone markup is attractive to a retailer because of its ease of calculation and the comfortable profit margin, it can leave a complacent firm vulnerable to serious competitive inroads, if competitors are content with more modest markups. Keystoning is especially dangerous to use for items whose price and quality are more easily compared to competing goods than they are with fashion goods. Discount stores and discount-catalog showrooms are growing today as consumers become more price conscious; and the discount stores are not keystoning.

Initial Markup and the Maintained Markup

The initial markup (sometimes called the markon) that we have been calculating is not always the actual markup realized when the goods are finally sold. The maintained markup, or the actual markup realized from sales, may be less because of markdowns and certain other discounts. The following example illustrates the difference between these two markups. Let us assume that a certain lot of goods was received at the beginning of the month (BOM). By the end of the month (EOM) none were left, and the sales results were as follows:

	Cost	*Retail*	*Markup*
BOM stock	$4,000	$7,000	42.9% (initial)
Markdowns		1,500	
EOM stock	0	0	
Sales	4,000	5,500	27.3% (maintained)

In this example, the size of the markdowns necessary to sell out the goods brought the realized or maintained markup down to the point of dubious profitability.

While the maintained markup can be figured for each purchase, it is simpler to apply it for a given period of time only to major merchandise classifications and entire departments. To cover the estimated reductions from the initially established selling price, a formula can be used to arrive at an initial markup percentage goal.

RETAILING TOOL—*How to Plan Markup for a Department*

A department manager needs to determine what initial markup percentage is necessary to cover estimated expenses and yield a desired profit percentage, taking into account probable retail reductions.

Problem   A maintained markup of 33 percent is set as a goal in order to cover expenses and make a satisfactory profit. Past experience has shown that reductions (markdowns, shortages, and discounts to employees) will average 5 percent of sales. What initial markup percentage should be sought?

Solution

$$\text{Initial markup percentage} = \frac{\text{Maintained markup} + \text{Retail reductions}}{100 \text{ percent} + \text{Retail reductions}}$$

$$= \frac{33 \text{ percent} + 5 \text{ percent}}{100 \text{ percent} + 5 \text{ percent}} = \frac{.38}{1.05} = 36.19 \text{ percent}$$

Thus, to achieve a maintained markup of 33 percent, an initial markup of slightly over 36 percent is needed.

For Further Analysis   Assume the role of buyer. Because of a cool spring, you are finding that your markdowns are running higher than expected and are about 6 percent of sales. You still hope to keep shortages and other reductions within the planned 1.5 percent. What initial markup percentage should you aim for at this point? Do you see any risks in striving for this higher markup percentage?

Cost of Goods and Gross Margin

While we have been referring to the cost of goods, a little examination is needed of what goes into this cost. The vendor's price to the retailer may include some discounts, especially a discount for cash payment (perhaps 2/10, net 30); there may be certain trade and quantity discounts as well. Then in-bound transportation charges will usually be involved. What is the cost to be used for determining markups and selling prices?

Merchandise cost is most generally defined as including any trade or quantity discounts that will deduct from the vendor's list price, and all transportation costs that will add to the list price. Cash discounts are usually not deducted from the billed cost to the department, but may later appear as an addition to the gross margin of the department.

Gross margin is similar to the maintained markup, except that it may include two adjustments to the maintained markup: adding cash discounts, and deducting any workroom costs, such as alterations for various clothing items. The relationship is as follows:

Gross margin = Maintained markup +
Cash discounts − Net workroom costs

The Need to Average Individual Markups

To arrive at the planned maintained-markup figure, it is seldom practical to give the same markup percentage to all items. To do so can leave a firm vulnerable to varying competitive prices and customer demand, and the degree of attractiveness of various items is completely ignored. Consequently, the skilled buyer attempts to mark up each item to a point that will maximize its total contribution to profit. This may mean that individual markups may be above or below the desired total markup percentage.

RETAILING TOOL—Buying to a Planned Markup

It is not unusual for a buyer to find that earlier purchases are not meeting markup goals. The situation might be remedied by raising selling prices on these goods, but this may be impractical for competitive reasons or because the demand would likely fall off sharply. Accordingly, to meet the planned markup the buyer may need to search for new purchases that will yield higher markups. The buyer needs to know what markup goals should be for the new purchases.

Problem: A buyer goes on a buying trip with an open-to-buy (OTB) of $86,000 (retail). (That is, the buyer has a spending allowance to purchase goods whose sale at retail will total $86,000.) The planned markup for these purchases is 40 percent. After the first few days, an examination of the records shows that $32,000 at retail has been spent, but that these purchases have an average markup of only 30 percent. How much does the buyer have to average on the remaining purchases in order to achieve the overall planned 40-percent markup?

Solution:
Cost of planned purchases at 40-percent markup:

$$C = R \times (1.00 - .40) = \$86,000 \times .60 = \$51,600$$

Cost of purchases already made at 30-percent markup:

$$C = 32,000 \times .70 = 22,400$$

	Cost	*Retail*
Planned purchases	$51,600	$86,000
Purchases already made	22,400	32,000
Remaining to purchase	$29,200	$54,000

$$\text{Markup percentage on remaining} = \frac{R - C}{R}$$

$$= \frac{54,000 - 29,200}{54,000} = \frac{14,800}{54,000} = 45.9\%$$

For Further Analysis   You have $50,000 at cost to spend for the next two months. Your department markup is planned at 42 percent. So far this season you have spent $62,000 at cost, but these goods only average a 39-percent markup. What must the markup on your remaining purchases be if you are to achieve your desired average markup percentage?

Top management sometimes has been guilty of insisting too strongly that markup-percentage goals be reached by each department. While per-unit contributions to profits are assured by markup goals, total profits may be diminished, since some items might have sold more with lower prices. In the past, such an inflexible markup policy has encouraged lower-price competitors. These discounters were not worried about markup-percentage figures, but rather about dollar gross margin figures; they were happy to sell goods at a much lower markup if this would produce good sales volume. To see how greater profits can come from lower markups that produce more sales volume consider the following:

Inflexible markup percentage policy:

> Markup percentage goal   40 percent
> Cost of Product A $3.00
> Selling price at 40 percent $5.00
> Sales at $5.00   250 units

Since each unit has a $2 markup, the contribution to profits is ($2 × 250 units) = $500.

Flexible markup percentage policy:

> Markup percentage permitted   33 percent
> Selling price of Product A
>   at 33 percent $4.50
> Sales at $4.50   500 units

Since each unit has a $1.50 markup, the contribution to profits is ($1.50 × 500) = $750.

As you can see, the buyer would be wiser in this instance to put a lower price and markup on these goods in order to achieve greater sales volume and more total dollars of profit. Of course, demand at different selling prices is not easily determined. Often an increase in sales will not be enough to compensate for the lower per-unit profit. For example, if only 300 units were sold at the lower price, the profits would have been $1.50 × 300 = $450. This would not be as much total profit as 250 units at the $5 price.

The point is that an overemphasis on planned average markups fosters inflexibility. Items with attractive sales potential may not be handled because of below-average markups at competitive prices. Other items may be priced according to the average-markup plan, without regard to handling costs, turnover, and demand elasticity.[3]

The better course of action is to price on the basis of individual item evaluation. By keeping track of how much the cumulative markup percentage on purchases deviates from the planned target, a buyer usually can come close to the target figure.

On the other hand, not to know how various classifications of merchandise are contributing profitwise as compared with other merchandise may result in pricing deficiencies not being noticed. Consider the following analysis of markups made by one store.

---

[3] Demand elasticity is an economic term pertaining to how demand varies with price. The more elastic demand is, the more sales will be affected by differences in prices.

RETAILING TOOL—Analyzing Markup by Class of Goods for a Housewares Department

Period IV

	Cost	Frt.	Landed cost	Retail	MU% w/o Frt.	MU% inc.Frt.
1. Alum. Cooking	10737	96	10833	16610	35.36*	34.78*
2. Stainless etc.	5873	22	5895	9568	38.62*	38.39*
3. Pantry	2971	11	2982	6026	50.70	50.52
5. Paper	2544	38	2582	4305	40.91	40.02
6. Fireplace	68	3	71	122	44.26	41.80
7. Plastics	3666	11	3677	6176	40.64	40.46
8. Cleaning	6485	52	6537	10906	40.54	40.06
9. Table & Stools	500	—	500	833	39.98	39.98
10. Game & TV Table	1173	59	1232	1986	40.94	37.97*
16. Bar BQ	13122	206	13328	18726	29.93*	28.85*
17. Shower Cur.	1746	8	1754	3041	42.59	42.32
18. Gadget	2589	58	2647	4527	42.81	41.52
19. Bath Shop	5699	284	5983	11199	49.11	46.58
22. Laundry	4921	137	5058	8786	43.99	42.43

Goal 38.7% *Below Goal

Comments Note again, as in the analysis of markups by vendor shown in the last chapter, the desirability of looking at markup percentages with freight added in (in other words, landed cost). You can see from the above analysis that some categories of merchandise are a drain on overall department profitability; indeed, the largest-volume category, Bar B Q, was way below the markup goal; the second largest volume category, Aluminum Cooking, was also below.

For Thought and Discussion What would you as a buyer do when faced with these figures? Defend your actions to your merchandise manager.

FACTORS INFLUENCING PRICING AND MARKUP DECISIONS

Certain factors influence both the general level of markups, and the markup and pricing decisions for particular lots of goods. How these factors are interpreted by the individual retailer determines the effectiveness of pricing policy and overall profitability.

Price Levels

A store faces a policy decision of how to price its goods relative to similar goods carried by competitors. To a large extent this should depend on the image a store has or is trying to develop, whether a prestige image, a discount image, or something in between. Markups and prices should vary accordingly.

If a strong retailer has already developed a quality and high-fashion image, for example, the market may not be large enough to support two stores seeking this same price level. And the stakes are often higher in trying to compete at this level. If it is to price above market levels, a store needs to offer certain unique attractions, such as more luxurious surroundings, better service, more exclusive and high-fashion merchandise lines, and a growing reputation for quality. On the other hand, the mass market may support several stores with price levels at or below the general market level; and the stake in decor and merchandise is not as great. This suggests that it is often easier for a new store to seek market entry as a low-price or promotional store, unless analyzing competition (perhaps with retailing mix scales described in Chapter 5) shows that the quality-conscious segment of the market is not being effectively served by existing stores.

Price Lines

In Chapter 11 we discussed the advantages of grouping merchandise into certain price lines, such as $2.98, $4.98, and $7.95, rather than having the confusion of many different prices. The number of price lines and the particular prices decided upon will affect markup decisions. Some goods may have to carry a lower-than-desired markup in order to fit in with a particular price line; other goods may carry a higher markup. Some attractive items may have to be turned down because they cannot reasonably be retailed at the price lines carried.

Promotional Pricing

A store's policy regarding promotions and sales will affect markup decisions for some goods. A major objective of any sale is to bring into the store people who may not have come otherwise. The merchant has two objectives in mind: first, that these customers will not only buy the item on sale, but regular-priced goods as well; or, second, that they can be traded up from the low-priced sale item to a higher-priced item. (Of course, clearance sales, which are usually run at the end of the season, also have the major objective of selling off seasonal stocks, so that no such goods have to be carried over for another year.) To achieve sale objectives, certain goods are selected as *leaders* and carry a lower-than-normal markup.

An extreme type of leader is a *loss leader*. Such goods are priced near or below cost so that they will draw as many customers as possible. Especially when offered by large stores for an extended time, loss leaders can have a devastating effect on stores with marginal resources. Fear of this during the depression of the 1930s led small retailers in a number of states to pressure their state legislatures to prohibit sales below cost or, in some states, below six percent above cost (costs were defined somewhat differently in the various states). In some states, these so-called *unfair-trade practices acts* pertain to all products; in other states, only specific goods, such as cigarettes, dairy products, and liquor are covered by such laws. Today, unfair-trade practices acts are seldom strongly enforced.

Maintained or Fair-Trade Prices

With some goods, a retailer is virtually forced not to sell below a certain list price. A manufacturer of a well-known brand, such as Magnavox, may refuse to sell to a retailer unless the suggested list price is maintained. The manufacturer's objective is to assure that a reputation for quality is not jeopardized by price-cutting retailers. The retailer gets an attractive per-unit profit margin, but does lose some control of the store's merchandising operation and some promotional opportunities.

There have been more formal controls over list-price maintenance. In the 1930s some forty-five states enacted *fair-trade laws,* which permitted the manufacturer to set the minimum price at which the product could be sold at retail. Less than ten percent of retail sales have ever been covered by fair-trade laws. Druggists, who have been the biggest advocates for such laws, were instrumental in pressuring state legislatures to enact them "to protect the weak and small against the large retailers." Since the 1950s, these laws in many states were either repealed or ruled unconstitutional. Finally, President Ford signed a law repealing, as of March 1976, the federal enabling legislation for fair-trade laws in all states still having these laws on their books.

Psychological Pricing

Retailers have long been enamored of the psychological appeal that *odd prices* have in stimulating sales. Consequently, a price such as $1.00, $5.00, or $10.00 is uncommon; instead we find 98¢, $4.98, and $9.95. The assumption is that these odd prices are more attractive to customers because the few cents below the round figures will be perceived psychologically as a substantially lower price. But in fact, there has been little confirmation of the psychological appeal of odd prices. Originally, odd prices were developed as a control device to force salesclerks to give customers change, which meant ringing the cash register and, thus, recording the sale, instead of pocketing the money and not ringing up the sale. Nowadays, with sales taxes almost universal, this rationale for odd prices no longer applies.

An interesting twist of pricing psychology sometimes occurs: an item may have less sales at a low price than when the price is raised. It may be perceived as inferior because of the "cheap" price (which in reality may reflect an excellent value). Of course, the reason for this is the price-quality perception mentioned before: the higher the price the higher the quality. Some products—aspirin and perfumes, for example—are very susceptible to customer fears of inferior quality.

PRICING ADJUSTMENTS

Sometimes, the retail price established when goods are first brought into the store needs to be changed. Perhaps the buyer's judgment was wrong, or perhaps competition had something similar that was priced more attractively. Maybe, as the season draws to an end, the scattered remains of the original assortment, no longer attractive or in peak demand, simply have to be reduced if they are to be disposed of. Or perhaps the buyer wishes to attract more customers through a special promotion and therefore may temporarily reduce some goods for the sale. The result is a markdown. *Markdowns* are the most frequent pricing adjustment made. When not held to moderation, they can wreak havoc on what otherwise might have been a successful season.

Occasionally, the buyer may have reason to adjust the price upward: perhaps the goods were originally priced for a special sale and, the sale being over, their prices can be raised. Or maybe, after viewing customer demand or competitor offerings, the buyer sees an opportunity for a larger-than-expected markup. Consequently, an *additional markup* will be made.

Markdowns

CALCULATIONS FOR MARKDOWNS   Markdowns are expressed as a percentage of net sales for that period. For example, if sales for a certain month amounted to $10,000 and the markdowns taken during that period were $600, then the markdown percentage is 6 percent:

$$\text{Markdown percentage} = \frac{\$ \text{ Markdowns}}{\$ \text{ Sales}}$$

$$= \frac{\$600}{\$10,000} = .06 \text{ or } 6 \text{ percent}$$

Store personnel need to keep careful records of all price changes made and an exact count of the number of items affected. Carelessness in recording markdowns will result in shrinkage, which has the same effect on company profitability as shoplifting.

The dollar amount of a markdown is a simple calculation. For example, a dress department buyer notes that certain $29.95 dresses are selling more slowly than expected. Concerned that the selling season may end with many of these dresses still unsold, the buyer orders them reduced to $24.77. The salespeople change the price tickets and count the dresses. The buyer records the count and markdown as follows:

74 dresses reduced from $29.95 to $24.77
74 × $5.18 = $383.32 total markdown

Two weeks later, 26 dresses still remain unsold, and the buyer orders another markdown to $17.77. An additional $182 is added to the markdowns taken for that month:

26 × $7.00 = $182.00

The total markdown is then

$$(\$383.32 + \$182.00) = \$565.32$$

In this example, you should note two things about the markdown calculations:

1. A markdown is recorded before the item is sold.
2. If an item has to be marked down further, this markdown is calculated from the last price (not the original price).

CAUSES OF MARKDOWNS   We will classify markdown causes under the following categories:

1. Buying errors
2. Pricing errors
3. Selling errors
4. Unusual events not predictable or under direct control
5. Certain sales policies

Few buyers can escape making some buying errors that will result in markdowns. But as every merchandise manager knows, some buyers are far more prone toward these mistakes than others. Overbuying is a common affliction and can be charitably described as too much enthusiasm. Poor timing is less easy to defend. It occurs most often with seasonal goods and fad items: a large order placed late in the demand cycle often results in unwanted goods. Even the most experienced buyer will make some bad decisions on colors, fabrics, and styles. We cannot always forecast the future and the fickleness of consumer choice. However, many of these buying mistakes could be prevented by carefully analyzing sales records and buying trends.

Pricing errors reflect errors in judgment that result in pricing an item too high. Overoptimism may account for this. Less to be tolerated by a buyer's superiors is unfamiliarity with competitive offerings and prices. A buyer must keep alert and know what the competition is doing.

Selling errors may not be as directly attributable to the buyer, but this does not relieve the buyer of all responsibility for them. Where buying and selling functions are separated, as they are in many large firms, the buyer is not directly in control of salespeople or sales and display effort. A department manager, sales manager, or store manager is responsible for this aspect of the operation. However, the buyer still exerts strong advisory influence in most organizations and is the acknowledged expert for the categories of merchandise he or she buys.

The buyer should be responsible for providing product information to salespeople and offering display advice. On the other hand, poor stockkeeping, careless handling, high-pressure tactics that result in high customer returns, and a generally weak salesforce may be beyond the buyer's control. However, a buyer can work with superiors to correct such deficiencies.

Sometimes unpredictable circumstances arise and create a need for heavy markdowns. Weather is the most common such factor, and the buyer of seasonal goods—whether air conditioners or snow boots—may be sorely tested. A labor disturbance or an unexpected layoff by a city's largest industry can seriously affect business and result in heavy markdowns.

Not all markdowns reflect errors or unexpected detrimental occurrences. Some are the result of aggressive promotional efforts. Some stores mark down certain regular-priced items for major sales events, such as anniversary sales. After the sales period is over, the remaining goods are marked up to the regular price (this is technically known as a *cancellation of markdown*). While many stores attempt to bring in special merchandise or manufacturers' closeouts for their sales so that there is only limited markdown of regular goods, "ragtails" usually are left, and these have to be marked down further to be disposed of quickly. Typically, a store with a strong promotional emphasis has higher markdowns than a prestige store that confines its promotional efforts to the twice-a-year seasonal clearance.

As you might suspect, certain departments in a store mark down far more than other departments. Those having a fashion emphasis—women's dress departments, shoes, sportswear, and hats—may produce three to five times as high a markdown percentage of sales as departments carrying staple items such as toilet articles, books, notions, linens, and bedding. In the high-markdown departments, the fault does not necessarily lie with poor buying or with poor sales and stockkeeping supervision. To maximize sales, many merchants have found it desirable to carry an adequate stock late into the season. Of course, sizable markdowns necessarily result, but the initial markup can be high enough to offset the anticipated markdowns.

CONTROL OF MARKDOWNS   Heavy markdowns will be a major drain on profits. High markdowns for clearance at the end of a season can negate conscientious performance during the entire period. But the alternative to such markdowns is to carry any unsalable stock over into another year, tying up investment and storage space with no assurance that such goods will be in demand another year. Many retailers need to seek certain controls to help minimize markdowns, even though controls offer no guarantee that markdowns will never be excessive.

Budgetary controls should be established. A planned markdown figure or target can be set for the period ahead, along with sufficient sales and profit goals. Such a plan not only focuses attention on markdown dollars and how they are accumulating, but also tends to bring more order into the trauma of reducing prices by crisis amid the sudden realization that something drastic must be done to get rid of slow-moving goods.

If markdowns are excessive, classification and analysis of their probable causes can be helpful for preventing similar occurrences in the future. Even placing them in broad categories, such as buying errors or selling deficiencies, will help direct attention to corrective action. A more finely honed breakdown is desirable: How much was caused by overbuying, bad timing of purchases, defective and broken goods, or shopworn items? A productive analysis may be to tabulate how many problems are attributable to certain vendors and what the markdown percentage of total business with these vendors is. Such an analysis may reveal that the goods of a few vendors account for as much as 80 percent of total departmental markdowns. In such a case, a reconsideration of future buying commitments may be called for.

Sometimes markdowns are taken too hastily or with a kind of defeatist attitude before other possibilities for getting rid of the goods have been adequately explored. Markdowns are the easy way out; no ingenuity is required to take a markdown, even though the consequent effect on profits is inescapable. But to move some goods without a markdown, or with a lesser one, requires effort and imagination.

RETAILING STRATEGIES—*Clearing Out Goods Without Markdowns*

Perhaps a fresh display, a change in location, a bit of advertising, or special motivation of salespeople will start the goods moving. Perhaps salespeople do not suggest or show the items because of insufficient product knowledge; better training sessions might be helpful. Sometimes a PM (or push-money) system may be used as an incentive for salespeople. Such a cash or merchandise bonus for sales of specially designated items can light a powerful fire under formerly lackadaisical efforts and may be less costly than taking a markdown.

Sometimes a vendor can be persuaded to take back poorly selling merchandise and thus eliminate the need for a markdown. Of course, the larger and more important the retailer is to suppliers, and the better the relationship, the more chances there are of doing this (a strong argument for doing business with a few rather than with many suppliers). Sometimes a retailer can use the services of a buying office to persuade vendors to take back merchandise.

Another alternative is to persuade a vendor to offer incentives to salespeople to push his or her goods: for example, vendor-sponsored contests have often been successful in cleaning out slow-selling goods by offering free merchandise to winning salesclerks. If a vendor's merchandise can be shown to frequently have high markdown ratios, the buyer may be in a strong position to gain some concession.

For Thought and Discussion   The ultimate success of getting rid of goods without markdowns would be the elimination of all markdowns. Can you give some arguments why such a seemingly attractive situation might really not be entirely desirable?

While markdown control and the hoped-for lessening of markdowns are very much to be desired, the alternative to taking needed markdowns can be more costly in the long run. Some retailers are reluctant to take necessary markdowns. They sit on goods that have long passed the point of salability. This ties up money in idle goods that eventually will have to be marked down, perhaps even completely written off, as they become more shopworn and obsolete. Insistence on markdown controls should not be at the expense of taking necessary markdowns promptly and completely.

HOW MUCH TO MARK DOWN?   The natural question at this point is how big a markdown to take on a slow-selling item. Too large a markdown will readily move out the goods but will be more costly than necessary. A markdown that is too small merely prolongs misery and may postpone the clearance of the item until so late in the season that drastic reductions have to be made. The ideal markdown is just great enough to sell the goods. A number of factors affect the chances of achieving this ideal.

First, a markdown must appear significant enough to customers to make the product more appealing. A dollar markdown on a $20 item will generate little additional business; a dollar markdown on a $5 item may be enough to sell it out. A 15–20 percent markdown is probably the minimum that the average customer would find significant. Of course, if a store is already offering a slightly lower competitive price, this percentage need not apply.

Second, the style or seasonal aspects of the product affect the urgency and extent of the clearance effort. Staple products may require less drastic actions.

Third, if a markdown is being considered early in the season, it can be smaller than one taken late, since there is still time for additional reductions while the goods are salable.

Fourth, certain end-of-season markdowns have become rather traditional. For example, many stores clear out their Christmas cards, tree ornaments, and some toys after December 25 at one third to one half off.

TIMING OF MARKDOWNS   The merchant faces several alternatives as to when to mark down. Perhaps the more difficult decision is whether to mark down at all or simply carry the seasonal goods over to another year. When markdowns have been running heavy, the latter decision is likely to be pondered. Some items may actually bring a higher price at the beginning of the season next year than they do at the end of the current season. With certain seasonal goods that have little risk of going out of style, carrying over may be attractive. Examples are air conditioners, snow tires, and Christmas toys, cards, and ornaments. But consider the following disadvantages:

1. Goods carried over are seldom as fresh and salable as new goods; they tend to become shopworn and broken.
2. There are labor costs involved in packing and storing, and further expenses for stockroom or warehouse space, interest charges on the inventory investment, and insurance.
3. Money invested in such goods cannot be used to purchase current merchandise and, therefore, the assortment is more limited, while merchandise turnover is reduced.

Many aggressively managed stores are reluctant to carry goods over until the next season. Opinions differ, however, on whether markdowns on individual items should be taken early in the season when justified, or held for a storewide clearance late in the season. These decisions depend on several factors: the store image, the kinds of products involved, the cost of overhead, and the amount of markup on the original price.

RETAIL CONTROVERSY—*Should We Take Markdowns Early or Late in the Season?*

Arguments for Early Markdowns

1. Stocks can be kept fresh and wanted by continually weeding out the poor sellers and replacing them with newer goods.
2. Smaller markdowns are needed to move these goods, since they are less shopworn and more desired in the height of the season than they will be later.
3. Many customers respond to sale and markdown items and may shop more often where there is a constant availability of some reduced prices.
4. Prices may be more attractive than those of competitors, who may have the same goods and be slower to reduce them.

Arguments for Late Markdowns

1. A store image of high quality and prestige may be better preserved by keeping bargains and marked-down goods to a minimum, except during a few large yearly sales events.
2. Sometimes demand for goods is unpredictable and erratic; a slow seller at the beginning of a season may suddenly become popular.
3. An early-markdown policy tends to discourage creative efforts to move slower-selling goods by other methods, such as display, change of location, developing salesperson enthusiasm, and so on.
4. By saving clearance efforts for a large storewide effort near the end of a season, a much bigger promotional impact is possible.

The arguments are strong on both sides. Some compromise has to be made, with the quantity on hand and rate of sale considered in the decision. Many successful merchants, however, tend to be rather quick to recognize a loser and take prompt action to get rid of it and bring in more salable goods for replacement.

For Thought and Discussion   How would you counter the argument that an early markdown policy discourages creative efforts to move slow-sellers by other methods?

AUTOMATIC MARKDOWNS   A few retailers set rather inflexible rules for marking down their slower-selling goods. *Automatic markdowns* may be taken particularly on fashion goods, because it is important that such goods continue to move out of the store before they become out of style and out of season. A policy may be established for marking down any garment after it has been in stock for a specific period of time, for example, four weeks. The best-known proponent of automatic markdowns is the basement store of Filene's of Boston. "All merchandise still unsold after twelve selling days is reduced 25 percent; each successive week an additional 25 percent markdown is taken. At the end of five weeks anything left is given to charity."

While such automatic policies assure that stocks will remain fresh, the inflexibility may result in higher markdowns and fewer efforts by store personnel to push the slower-selling goods. Also, conditions other than customer demand (for instance, the weather) may be to blame for slow sales, especially of goods that arrive early in the season.

CUSTOMER RELATIONS AND MARKDOWNS While one might think that the markdown can do nothing but better customer relations and produce good will, the opposite is sometimes true. Whenever regular stock is either marked down for a temporary sale or marked for clearance, customer-relations problems can arise. The customer who bought the same item a few days before at a higher price is disturbed and resentful to find it now priced lower. Usually, few of these grievances reach the attention of responsible executives; most customers suffer in silence. For a store that promotes frequently, the problem can be especially serious, and it is a particular problem for stores that mark down early. What can a store do to improve this situation?

A simple remedy—and one that many stores practice surreptitiously, without publicity—is to give the complaining customer who bought at the higher price a refund for the difference. The trouble is that the customers who do not go back to the store to complain may be just as offended. Good public relations would argue for more publicity for such a refund policy. They would also argue for informing salespeople several days before planned price reductions, so that they can advise interested customers of what is coming.

An alternative to this procedure is to mark down the goods a week or so in advance of the sale announcement. Regular customers who shop during this period may take advantage of the unannounced sale prices. This creates good will and also makes the time frame between the regular price and the announced sale or marked-down price less hectic.

Discounts to Employees and Customers

Most retail firms, with the notable exception of food retailers, give a purchase discount to their employees. An *employee discount* typically is

10 percent of the selling price, although it sometimes goes as high as 20 percent for clothing items, especially those that might be worn on the job and thereby enhance the appearance of the employee.

It is not uncommon to give similar discounts to certain categories of customers who thereby enjoy special status. For example, drugstores may give discounts to physicians and hardware stores to contractors; other businesspeople may be given discounts by some retailers; members of the clergy sometimes receive discounts.

These discounts represent a reduction in the retail price as real as a markdown. While most retailers consider the extra business generated and the good will gained as worth the discounts, such lower prices do have an impact on gross margin and net profit. And they should be considered in merchandise and markup planning.

Improving the Gross Margin

The gross margin is the gross profit figure from which operating expenses are deducted to yield, hopefully, the net profit. If the gross profit percentage of sales can be increased without hurting sales, then it stands to reason that more money is available to cover expenses and to yield more net profit. The buyer has a number of alternatives available to increase the gross margin ratio. Some will be more practical and feasible than others, but all deserve at least passing consideration.

Recall that Gross margin = Maintained markup + Cash discounts − Net workroom costs. And Maintained markup = Initial markup − Reductions, which can be markdowns, shortages, and discounts to employees and special customers. Therefore, the following will increase the gross margin:

1. Increase cash discounts: This represents a possibility for increasing gross margin, primarily if the store has been lax in paying invoices on time. Occasionally, a buyer may be able to negotiate for a higher cash discount from a vendor, but often at a sacrifice of lower merchandise costs and advertising allowances.
2. Decrease alteration and workroom costs: Two alternatives are possible here. Neither may be feasible in most operations; yet they should at least be evaluated as possibilities. If workroom productivity could be improved, this would have a favorable effect on gross profit. The profit picture would also be improved by charging customers more for alterations and other workroom costs. The possible impact of such an action on sales—and, of course, on the store's competitive stance—would have to be seriously weighed.

3. Increase the initial markup:
   a. Buy at a lower cost while keeping the same selling prices: One way to do this is to increase the emphasis on quantity purchases that carry higher discounts, and on special expeditious buys that can be sold at above average markups. Many firms have found that through their own private brands they can obtain higher markups than with nationally advertised brands. Some buyers are careless in specifying the routing of their orders, and can achieve transportation savings by allowing more time and specifying cheaper modes of transportation. Finding new sources of supply and making use of harder negotiation may sometimes result in lower cost prices.
   b. Raise selling prices: Competition usually is a major constraint to raising selling prices. However, if some brands and goods can be handled on an exclusive basis (that is, without the manufacturer making them available to competing stores) then higher prices often can be charged without a competitive disadvantage.
   c. Sell a greater proportion of higher-markup goods: This represents one of the more practical ways to increase the gross margin ratio. It can be done by giving more emphasis in the advertising, display, and sales force efforts to such goods over the lower-markup items. This approach, of course, requires that the relative profitability of the various items of merchandise be well communicated to those involved in selling them.
4. Reduce the reductions:
   If markdown losses can be reduced, this will have a marked effect on gross profit. If merchandise shortages can be reduced, the effect is also significant. The last alternative for reducing the reductions concerns discounts to special customers and to employees. Allowable discounts are usually store policies, and not controllable by departmental executives. However, in certain cases there may be merit in restricting overly generous discount policies, especially if these are out of line with those of other retailers.

■ Summary

Initially, pricing is treated both from the retailer's viewpoint and the consumer's. Pricing abuses do occur but reputable retailers should beware of the temptation to have fictitious comparative prices, false sales, and deceptive bait and switch practices. Calculations of markups are discussed at some length and should be carefully studied since they are essential to an on-target merchandising operation. Pricing adjustments, especially markdowns, are important to the merchandising function and can hardly be prevented. Ideally, they should be taken promptly to avoid allowing old goods to remain in stock tying up capital and becoming increasingly shopworn. At the same time, by giving careful attention to controlling markdowns, a department or a store can significantly increase its profitability. In the next chapter, we will examine the important topic of controlling the merchandise investment and maintaining a satisfactory turnover. If successfully carried out, these merchandising activities can help minimize markdowns and satisfy customer demand.

■ **Key Terms**

Additional markup	Loss leaders
Automatic markdowns	Markdowns
Cancellation of markdown	Markup percentage
Comparative prices	Odd prices
Employee discounts	Open-to-buy (OTB)
Fair-trade laws	Price differential
False sales	Price-quality image
Fictitious comparisons	Unfair-trade practices acts
Keystone markup	Unit prices
Leaders	

■ **Discussion Questions**

1. How do you account for the fact that so much retail advertising features lowest prices, while surveys of consumers suggest that low prices rank below many other appeals?
2. Can you give any examples, based on your own experience, of the price of an item not bearing the correct relationship with its quality? How do you account for this?
3. Are there any advantages to unit pricing from the firm's viewpoint?
4. Explain how a firm might make more money with a lower-percentage markup rather than a higher one. Is the reverse more likely to be true? What factors might determine this?
5. Describe how poor stockkeeping can result in heavy markdowns.
6. "Basing markup percentages on the selling price instead of on the cost price is simply a trick to deceive the public." Comment on this statement.
7. Compare the arguments for marking down snow tires at the end of

winter to clear them out with carrying them over to the next fall.
What might your decision depend on?

■ Project

Survey retailers in your community to ascertain if there are any who do
not use comparative prices. If any are found, determine their reasons
for not doing so. Then evaluate these reasons and any competitive
impact they may have.

■ Exercise in Creativity: Role Play

You have managed to obtain some imported running shoes of relatively
high quality; that is, several local athletes who have participated in
races, including the Boston Marathon, have strongly approved of them.
You have the exclusive right to sell these in your area, but the brand is
unknown. While the landed cost is $14 a pair, you believe the shoes
should sell at a much higher markup than normal. How would you go
about trying to come up with the best price for these shoes, one which
will yield the most total profits?

■ Retailing in Action

Crestmont Electronic Stores have grown rapidly through heavy promotion and sharply competitive prices. A recent successful promotion
was a heavily advertised loss leader of a famous brand of CBs (citizens
band radios) that had an excellent reputation and a strong sales pattern
nationally. Crestmont advertised these at one-third lower than the
usual price, and customers flocked to the stores in the chain.

However, the manufacturer was unhappy. Martha Rubenstein, vice
president of sales for the manufacturer, called Sid Krauss, the president
of Crestmont:

"Mr. Krauss, we must ask you to stop selling our CBs at that price.
Our other retail customers are screaming about this."

"Now, now, Miss Rubenstein," Sid Krauss responded. "We don't
believe in being coerced into price fixing. We only want to give the
consumer the best buy we possibly can. That's all we have in mind with
this promotion. We love our customers."

1. Do you think the CB manufacturer has any justification for being
   concerned?
2. What can Martha Rubenstein do about this situation?

3. Do you think Sid Krauss's position can be criticized?

4. If you were another retailer selling this brand of CBs, what would your reaction be to Crestmont's use of them as loss leaders?

■ Retail Math

1. A shirt costs $89 a dozen and retails for $12.98. What is the markup percentage on retail?

2. If a chair costs $70 and the buyer wants to achieve a 50-percent markup on retail, what would the selling price be?

3. An item is selling for $4.98 and you know that the markup percentage is 40. What is the cost?

4. If a buyer wants goods to sell for $15.95 and he is seeking at least a 40 percent markup, what is the lowest cost he should seek? What if he wants to sell them at $19.95?

5. A men's department bought 100 tropical suits to sell at $90. They cost $48. At the original retail price, 60 were sold. The rest were marked down $15 from the original price, and 18 were sold then. Those still left were marked down another $20 before they were finally sold. Compute the markdown percentage for this purchase.

6. A lingerie buyer finds that, according to her records, the inventory of her department consists of merchandise worth $28,000 at cost and $42,000 at retail. Orders have been placed for delivery over the balance of the season amounting to $80,000 at cost and $170,000 at retail. She has $30,000 at retail left to spend. If the department plan calls for an average markup of 44 percent, what should be the markup on her remaining purchases?

14　Merchandise Control

Controlling the merchandise investment is vital to all retail firms. Control means maintaining assortments of merchandise that are in balance with customer demand. The merchant in a small enterprise may use *eyeball observation* of stock and its movement, rather than detailed record-keeping. In large operations, however, formal records and controls of some type must be set up and followed if the stock of goods is to be balanced and compatible with customer demand. More than this is needed for an aggressive merchandising strategy; the contribution that a good rate of turnover can make to profitability and merchandise attractiveness must also be sought.

IMPORTANCE OF MERCHANDISE CONTROL

The investment in the stock of goods available for resale represents a major part of the total capital outlay of a retail firm. How this inventory is managed is crucial to a firm's profitability. Note two things here. If the goods do not meet customer wants well enough, sales will be slim and the store cannot expect to survive without some major change. However, there is a limit to how large a stock of goods can be offered. While more wants can be satisfied with more goods, only so much money and space are available for investment, usually less than is desired. Accordingly, some balance must be found between satisfying customer wants and keeping the investment within practical limits. This problem creates the need for merchandise control.

A careful analysis of purchases and sales is necessary to maintain a lean and healthy stock. A buyer's decisions are more likely to be on target, both in quantity to purchase and in such aspects as sizes, styles, and colors, if there are up-to-date records of sales, trends, and goods on hand and on order. While the past is not always indicative of the future, making buying decisions without facts about past performance is rather like traversing an unmapped terrain.

Certain side benefits can come from having a healthy stock that is well geared to customer demand:

1. Markdowns can be minimized, since slow-selling sizes, colors, and prices are more easily recognized and avoided.
2. Stock shortages may be lessened by pinpointing trouble areas and taking corrective action.
3. Turnover of merchandise can be increased, and this can have a marked effect on profitability.

MERCHANDISE TURNOVER

Calculation of Turnover

By *merchandise turnover* or stock turnover we mean the number of times the average stock is sold during a given period, usually a year. The formula is

$$\text{Stockturns} = \frac{\text{Retail sales (for the period)}}{\text{Average stock at retail (for the period)}}$$

If, for example, a store had sales of $120,000 during 1980, and the average inventory (as calculated at the selling price) was $36,000, then the turnover was

$$\frac{120,000}{36,000} = 3.3 \text{ turns}$$

Turnover can be calculated at cost figures rather than at retail; it can also be figured by units sold rather than dollar sales. But by far the most common method is to use selling price, as in the example above. If the inventory is calculated at selling price, this presents no problem.

Calculating *average stock* deserves a brief discussion. Since retail business is seasonal, with November and December business many times greater than January and February sales, retail stock will vary greatly from month to month depending on expected sales for the period just ahead. The average stock is best calculated by adding the beginning stock for each month plus the ending stock for the year, and dividing by 13 (not by 12, since there will be 13 stock listings).

RETAILING TOOL—*Deriving Merchandise Turnover*

Problem   Find the number of stockturns for a men's clothing store that had sales of $65,000 in 1979, and the following monthly inventories:

Jan. 1	$ 8,000	July 1	$ 9,000
Feb. 1	9,000	Aug. 1	11,000
March 1	12,000	Sept. 1	12,000
April 1	14,000	Oct. 1	13,000
May 1	10,000	Nov. 1	16,000
June 1	9,000	Dec. 1	17,000
		Dec. 31	9,000
		Total	$149,000

Formula

$$\text{Stockturns} = \frac{\text{Retail sales for year}}{\text{Average stock during year}}$$

$$= \frac{65,000}{149,000 \div 13}$$

$$= 5.7$$

For Further Analysis If the same firm took $5,000 of markdowns in December 1979 to clear the stock of slow sellers before taking inventory, what would the turnover be?

Importance of Turnover

Turnover provides a measure of the efficiency of a department or store, and of the buyer and manager involved. To furnish such a measure, however, latest turnover results need to be compared to (1) turnover figures in prior periods (to show whether performance is better or worse), and (2) turnover figures for other comparable departments and stores.

Comparing the present with past results is simply a matter of looking back at old records, which any retailer should have. Small retailers in particular tend to be so preoccupied with day-to-day business and its inevitable problems that they neglect to make this simple comparison. What harm is done? Perhaps none; but, on the other hand, a lower rate of turnover may be a danger signal that something is not right. Inventory levels may be getting out of balance, or—most insidious of all—severe stock shortages may be accruing due to pilferage or bad record-keeping.

A small retailer may have difficulty in comparing his store's performance with that of similar stores. However, if a retailer belongs to a trade association, such data are usually shared by member stores. Trade journals often provide usable comparison statistics. Personal acquaintance with managers and owners of similar stores that are noncompeting (that is, located some distance away) often leads to shared performance data.

One of the advantages of chains is that performance data are shared among the various units, and this provides both a measure of individual efficiency and an incentive to do better. Poor performance of executives is quickly spotted, while the top performers are easily identified. A department store can usually obtain turnover and other operating statistics comparisons from its resident buying office or other affiliates, as well as from trade associations and leading business periodicals.

Deviations from the turnover rates of other stores may not necessarily mean that a particular store is doing a better or worse job. Differences may be due to the size of the store, the presence or absence of good local wholesalers, the distance from sources of supply, or differences in operating and merchandising policies. For example, if a store is located in a smaller community with no strong local wholesalers to aid in quick replenishment of stock, and has rather poor transportation facilities, then a larger stock and consequent lower turnover may be necessary to maintain a good in-stock condition. Store policies of some stores prescribe that wide assortments of goods be carried in order to reach certain target consumers; this tends to increase the amount of stock and to decrease the merchandise turnover as compared to the average firm.

Higher turnover can play a substantial role in increasing profits. This is the greatest incentive for emphasizing stock turnover, although its importance escaped most retailers until discounters came on the retail scene with high turnover as one of their trump cards. How does turnover have such a key relationship with profits? First, we have to define what profits we are talking about. Net profit dollars as a percent of sales is the commonly thought of measure of profitability—and it is *not* directly affected by turnover.

The more sophisticated and more basic indicator of profitability is *return on investment.* This is the profit that one gets for the money invested. This figure is what financial analysts and expert investors are looking for: the 15 to 20 percent return, and more, that they can get on their investment. The following examples illustrate how increasing stock turnover directly affects return on investment.

Example 1: The relevant statistics for a small department store in 1978 were as follows:

Sales	$5,000,000
Net profit percent	5
Net profit dollars	$250,000
Stock turnover	4
Average stock at retail price (5,000,000 ÷ 4)	$1,250,000
Average stock at cost, if gross margin is 40% (1,250,000 × 60%)	$750,000
Investment in furniture and fixtures	$250,000
Return on investment	

$$\frac{250,000 \text{ (net profit)}}{750,000 + 250,000 \text{ (investment)}} = 25\%$$

Example 2: For the same store in 1979, the stock turnover was increased to 5, while sales and profits remained the same:

Sales	$5,000,000
Net profit dollars	$250,000
Stock turnover	5
Average stock at retail price	
(5,000,000 ÷ 5)	$1,000,000
Average stock at cost, with gross margin of 40%	
(1,000,000 × 60%)	$600,000
Investment in furniture and fixtures	$250,000
Return on investment	

$$\frac{250,000}{600,000 + 250,000} = 29.4\%$$

In these examples, increasing the rate of turnover from 4 to 5 resulted in increasing the return on investment from 25 percent to almost 30 percent, a substantial increase. However, we assumed that sales remained the same, while the stock necessary to produce those sales was cut one fifth. How realistic is this? It may come as a surprise that sales may even increase with a lower stock because the stock may be fresher and more attractive. Even the enthusiasm of salespeople may be spurred because of the continual arrival of new and interesting merchandise. There may be more opportunity to pick up special purchases when a department or store has money available and is in an open-to-buy situation (described further later in this chapter). These purchases may stimulate sales.

A high turnover may improve not only sales, but also net profits. Markdowns are usually minimized, since heavy markdowns usually come from heavy stocks. Also, there tends to be a correlation between heavy stock and heavy stock shortages (as we will see later in this chapter). Furthermore, the lower average stock that goes with a higher turnover means less insurance on inventory and lower personal property taxes. Less storage space and lower stockroom handling expenses also contribute to lower operating costs and increased net profits.

Differences in Turnover

Different categories of merchandise and different types of retail firms make for different numbers of stockturns. For example, the following compares the approximate stockturns commonly found for various goods.

Category of Goods	Approximate Number of Yearly Stockturns
Meat	40
Gasoline	21
Candy	11
Millinery	10
Liquor	6
Women's dresses	5
Women's hosiery	4
Boy's wear	3
Furniture	3
Hardware	2
Men's clothing	2
Shoes	2
Jewelry	1.5

This photograph shows great depth in men's suits. Such a variety of styles, patterns, and colors is very appealing to customers, but for the merchant it represents a major investment in inventory. Men's clothing departments typically have one of the lowest turnover rates of any department, averaging only two turns a year. (F. B. Grunzweig/ Photo Researchers. Inc.)

To a large extent the differences in turnover rates reflect the frequency of purchase: gasoline, food, and candy are purchased frequently; furniture, jewelry, men's clothing, and shoes, are purchased much less frequently. Since more money is usually involved in the less-frequent–purchase categories, the customer wants to choose from a fairly wide assortment of goods.

Because of the wide differences in turnover rates, you can see how these should be analyzed by department or merchandise category, rather than by overall store figures. The overall turnover rate may mask variations in departmental performance, some of which may need corrective action even though the total storewide figure seems acceptable.

RETAILING ISSUES—How Much Turnover to Seek?

Advantages of High Turnover   So far, the attractiveness of the highest possible turnover has seemed inescapable. Not only is return on investment substantially improved, but markdowns are fewer, stock shortages are prevented, there is less wear and tear on goods, and less storage space and handling and inventorying of goods are required. What incentive is there to seek anything but the highest turnover, which is achieved with the leanest stock?

Disadvantages of Excessive Turnover   As with most things in life, moderation is to be preferred. A quest for ever-higher turnover rates means more frequent orders for small amounts, and may add to expenses in the following ways:

1. Quantity discounts are usually sacrificed when buying is hand to mouth.
2. Transportation costs are often more per unit for small shipments than for large ones.
3. Clerical and handling costs invariably are higher for several small shipments rather than for one large one.
4. The buyer's and assistants' time will be taken up with more stock analysis and reordering, leaving less time for other aspects of management.

These disadvantages are usually not serious and will probably be outweighed by the inherent advantages of moderately high turnover. However, another drawback to excessive turnover is serious, and should place a limit on how much turnover a store seeks. Excessively lean stock may result in lost business, since the assortment of goods is reduced, affording customers less choice, and the depth of goods may be so shallow that out-of-stocks are frequent.

Customers do not need to be disappointed many times before they go elsewhere. A store with a reputation for having large assortments is in a strong competitive position. But it may not have an enviable turnover picture.

A more insidious danger for the store seeking the most rapid turnover possible is that its image may become bland and nondescript, and it may lose distinctiveness in customers' minds.

Conclusion   Some sort of compromise has to be made by most stores. The advantages of lean stocks are undeniable. But to make this a siren call to which all actions are geared and by which all performance is judged may lead to competitive vulnerability.

For Thought and Discussion   Two women's dress stores in the same city have the following operating results: Store A has achieved a turnover of 8, while markdowns are 9.0 percent (low for dresses); Store B has a turnover of 3, with markdowns 12.5 percent. The town has a rather homogeneous middle-income population. Based on this information, what conclusions might you make about the operating strengths of these two stores? What else would you want to know in making a judgment?

Causes of Low Turnover

A low turnover does not necessarily mean more choice and better-satisfied customers; it may mean instead more merchandise duds. Turnovers in many departments and stores can be raised without reaching the excessive levels described above. The following are some causes of low turnover:

1. Many firms accept seasonal goods far in advance of the main selling season. For example, toys bought for Christmas selling may be accepted in late summer. While some are sold then, the great bulk will not be sold until November and December. Manufacturers offer various inducements to encourage such advance-of-the-season buying. Each retailer has to weigh the pros and cons of seasonal discounts and seasonal datings which may lead to higher handling costs and goods shopworn before the peak selling period.

2. Goods, especially seasonal and fashion items, tend to be accepted by merchants regardless of late delivery. By not adhering to order

cancellation dates merchants find themselves with goods received at the tail end of a selling season. Such goods invariably are carried over to another year or else are found on clearance counters after heavy markdowns.

3. Bad buying, unrealistic pricing, reluctance to take necessary markdowns, and attempts to please all customers, which usually result in too-wide an assortment to be practical and efficient, are other causes of low turnover.

4. Some causes of poor turnover are not directly the fault of the buyer, except that he or she should not tolerate conditions adversely affecting performance. For example, delays in checking incoming merchandise—and therefore not getting goods to the selling floor—may result in lost sales and inactive stocks. Poor stockkeeping and unknowledgeable salespeople may lead to lost sales even when the goods are available. Promotional efforts and displays may do no justice to merchandise.

Buyers today are under strong pressures to stock more goods. This often results in decreasing the turnover rate. For example, a few years ago most of the business in men's dress shirts could have been done with one or two prices of white shirts and a few colored numbers. Now a large variety of colored or patterned shirts is required, while the standard white shirt has declined markedly in sales (although there is some indication of a reverse trend).

METHODS OF MERCHANDISE CONTROL

There are two major methods of merchandise control: by dollars and by units. With *dollar control,* analysis and planning of merchandise requirements is in terms of dollars, broken down into various classifications such as men's ties, dress shirts, sport shirts, underwear, and the like for a men's furnishings department. Total figures of stocks and planned sales for an entire store or even a department furnish little guidance in the quest for balanced stocks of specific items. For example, figures for expected sales, total stocks, and on-orders for an entire store are rather meaningless bits of information for the men's-wear buyer attempting to place orders for neckties for the Christmas season. The buyer needs specific information including how many ties in what price lines were sold the previous year and what present stocks are on hand and on order.

Unit control is a further refinement of dollar control. Rather than dealing with broader merchandise classifications, it provides more specific information in terms of units sold, on hand, on order, and expected to sell. The procedures involved for the two systems, as well as the advantages and disadvantages, are examined in the following sections.

Dollar Control

Without some sort of planning and comparing of results with these plans, merchandise control is futile. The small firm, of course, can get by with less formal controls than the large, decentralized firm. Also, if merchandise is relatively staple and unvarying in its demand, you would not expect planning and control to be so rigorous. But where style and fad factors are at work, and also where there is a considerable lag between the time of placing orders and when they are received, rather detailed planning and control are needed.

Merchandise control involves planning for the following:

Sales
Stock on hand
Markdowns
Markups
Purchases

This planning is most often done twice a year—with six-month plans—but with some flexibility built in so that a change in sales or other conditions affecting turnover can be accommodated. An important result of such planning is *open-to-buy budgeting,* whereby a department and store develop broad guidelines for their immediate buying decisions. In planning the open-to-buy (OTB) for each month, all of the above elements are considered by the manager in reaching decisions on ordering merchandise.

OPEN-TO-BUY PLANNING   Open-to-buy planning means just what it says: planning the amount of purchases that a buyer can make in any particular month and still keep within his budget. It can be computed, in terms of selling prices, by the following formula:

Planned purchases or OTB = Planned stock at end of period + Planned sales + Planned reductions − Stock on hand and on order at beginning of period

We will show a specific example of how this formula is used in a practical way. But first, let us examine some of the components of it.

Planned sales can be estimated by considering past sales records, any significant trends upward or downward, any unusual promotions planned for the coming period, as well as forecasts of local business conditions. Sometimes an element of confidence (or optimism) is thrown in, especially when there has been a change in management. As we know, retail sales tend to be very seasonal, with the Easter season and November/December accounting for a major part of the total year's business for many types of goods.

Planned stocks are related to planned sales, although a certain minimum stock must be maintained, regardless of sales estimates, to assure reasonable assortment. Furthermore, as we have noted before, stocks have to be built up in anticipation of a peak selling season. Markdowns are almost inevitable; therefore, they should be planned for in advance. Again, efforts should not be directed toward not taking markdowns (and thus postponing problems), but should be geared toward trying to stay within the plan. It should be recognized in this planning process that reductions or markdowns will not come evenly throughout the year. Some months, particularly those at the end of a season, will generally require much higher markdowns than other months. For example, clothing departments will usually find higher markdowns in July and August due to clearance of summer clothing and sportswear. The result of all the estimated or planned figures is a purchase or open-to-buy budget.

RETAILING TOOL—*Calculating Open-to-buy*

Problem   What is the open-to-buy (OTB) for a children's store with the following figures:

Planned stock, August 31	$42,000
Planned sales for August	87,000
Planned markdowns and shortages for the month	4,000
Actual stock on hand August 1	48,000
Goods on order	36,000

Solution

Planned purchases for August (OTB)
= Planned stock August 31 + Planned sales
  + Planned reductions − Stock on hand
  − Stock on order Aug. 1
= (42,000 + 87,000 + 4,000
  − 48,000 − 36,000)
= 49,000

For Further Analysis   In the above example, if sales were running 20 percent ahead of plan by the second week of August, what revised figure for planned stock August 31 and additional OTB would you submit for approval to your merchandise manager?

It should be noted that such planned purchases or open-to-buys can be applied to an entire store, department, merchandise category, price line, and even to a style number. The formula can also be used with physical units as well as dollars. While the effectiveness lies in the accuracy of the judgments regarding planned sales and reductions, it is not too much to expect fairly good estimates to result, unless unforeseen circumstances occur, such as unseasonal weather or a strike.

Sometimes the open-to-buy figure is used as a sacred limit, beyond which no buyer may trespass. Such a position reflects an uncompromising merchandise manager or top management policy. But as was suggested in Chapter 11 in the discussion of staple merchandise and never-out items, such arbitrariness is misguided. While a buyer may have been too rash (or optimistic) and exceeded the planned purchase figure, to deny the buyer needed funds for staple, fast-selling merchandise penalizes that buyer and the store. A degree of flexibility should always be permitted.

Those of you who become buyers will quickly be exposed to the practical consequences of open-to-buy restrictions. The great tendency is to become overbought and to have open-to-buy seriously constrained, even for the most needed purchases. Whether or not the open-to-buy figure is a rigid limit, most buyers sooner or later—usually sooner—find their purchasing requirements deterred. In this not uncommon circumstance it is good to know how the open-to-buy figure may be increased to accommodate necessary immediate purchases.

There are six possibilities for increasing open-to-buy. Three of these depend on vendor or other store or department cooperation; three have to do with changing planning estimates:

Cooperation of vendors and/or other units of firm:

1. Reduce stock on hand by transferring to other units or by returning to vendor.
2. Postpone outstanding orders to a later month.
3. Cancel outstanding orders.

Changing planning estimates:

4. Increase planned sales.
5. Increase planned markdowns.
6. Increase planned closing stock.

First, the stock on hand can be reduced by returning some goods to vendors, or transferring them to another unit of the company. Doing this is unlikely unless the store has extremely good relations with the vendor or unless other branches or store outlets are in immediate need of these particular goods.

Second, the outstanding orders can be postponed to a later month. This represents a more reasonable way to free up immediate open-to-buy by simply postponing some of the orders; of course, open-to-buy in these later months will necessarily be curbed. Vendors will usually be willing to extend the delivery period if the goods have not yet been shipped.

Third, outstanding orders can be canceled if the goods are overdue and if the buyer deems that this merchandise deserves a lower priority than other needed purchases. While some vendors may grouse at such canceling of orders, if they have not fulfilled the delivery conditions of the contract the cancellation will stand.

Fourth, the planned sales figure for the present month or for the next month can be increased, if favorable market conditions warrant a more optimistic plan. However, to do this without sales justification, in order to free up buying funds, is simply leading to a worsening inventory situation in the near future.

Fifth, more markdowns can be taken than originally planned. But this is a most costly way to free up open-to-buy unless a slow moving stock really warrants it.

Sixth, the closing inventory can be revised upward. This is usually not justified, but may be an emergency measure to free up badly needed funds. The rationale for increasing the planned closing stock rests on present sales running higher than expected so that sales for the succeeding period can reasonably be expected to do likewise.

BOOK INVENTORY   Dollar control permits the investment in inventory to be regulated so that planned sales can be achieved and turnover figures kept in line. If such control is to be realized, a "book" inventory system must be maintained that accounts for: (1) beginning stocks, (2) stock received, (3) markdowns and additional markups, (4) employee discounts, (5) merchandise returned by customers, (6) merchandise returned to vendors, and (7) sales. By keeping a close and accurate tally of these items (usually according to the retail value of each), a running record can be kept of the dollar investment in merchandise. Usually such a book inventory will not agree with the physical inventory that is taken periodically. The book figure will then need to be adjusted for any shortages or overages.

RETAILING TOOL—*Calculating Book Inventory*

Problem   For the children's store described in the previous example, calculate the book inventory as of the end of August. The additional data needed are:

Sales for August	$88,000
Goods received in August	83,000
Returns to vendor	500
Returns by customers	400
Markdowns	3,500
Employee discounts	500
Additional markups	800

Solution

		Retail value
Beginning stock, August 1		$48,000
Plus: Additions to stock		
Goods received during August	$83,000	
Additional markups	800	
Returns by customers	400	84,200
Total stock available		132,200

Less: Deductions from stock
  Sales $88,000
  Markdowns   3,500
  Employee discounts   500
  Returns to vendor   500   92,500

Ending stock August 31 (book inventory) $39,700

For Further Analysis   If the other figures remain the same how would higher sales affect the book inventory? Higher markdowns? No returns to vendors?

Unit Control

So far we have been talking about apportioning dollars among various merchandise and departmental categories. Unit control concerns the physical units of stock rather than the dollar amount in broader categories: for example, how many units of a particular item are on hand, on order, have been sold, or should be bought. As such, it is not a substitute for dollar control, but rather a supplement. Unit control is the universal ingredient of merchandising, since practically all stores, even the smallest, keep track by units. Dollar control, on the other hand, involves more sophisticated techniques of budget planning that may be almost disregarded by small merchants.

ADVANTAGES OF UNIT CONTROL   Formal unit controls can be designed to provide such useful information as the following:

1. The age of stock, thereby quickly pointing out markdown candidates and slow sellers
2. Vendor information, such as salability of vendors' products, promptness in shipping, number of returns, and markdowns taken
3. Sales by colors, sizes, and other factors, and their seasonal variance, thereby being an important aid to future buying
4. Data on customer preferences, to be used in model stock plans, basic stock lists, and never-out lists in order for them to be kept up to date and geared to proven customer wants
5. Automatic reorder points, which can be established for staple merchandise and computerized

DEVELOPING THE UNIT CONTROL SYSTEM   Unit control can be crude and unsystematic. Small retailers may simply "eyeball check" the units on hand and make a quick calculation of what should be ordered, perhaps while a vendor's sales representative is waiting. But unit control is much more complex in major stores, even to the extent that each sale is recorded along with receipts and any returns, so that the units on hand are *perpetually* recorded. The use of computers for print-outs of item sales and receipts is becoming widespread in chains and department stores with branches.

However, as systems become more complex in order to furnish more information, requirements for clerical work increase. The cost and the likelihood of errors in recording merchandise data become factors to be reckoned with and are disadvantages of complex unit control systems.

Various forms and control cards are used to record the information in the kind and the form wanted. These forms may be kept as cards and filed in special cabinets, or they may be maintained in loose-leaf binders. The breakdown of information can be as detailed as desired, and may be specific as to size, color, style, fabric, price, vendor, and even weight.

Regardless of the bookkeeping forms to be used, two major alternatives are available for the posting of the stock and sales information: *periodic stock counting* and *perpetual inventory.*

PERIODIC STOCK COUNTING   A periodic check of the stock on hand is simpler than a perpetual inventory system. This is the procedure used by the small retailer in his eyeball or visual check. Usually such a visual control is most effective for the small retailer who is in constant touch with his goods and who can get fill-in orders quickly from a local wholesaler.

Such a visual control tends to be cursory and sporadic. However, it can be satisfactory for items of low unit value where sales are steady and where replenishment can be made quickly *if* someone is given definite responsibility to make such visual checks at regularly scheduled times. Grocery departments can operate with visual controls. Drug and hardware stores usually find this quite satisfactory, although care must be taken that changes in rates of sale are quickly recognized and adjustments made in stock depth.

Most periodic stock counting systems involve just that: periodically counting the units on hand of various categories of goods, recording this information and any on-orders on stock cards (or pages), computing sales, and placing needed orders. Such a physical count is often taken monthly for each merchandise category. However, in order not to overburden the workforce, only certain categories usually are scheduled for counting each week, so that by the end of the month all goods have been counted. Many lines of merchandise typically are controlled in this way, including notions, men's furnishings, toys, cosmetics, lingerie, shoes, jewelry, sporting goods, and most variety-store merchandise.

Periodic and frequent stock counts have some disadvantages. Since there is no record of goods on hand between these periodic counts, some goods may be sold out in the period between counts and not reordered until after the next scheduled count. (Of course, if the sales organization is alert and well motivated, the last unit sold would be brought to the buyer's attention before then.) The actual physical counting of goods is time consuming, and usually must be handled by salespeople as they find time (that is, between customers). Sometimes the worst situation happens: customers are given poor service and lost sales result. Otherwise, the counting of stock can be delayed or the count may be inaccurate because of interruptions.

PERPETUAL CONTROL   Under a perpetual inventory system, each item is recorded as it is sold. This provides an instant reference of the stock on hand at any time. Sales information may be derived from sales checks, punched cards, price tickets, or cash registers that feed data into computing machines.

While theoretically such a perpetual inventory would seem to eliminate the need for any physical counting of goods (since the books and stock records would show all sales, receipts, stock on hand, and any returns) actually, more than enough errors creep in. Perhaps a stock number was misrecorded, or a price ticket lost, or someone became careless and forgetful. Shoplifting might have occurred, or maybe some damaged goods were removed but not recorded. In any case, a physical inventory needs to be made periodically to ascertain the differences between the book inventory and the actual goods on hand.

A perpetual inventory control system is considerably more costly than using periodic stock counts, and therefore is not practical where units are of low value, such as notions and cosmetics. However, for furniture, men's clothing, and women's dresses and coats, it is frequently used. The automatic systems, which usually are tied in with a cash register especially fitted to provide merchandise information input into a computer, eliminate the tedious manual posting of perpetual unit control systems. However, errors in punching the cash register have led to problems, which often can only be reconciled by taking fairly frequent physical counts.

The Need for the Physical Inventory

Book inventory figures, no matter how carefully kept, do not eliminate the need for periodically taking a complete physical count of all the merchandise in the store. If for no other reason, this has to be done to determine the profit or loss of the firm during the year and to report this for income tax. Shoplifting, employee thefts, and clerical errors occur frequently enough that most stores find their *physical inventory* of goods to be somewhat less than the book inventory figures indicate. This difference is the *stock shortage.*

Physical inventories are taken at least once a year, usually at the end of the fiscal or the calendar year. For a calendar year, the physical inventory is taken at the end of December. This is a time when stock should be at its leanest, but it is also a time still hectic from the aftermath of peak Christmas sales. The end of January is becoming more popular for taking physical inventories. This coincides with the needs of stores reporting on a fiscal-year basis, and the January clearance sales help with inventory reduction. Some stores and departments take a complete physical inventory more frequently. This especially is true of fashion departments and those that have experienced a severe stock shortage on the previous inventory.

RETAILING ERRORS—*Consequences of Inaccurate Physical Inventory*

It is no simple thing to take a complete and accurate physical inventory. Any inaccuracies confound the situation and the determination of profitability. More than this, the inaccuracy affects the succeeding period as well. The following consequences may result from inaccurate inventories:

1. If the inventory for the end of the period is understated, this will make the cost of goods sold appear to be higher, and serious stock shortages will be apparent and therefore decrease the profitability for that period.
2. If the inventory is overstated, cost of goods sold will appear to be lower, and profitability will be overstated.

If the inaccurate inventory is not corrected, the period after will show the reverse situation, with profits overstated in the first instance, and understated in the second. The reason for this rests on the relationships among the beginning and ending inventory figures, the cost of goods sold, and the gross margin. The following computations will clarify this:

	If end-of-year inventory		
First period	**Is correct**	**Is understated**	**Is overstated**
Sales	$150,000	$150,000	$150,000
First-of-year stock on hand	$ 10,000	$ 10,000	$ 10,000
Purchases	100,000	100,000	100,000
	$110,000	$110,000	$110,000
Less end-of-year inventory	$ 15,000	$ 10,000	$ 20,000
Cost of goods sold	$ 95,000	$100,000	$ 90,000
Gross margin	$ 55,000	$ 50,000	$ 60,000
Next period			
Sales	$180,000	$180,000	$180,000
First-of-year stock on hand	$ 15,000	$ 10,000	$ 20,000
Purchases	120,000	120,000	120,000
	$135,000	$130,000	$140,000
Less end-of-year inventory	$ 20,000	$ 20,000	$ 20,000
Cost of goods sold	$115,000	$110,000	$120,000
Gross margin	$ 65,000	$ 70,000	$ 60,000

It is assumed in this example that only the inventory at the end of the first period was incorrect. Since such an incorrect ending inventory becomes in turn the beginning inventory for the following period, the error is extended into that period (even though the ending inventory for the second period is assumed to be accurate at $20,000).

A moment's reflection will suggest how a manager can be a hero in one period (if the inventory is erroneously overstated) and a flop the next period. More than this, if a buyer or manager is transferred shortly after the inventory is overstated, his or her successor will face the consequences of a lowered profit performance. For this reason, some careful buyers and store managers insist on verification of the inventory before they accept the responsibility of a new position.

> *For Further Analysis* You have been promoted to store manager on April 1, 1979. Your predecessor, after two outstanding years, left the company and became general manager of a large department store. On spot checking some of the inventory records with actual goods on hand and sales information, you have reason to suspect that the December 31, 1978, inventory was overstated. Further investigation, including querying of employees suggests that the December 31, 1977, inventory was also overstated. In consulting with your superiors, a general agreement is reached that the 1977 inventory was overstated by $15,000 and the 1978 inventory by $21,000. If these figures were not corrected, what would have been the effect on your profit for 1979?

Procedure for Inventorying

If maximum accuracy is to be obtained, careful planning and indoctrination of the people who will be involved in the actual counting and recording of goods are essential. It is obvious that goods must be straightened, arranged in an orderly manner, and correctly price-ticketed. All goods in stock must be found and counted—but only once. To lessen the possibility of some goods being counted twice, inventory tags are often affixed to the various clusters of goods, and these are carefully pulled and collected by the manager or other responsible executive after everything has been counted. These tags can then be tabulated, total prices computed, and the total value of the inventory built up in this way.

While procedures vary from firm to firm, the following are some that are in general use in the quest for accuracy:

1. While stockroom counts are being made—perhaps several days before the actual physical count on the selling floor—no merchandise can be sent to the selling floor unless carefully supervised procedures are used.
2. Stock counts on the sales floor are often done on Sunday or after the store is closed, in order to prevent misplacement of goods and missed deductions from stock due to a sale.
3. Inventory forms are numbered consecutively, and all forms must be accounted for. (The author remembers one occasion where a frantic search for a missing form was carried on all night before it was finally found buried under some goods.)
4. Some chains, in order to assure objectivity and prevent any inven-

tory manipulations, assign store managers to different stores than their own during the inventory procedure.

Tedious but necessary. That is how most workers and supervisors view the physical inventory process. But the executives responsible may wait anxiously for the results. A severe stock shortage can mitigate a whole year's efforts, not only destroying profits, but informing top management that serious personnel, operational, and/or security problems exist.

STOCK SHORTAGE

Stock shortages are unexplained differences in the value of goods on hand, as determined by physical count, from the goods which stock records show should be on hand. This is sometimes called *invisible shrinkage.* For example, if the book inventory figure (which has carefully recorded all purchases, sales, markdowns, merchandise transfers, employee discounts, returns to suppliers, returns from customers, as well as any *visible shrinkage* due to breakage or unsalable shopworn goods) is $180,000, and the actual physical inventory count can only come up with $157,000, there is $23,000 of invisible shrinkage.

Many things can account for the discrepancy between book and physical inventory figures. (If the physical inventory is more than the book inventory, this is an *overage*.) They can be categorized as follows:

1. Theft, not only by shoplifters, but also by employees
2. Physical loss in the store due to unrecorded breakage, misweighing and mismeasuring, as with candy and piece goods
3. Clerical errors which can involve a wide range of possibilities, from careless receiving of goods (and thereby not catching shortages from vendors), to errors in recording prices, markdowns, tabulations, and so on

Since so many ingredients are covered in the stock shortage figure, you can see how difficult it is to focus blame and to know just where remedial action should take place. And if the physical inventory itself is inaccurate, even the shortage figure will be distorted. In Chapter 18 we will take an in-depth look at this serious problem of shrinkage, and particularly at the security problems and remedies for it.

■ **Summary**

Turnover, its importance, and its calculations are described early in the chapter. The issue of how much turnover is desirable is also studied. Low turnover is more common than too high a turnover, and causes of low turnover are identified for possible improvement of the turnover rate. The basic merchandise-control concepts of open-to-buy, dollar control, and unit control are discussed. The chapter goes on to describe the physical inventory and the consequences of an inaccurate physical inventory, as well as procedures for taking the physical inventory. Finally, the ominous subject of stock shortages is introduced, but will be discussed in more detail in Chapter 18. Chapter 14 concludes a very important section on merchandising. Next we turn our attention to promoting goods and services and operating the store so as to enhance the goods supplied by the merchandising function.

■ **Key Terms**

Average stock	Overage
Book inventory	Periodic stock counting
Dollar control	Perpetual control
Eyeball observation	Physical inventory
Invisible shrinkage	Return on investment
Merchandise control	Stock shortage
Merchandise turnover	Unit control
Open-to-buy budgeting	Visible shrinkage

■ **Discussion Questions**

1. How do you account for some categories of goods typically having much higher merchandise turnover rates than others? Does this situation mean that there are big differences in managerial efficiency?

2. If a certain department or store has a much lower turnover rate than that of similar stores, what would you conclude? Why?

3. Why is return on investment a better measure of profitability than net profit percent of sales?

4. Distinguish between dollar control and unit control.

5. Why is merchandise turnover of major importance to retail management?
6. What is meant by visual control? Who would most likely use it? How effective a technique is it for merchandise control?
7. If the book inventory is carefully recorded and the physical inventory is accurately taken, will they be approximately the same? Why or why not?
8. Why is it important for a newly transferred buyer or manager to be reasonably sure that the last physical inventory was correct? What can be done to assure that this is so? If you have been told that company policy requires that a manager could not be present when his or her own store was being inventoried, would this relieve your concern? Why or why not?
9. What is the importance of open-to-buy budgeting?

■ **Project**

Look up the standard turnover rates for: (a) a housewares department, (b) drugstores, (c) camera and photographic equipment, (d) a handbag department, and (e) men's ties. Be sure to note the sources used in obtaining these figures.

■ **Exercise in Creativity**

You are the buyer of linens and bedding for a four-unit discount chain, all units being in the same metropolitan area. Pressure from top management to pare the number of employees has resulted in stock counts for your merchandise either being seriously delayed or badly in error. What might you do to try to correct this situation so that you can maintain adequate stocks of sheets, towels, bedspreads, blankets, and related goods? How about if the company expands to four more stores located in other cities?

■ **Retailing in Action**

You have been brought into a small dress chain as buyer of sportswear. Sales and profits for this department have been declining for the last several years. You believe that part of the decline in sales is due to overemphasis on merchandise turnover, since the chain's figures are higher than for comparable departments in other firms. You propose to build up stocks to the point where the turnover rate will be lower than for comparable stores.

1. What arguments can you present to top management to persuade them to let you change the high turnover goals?
2. What assurances can you give that in the process of building up stock assortment you will keep markdowns from becoming excessive and still maintain fresh and current stocks?

■ **Retail Math**

1. Last year a certain department had net sales of $60,000 and a turnover rate of 4. A turnover of 5 is desired in the year ahead. If sales volume remains the same, by how much must the average stock be reduced? How would you go about achieving this higher turnover?
2. What sales volume is required to secure a stockturn rate of 8 times a year on an average inventory at selling price of $150,000? If the inventory is $100,000 at cost and the gross margin is 33 percent?
3. Calculate the inventory for the end of the period:

Sales	$87,000
Purchases	76,000
Opening inventory	38,000

4. If the book inventory is valued at $56,000 and a physical inventory taken at the same time totaled $54,500, which would you use for your financial statements, and why?
5. Calculate the open-to-buy for November and December:

Planned sales for November	$45,000
Planned sales for December	75,000
Planned markdowns for period	8,000
Anticipated shortage	3,500
On hand and on order, November 1	80,000
Planned stock, December 31	30,000

Cases for Part Four

GETTING A HIGH MERCHANDISE CHECK

"It is extremely important that we get a high merchandise check the next time Mr. Warren [the district manager] visits us," Mark Grand, the manager of a variety-store unit of a major chain, was telling Andy Brennan, his new assistant manager. "The last time he checked us, about six months ago and before you had been transferred here, we checked only 89 percent of required merchandise items on hand. As you know, that's pretty bad, and I don't want to jeopardize my job, or your's either, with another poor check."

"It has always baffled me, Mr. Grand, how we can maintain an adequate stock assortment—with no out-of-stocks—and still keep our turnover as high as we're supposed to," Andy complained.

Mr. Grand agreed. "That's the dilemma, of course. We have to maintain a lean stock in order to have a good turnover, but it does increase the risk of having out-of-stocks and a low merchandise check."

"How can we possibly come up with a decent check then?"

"Our problem is no different than that faced by the other stores in our district, or even in the company. We really are in competition with them, Andy. We need to come up with as good a showing, or better, than they do, if you and I are to be considered top candidates for promotions to better jobs." Mr. Grand was certainly serious about this, Andy thought, for he was pounding his fist on the desk. But granted the desirability of having a high check, how does a store go about achieving it?

"Andy," Mr. Grand was saying, "The only way we are going to be able to come up with a decent check is for you to see that the salespeople put under the counter some of the high-point items that we are getting in short supply of. This will mean that you will have to check the in-stock situation of the high point items on the checklist every few days or so. If something is getting low, it had better be removed from the counter. Then when we get word that Mr. Warren is on the way here, we can quickly get these out from under the counter and have them adequately displayed so as to receive full credit. I'm going to depend on you to supervise this. Any items that carry checklist points of ten or more will need to be so scrutinized."

"But won't this take away from sales?" Andy was troubled.

"It will, of course, to some extent. But right now in this company a high merchandise in-stock check is more important than achieving maximum sales."

Mr. Grand paused, and spoke a little more quietly. "I can see the company's rationale for insisting on high checks. In theory, a high proportion of desired goods on hand, which translates to a minimum of out-of-stocks, should result in few lost sales; in other words, it should lead to maximizing our potential sales. But, Andy, all the other stores are withholding merchandise from sale also, in order to have high checks. So, in practice, the logic of the system breaks down."

He put his hand on the younger man's shoulder. "Our futures depend on a high check, Andy. Don't let us down."

Questions

1. In light of this example, discuss the pros and cons of a company insisting on high merchandise in-stock checks. Can a company prevent the self-defeating practice of withholding desirable merchandise from sale in order to save it for a high check?
2. Why do you suppose it is so difficult for a store to maintain a high in-stock check, such as a 95 percent check? Is a 100 percent check likely to be achieved? Why or why not?
3. Evaluate Mark Grand's strategy to maintain a high merchandise check. Are there any other alternatives he ought to consider?

RELUCTANCE OF A SMALL STORE TO TAKE MARKDOWNS

Mike Rodriguez opened a small piece goods store in the fall of 1976. Before this he had been a buyer for a large department store and, by carefully saving his money, had accumulated enough for this venture into entrepreneurship.

His efforts were not overwhelmingly successful, although there was no danger of bankruptcy. The first three full years of his operation showed the following results:

	1977	1978	1979
1. Sales	$91,000	$96,000	$98,500
2. Inventory at end of year	31,000	38,000	49,000
3. Investment in fixtures	10,500	11,000	11,000
4. Net profit percentage	6.0	5.5	5.5
5. Net profit dollars	5,460	5,280	5,318
6. Percent return on investment: $\dfrac{5}{2+3}$	13.1	10.8	8.1

While Mike was experiencing some increase in sales, the investment in inventory was resulting in a drastically deteriorating return on investment, from 13.1 percent to 8.1 percent. Most of this increase in investment, which meant that Mike was pumping more money into the enterprise than he was actually realizing in net profits, came from inventory buildup due to a reluctance to take any markdowns.

"I don't want to adversely affect my net profit by taking substantial markdowns. Such markdowns would come right out of my profit. And my old stock is perfectly salable. So it moves out a little more slowly than some of the other merchandise. This doesn't mean that it's bad, or should be marked down. It's different when you're working for a big firm and using their money. When it's your own, you naturally play things closer to the vest," Mike maintained.

Despite being warned about a deteriorating return-on-investment situation, Mike was adamant in his refusal to mark down: "This is perfectly good merchandise. Why should I sell it at cost or below? These big chain stores make a mistake in my judgment in being so eager to mark down. Of course, I'm not saying that if some merchandise is damaged or defective that I won't mark it down. Sure, I'll be quick to do so in that case. But slow sellers, who can say that they won't turn out to be big demand items in another few months or in the next season?"

Questions

1. Evaluate Mike's reasoning.
2. If Mike could be persuaded to take $10,000 in markdowns this next year, what do you think would be the likely effect on the 1980 operating results? Defend your rationale.
3. Which is the more important measure of profitability, net profit or return on investment? Why?

5

Sales Promotion and Store Operation

15 Sales Promotion: Advertising, and Some Cautions

You may have heard of the drugstore in Wall, South Dakota. The town has a population of 800; nearly a third of the families in the town work for this drugstore. If you are a world traveler, you have heard of it: in the Paris and London subways, the canal boats of Amsterdam, in Vietnam, the South Pole, or Shanghai. Certainly, if you have ever driven across South Dakota and adjoining states, you have seen Wall Drug signs, which, in some places, are thicker than one per mile. They promise free ice water—as they have since 1936—among other things. Most signs are corny, such as:

> *Slow down the old hack*
> *Wall Drug Corner*
> *Just across the railroad track.*

The store itself offers merchandise ranging from the usual drugstore items to all kinds of souvenirs: steer skulls, Sioux-made moccasins, snake-bite serums, lariats, and leather chaps. Snake ashtrays made from plaster of Paris and painted to resemble rattlesnakes are bestsellers. Another popular item: Jack-a-Lopes. Made by a local taxidermist, they are stuffed jack rabbits sporting antelope horns.

The advertising pays off: one survey found that 45 percent of all westbound autos on the interstate highway near Wall, and a slightly lower proportion of those eastbound, turn off to visit the store. It now attracts some 10,000 customers a day during the tourist season and has sales of over $1 million a year.

Sources: The Wall Drug phenomenon has received considerable publicity. Sources include numerous articles, a case, and even an entire book. For example: "Wall, S.D., Has Population of Only 800, but Its Drugstore Draws 10,000 a Day," *Wall Street Journal,* September 5, 1973, p. 8; James D. Taylor, Robert L. Johnson, and Gene B. Iverson, *Wall Drug Store* University of South Dakota case study; Dena Close Jennings, *Free Ice Water: The Story of the Wall Drug* (Aberdeen, S.D.: North Plain Press, 1969).

For Thought and Discussion

1. Can you think of other examples of successful billboard retail advertising?
2. What factors do you think account for the effectiveness of Wall Drug's advertising?

Few retailers can match the advertising success of Wall Drug, but all retailers are aware of the need to promote their store and its wares. Large retailers spend millions of dollars in mass media and other types of advertising, but small stores can also make use of promotion—whether it be by purposely letting the smell of good food or fresh baking to waft out to the sidewalk from a small restaurant or bakery, or by using display windows forcefully to lure passersby inside.

Where properly used and coordinated, advertising provides many opportunities to the aggressive retailer. Strong and well-designed promotional efforts may draw far more patronage than the competitive attractiveness of a store would. More than this, effective promotion, combined with satisfactory merchandise and service, will build a favorable image and a large number of loyal customers.

However the temptation to exaggerate has often resulted in deception: it is very easy to claim that an item or a sale is better than it is. As we have noted, the word *sale* is often used unjustifiably. Today's customers (and the government) are more alert to deceptive practices, and ready to contest them.

INGREDIENTS OF SALES PROMOTION

Retail promotion has three main ingredients: advertising, display, and personal selling. The retailer most often uses these in combination, and where efforts are coordinated—as with newspaper ads, window and counter displays and signs, and the efforts of salespeople all concentrated on the same theme—more powerful promotional punch can result. Especially with advertising, a variety of alternatives are available, not only as to what media to use, but also how much, how often, how widespread (that is, whether storewide or more limited), and what themes (such as price, or newest fashions). The use of stamps and games is another type of advertising alternative that some stores have found to be attractive.

COMPATIBILITY WITH STORE IMAGE   With so many alternatives available, some constraints should be recognized. The advertising and display budget necessarily places limits on and narrows the number of alternatives, especially for smaller stores. Just as important a restriction, and one not always so quickly recognized, is compatibility of promotion with *store image.* In several previous chapters we discussed the need for a store to develop a distinctive image—one that appeals to target customers. Once again we want to emphasize that the decor, fixtures, merchandise, and prices all affect this rather nebulous image or customer perception of a store. But promotional efforts may have even more influence. It is important that they harmonize with the desired image and with the other aspects of the store's merchandising program. For example, the following Lord & Taylor ad typifies that store's image:

> *We live for beauty*
> *And search*
> *The world over*
> *To find it.*

COORDINATION OF PROMOTIONAL EFFORTS   If promotional expenditures are to be effective—indeed, if they are not to produce more ill will than good will—then some basic *coordination of promotional efforts* must be attended to. When a particular product or category of goods is featured, it is essential that merchandise to support the promotion be in the store in reasonably sufficient quantities. This probably seems obvious; but unless care is taken, delays in placing the orders, shipping, unpacking, marking, and getting the goods to the sales floor may kill the impact of the promotion. Hence, a major need is to coordinate merchandise and promotion.

Coordinating operations and promotion may also be important, especially for sales events that generate heavier-than-usual customer traffic. Extra personnel, additional cash registers, sufficient bags, string, salesbooks, and so on, are all details necessary for smooth functioning and maximum utilization of sales opportunity.

Efforts of salespeople should also be coordinated with promotion. They should be fully informed about the promotion; where the merchandise is; its prices; key selling points; and any special policies about delivery, alterations, return goods, and the like. Special efforts should be made to inform part-time people, who often are neglected because of their shorter schedules.

ADVERTISING

A store typically spends the greatest portion of its promotion budget on advertising. The ability to reach out with a selling message to large numbers of people makes advertising particularly potent in comparison with a display, which can only influence passersby, or a salesperson, whose influence is limited to the few persons he or she can talk to.

The following discussion will not go into the technical and specialized aspects of advertising, such as layout, artwork, and copywriting. Rather, we will be concerned with advertising from the buyer or manager's perspective.

Planning the Advertising

A department store may spend 3 percent of sales or more for advertising. For such a commitment of funds, efforts should be well planned. In the larger store each department may be given a total advertising budget, and, with that in mind, the timing, the media to be used, and the merchandise to be featured must be planned. Past years' results are helpful here and may serve as guides, especially if a diary of successes and failures of promotional efforts has been maintained. Trade associations, such as the National Retail Merchants Association, and various trade publications offer *promotional calendars* and guides for various months throughout the year.

An example of a form used to record promotional results, factors affecting such results, and suggestions for improving the next year, is given in Figure 15.1. The major scheduled events for four weeks of July are listed so that individual departments can plan their efforts accordingly.

Usually the total advertising allotment for the year (or for a six-month period) is apportioned to each month according to estimated sales figures: the higher the expected sales, the more the share of advertising dollars. However, some retailers are now recognizing that peak traffic months, such as November and December, can thrive with less advertising.

After advertising funds have been allocated for each month, they can be assigned to individual promotions by days and weeks. It is good to set aside some money for promotions of expeditious purchases and special clearances. The experience of previous years can help in this planning, but it should not be such an anchor as to thwart originality.

TIMING THE ADVERTISING   *Timing* is important in advertising effectiveness. Certain days of the week are traditionally heavy days for retail newspaper ads. As you know, most supermarkets advertise heavily toward the end of the week, often on Thursday, in anticipation of the peak weekend grocery shopping. Department stores tend to concentrate ads in Sunday papers, which presumably are read more carefully than daily papers. But there are some retailers, too courageous to follow the crowd, who choose instead to advertise in less busy days of the week, when there are fewer competing ads.

Weather can play an important role in the advertising of seasonal goods. An unseasonably warm or cold spell may completely ruin the effects of some advertisements. On the other hand, matching the weather can be a boon. Perhaps nowhere is this more important than with rubber footwear: rubbers, overshoes, boots. Many stores have these ads prepared in advance and in the hands of the newspaper. Long-range weather forecasts are closely watched, and when the first major snow of the season is forecasted, the go-ahead is hurriedly called in to the paper.

A difficult decision is how far in advance and how much emphasis

FIGURE 15.1 PROMOTIONAL CALENDAR FOR PLANNING AND REVIEWING

	Scheduled events	Weekly review Per. VI Year Dept.		
Sun.		1. Results of advertised events?		Week 1
3.	Pre-4th Sales			
4.	HOLIDAY	2. Comments concerning competition, weather, special events, stock condition, customer trends, etc.		
5.	After-4th Clearance			
6.				
7.		3. How to improve next year?		
8.				
Sun.		1.		Week 2
10.	(SFH White Sale) (Annual Doll Sale)			
11.	(Appliance Week)	2.		
12.				
13.				
14.		3.		
15.	HFS Out-of-Town Courtesy Day			
Sun.		1.		Week 3
17.	HFS Regular Courtesy Day			
18.		2.		
19.	HFS Package			
20.	"			
21.	"	3.		
22.	"			
Sun.		1.		Week 4
24.	Swim Suit Break July Sales & Clearance			
25.		2.		
26.				
27.				
28.		3.		
29.				
Sun.	SFH = Store For Homes HFS = Home Furnishings Sale	1.		Week 5
		2.		
		3.		

Use reverse side for additional notes

COMING
THIS SUMMER:
BILL RODGERS
RUNNING CAMP
AUGUST 27-31

BILL RODGERS
RUNNING CENTER

Women's Clothing & Shoes
Also—the Bill Rodgers Running Line

North Market Place
Faneuil Hall
Boston, Mass
723-5612

372A Chestnut Hill Ave
Cleveland Circle
Boston, Mass 02146
734-7317

This seasonal ad capitalizes on the fame of Bill Rodgers, record holder for the Boston Marathon. The ad is of particular interest because it shows how a celebrated athelete can use his reputation successfully to promote commercial endeavors related to his sport. (Ad as appeared in *Equal Times*)

should be given to advertising certain seasonal goods, such as sportswear, bathing suits, ski equipment, and Christmas cards and ornaments. Some think that the long-range results of early advertising efforts are significant. Other retailers insist that only ads run close to the time of purchase have any impact. The latter may be closer to correct. Although advance-of-season ads do keep the name of the store before the public, merchandise already wanted and in season deserves priority and yields more tangible sales results.

CHOOSING THE MERCHANDISE   The choice of merchandise to advertise is critical. Even the best ad will not produce satisfactory results when the merchandise has little customer appeal. How does one determine what is wanted merchandise? Judgment has to be used here, and some feel or intuition may be helpful for the experienced buyer. But there are also guidelines:

1. Success in past sales and in the preceding year is most helpful, especially for goods that are not high fashion.
2. Merchandise that is presently selling well, or that in pretests of

samples showed promise, is a good candidate, provided the merchandise is still in season.

3. Experiences of other stores, as obtained by feedback from resident buying offices, vendors, trade associations, other units of the chain- or department-store group, and so on, may focus attention on possibilities.

4. For the new buyer, an important source of input can be the advice of experienced salespeople in the department.

None of these sources of information guarantees success: some ads will be duds and others will be surprisingly successful. But this makes the business of merchandising challenging. (It also makes it less secure and comfortable than some would like.)

Types of Advertising

Retail advertising can be categorized as (1) *product-nonpromotional,* (2) *product-promotional,* and (3) *institutional.* Although the objective of all advertising is to generate more sales than would be likely otherwise, some ads are geared to do this more directly than others. And some advertisements have such an uncertain effect on sales that the most an advertiser really expects is some change (for the better) in the way people view the firm.

PRODUCT-NONPROMOTIONAL ADVERTISING We typically find certain stores trying to assert a quality or fashion image, or an image of having the newest merchandise or a large assortment. Most of their advertising will be of featured items, sometimes only one or two to an entire ad, with regular prices (nonsale prices) presented in small print (almost, it sometimes seems, as if price were something customers are not really interested in). Much cooperative advertising (see page 388) is of this type—but the brand name is prominently displayed.

PRODUCT-PROMOTIONAL ADVERTISING This is the most common type of retail advertising. Here one or more products are featured at a sale or special price. The intent is to generate immediate store traffic, and the items advertised presumably are at such prices only for a limited time. It is expected that the increased customer traffic resulting from such items will boost sales of regular-priced goods also. Some product-promotional advertising is directed to clearance and end-of-season goods. Many stores use a combination of promotional and

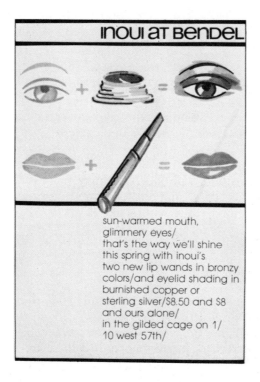

sun-warmed mouth,
glimmery eyes/
that's the way we'll shine
this spring with inoui's
two new lip wands in bronzy
colors/and eyelid shading in
burnished copper or
sterling silver/$8.50 and $8
and ours alone/
in the gilded cage on 1/
10 west 57th/

Here we have a large product-nonpromotional advertisement. The ad features only two related items with price presented inconspicuously. Note the large amount of white space and the connotation of quality this lack of clutter imparts. One criticism might be leveled at the advertising copy: the personal pronouns *we* and *ours* might better have been changed to *you* and *yours*. (Henri Bendel, 10 West 57th Street, New York City)

nonpromotional product advertising, with some items advertised at regular prices along with those on sale. Supermarkets often use combination ads.

INSTITUTIONAL ADVERTISING   In *institutional advertising*, no product is even mentioned; there is no persuasion or attempt to generate immediate extra customer traffic. You may wonder why a firm would spend money on such seemingly unproductive efforts. This advertising is used to promote good will by trying to show that the store is a good place to shop, has pleasant and happy employees, is interested in the community, or perhaps is particularly consumer-oriented.

   The effectiveness of institutional advertising is virtually impossible to measure, but there are certain potential advantages in having the

Do a good turn for your country.
(And save energy.) Happy fourth!

Neiman-Marcus

This large, expensive institutional ad features no product, but only a public service message. Even the name of the sponsor is unobtrusively presented. Do you think such an ad is worthwhile to the store? (Neiman-Marcus Co.; Art Director, Richard Nelson; Copywriter, Marion Kennedy.)

name of the store presented in a most favorable light in a nonselling context. Institutional advertising may (1) win new customers or better relations with present customers; (2) develop the reputation of the store as a good place to work, thus bringing better employees; (3) develop a store's stature as a community leader and enhance the influence of store executives with local governmental bodies, chambers of commerce, and the like.

Stores located in or near a ghetto or that have a large proportion of lower-income shoppers—and many downtown stores are facing this—have a special need for institutional advertising, but of a different kind than simply a nonproduct newspaper ad. Store involvement in community affairs, such as with local athletic teams, sponsorship of special activities and bazaars, contributions to churches and organizations, and consumer education are possibilities for institutional advertising directed to a particular audience. This may contribute to less shoplifting and vandalism, and produce more loyal customers, as well as community betterment.

Advertising Media

Media refers to the different ways in which an advertising message can be projected, such as newspapers, magazines, radio, television, direct mail, billboards, and others. The choice of which to use depends on several factors:

1. Cost
2. Audience to be reached
3. Message or product to be advertised
4. Extent of coverage afforded by the available media
5. Amount of advance or lead time required
6. Custom and past ways of advertising

NEWSPAPERS   Newspapers have long been a favorite medium for retailers. It is easy to see why. They are ideal for reaching the store's market area. This coverage can be provided at a relatively low cost per reader. Not very much lead time is required. (This is important so that the retailer can make last-minute price changes or merchandise substitutions.)

The large city newspapers, however, favor the large merchant, or the one who has several stores scattered throughout the metropolitan area, so that the cost of advertising can be spread over more than one outlet. A small retailer often cannot afford the wasted coverage that a large paper would provide, since his geographical draw of customers is small. Sometimes local neighborhood or suburban papers are better.

MAGAZINES   Magazines are a much less important medium to most retailers, because they require a long lead time. Since they are usually nonlocal, they are practical only for chains or other firms with a national reputation and widespread charge-account customers. Magazines are occasionally used by retailers who offer mail-order service.

RADIO AND TELEVISION   The media of radio, and to a lesser extent, television, have in the past mostly been used as a supplement to newspaper advertising. Occasionally when newspapers are on strike, radio spots are substituted because of the rather low cost and short lead time required. However, the fleeting nature of the sales message through radio makes this alternative not particularly attractive under normal conditions. Local TV spots are sometimes used by large retailers, usually for special storewide sales events, or for major volume periods such as Easter and Christmas.

Until recently, national network TV was out of the question for retailers, even big ones, since too many potential viewers would be out of their market areas. Even a large firm like J. C. Penney Company, for example, has the bulk of its sales west of the Mississippi River, where only 35 percent of the nation's population lives. And the major department-store corporations, such as Federated, have major market coverage only in scattered locales, so that much TV coverage would be wasted.

Today, retailer use of TV has changed decisively. Sears led the way, expanding its emphasis on national advertising to establish more than a score of its private-brand products, from hosiery to auto batteries. By 1976, Sears was spending over $51 million for network TV and over $22 million for local TV spots.[1] J. C. Penney Company tried network TV for national exposure during a presidential election campaign. More and more, department stores are finding local TV spots an effective way to advertise major sales events or to impart a credible fashion image. But one of the most avid retailers to use TV is a retailer of hamburgers, McDonald's.

SUCCESSFUL RETAILING STRATEGIES—Massive TV Advertising: McDonald's

McDonald's sales were $1.38 billion in 1977. It has been the nation's biggest dispenser of meals for more than half a decade and during that time has budgeted $50 million or more each year for advertising, most of this on TV (in 1976, network and local TV expenditures reached $57 million). *Time* magazine commented: "The company's relentless advertising campaign has made the McDonald's jingle, 'You Deserve a Break Today,' almost as familiar as 'The Star-Spangled Banner.'"

Why did McDonald's make the decision to place most of its promotional

---

As reported in *Advertising Age,* August 23, 1976, p. 74.

dollars in TV advertising? Fred Turner, the president, explains: "Our move to the suburbs was a conscious effort to go for the family business. That meant going after the kids. We decided to use television, so we created our own character, Ronald McDonald." Today there are fifty Ronalds who make appearances at parades, county fairs, and store openings. In addition, one Ronald is stationed permanently in Hollywood to appear in the firm's television commercials.

And how successful has this advertising strategy been? In a survey, 96 percent of the schoolchildren identified Ronald McDonald, ranking him second only to Santa Claus.

Sources: *Forbes,* May 15, 1978, p. 268; and "The Burger That Conquered the Country," *Time,* September 17, 1973, pp. 84–92.

For Thought and Discussion

1. Do you think the massive use of TV advertising was a vital factor in the success of McDonald's? Why or why not?
2. How would you evaluate the effectiveness of this type of advertising?

DIRECT MEDIA   Some promotional messages go directly to the consumer. Letters, catalogs, bill enclosures, handouts, package inserts, even sales messages delivered by telephone, may be used. The advantages are that the number and type of persons who receive the advertisements can be carefully selected. This flexibility makes direct media ideal for the smaller store or for the one seeking a special segment of consumers difficult to reach otherwise. Many stores send promotional enclosures to their charge customers with bills. But although there are almost endless possibilities with direct media, many of these messages receive scant attention from recipients.

YELLOW PAGES   The Yellow Pages of the telephone book—or, in larger cities, in a separate book—are an important advertising medium for smaller retail and service establishments. Directories are especially well adapted to establishments geared to emergency service and to allowing the consumer a quick comparison of offerings. For example, the TV set that stops working before the big game needs the prompt service that can be found by consulting the Yellow Pages. Restaurants find the Yellow Pages an important medium for promoting their specialities and providing their addresses.

The telephone company has long urged consumers to use the Yellow Pages: "Let your fingers do the walking through the Yellow Pages."

This promotional message is geared to less urgent business where the consumer can use the phone as a shopping device to compare the offerings and prices of similar firms.

A firm can opt either for a boldface listing under its product or service category, or for a larger display listing. For either of these options the firm must pay: up to $2,000 per year for a quarter-page ad in a directory for a city of 500,000.

BILLBOARDS AND MISCELLANEOUS Highway signs, even skywriting, may occasionally be used, especially as supplementary media for special sales events or new store openings. These must be recognized as secondary, even novelty, media, and their effectiveness is difficult to assess. However, there are some examples of the use of highway signs that have been outstanding contributors to success (most notably that of Wall Drug, described at the beginning of this chapter).

Here is an example of highly innovative advertising. Pictured is the top of a candy delivery truck for a New England franchise restaurant and candy chain. The painting of an open box of candy with an enclosed note is a real eyecatcher from high-rise offices and apartments. (Courtesy Brigham's Division of Jewel Companies, Inc.)

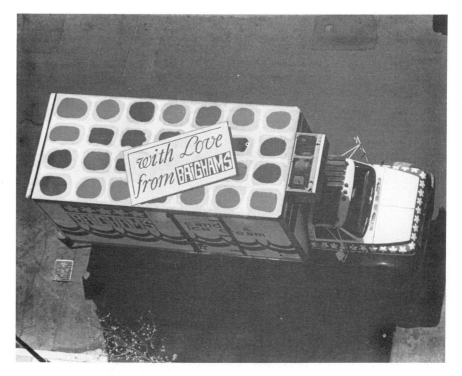

Cooperative Advertising

As noted in Chapter 12, manufacturers sometimes reimburse retailers for part of the cost of ads that feature the manufacturers' goods. This is known as *cooperative advertising,* and a manufacturer may pay as much as 50 percent of the cost, up to a certain percentage—often 5—of the retailer's total purchases from the manufacturer. Such a subsidy can be attractive from the retailer's viewpoint, and it enables a store to do more advertising than would be possible otherwise. But judgment must be used in choosing the best deals, ones that will appeal to the retailer's

Here is an example of a cooperative ad. The famous designer and dress manufacturer, Diane Von Furstenberg, shares the cost of the ad with retailer. Again, we see a lot of white space and a quality image. Note that the ad solicits mail and phone orders. (Courtesy of Cain-Sloan, Nashville, Tenn. 37219. Registered trademark ® of Diane Von Furstenberg.)

IT'S TULIP TIME!

A fresh, new look for the new season! This famous designer takes the outline of a tulip and inverts it on the hem of this button-front dress. Then fashions it all of silk-like, mint green polyester jacquard, for sizes 4 to 14. A unique and timeless design . . . $88.00, from Better Dresses. Mail or phone orders filled; dial 255-4651, ext. 4700.

CAIN-SLOAN
A UNIT OF ALLIED STORES

customers. Since manufacturers typically want these ads run at regular prices, a promotion-minded retailer may see little advantage here and may be quite selective in using it.

Manufacturers benefit in cooperative advertising because of lower local advertising rates and because retailers will show greater interest in the products so advertised. However, care must be taken that no discrimination is shown to other retailers and that advertising allowances are available to all customers on proportionally equal terms. Otherwise there may be a violation of the Robinson-Patman Act of 1936.

Evaluating Advertising Results

One of the problems that has long faced advertisers is how to determine the effectiveness of an ad or even of an entire campaign. Related to this is the problem of how much should be spent.

With institutional advertising, the task of evaluating results is practically impossible. With product advertising, some feel that the results can be measured by tallying sales of the advertised product for three days to a week after the ad has been run. Along with such a tally, which can be conveniently made on a tear sheet of the ad, certain other factors affecting sales results can be noted: the weather and any competitive ads. Such a check on specific advertisements is a useful guide for planning the following year's advertising. In the case of a particularly successful ad, it may be worth repeating in several months.

Such tallies are useful and should be maintained scrupulously. But they still tell little about certain other contributions of the ad. As we observed before, one expectation from advertising—particularly promotional advertising—is that sales of unadvertised products will also benefit from the increased traffic. But it is difficult to get a direct measure of this and to determine how much is due to a particular ad. Also, we cannot measure the long-range effects of ads. An ad that produced little extra immediate business, may have affected sales weeks later.

MAJOR PROMOTIONS

Some stores have a special sale every week. With supermarkets this is almost axiomatic; but many other retailers do also—furniture stores, discount stores, renowned department stores. Sears, for example, typically features special sales the last four days of every week. Certain occasions for periodic sale events that have become commonplace with many retailers include: anniversary sales, white-goods sales, back-to-school sales, one-cent sales, dollar days, January clearances, and August fur sales. Then there is the fire sale for the merchant with rare opportunity, and the going-out-of-business sale.

Some of these periodic sales are major store events, with merchandise specially priced in all departments, with heavy advertising, special window displays, interior trim, even perhaps special catalogs or brochures sent to all charge-account customers. Planning for some of these major events may take months. The customer traffic produced by a major sale event in a large store may be tremendous. Main traffic aisles may be almost impassable. Buying may become so frenzied that customers actually shove and attempt to grab things from each other. Keeping counters replenished and in some semblance of order may be almost impossible. And it invariably seems to happen, just as the crowd around a cash register becomes heaviest and most impatient, that the register tape runs out and has to be replaced. (The answer here, of course, is to check all register tapes before the doors open.)

Limitations of Major Sale Events

The tremendous traffic and sales volume generated by a successful major storewide sale does have disadvantages, however. Usually these do not outweigh the advantages and the problems can be minimized if not eliminated. But these potential disadvantages or problems ought to be recognized: (1) Deception must be avoided if customer confidence is to be maintained and even government investigation prevented. (2) If special sales are used too frequently, they tend to lose much of their punch. Customers become indifferent to them or perceive them not to be special. (3) Although special sales with outstanding bargains may produce tremendous business, unless regular-priced goods are also prominently displayed, their sales may be adversely affected. (4) Major storewide events, which require considerable preparation and often are anticipated by knowledgeable customers for several days or even weeks, tend to detract from business preceding and following the events. (5) Major sales peaks lead to built-in inefficiencies because part-time, marginal, and inexperienced employees must be used for adequate staffing; and because mistakes in making change, ringing cash registers, making out delivery slips, and so on, are likely.

In general, efforts should be taken to insure that the demands of special promotion buying and operational planning do not result in neglecting or giving a lower priority to other important store duties and responsibilities.

Nonprice Promotions

Not all special promotions need be on a price basis. Some stores have conducted major *nonprice promotions* on different themes with notable success. For example, Hess's of Allentown, Pennsylvania, has gained a reputation as an exciting store, and it draws customers from a hundred miles away, although it covers only one quarter of a midtown block and serves a city of less than 120,000 people.

These shoppers are lured by major once-a-year extravaganzas: for example, the annual flower show. This lasts a full week, and the first floor of the store looks like a forest primeval—with 250,000 flowers, shrubs, plants, and trees choking the aisles, countertops, and merchandise racks. The promotion takes twelve months to prepare, draws upward of 135 busloads of out-of-towners, and gives Hess's one of its biggest sales weeks of the year.

In recent years, some stores have effectively jumped onto the physical fitness bandwagon and developed major storewide promotions with this theme. Perhaps Dayton's in Minneapolis is the best example of how retailer sensitivity to changing lifestyles can be made not only into a storewide promotion but also a communitywide major event. In the spring of 1978, they called it "Getting into Gear at Dayton's." It was a two-week event that included seminars and clinics on exercise and diet, talks of preventing aching back problems, free EKG tests, and aerobic dancing demonstrations; it culminated in two races, a 26.2-mile marathon, and a 10-kilometer (6.2-mile) run. Cooperation and participation of many organizations in the community and elsewhere were obtained, ranging from the local YMCA, North Memorial Hospital, the Minneapolis Park Board, both city newspapers, and the Prudential Insurance Company, to Nike, a manufacturer of running shoes, and Danskin.

In addition to initiating and planning the event and drumming up community support and publicity, Dayton's directly benefited from a strong merchandising tie-in supported by a twenty-four-page four-color catalog illustrating apparel and equipment available at Dayton's for all kinds of outdoor sporting activities—from running and swimming to the racket sports. Displays throughout the store announced the theme and set the mood. Of course, footwear departments had beefed-up stocks and abundant displays. James Fixx, author of *The Complete Book of Running,* the number one nonfiction best seller of 1978, spoke to a standing-room audience. The excitement engendered, the good will gained, not to mention the extra business fostered, made this super promotion one of the more memorable events of a bitter winter. And the race? When race day, April 15, came, over 3,500 runners of every age and degree of fitness started the marathon, and over 1,400 others participated in the shorter race, with thousands of spectators cheering the runners on.[2]

Such extra promotions require much planning and are costly, but they can have the following benefits:

1. They make the store exciting, not only for customers, but for employees as well. They move away from the routine and commonplace; they have an element of innovation that can permeate other aspects of the operation and last longer than the actual event.
2. Customer traffic is generated, which invariably results in additional sales throughout the store.
3. Often these events are of such interest that considerable free local (and even national) publicity is provided. This not only furthers the public relations and image of the store, but directly produces added traffic.
4. Certain promotions can cement relations with significant customer segments: as an Italian-import promotion favorably influences a large Italian ethnic group; and a flower show, a large number of horticultural buffs and environmentalists.

Major promotions are not limited to department stores and individual retailers. Some shopping centers do an outstanding job of sponsoring promotions of various kinds that can bring masses of people into the center, with all merchants benefiting. Some promotions have become rather traditional: sidewalk sales, arrival of Santa Claus (perhaps by helicopter, or even by parachute), George Washington's Birthday sales, and dollar days. The enclosed mall type of shopping center is particularly well suited for innovative ways to lure customers, such as auto shows, art exhibits, minicircuses, special exhibits of all kinds, and many types of entertainers from rock-and-roll bands to magicians. One of the more imaginative recent promotions took place at Randall Park Mall in Cleveland:

---

[2] For more details, see "Running, Jumping, and Getting into Gear," *Stores,* July 1978, pp. 30–32.

FANTASY ON ICE—The biggest Mall of all is presenting a Fantasy on Ice, but without the ice. It's a most unusual show with expert figure skaters performing on a specially treated surface. You'll see dazzling figure skating, jugglers, and a fun-filled comedy act.

With more than 200 stores sharing the costs of an extravaganza of this kind, and reaping the harvest of the resulting customer traffic it is obvious that large malls have a decided advantage over small shopping centers, if promotional opportunities are used innovatively and aggressively.

CAUTIONS IN USE OF PROMOTIONS

A store with a heavy promotional bent needs to be extra cautious in today's business environment. We have noted before the temptation to exaggerate a little, or to use quasi-deceptive methods such as fictitous comparative prices, bait-and-switch techniques, and a false use of the word *sale.*

So-called fire sales and going-out-of-business sales have often been vehicles for promotional deception. Fire sales have dragged on for months, long after the original fire-damaged goods have been sold out. In these instances, replenishments are continually made with distress goods obtained from a variety of sources, and these are promoted as original fire-damaged goods at fantastic savings. Going-out-of-business sales sometimes last interminably, also. The author, on some of his periodic buying trips to New York City, found a store on Fifth Avenue with its windows plastered with "going-out-of-business" signs, month after month after month.

In order to curb some of the abuses of fictitious sales, particularly of the fire and going-out-of-business breed, some cities now require licenses for such sales. The cause of the sale then has to be validated and a definite final date of the sale, or termination of business, specified.

Retailers face a different business environment today than they did even a decade ago. Practices that were then commonplace are becoming unacceptable today. Consumers are more alert to abusive and deceptive practices; sometimes in their agitation they even perceive deception where there is none. Government agencies are responding to consumer outcries. The Federal Trade Commission, at the national level, is becoming a more vigorous consumer defender, and is taking particularly strong action against any deception in advertising. Local consumer offices also have been set up in many metropolitan areas to process consumer complaints and exert pressure on the merchants involved. And retailers have long attempted to regulate themselves through the better business bureaus described in Chapter 4.

This suggests that a store concerned with its reputation and the loyalty of its customers needs to take measures to insure that its sales are legitimate and that comparative prices are not exaggerated. Such policing can be difficult in a large multidepartmental store. The objective of department managers and buyers is to make a good sales and profit showing. Executives are evaluated on this; it is crucial to their promotional opportunities and their continued employment with the firm. They are sometimes tempted to mislead a little, in order to make a better showing. To prevent this, a few retailers are establishing as a company policy, that

1. Any item stipulated either in an advertisement, a counter display and sign, or in a salesperson presentation, as being on sale, must be at least 15 percent under the price it is regularly sold at, or else must be a special purchase carrying a below-average markup.
2. Comparative pricing will be eliminated, so that exaggerated original prices are prevented.

Although such policies seem drastic to many promotion-minded stores, the long-term effects on customer confidence and loyalty can be worth it. Sometimes there is merit in being a leader in raising the image and practice of business to a higher level.

SEARCH FOR INNOVATION

Many alternatives are available in promoting a store and its goods. The fact that a certain way of advertising and promoting is commonplace, traditional, or is being practiced by all competitors does not mean that a different approach might not be successful.

A new promotional concept can, of course, easily be copied by other retailers. Then the once-fresh idea becomes commonplace and less effective, and the search goes on for another innovative approach.

Sometimes innovation can include appealing to a different customer segment, for extra business.

In Chapter 5 we noted that rural, small-town consumers are dissatisfied with their local shopping environment but reluctant to brave the unfamiliarity, impersonality, and congestion of large cities, where they would have a better assortment and quality of goods to choose from. What might big-city retailers do to woo these dissatisfied but reluctant consumers? Here innovative promotional efforts could make a significant contribution. For example:

Many large stores have personal shoppers. . . . For the rural consumer unfamiliar with a big store, the availability of a personal shopper as a knowledgeable and friendly escort for the first visit would do much to wither the negative image of impersonality and give concrete evidence of the "personal touch."

Free parking privileges for out-of-town shoppers . . . would be a tangible indication of the retailer's concern for a customer unused to the difficulty and expense of parking in the big city.

Promotional efforts could be directed to these consumers, with instructions—perhaps a map—showing the best way to reach the store.[3]

■ **Summary**

Retail advertising can utilize a number of different media, although the newspaper is the most customary one. But even billboards can be extremely effective under certain conditions, as they long have been with Wall Drug. Important considerations in planning the advertisement are: budgeting the expenditures, timing, choosing the merchandise, and deciding on the advertising media. Cooperative advertising is commonplace and beneficial to both parties. Some stores and shopping centers have achieved great success with imaginative major promotions, even though these may involve extensive planning and heavy expenditures. In the next chapter we will consider other promotional activities as well as the role of the sales staff.

■ **Key Terms**

Cooperative advertising

Coordination of promotional efforts

Institutional advertising

Media

Nonprice promotions

Product-nonpromotional advertising

Product-promotional advertising

Promotional calendar

Store image

Timing

[3] Examples taken from Robert F. Hartley, "The Rural Market Offers a Challenge for Extra Business," *Stores,* January 1969, pp. 45–46.

■ **Discussion Questions**

1. Do you think a retail store can get along without newspaper advertising? Why or why not?

2. Why, at least until recently, have so few retail stores advertised on TV?

3. Discuss how stores can evaluate the effectiveness of their advertising. What are some of the problems in making valid evaluations?

4. Some people have suggested that, since retailers have peak traffic during November and December, they could cut down on advertising expenditures during these months. This would permit them to advertise more heavily in the less-busy months. If you were a retailer, how would you respond to such a suggestion?

5. Rain checks are used by some stores when an advertised item is not available, perhaps because of late shipment or heavier-than-expected demand. A rain check entitles the customer to buy the product at the advertised price at some later date, when it is again in stock. Evaluate the use of rain checks, from the viewpoints of customer satisfaction and operational efficiency.

6. Why is coordination of advertising with other aspects of the operation important?

7. As a small store owner in the suburbs, you feel that advertising in the metropolitan paper is too expensive and has too much waste coverage (that is, people are hardly going to come from the other side of town to shop in your store). What other advertising media alternatives would you consider? How effective are these likely to be?

■ **Project**

Check through the ads of a Sunday newspaper and classify those that are (1) product-nonpromotional, (2) product-promotional, and (3) institutional. Can you make any conclusions about the types of stores that use the various types of advertising? Why are there so few institutional ads?

■ **Exercises in Creativity**

1. Assume the role of assistant manager of a shopping center. The center has been very effective in the past in using special showings, exhibits, and promotions on a centerwide basis. These have sometimes drawn throngs to the center, who then shop in the various

stores. How many ideas can you come up with to help generate traffic in the shopping center? Be as creative (and even flamboyant) as possible.

2. As the sales promotion manager of a large department store, what ideas do you have for major storewide promotions? Evaluate your ideas for practicality and effectiveness, and develop a list of six, with supporting arguments, suitable for submission to top management.

■ Retailing in Action

1. Through no fault of your own, a pocket calculator that you had advertised at a "hot" price was delayed in shipment and did not arrive until ten days after the ad ran. The result was numerous customer complaints and resentment; some even complained to the Better Business Bureau and a letter of reprimand had been issued by it.

   What would you do to be reasonably sure that this would not happen again? Can such a situation be absolutely prevented?

2. Assume the role of manager of a small Ben Franklin variety store. All merchants are promoting Dollar Days, a promotion that has been successful other years in drawing considerable customer traffic downtown. This year you select 39¢ women's panties to advertise at 3/$1.00, and children's stockings at 4/$1.00. The sales results are disappointing.

   In retrospect, how might you assess the reasons for the lack of success? Assuming that Dollar Days come in February, are there other items you think might have been more successful?

16 Sales Promotion: Sales Incentives, Display, and the Salesperson

Although advertising can play a powerful role in bringing customers to a store, most retailers do not rely on this alone to produce sales. Attractive displays can entice the customer brought into the store by an advertisement to buy other goods. Some stores without much money to commit to advertising have to rely primarily on displays—usually window displays—to bring customers into the store. In most stores a salesperson is needed to close or "wrap up" the sale, even though an advertisement or display may have stimulated initial customer interest. Some stores have found that various sales incentives, such as trading stamps, games, giveaways, premiums, and contests help attract extra business. In this chapter, we will examine these other promotional tools.

STAMPS, GAMES, PREMIUMS

A variety of sales incentives is used by some retailers. Most are long-term, designed to produce some store loyalty or repeat business. For example, a store with a certain kind of trading stamps will find that the customer interested in collecting such stamps is, at least temporarily, a very loyal shopper. Similarly, with games and contests and with premium programs, the objective is to draw the customer back to the store again and again, not so much to purchase any particular items (as in the case of advertising), but to do general shopping.

Such promotional devices are not new. The 1960s in particular saw a great flurry of them, especially of *games* and *contests*. Some were quite ingenious, and they made shopping more exciting for some customers. However, the sheer abundance of games and contests among many different retailers lessened their competitive impact. By 1970 games and contests were receiving unfavorable publicity: there seemed to be a scarcity of winners despite claims of many prizes being awarded. This, along with increased government surveillance, lessened the enthusiasm of both consumers and retailers.

Supermarkets were the biggest users of *trading stamps*. (At one time during the 1960s between 60 and 70 percent of all stamps were distributed by supermarkets.) Many other noncompeting retailers, such as gas stations, drugstores, and various specialty stores and services, used the same stamps for mutual advantage, since consumers are inclined to buy from stores offering the stamps they are currently saving. But by the early 1970s the use of trading stamps was waning.

RETAILING CONTROVERSY—*To Give or Not to Give: Trading Stamps*

The main reason for any retailer to give stamps is to gain customers who are attracted by stamps. By the mid-sixties, roughly four families out of five in the United States were collecting stamps, pasting them in books, and exchanging the books for a wide variety of consumer goods, ranging all the way from fishing tackle to jewelry and free vacations. Furthermore, the customer who collected S & H Green Stamps, for example, was inclined to shop at stores offering these stamps in preference to stores that had Gold Bond or some other kind of stamp.

The early 1970s brought a lessening of interest in stamps. The 2 percent of sales cost of stamps to retailers was a factor, as stores, especially supermarkets, sought to pare prices to the bone. And the gasoline shortage beginning in 1973 was hardly the type of environment in which a service station dealer could continue to offer stamps. But even before this, many stores found that the competitive effectiveness of stamps was decreasing. Many turned to stamp promotions and extra stamp giveaways, and a costly market saturation of stamps resulted. More and more consumers became interested in price savings, rather than in the tedium of collecting stamps.

For Thought and Discussion

1. Is it likely that stamps will ever disappear from the marketplace altogether? Why or why not?

2. If you operated a small children's goods store, with a department store branch and a discount store (neither of which offered stamps) as competitors, would you consider offering stamps? What other information might you want before making your decision?

In the fall of 1978 there were indications that after several years of a downward trend, perhaps trading stamps were reviving in the same way they had a number of times in the past. When only a few firms are using stamps, they can be an attractive competitive strategy. A&P started what looked like a new trend in trading stamps by testing them in 600 of its stores in the Northeast and Midwest. It was expected that other major food chains would be forced to follow A&P's lead in order to maintain their market share.[1] Despite retailer reluctance, if consumers after a period of abstention were again ready to embrace trading stamps, it seemed there was little recourse but to follow the leader. But by early 1979, A&P halted stamps in 314 stores, while still continuing in others. The reason: "They just weren't getting the volume of business we expected. The initial response was favorable but this wasn't sustained."[2]

Games and contests, such as Bonus Bingo and Let's Go to the Races, often replaced stamps, as retailers began seeking a competitive advantage from the stamp saturation of the mid-1960s. But these were

---

[1] "A&P's Newest Ploy: Trading Stamps—Again," *Business Week,* August 14, 1978, pp. 29–30.
[2] "A&P Quietly Drops Its Trading Stamps in Over 300 Stores," *Wall Street Journal,* February 6, 1979, p. 11.

quickly duplicated by other retailers, and any advantage was lost. *Premiums* also have been widely used by both retailers and manufacturers. The premium often is a tie-in that the customer can obtain either as a gift or for the payment of a small amount. This can be a single transaction offer, as with many premiums in cereal boxes. With *continuity offers,* premium offers extending over a period of time, a supermarket, for example, may offer a different volume of an encyclopedia each week with a certain minimum purchase. But as with the other sales incentives, premiums are mutually neutralizing and can be easily matched by competitors. Furthermore, incentive promotions appeal to only a small part of the market.

DISPLAY

Display as a promotional tool involves both exterior windows and inside the store *point-of-purchase displays.* Both are important, but in somewhat different ways. Window displays play a role similar to advertising—although not as effectively since the audience usually is smaller. They draw people into the store. Point-of-purchase or interior displays may be instrumental at the final moment of decision when a sale is culminated. They may also act as magnets, stopping a customer in a headlong rush down an aisle, and encouraging him or her to consider, to ask, and perhaps to buy on impulse. The growth of self-service, in particular, has made interior displays much more important, since they do the selling job of an absent salesperson.

We will neither treat the technical aspects of display, such as planning and trimming windows or interior displays nor deal with the variety of fixtures and props available for display purposes. Rather, we will be concerned with a general managerial overview of display.

Window Displays

Windows traditionally have been considered an important facet of retail operation, especially by the big retailers.

Windows are the "face" of the store. They are of great importance since they constitute the first impression that the store makes on the customer.[3]

---

[3] Charles M. Edwards, Jr., and William H. Howard, *Retail Advertising and Sales Promotion* (New York: Prentice-Hall, 1943), p. 520.

These words written thirty years ago are still valid today. For a store in a busy customer-traffic location, the importance of windows is unmistakable. Windows can compare favorably as an advertising medium with the newspaper.

R. H. Macy Company counted the number of people passing the corner of Broadway and 34th Street, New York, on an average day and found the total to be in excess of 250,000. This is the equivalent of the circulation of a large metropolitan newspaper.[4]

Although not all passersby would stop to look at the window displays, not all readers of newspapers stop to read the ads, either.

With large retailers in prime locations attaching such importance to their windows, it is not surprising that they employ specialized staffs of artists and display people. At Christmastime, a single window may cost as much as $50,000 and be months in the planning.

Window displays have at least two major objectives. First, the prestige of the store may be enhanced by imaginative special-event windows, such as novelty Christmas or Easter windows that may display no merchandise at all but draw hoards of passersby. Of course, the direct contribution of such windows to sales is impossible to measure. Second, the merchandise featured in regular window displays may generate business, much as advertising does.

Many small retailers try to show a variety of styles in their windows. Shoe stores may identify the displayed item by number so that a customer can easily single out a particular style to try on. For a department store with its many departments and thousands of items, a certain fashion touch or novelty flair often has the priority for window placement: a single color or style may be highlighted in a particular window.

There is some question today whether windows are as important as they once were. Some retailers are finding glass fronts, through which passersby can look directly in to the selling floor with its interior displays, to be more desirable than display windows. Certainly they are easier to maintain than frequent window changes. Windows can exert a negative image, if they are dirty, unimaginative, cluttered, or infrequently changed. Such windows may suggest an inefficient, unprogressive, careless firm. Furthermore, as noted in Chapter 6, there is even evidence that windows are becoming less important for multifloor downtown stores, since many of their passersby (often on lunch breaks) are interested in fast shopping, and taking time to find an item seen in the window of a large store is not practical for them.

Windows today may have a greater selling role in small towns, where

[4] Ibid.

window-shopping is often an accustomed activity, than in large cities. Of course, there are exceptions to this: Fifth Avenue in New York City still draws multitudes of people; other downtowns, such as that in Minneapolis, are attracting window-shoppers and casual strollers through pedestrian malls.

Interior Displays

Although there is some question of the importance of the window display today, interior displays are clearly becoming more important. For a self-service store, the interior display has to do almost all the selling. But even when salespeople are present, a display may have presold a customer waiting for a busy salesclerk. Furthermore, a display can often help sell related merchandise, such as a tie with a shirt or suit purchase, or a handbag with shoes.

We may categorize interior displays as (1) *nonselection displays,* which are separate from the goods available for sale; and (2) selection or *point-of-purchase displays.*

Separate, nonselection displays have the same objective as window displays: to attract customers to the department where the goods are available. Some department stores like to use main-floor traffic locations to display certain selected items from upstairs departments, and thereby induce customers to move through the store. New merchandise and fashions may be displayed at various strategic locations, both in the department and outside it, such as near elevators or escalators. Displays of related items may subtly encourage additional sales, such as luggage with cruise apparel and sporting goods with sportswear. There is ample opportunity for creativity with interior displays, and many types of equipment and manikins are available to help achieve any desired effect.

Selection displays include counters, racks, shelves, tables, and other areas where goods are stocked, as well as appropriate descriptive signs, showing price, size, and other features. Overhead displays, such as blouses on bust forms, may also be used. With merchandise coming in many different shapes and sizes, considerable ingenuity is required to develop the most effective selection display. Where pilferage is a problem, sample items only may be on display, with a salesclerk required to obtain the item from stock. Some goods may have to be displayed under glass, although this does not maximize sales. A store may have to compromise between maximizing sales and minimizing pilferage.

In selection displays it is important that goods be systematically arranged for easy selection. Finding the correct size is often a major problem on a busy day when merchandise becomes rumpled and misplaced. Glass bins may help here, but sufficient sales help to maintain reasonable order is the only real solution. There are times, however, when a jumbled display is more conducive to sales than a neat one, since customers then have no qualms about handling the goods, and in the process are more likely to buy something. Furthermore, such a jumble can add to the bargain image.

The role of selection displays is particularly important because of *impulse buying.* On occasion we all buy without preplanning. A display may catch our eye, or a sign or counter loaded with fresh goods may cause us to pause, examine more closely, and buy. Some restaurants and bakeries have been known to install fans to blow tempting aromas out to the sidewalk.

Another type of purchase decision may also be called impulse buying. As an example, you may go to the store for some dog food. You have seen several brands advertised on TV, but your attitude toward the competing brands is about the same. The decision to buy a particular brand will then be made at the point of purchase, and the brand bought will be the one that makes the best last impression: it may have a bigger stock on the counter or a better display. Because of this common phenomenon of the final buying decision, the point-of-purchase display assumes great importance. Consider the following data on the importance of displays and location in supermarket selling.

RETAILING STRATEGIES—*Importance of Spacing and Display in the Supermarket*

A shopper may go to a supermarket with a shopping list in hand; most likely it is a short one and is not scrupulously followed. Going down the aisles, the shopper is attracted by various signs and displays. The shopper's eyes may sweep from one side of the aisle to the other—most often at eye level only—and focus on various items as he or she mentally contemplates whether the household needs or wants them. Studies have shown that about half the purchases in supermarkets are not planned.[5]

With unplanned purchases and impulse buying looming so important, a number of studies dealing with the sales impact of changing displays and

---

[5] For example, those studies mentioned in James F. Engel, David T. Kollat, and Roger D. Blackwell, *Consumer Behavior,* 3rd ed. (New York: Holt, Rinehart and Winston, 1978) p. 483.

shelf position have been made for supermarkets. We have some rather convincing evidence of the sheer importance of display. For example:[6]

	Percent change in unit sales
Maintaining a fully stocked shelf rather than a normally stocked shelf that would have some low-stock and even out-of-stock conditions	+20
Using special shelf signs to highlight certain items	+152
Displaying individual items in combination with related goods rather than presented by themselves elsewhere in the store	+418
Using "as advertised" and "cents-off" signs	+124 and +23
Moving an item:	
from waist level to eye level	+63
from waist level to floor level	−40
from floor level to waist level	+34
from floor level to eye level	+78

Other studies have shown that an average display can boost sales as much as 536 percent over normal shelf position.[7]

For Thought and Discussion   Since changing the position of an item or adding a sign or display can have such a strong impact on its sales, the choice of merchandise for special treatment becomes important. What criteria would you use in selecting an item to give a special display or eye-level location?

A multiplicity of *vendor displays* or point-of-purchase material is available to retailers, ranging from signs and banners to display racks, expensive turn-tables, and mobile displays. However, many of these materials are not used by retailers, either because they are too big or are otherwise unsuitable for the space, or because so much material is offered that the retailer has a problem in selection. An example of the mutual success that can come from a well-designed vendor display,

[6] "Colonial Study," *Progressive Grocer*, January 1964, pp. C123–27; "How In-Store Merchandising Can Boost Sales," *Progressive Grocer*, pp. 94–97, October 1971; "How the Basics of Special Display Affect Sales and Profits," *Progressive Grocer*, January 1971, pp. 34–45; "How to Make Displays More Sales Productive," *Progressive Grocer*, February 1971, pp. 34–45.
[7] William W. Mee, "How Point-of-Purchase Is More Efficient as an Advertising and Sales Medium," *Media/Scope*, September 1963, pp. 55–56.

coordinated with strong advertising and servicing, is L'eggs pantyhose, described in Chapter 12. The distinctive 2½-square-foot selling display to hold the pantyhose, packaged in super-ostrich-egg-sized packages, made this the largest-selling brand of hosiery in supermarkets and drugstores.

Signing is important for both window and interior displays. What is said on the sign can stimulate sales many times greater than would be the case with no sign. The following is an illustration of the power of words.[8] A blind man on a street corner was begging for coins with the sign:

I Am Blind

Imagine his success with this sign:

It is Spring
and
I Am Blind

Buyers and their assistants usually furnish the sign copy for their merchandise, since they are most knowledgeable about the goods. But they may give scant attention to this phase of their promotional operation, and an ineffective sign results. Just as with advertising copy, there is no set formula that assures good results. But an effective sign should be informative and accurate, yet not verbose or flamboyant. If too wordy, it is not likely to be read; if flamboyant, customers may be impressed with the sign's cleverness and overlook the merchandise. For example, the following sign would hardly create much buying interest:

Shoes 2 / 95

But when changed to this, sales might well be stimulated:

Shoes that Stir Excitement

adjustable straps
cork platforms for lightness
newest colors for spring

2 / 95

---

[8] Example taken from Emily M. Mauger, *Modern Display Techniques* (New York: Fairchild Publications, 1966), p. 118.

What might you say for:

Handbags
Tablecloths
Cotton dresses
Slips
Nightgowns
Luggage
Men's jackets
Pots and pans
Boys' trousers
Printed sheets

PERSONAL SELLING

A Diminishing Role?

The trend for the last several decades has veered sharply away from the importance of the retail salesperson. Many stores have turned to self-service in an effort to cut selling costs; others have been virtually forced to it because of increasing difficulty in getting and keeping good people. Some suggest that the absence of a salesperson may actually increase sales.

> . . . *The mere presence of the salesman prevents large numbers of persons from looking at things that they are not seriously interested in, because of the presumed social obligation to buy. . . . Lack of such pressure in the self-service store allows the shopper to look around at his leisure, incurring no social debts. . . . Such leisurely perusal of merchandise seems to do as good a job of suggestive selling as many experienced salesmen, and accomplishes more than the mediocre salesclerk at less expense.*[9]

Discount stores and vending machines in particular have thrived in the absence of salespeople. But many other retailers, including major department, chain, and specialty stores, use personal selling. The trend may be reversing. Today more good people are becoming available for retail sales jobs, as other job markets are becoming saturated. Some customers, tired of the impersonality and monotonous similarity of most self-service stores, are returning to full-service stores.

[9] W. T. Tucker, *The Social Context of Economic Behavior* (New York: Holt, Rinehart and Winston, 1964), pp. 76–77.

This is an excellent example of the personal involvement required of retailers who specialize in quality and service. Note the number of shoe boxes already brought out. Would you say that this customer is unreasonably hard to please? (Eliot Erwitt/ Magnum)

Certain types of merchandise can be sold only by salespeople. One can hardly imagine buying a car by mail order or self-service. Nor would a sewing machine or television set—where demonstration and possibly a trade-in are involved—be bought without the help of a salesperson. In general, items of relatively high price, and items where specialized requirements need to be satisfied should be serviced by salespeople. But a good salesperson can help the sale of many items by pointing out attractive features, by furnishing desired product and store information to customers, and by conveying an air of integrity and good will.

Need for Improvement

Although it is unlikely that self-service or automated retailing will ever completely supersede the salesperson, we know from our own experiences that the quality of retail selling has sometimes been poor. There are salesclerks who are discourteous, slow, careless, uninformed, and unintelligent.

But though we recognize the need for improvement, reasons for such poor selling should also be noted, if corrective action is to be taken. Some of the more common causes are listed below.

Poor selection and training
Inadequate supervision
Inadequate product and store-policy communication to salesforce
Heavy stockkeeping responsibilities, with underemphasis on serving customers
Lack of incentives to give better customer service
Lack of management commitment to good customer service
Increased diversity and complexity of products

In certain cases the corrective action is obvious but not easily achieved. For example, poor selection of salespeople may not be so much the fault of the personnel department as of a job market that brings in few top caliber applicants. Retail pay has not helped here, being notoriously low compared with other employment alternatives. And the poor prestige of some retail selling, or clerking, as it is often called, has not helped. Another cause of poor retail sales service, stockkeeping, is certainly a necessary activity. Cleaning, replenishing, straightening, stock counting, and making layout changes should normally be sandwiched in between customers. Sometimes, however, the temptation is to reduce the work force, and this may prove inadequate for serving customers and servicing stock.

Some causes of poor selling are more easily controllable, and the blame for them must be shouldered by management. Inadequate supervision of selling activities often results when the buyer is responsible for both the selling and buying in a department. The solution may be to divorce buying and selling responsibilities, placing salespeople under sales managers (a trend we noted in Chapter 8). A lack of adequate product information must be blamed on inadequate management efforts to communicate with the sales force. A store with a continuing problem of poor selling efforts may need to examine the compensation plan and the criteria for evaluating employees. In order to motivate greater efforts in selling, some kind of bonus or commission may be started, with raises and promotions tied to adequate sales performance. *P.M.'s* (prize money that amounts to a small cash bonus) may be paid for selling certain types of merchandise, usually items that are slow-selling, in heavy stock, or near the end of the season. Sales contests may be worth testing in the quest for a more enthusiastic sales force. (See Chapter 10.)

An often-unrecognized factor underlying shabby sales performance is a management unconcerned with good customer service. It is easy for management time to be directed to more pressing and vital matters. Yet what is more important than satisfied customers?

Types of Retail Selling

Retail selling jobs can be depicted on a continuum, ranging from order filling to *creative selling:*

Order filling ⟷ Creative selling

Certain departments and selling situations require more order filling than creative selling. The perceptive retailer may need to juggle salespeople to maximize their abilities. Although creative selling is normally accorded the higher stature and higher pay, this need not be so. The extremes of these two selling roles are found in the candy salesperson and the furniture salesperson. In between are sales jobs requiring some combination of skills, such as the men's furnishings salesperson who is more effective as a rapid order filler during peak-traffic times, and also a creative salesperson during less-busy times, and with certain customers and merchandise.

The effective order filler must be able to work rapidly and accurately, and avoid long entanglements with customers. In a volume shoe department a salesperson may handle four or five customers at a time, with little chance for creative selling, but achieve a high sales volume because of sheer number of transactions handled. Probably in no other retail enterprise does order filling reach the state of virtual automation than it does at McDonald's.

SUCCESSFUL RETAILING STRATEGIES—*The Automated Order Filler: McDonald's*

Winking lights on grills tell McDonald employees exactly when to flip over hamburgers, cybernetic deep fryers assure that French fries come out with a uniform degree of brownness, and specially designed scoops make it almost impossible to stuff more than the specified-by-headquarters number of French fries into a paper bag.

Strict rules are also demanded of McDonald employees regarding conduct with customers and even personal appearance. The strict rules, the grueling tedium, and the robotlike working conditions result in high personnel turnover: the average teen-age worker quits after four months.

Whereas such personnel turnover would be catastrophic for most businesses, in the fast-food business where training and experience requirements are minimal it means that almost everyone is paid the minimum wage and almost no one gets a merit raise or joins a union.

The success of McDonald's is undeniable. In 1977 it was selected by *Dun's Review* as one of the five best managed companies in the United States.

Sources: "The Burger That Conquered the Country," *Time,* September 17, 1973, pp. 84–85; "McDonald's Grinds Out Growth," *Dun's Review,* December 1977, pp. 50–52; "Low Pay, Bossy Bosses Kill Kids' Enthusiasm for Food-Service Jobs," *Wall Street Journal,* March 15, 1979, pp. 1, 27.

For Thought and Discussion

1. What arguments can you present for urging McDonald's to reduce its high employee turnover?
2. What suggestions do you have for reducing this turnover?

The creative salesperson in a dress or coat department, a furniture department, or a men's suit department, has more time to spend with individual customers, and the unit sale is much larger than that of the order filler. Accordingly, he or she should be able to arouse demand, persuade, overcome objections, and smoothly close the sale—all steps in the traditional sales transaction.

The Art of Personal Selling

Unless you enter retailing in some specialized staff position, such as accounting, data processing, or advertising, the chances are that you will be involved with personal selling. Even self-service stores and discount stores have certain departments that require salespeople to explain the features of rather complex products, like cameras and appliances. As you assume merchandising and supervisory positions, you will find that the success of your department or store will be helped or hindered by the selling efforts of your subordinates. You may need to coach them and evaluate their selling effectiveness. Some say that good salesmanship is an art, or that selling skills are best learned from experience in the actual selling situation. But a book on salesmanship can help one avoid certain pitfalls and provide ideas for more effective sales presentation and interaction with customers.[10] The following is a brief description of the personal selling process.

RETAILING TOOLS—*The Personal Selling Process*

The possible progression of a customer to the final buying stage has traditionally been described as going from attention to interest to desire, and finally to action, at which point the goods are bought. For many years this has been known as the *AIDA* framework for selling. It furnishes a useful tool for examining retail selling, and we will use it here.

In the first step, the *attention* phase, the customer's attention must be gained. A display may help; perhaps an advertisement has already aroused sufficient attention and interest to bring the customer to the store. The salesperson may gain attention by pleasantly greeting the customer and perhaps making a comment about the merchandise the customer has stopped to examine. The progression should then be made rather quickly to the important next step—creating interest.

The *interest* stage involves determining the customer's wants and then presenting merchandise to meet those wants. Usually a few well-chosen questions are needed to find out specifically what the customer is looking for. For example, the questions might concern the purpose for which the product is wanted, or the type of material desired.

Caution: Asking questions about price early in the sales process tends to focus attention too much on it and may limit the salesperson in showing certain goods that might better meet the needs of the customer.

Presenting merchandise effectively requires that the salesperson know what the store has available for sale as well as the major features of such goods. Often customers do not really know what they want; the judicious presentation of goods may help them decide.

The *desire* stage should move smoothly from this point on. With the customer's interest aroused, the salesperson can point out outstanding features, how the product is used, what makes it distinctive, and any other features that might be of interest to the customer. Where possible, the product should be demonstrated and the customer invited to handle the

---

[10] Many books have been written about selling. Perhaps this is because a typical salesperson tends to grow discouraged from time to time and finds that a book may provide a little inspiration, and possibly some concrete help. The following is a sampling of the available books: W. J. E. Crissy, William H. Cunningham, and Isabella C. M. Cunningham, *Selling: The Personal Force in Marketing* (New York: Wiley, 1977); David L. Kurtz, H. Robert Dodge, and Jay E. Klompmaker, *Professional Selling,* rev. ed. (Dallas: Business Publications, 1979); and Annalee Gold, *How to Sell Fashion* (New York: Fairchild Publications, 1968).

goods. At this point, objections may need to be dealt with, such as those involving price, delivery time, certain product features, or fit.

As objections are answered, the salesperson should move into the *action* stage and attempt to close the sale. He or she may need to ask for the order directly. Or a more subtle approach may be used, such as:

"Let me have our tailor check the fit."
"Will this be cash or charge?"
"Would you like it delivered, or will you take it with you?"

With the sale made, the salesperson should express appreciation and also assure the customer that a wise decision was made. Other merchandise can often be effectively suggested at this point.

Sources: The above is synthesized from many sources. The AIDA concept may have first appeared in M. S. Heidingsfield and A. B. Blankenship, *Marketing* (New York: Barnes & Noble, Inc., 1957), p. 149.

For Thought and Discussion

1. How would you handle these objections?
   "I really haven't time to try it on now."
   "The price is too high."
   "I like the chair, but I don't want to wait six weeks for delivery."
   "I don't like the style of these shirts."
2. How would you handle this resistance to closing the sale?
   "I want to think it over before buying."
   "I want to talk this over with my husband."
   "I'd like to look at another store before I decide."

SUGGESTION SELLING Once a customer has decided to buy, the mood is often such that any additional items, somewhat related to the item purchased, will be favorably considered. Consequently, if the salesperson is alert to opportunities, *suggestion selling* can pay off in sales of additional merchandise. The following are some ways in which suggestion selling might be done.[11]

1. Suggest related merchandise—such as ties with shirts, and curtain rods with curtains.

[11] Adapted from O. Preston Robinson, Christine H. Robinson, and George H. Zeiss, *Successful Retail Salesmanship*, 3rd ed. (Englewood Cliffs, N.J.: Prentice-Hall, 1961), pp. 425–431.

2. Suggest larger quantities, thereby saving the customer time and possibly money.
3. Suggest higher-priced merchandise—when advantages of purchasing better-quality goods can be effectively pointed out.
4. Suggest new merchandise. (Customers are often eager to learn about new merchandise.)
5. Suggest specials or specially advertised goods. A customer may have overlooked advertised merchandise but be interested once the initial shopping need has been satisfied.
6. Suggest new uses for merchandise. New or little-known uses for certain merchandise may widen the sales appeal. This is especially true of food products and food utensils, where new uses and recipes may offer an opportunity to increase the size of the sale.
7. Suggest merchandise for special occasions. Holidays in the near future present prime opportunities to sell more merchandise by suggesting that gift problems are solved more easily now than when the shopping rush begins.

Unfortunately, suggestion selling is little practiced in many stores, despite the fact that tactful suggestions are appreciated by customers and can add substantially to total sales volume.

Evaluating Sales Performance

Some salespeople will naturally be more effective and productive than others. Of course, we cannot all be standouts. But a manager may find some employees so marginal that replacement is desirable. Although simple observation of salespeople may furnish clues as to which are giving below-par performance, more objective measures are usually needed.

The evaluation method most used is simply to tabulate sales by salesperson to see how each compares with fellow employees. Selling cost is also frequently used in measuring productivity. However, these measures assume that all salespeople are spending an equal amount of time on the salesfloor and have the same opportunity for sales.

Some time ago a study of sales personnel activities showed that the average salesclerk's time during the day was spent as follows:[12]

---

[12] Robert J. Paul, "Scientific Determination of Performance Standards for Non-repetitive Duties," *Journal of Retailing*, Fall 1967, p. 54.

Selling	25 percent
Stock work	12 percent
Awaiting customers	34 percent
Absent	15 percent
Miscellaneous work	14 percent

But the following results of another study are of more interest to managers in singling out what makes some salespeople more effective than others.[13]

1. *There was a significant difference in the way in which highest dollar volume and lowest dollar volume salespeople spent their time.*
2. *The activity difference was greatest in the "selling" and "idle time" categories.*
3. *Highest dollar volume salespeople spent a higher percentage of the work period doing stock work and miscellaneous activities than did lowest dollar volume salespeople.*
4. *Highest dollar volume salespeople tended to work at a faster pace than did lowest dollar volume salespeople.*
5. *Higher volume salespeople were absent from their departments significantly less than were low dollar volume personnel.*

Time spent working, and number of transactions accomplished then become important measures of retail salesperson performance. Although such criteria will vary somewhat depending on the type of goods—for example, furniture and expensive clothing require a longer transaction period—the evidence suggests that the effective salesperson in all departments is quicker in closing sales and in processing them. The supervisor may help here through better training and, if necessary, revising the sales-processing system and department layout so that sales transactions can be handled more speedily by all employees.

Telephone and Mail-Order Selling

Although telephone and mail-order business is not technically personal selling, it is most akin to order filling, and will be discussed here. In their ads many stores encourage this kind of business. A growing

[13] Robert J. Paul and Robert W. Bell, "Evaluating the Retail Salesman," *Journal of Retailing,* Summer 1968, pp. 20–21.

number of stores issue small catalogs, especially during the Christmas season, to stimulate this business. And there are giants in this field: Sears, Ward, Spiegel, and Penney.

Telephone and mail-order selling caters to customers' desire for convenience. Retailers can gain considerable extra business in this way, without having to gear up for extra customer traffic. But some retailers see it as a disadvantage. They are reluctant to use such forms of sales promotion because they fear customers will not then visit their stores. It is not unusual to see ads carrying the notice, "no mail or phone orders."

Admittedly, to do a good job in attracting and handling phone and mail-order business, some logistical planning is required. Extra telephone lines may be needed (to prevent interminable busy signals), as well as extra operators, and a procedure established for getting orders to departments for filling quickly. But these are not difficult requirements, and the extra business can provide a sales boost.

The telephone can also be a business builder. Salesmen can use it to advise customers of new merchandise or sales. New residents can be welcomed and invited to visit the store. Even inactive credit accounts can be stimulated. Occasionally a retailer may randomly call numbers from a phone book or from a list of charge customers with a brief selling message about some outstanding special.[14]

Importance of Salespeople in Customer Relations

It is rather obvious that the salesperson is important to a customer's satisfaction or dissatisfaction with a particular store. In reality, the salesperson acts as the store's representative or ambassador; often he or she is the only contact a customer has with the store. Thousands of dollars may be spent in advertising to woo customers and build a favorable image, only to have this lost by an uncaring salesclerk.

The importance of this role should lead a store to the most determined efforts to improve both the face-to-face confrontation of its employees with customers, and any telephone contacts. We will discuss this at more length in Chapter 17.

■ Summary

In the past, some retailers have had success in offering consumers sales incentives, such as trading stamps, games, and contests. Although these

---

[14] For a helpful book dealing with telephone selling, see Murray Roman, *Telephone Marketing: How to Build Your Business by Telephone* (New York: McGraw-Hill, 1976).

created some shopping excitement, they added to the costs of doing business and were easily imitated by competitors. Displays, both window and interior, add to the appeal of merchandise and can induce impulse buying. Some retailers have been plagued by an inability to attract and keep good salespeople, and this has encouraged more and more to turn to self-service. But many stores still find that salespeople are required to sell their type of merchandise and to promote the store's desired image. Effective retail salespeople can be instrumental in creating good customer relations and can increase sales by suggestion selling and effectively catering to customers' needs. Retail management faces a challenge in developing effective salesperson performance.

■ **Key Terms**

AIDA (attention, interest, desire, action)

Continuity offers

Creative selling

Games and contests

Impulse buying

Nonselection displays

P.M.'s

Point-of-purchase displays

Premiums

Selection displays

Suggestion selling

Trading stamps

Vendor displays

■ **Discussion Questions**

1. What types of stores are giving trading stamps in your community? What can you conclude from this regarding the present success of stamps as a promotional device?

2. What are the arguments for using P.M.'s? Are there any counter-arguments?

3. Contrast the personality and behavioral characteristics of the effective order filler and the creative salesperson.

4. Some stores, particularly clothing and furniture stores, have salespeople waiting to pounce on any customers entering the store. In other stores a customer has a difficult time finding a salesperson. What types of customers do you think would be attracted and turned off by these two contrasting sales approaches?

5. What factors would you want to consider before using a display furnished by a vendor?

6. What problems does a manager face in trying to build up the productivity of salespeople?

7. The Bi-Rite supermarket has used trading stamps for years. Re-

cently its competing supermarkets have given them up. Evaluate the desirability of Bi-Rite also abandoning trading stamps.

■ Project

Visit several stores in your community and observe whether the windows express what you think is the image the store is trying to achieve and whether the caliber and appearance of the sales force are similar to the image of the rest of the store and its merchandise.

If there are any discrepancies, how do you explain these, and what recommendations would you make?

■ Exercise in Creativity

In opening a new men's clothing and sportswear store near a college campus, what sales promotion techniques might you want to consider? (Be as innovative as possible.) Design a promotional program for the initial opening and for the next three months, assuming that limited funds prevents using most types of advertising.

■ Retailing in Action: Role Play

1. You are the assistant manager of a medium-size chain department store. The time is early December. A large shipment of a hot toy item has just arrived, and you plan to feature it in an ad. Your store manager tells you:

   "Ned, let's be sure to say at the bottom of the ad that we will accept no telephone or mail orders. The last time we ran a similar item it took us three weeks to clean up the mass of orders, and we lost all that customer traffic."
   a. What would you recommend in this situation?
   b. What factors would you want to consider?
   c. If your ideas on this are different from those of the store manager, what arguments would you use?
2. As a newly promoted department manager, you realize that suggestion selling can substantially increase sales. What inducements and guidance would you offer your salespeople to help motivate them to practice suggestion selling?

17 Customer Services and Limits to Services

Many ingredients of the retailing mix come under the broad umbrella of "service." The store itself, its decor, amenities such as carpeting or piped-in music, air conditioning, restrooms, convenient parking facilities—these are all part of the service package. The presence of salespeople instead of self-service is a major form of service. Then there are the traditional services: credit, delivery, alterations, gift wrapping, return-goods privileges. Possibilities for extra services include baby-sitting for shoppers, bridal consulting, home decorator, personal shopping, amusement-ticket service, and handling of utility-bill payments.

As you can imagine, some of these services, such as delivery, are costly. A store may come close to breaking even on others, but this may not be the best use of store resources. The question arises: Why provide services that do not make money? The answer is simple: To make the store more attractive to customers.

SCOPE OF CUSTOMER SERVICE

Some services are demanded by customers today. A store has to provide them to be competitive. Few retailers can do without credit, except for food retailers, and they must set up check-cashing procedures. Amusement-ticket service, accepting payments for utility bills, and being a post office substation draw people into the store. Services such as baby-sitting and children's playrooms make shopping more leisurely and restful for some customers, and they are then in a better frame of mind for purchasing freely. Other services are necessary if certain goods are to be sold: delivery, alterations, and gift wrapping. The question then becomes not so much whether to provide a service, as how to fund it: Should it be free? Should there be an extra charge to defray part or all of the costs? Or should costs be hidden in a higher selling price?

Another type of service is becoming common in many large stores. *Income-producing services* are offered with the same objective as regular merchandise departments—that is, to make money. Examples of income-producing services are repair and cleaning (such as rug cleaning, watch repair), reupholstery, television repair, custom-made draperies and slipcovers, and fur storage. Instruction courses are offered, such as golf schools, ski instruction, knitting courses, and charm and self-improvement courses. Some retailers, notably Sears, are adding separate departments for mutual funds, insurance, and travel bureaus. Auto service centers, beauty salons, and restaurants and snack bars can also be classed as services. Rental services have grown rapidly and offer profitable opportunities for small as well as large stores in renting such things as tools, party goods, and extra furniture.

The customer-service impact of the store and its furnishings was discussed in Chapter 7. The services provided by salespeople were treated in the last chapter. In this chapter, services will be examined that (1) require a major commitment by the firm, such as credit and delivery; (2) focus on customer relations; and (3) represent nonmerchandise diversification into income-producing activities.

CREDIT

The importance of credit in spurring sales can be seen in the following example. From its beginning in 1902 in a little mining town in Wyoming, the J. C. Penney Company had stoutly maintained a cash-and-carry policy: no credit. Not until the late 1950s did top management become flexible enough to test the use of credit in their 1,600 stores. At that time they selected several hundred stores to run a lengthy experiment on the feasibility of providing credit.

One of the experimental stores was in Superior, Wisconsin, a store whose sales in a relatively economically depressed community had remained static for over three years. The first year that credit was offered, sales increased dramatically, over 30 percent. Shortly afterward the Penney Company adopted credit nationwide.

KINDS OF RETAIL CREDIT

Most retail credit plans can be classed as regular charge, installment credit, and revolving credit. There are some variations, such as issuing coupon books in place of a revolving credit plan, with such coupons being used as cash while the book is paid for on a time-payment plan. Banks and commercial credit firms are important in providing retail credit, especially for smaller retailers. They issue a credit card to eligible customers, which is accepted by affiliated retailers for charging purchases; the bank or commercial credit firm then pays the merchant for the credit purchases, less a 5 or 6 percent service charge; the customer is billed and pays the credit card firm. Although credit-card plans have a high cost, most retailers consider the extra business gained under a widely accepted plan to be worth the cost. Furthermore, it is unlikely that many retailers—especially the smaller ones—can manage their own credit function and keep costs as low.

Bank credit cards have become very popular today: over 37 million people have Master Charge cards, and 31 million have Visa (formerly BankAmericard). About 1.7 million merchants throughout the world accept Master Charge; about 1.8 million accept Visa.[1] Another popular category of cards are travel and entertainment (T&E) cards, notably Diners Club, American Express, and Carte Blanche. These were originally designed for use by travelers, and were initially honored by

[1] William Flanagan, "Playing Your Credit Cards Right," *New York,* June 7, 1976, p. 90.

restaurants, hotels, airlines, and other travel-oriented businesses, but now are accepted by merchants also. The primary distinction today between bank credit cards and T&E cards is that bank cards have been given free (although this is changing as the costs of credit and processing go up) whereas the T&E card companies charge a small annual fee.

A noncredit plan with some similarity to credit plans (in that payments can be delayed) is the *layaway plan:* a store holds goods for a customer until they are completely paid for. Before it adopted credit, the J. C. Penney Company promoted its layaway plan for expensive items and for merchandise sold in advance of the season, such as during its July Blanket Event.

REGULAR CHARGE ACCOUNTS These are sometimes called *open-account credit.* No interest is charged if goods are paid for in full, usually within thirty days. For certain large purchases a customer may be permitted to pay one-third each month, rather than the whole bill within thirty days. (Some stores call this a *three-pay plan.*) This option is usually offered without interest charges and can thereby stimulate sales of higher-priced items.

With this type of account the store is providing a convenience to the customer without charge for the risks involved, the overhead billing costs, and other miscellaneous credit department expenses. However, the store expects to gain by having more loyal customers. Furthermore, because purchasing is easy it is not unusual to find customers buying more than they otherwise would. The list of charge customers also provides a ready mailing list for special promotional material. For example, some stores send these customers a listing of sale merchandise and extend them a "courtesy day" for shopping before major sale events are publicly advertised; for some stores such courtesy days can be the biggest volume days of the sale event.

INSTALLMENT CREDIT Large durable goods purchases, such as appliances and furniture, which are relatively high priced, are usually offered under an *installment credit* plan. A customer is permitted to make monthly payments, perhaps for twelve or eighteen months, thereby easing the burden of paying and also creating an incentive to purchase a more expensive item. A contract is signed and repossession in case of default provides some security to the seller. It should be recognized, however, that repossession is not a desirable thing for most retailers since there can be considerable expenses in reclaiming and disposing of such merchandise. Carrying or finance charges are included with this type of credit, and help defray some of the costs of credit (including bad debt losses), and can contribute to income over and above the costs.

REVOLVING CREDIT In contrast to installment credit, which permits customers to enjoy major purchases while they are still being paid for, *revolving credit* is tailored to smaller purchases, in essence giving the customer a line of credit. A rigid limit may be placed on how much a customer can have on account at any time, and this is often six times an agreed-upon monthly payment. For example, if $30 is the amount that a customer can or wants to pay monthly, the credit limit would be established at $180. Sometimes flexible-limit plans are offered with no rigid limit set, but a customer is expected to pay one sixth of the outstanding balance each month. Interest charges, often of 1.5 percent per month on the unpaid balance, are added.

An option plan is a further refinement. Under this, the customer has the option of paying off the entire balance within thirty days from the date of statement and having no interest charges to pay. Otherwise, the bill may be paid in installments, and the interest charge is incurred.

We should note that an interest rate of 1.5 percent per month really adds up to 18 percent a year, hardly a middling amount. Under the Federal Truth-in-Lending Law enacted in 1968, the equivalent annual percentage rate must be shown for all finance charges. Before this law, these were often hidden or disguised under a variety of service, handling, or billing charges. Many retailers fought bitterly to prevent this disclosure requirement while the legislation was being considered by Congressional committees. They feared that by informing credit customers that they actually were paying 12 to 18 percent interest, this lucrative credit business would dry up.

Retail Credit Management

Operation of the credit system involves a number of policy decisions and their implementation. Once credit standards and standard operating procedures have been established, much of the work becomes routinized and repetitive. The computer can play a major role in speeding service and reducing costs, especially for the large credit operation, although as we will shortly note, it is not without deficiencies.

CREDIT POLICIES Policies must be established as to how rigid or moderate the standards for granting credit will be: what criteria of income, employment, past debt history, and so on, will make the credit application acceptable or unacceptable. Related to this is the establishing of limits on the accounts, and how rigid or flexible these should be. And these policies are subject to considerable disagreement.

RETAILING CONTROVERSY–How Restrictive Should Credit Be?

Basically, a credit function has two objectives: (1) to increase sales, and (2) to minimize bad credit losses. The problem is that they are incompatible. Usually some compromise has to be made, and organizational pressures may pull one way at the expense of the other.

If credit is freely and easily given to most customers, then sales should be stimulated. However, in granting unrestricted credit, many marginal accounts will be set up and the bad debt ratio may rise markedly. At the other extreme, to grant credit only to those with impeccable credentials would seriously limit the sales efforts of the store, since many interested customers would not qualify and would undoubtedly go to competitors. You can probably imagine the pressures on the credit manager: the merchandising people complaining bitterly about tight credit policies costing them business, while the controller's department will constantly hound for better screening and fewer uncollectible accounts. Normally, neither party is completely satisfied.

For Thought and Discussion: Role Play   You are a newly transferred merchandise manager in a large store in a deteriorating neighborhood. Sales have been declining for some years. You suspect that credit policies are too restrictive, and you want to persuade the general manager to order a loosening of some credit restrictions.

1. What data would you want in order to support your contention that credit policies are too restrictive?
2. What arguments would you make for lowering credit application standards?

Procedures must be set up for opening new accounts and handling rejections. Is an interview to be used? How much outside information is to be required, especially for new residents whose records are not on file with the local retail credit bureau? Furthermore, a large store needs to establish some system for keeping credit information current. This may require periodic review of its charge accounts to determine any with deteriorating performance. It may also require subscribing to rating books issued by private credit bureaus to determine any changes in ratings.

An important procedure is that of identifying credit customers as well as their credit limits. Since this usually has to be done under the urgency of the sales transaction by the clerk on the salesfloor, a system must be set up so that this identification can be quickly and easily made, as well as insuring that charges cannot be credited to the wrong account. Charge-a-plates, or credit cards, are often issued to approved charge customers, and these are given to the salesclerk to expedite the credit transaction. For purchases over a certain amount, perhaps $25, policy may require a call to the credit department for approval. The computer can be an aid here in faster credit approvals.

A local *retail credit bureau* provides a good source of information for merchants in evaluating the credit worthiness of customers. Such credit bureaus can provide the credit history of an applicant—including employment verification, records of credit and payments, and any derogatory information such as slow payments or personal bankruptcies—for a fixed annual fee and a small per-request charge. An individual's file is updated by contacting various merchants in the community who share their credit information with the bureau.

If a large credit operation is to be handled, billing procedures need to be streamlined and systematized so that they become mere routine. Charges must be accurately recorded to respective accounts and payments and any adjustments accurately tallied. Otherwise, a serious source of shrinkage can occur (if charges are not completely recorded) and customer complaints will be unrelenting (if accounts are charged incorrectly for purchases not made, and if payments are not recorded). Some retailers, especially smaller ones, have found it advantageous to accept Visa or Master Charge or a similar central credit plan rather than setting up their own credit department. Although a fee is paid for the use of these services, it is often less than the cost of a store's own credit operation.

THE COMPUTER AS AN AID TO CREDIT OPERATION   In a large store the credit operation can involve recording and billing for as many as several hundred thousand customers. Furthermore, innumerable requests will come from the salesfloor for credit authorization. A computer is almost indispensable today in such large operations; the alternative is a manual operation with greater time requirements and a much greater clerical staff. Even smaller retailers can have their data processed through commercial computer service centers at a reasonable cost.

But the computer has some potential flaws, and these have been widely publicized in the popular press. Flaws are likely to crop up especially during the period of conversion from a hand-operated system to the electronic; this is when bugs invariably occur. Most experts recommend maintaining both the manual system and the electronic, side by side, for however long it takes for the transition to be smoothly completed.

A common computer term is GIGO: "Garbage in, garbage out." In other words, the output of a computer is only as good as the input. If a mistake is made in punching data into the system, a customer will receive an erroneous bill. Establishing procedures for taking care of mistakes has been notoriously weak in some credit operations. Customers' bitter complaints may go unheeded and unremedied even for months. Meantime a bad credit rating may be issued for the "offending" customers. The impersonality of a computer operation should not entirely supersede human responsibility and communication for corrective action.

COLLECTION MANAGEMENT   The credit department is also responsible for collecting the amounts due on customer accounts. Although the objective is to minimize losses, retaining customer good will should also be carefully considered. It is advisable at first to send out gentle reminders on delinquent accounts. As a delinquency continues, of course, less-subtle pressure may need to be exerted, through telephone calls or collectors. The final recourse is legal action and possibly a *garnishment* order—a court-issued order that directs the debtor's employer to pay a certain portion of his or her wages to the seller to satisfy the debt. Bad debt losses usually occur where the amount involved is too small to warrant the expense of legal action or where the debtor moves and cannot be traced. Procedures and timing should be carefully devised for handling delinquent accounts. Also some flexibility is needed so that the customer who falls behind because of unexpected problems can still be accommodated and not subjected to the same harsh measures as a habitual delinquent.

EVALUATING THE CREDIT DEPARTMENT   A retailer is wise to evaluate periodically the performance of the credit function. For some retailers, such a measurement of performance can be crucial since an insidious building up of overdue customer accounts and the likelihood of consequent heavy bad debt losses can actually lead a firm to bankruptcy. For other retailers, a periodic evaluation of credit department effectiveness may point to the need to be more selective in granting credit or to give more emphasis to collection procedures.

A major tool for evaluating the credit function is to *age the receivables.*

TABLE 17.1 EXAMPLE OF AGING THE RECEIVABLES

Customer Balances by Days Overdue	Dollar Amount Outstanding	Percent of Total
Not due	$165,680	70.7
0 to 30 days overdue	44,200	18.9
30 to 60 days overdue	15,700	6.7
60 days to 120 days overdue	3,460	1.5
Over 4 months overdue	5,200	2.2
Total	$234,240	100

This analysis usually is provided by the accounting department and it lists the outstanding balances in customer accounts by time overdue. Table 17.1 gives an example of customer accounts classified by age.

Two important comparisons should be made from a schedule like the one in Table 17.1. First, trend information should be examined: that is, how does the present age of overdue customer accounts compare with past figures—is it getting worse, or improving? Second, a firm can compare its credit experience with that of other similar retailers, perhaps other stores in the chain, other stores in the trade association, or industry figures supplied by the National Retail Merchants Association. Adverse comparisons strongly suggest the need to identify the cause of the poor or worsening performance and then to take corrective action.

CREDIT IN THE GHETTO The ghetto is a unique situation, one that puts the greatest demands on any credit system. But it is also an environment almost wholly dependent on credit, at least for anything beyond the smallest day-to-day purchases. The merchant entering the ghetto market faces a condition in which credit is essential to the consumers, since they have limited income. If one retailer does not give them the credit they want, they will go to another.

The credit risks are far greater than in nonghetto areas. The result is that if a store expects to do business in the ghetto, it must be prepared to lower its standards for credit applications and to accept more bad credit risks. It must also beef up its collection procedures and, in particular, be prepared to repossess merchandise for nonpayment and use the necessary legal remedies and garnishments. The acceptance of a much higher credit-loss ratio to sales may force the merchant to compensate for this increased expense by higher prices.

Where large retailers have gone into the ghetto with the same credit practices they employed in other outlets, they have often wound up with few credit customers—if any customers. The ghetto consumers simply turn back to the high-priced ghetto merchants—despite dirty stores, exorbitant prices, and deceptive practices—who offer easy credit.

Laws Regulating Credit

The government (not only federal, but state and local as well) is beginning to regulate consumer credit practices. Various states and cities have enacted widely varying laws dealing with installment purchases, maximum rates for finance charges, various contract provisions, and even "cooling off" periods, which give the buyer the right to cancel a contract within two or three days of signing. Review Chapter 4, for recently enacted major federal legislation dealing with credit.

DELIVERY

Delivery of customer purchases is a necessary service for some types of goods; for others it is an expensive luxury service. Furniture, heavy appliances, and other bulky items usually have to be delivered. But delivery of smaller items, such as clothing, may be discouraged (except for mail and phone orders).

A store may have its own delivery facility; it may contract with an independent delivery firm; in some cities or some shopping centers retailers have formed mutual or cooperative delivery systems. Parcel post and express shipments are used most often for long-distance shipments.

A store may choose to have its own delivery system and trucks in order to have more control over this phase of the operation. This also can provide advertising and prestige for the store, especially if the trucks are well maintained and the drivers are uniformed. When the volume of deliveries is sufficient, as it often is for a major furniture retailer, a store's own system may be less costly than using an independent delivery organization. However, such independent delivery firms are rapidly growing, and the largest, United Parcel Service, has facilities in forty-four states. One not-so-obvious advantage of having an independent delivery system instead of a store-owned system is to minimize chances for union incursions: drivers of store-owned delivery departments often are the first retail employees to embrace a union.

Cooperative delivery systems afford the possibility of lower delivery costs for participating stores; however, problems are often encountered in organizing and operating the system to the satisfaction of all members.

The full-service department or furniture store may provide free delivery, or free delivery with a certain minimum purchase. The costs of this service can run as high as 1 percent of sales. A less than full-service store, such as a discounter, usually must have delivery available for bulky purchases, but will often charge for this service. Of course, charging for delivery discourages unnecessary use, such as for light and nonbulky packages. Further, it gives the appearance that the take-with customer is not subsidizing the customer who insists on delivery.

Some stores have had success in not offering delivery service, but, instead, encouraging customer involvement. For example, Name Brand, a Midwest furniture outlet, provides no delivery. But they offer their customers the free use of trailers to cart their purchases home. By offering lower prices than conventional furniture stores, self-service delivery reinforces the discount image while affording a practical way of handling the necessary delivery.

It is unlikely that delivery costs will lessen. Rising labor costs preclude this. But any store can make a conscientious effort to promote take-withs, by having salespeople remind customers that "the package you carry gets there first."

A store should weigh the promotional use of free delivery, especially if considering limiting it or charging for it. Free delivery is necessary in promoting mail- and telephone-order business, and it is important that such orders be delivered promptly. Unfortunately, this can pose serious logistical problems, especially after a successful sales campaign or during the Christmas season when sales volume can be many times greater than at other times of the year.

OTHER SERVICES

Many possibilities exist for providing services to customers and thereby increasing the attractiveness of the store. But some are more essential than others. Alterations, for example, are necessary for stores selling clothing. Retailers disagree, however, as to whether this should be a free service, or one that is charged for. Gift wrapping is perhaps less essential, but is rather important during the Christmas season and is a stimulus to gift sales at all times of the year. Again, as with alterations, some stores charge and others charge only for certain elaborate wraps. Personal shopping service is provided by many department and specialty stores. In response to telephone or mail requests, this service will select merchandise and may even provide escort shoppers to accompany customers from department to department to assist them in their purchasing.

Some services obviously induce more customer patronage than others. With all decisions regarding service, judgment is needed concerning whether the gain in business or in good will justifies the costs involved. Sometimes retailers are bound by traditional service offerings and fail to note service opportunities that would involve minimal cost and yet be greatly appreciated by certain customers. For example, in many suburban shopping centers, a preponderance of customers are families with young children. Often the mother has to shop with youngsters in tow. Some stores are providing strollers to use while in the store; most stores ignore the convenience and good will that might be gained from such a simple service offering.

A retailer can provide services that will be greatly appreciated by some customers. In so doing, the retailer can gain invaluable good will, often at modest cost. For example, services provided for children, such as the play area shown in the photograph, make shopping easier and more attractive for parents with young children. (Jan Lukas/Photo Researchers, Inc.)

Convenient and inexpensive or free parking is a service that can have direct impact on sales. In suburban stores, free parking is taken for granted. Difficulty in finding on-street parking and costs of garages or parking lots is often a factor in people deciding not to shop downtown. Some retailers have provided their customers free or low-cost parking in nearby facilities. Sometimes these are owned by the store, or stores provide validation for their customers in public lots.

CUSTOMER RELATIONS

Good customer relations may be viewed as a type of service. Certain facets of it, such as return-goods privileges and systematic procedures for handling customer complaints and making adjustments, certainly are services. But it may be a mistake to think of customer relations as a service. This implies something extra that is provided by a store, something it doesn't have to provide, an option. It is true that some small retailers, usually certain shops, do not permit customers to return goods if they merely change their minds. Few larger retailers can be competitive without doing so. Other facets of customer relations are part of doing business, not something extra to be provided if and when the retailer sees fit. But there are all degrees of handling customers, from the marginal and counter-productive to the maximizing of customer satisfaction and good will.

Handling Customer Complaints and Adjustments

It is inevitable that customer complaints will arise, even in the best-run store. Complaints may be about an item of merchandise, about errors originating on the salesfloor, delivery delays, errors in billing, poor servicing of such things as television sets and appliances, and so on. And some complaints are unjustified: certain customers expect an impossible level of perfection in merchandise and service.

Whether justified or not, the complaint should be handled in a way that maintains good will. Even where a complaint is unjustified, the customer may think it is a legitimate grievance, and careless or rigid store actions may lose the customer. Eventually a store may have to refuse to honor an unreasonable complaint, especially by a chronic complainer. But a retailer should beware the tendency on the part of employees to view all complainants as chronic and unreasonable.

CUSTOMER COMPLAINTS AS A SOURCE OF FEEDBACK   Complaining customers can provide market information by which a store can be better attuned to problems with certain categories of merchandise and certain aspects of the operation. Such feedback can help a store identify particular problem areas and take corrective action. As a consequence, the number of complaints is probably reduced.

Unfortunately, in most stores there is no systematic procedure for tabulating and analyzing complaints and for getting this information into the hands of responsible executives. Much of this feedback is fragmented, especially where the complaining customer goes back to the person or department where the purchase was made. Most buyers and department managers have a vested interest in playing down the number of complaints they receive—in other words, in not passing this information on to higher executive levels—since the number and seriousness of customer complaints are to an extent a reflection on the competence of the departmental management.

PROCEDURES FOR HANDLING COMPLAINTS   In a small store, the manager or the proprietor often handles most or all the complaints and authorizes any adjustments. In a larger store, there may be *decentralized adjustment handling,* which can be rather unsystematic, with each department or floor manager having authority to make adjustments if the salespeople cannot readily handle the matter. However, this arrangement has several disadvantages. There is a lack of uniformity in handling complaints and in maintaining good will. The fragmented feedback may not provide any systematic analysis of data to detect and correct serious or worsening situations.

To minimize these disadvantages, some stores have *centralized adjustment handling*—a department for any complaints not readily handled on the salesfloor. There are some disadvantages here also. Customers may resent the time and effort required to go to an adjustment department, and may receive a negative impression of the store from seeing a long line of other persons with complaints. A tangible disadvantage is that more refunds as opposed to merchandise exchanges tend to result from a centralized system, since merchandise exchanges cannot be made easily away from the selling floor. There is no easy solution to the problem of customer complaints.

Return-Goods Privileges

Related to handling customer complaints is a store's policy regarding *return-goods privileges*. Some stores have a liberal policy. In certain departments, such as dresses and sportswear, salespeople may encourage customers to take several items home on approval, and return the one(s) not wanted. In this situation, returns can range as high as 25 percent of sales.

Such practices are attractive to some customers who have difficulty making quick decisions. But extra costs can result. If delivery is involved, there is a double expense when the store has to pick up the goods again. Returned goods usually have to be re-marked and perhaps repackaged; often such goods are shopworn and as many as half the returns may have to be marked down. Additional recordkeeping has to be done. And finally, additional effort is required to resell the goods.

The most costly returns for a store to accept are those that come back long after the original sale, perhaps at the end of the season or when comparable stock is all but closed out. A not uncommon example is a customer bringing back for a refund in early March an unworn jacket purchased the previous fall. By March most stores have closed out all winter apparel except a few odds and ends on a clearance rack. What should the store do? It must decide whether to give a refund for the full price the customer paid or for the present reduced clearance price.

At the end of the Christmas season, many stores attempt to put some urgency into the return of unwanted gift items by announcing acceptance of returns only for a stipulated period after Christmas, perhaps two weeks. Where such a policy can be made jointly with other stores, it is effective and is usually entirely satisfactory to customers. These stores are not faced with returns dribbling in for months afterward.

Some return goods result strictly from customer indecision and mind changing (or perhaps a spouse criticizes the purchase). There is little a store can do about these, short of refusing to accept returns, and this may be unwise competitively. Then there are those customers who return a party dress the day after the party, or return suits and shirts (dirty) the day after the wedding, along with a punch bowl set with the punch dried in the cups—this has been termed, *fraud by consumers.*[2] On the other hand, returns may be due to high pressure or overselling, which may be curbed with less aggressive sales efforts. And returns due to faulty handling or delayed deliveries certainly justify corrective action.

ROLE PLAY—*Handling Customer Returns of Merchandise*

You have been sent to Central City to take over management of the Golden Rule Department Store. Although the Golden Rule is the largest store in

[2] Noel B. Zabriskie, "Fraud by Consumers," *Journal of Retailing,* Winter 1972–1973, pp. 22–27.

Central City, the owners of the parent company are concerned with the low return on their investment. "If you can get profits up to where they belong, we'll have a good place for you in the home office," you have been told.

Upon assuming your new position and probing into ways of reducing operating costs, you are particularly concerned with merchandise return figures. "From now on," you announce to your assistant, "we will accept no returns that do not have the price tags and the sales tickets attached. And tell our people not to take back any merchandise that was bought more than a week before. And let's not make it so convenient to return goods. Instead of having customer-service desks on each floor, we'll have only one return desk on the eighth floor."

For Thought and Discussion

1. Do customer returns really add to operating costs?
2. What consequences do you think might come from this decision to tighten up procedures for handling returns?
3. What other methods might you use to reduce customer returns?

Intangible Customer Services

As retailers become larger, with more customers and the impersonality brought about by computerized billing, the customer-relations climate tends to become indifferent. A single lost customer is not fretted about, in view of the size of the total business. But when one is multiplied by other lost customers—and the adverse publicity they give their friends and neighbors—the impact may be greater than many firms realize. There is no real measure of this impact. The complaints that reach the ears of responsible executives are only a small proportion of the total.

In order to minimize such draining away of business, another group of services—*intangible customer services*—deserves attention. These may be called *overtones,* in that they enhance customer needs for self-esteem, thereby being ego-gratifying.[3] These ego-satisfying services are simple ones, such as courtesy and respect, prompt attention, and consideration. Are these not lacking in too many instances?

Usually far more executive time is spent in supervising and controlling aspects of the operation other than customer relations. There are reasons for this. Operational problems intrude for management attention, such as a decision on advertising scheduling that cannot be de-

---

[3] The term *overtones* and some of the philosophy of this section are adapted from Alfred R. Oxenfeldt, *Executive Action in Marketing* (Belmont, Calif.: Wadsworth, 1966), pp. 628–41.

layed, new seasonal buying commitments that must be made on time, a new display or merchandising program that must be submitted to higher management. The customer who is antagonized, who is ill-treated, whose special needs are disregarded, and who quietly fades away never to return often is ignored in the pressures of "more important" matters.

Even the promptness and quality of response to customer mail and telephone inquiries can result in positive or negative overtones. Many firms could benefit from devoting attention to this aspect of the store-customer interaction. Special training of employees may be needed, special policies established, and some type of periodic follow-up used to assure that the company's image does not deteriorate, that a positive contribution is made to customer relations and not a negative one.

The customer-relations climate of a store to a large extent rests with management; a poor climate cannot really be blamed on uncaring and inexperienced employees. Management must make a commitment to optimize customer service. This should be a frequent topic at meetings and training sessions. It should be part of the initial job orientation— what is expected for good customer overtones. It must be given major priority, or else other problems will intrude and dominate. Without constant management pressure and encouragement, and without suitable controls to provide feedback, an organization tends to become indifferent to customer relations.

An example of top management shortsightedness regarding customer relations was cited about Hudson's in Detroit, as it faced declining profits. *Business Week* noted that Hudson's was ". . . a long way from coddling the customer. When shoppers returned defective Lady Schick hair dryers, for instance, they were told to 'tell Schick'—in other words, ship the dryers back to the manufacturer themselves."[4] With such dictates coming down from a new top management concerned with maximizing efficiency and cutting costs, customer relations suffers.

LIMITS TO SERVICES OFFERED

There is no limit to the intangible, ego-satisfying services that can be offered, but there is a limit to the tangible services. These services generally cost a store money. Some, such as free delivery, can be a significant drain on earnings, or they can force a store into charging higher prices in order to reach for a profit.

---

[4] "A Swinging Merchant Goes for Growth," *Business Week,* November 18, 1972, pp. 60–61.

Services Versus Low Prices

A basic incompatibility exists between offering customers the lowest prices and providing them with bountiful services. Although the costs of providing the many kinds of services possible vary widely, they all involve some cost, even if it is only one person's time (as in handling ticket sales for cultural and sporting events). The temptation for the store trying to increase its market share or to revive failing business is to offer more and more services.

But several questions should be considered before such a decision is made:

1. Are there potentially attractive-to-customer services that are not being offered by competitive stores?
2. Will the costs of providing such services be likely to force prices to a level too high for our customers?
3. Is our actual and desired store image compatible with being a full-service store?

A heavy approach to service offerings may be less effective if a major competitor is committed similarly. Sometimes, however, an imaginative combination of services may be effective in this competitive situation, such as offering mothers with young children special shopping conveniences. At other times the opposite approach may be best. This was the opportunity that discount stores capitalized on in the 1950s when conventional retailers had become full-service and high-price operations and were vulnerable to new competition featuring minimum or no services, no frills, and lowest prices.

But there is a compromise position that a store can take: that of charging for services used.

RETAILING CONTROVERSY—*Should a Customer Pay for Services?*

A store may use a compromise approach to service. It may provide many services, but charge for those that are used. Therefore, it would charge for delivery, for installations, for gift wrapping, perhaps even for check cashing, children's playrooms, and personal shopping. What are the advantages and limitations of such a policy?

Advantages of Charging for Services

1. Costs will be kept in line, since availability of services will not be an additional expense.
2. Use of services will not be abused as often as is the case where service is free and, for example, customers have purchases delivered that they could easily take with them.
3. There should be no resentment by customers who do not use services over having to subsidize other customers who do, since no higher selling prices should be needed to cover the costs of services.
4. If a store wishes to promote itself as one having lower prices and best buys, this may be the best approach to services, even better than offering little or no service.
5. A store may be able to attract several disparate customer segments: those who want many services, as well as those who want little or no service.

Disadvantages of Charging for Services

1. This policy is not compatible with a high-quality store appealing to a high-income clientele.
2. Some customer good will may be lost, and some business will shift to stores that do not charge for certain services, such as alterations and installations.
3. If costs of services are carefully analyzed and fully prorated to individual transactions, some customers may see such charges as exorbitant and unwarranted.
4. Charging for some services, such as check cashing, may seem petty and unreasonably profit-oriented, and good will may be lost.

For Thought and Discussion

1. How would you evaluate the pros and cons of charging for service for:
   a. a medium-price department store
   b. a small men's clothing store
   c. a discount store
2. If one store charged for services and a competitor did not, do you believe the former could maintain its position? Why or why not?

Service Alternatives

The many different service (and price) packages that a firm can offer are illustrated by the following typical examples of supermarkets competing in one metropolitan area.

Supermarket A.   The emphasis is on discount prices, with everyday low prices and strong "leader" bargains for the weekends. Services are minimal, with long lines at the checkout counters during busy times. Customers are expected to carry bags in shopping carts to their cars.

Supermarket B.   The atmosphere might be termed flamboyant. An exciting circus and promotional emphasis predominates, with mass displays, bright signs, demonstrations, and hoopla. Prices are moderate. Services are the usual found in supermarkets, with some help usually provided in putting shopping bags in cars.

Supermarket C.   A maximum commitment is made to service, with courteous, well-trained employees and clean stores. Although the operation is self-service, boys will carry the grocery bags from checkout counters directly to customers' cars. Other services include a supervised playroom for children while their mothers shop, nutrition guidance and informative labeling, unit prices, weekly shopping guides listing the best buys—even a hospitality bar with free coffee. Prices are moderate to high.

Supermarket D.   This food chain is best described as a composite of the other three. It has low prices, although not as low as A. It has some seasonal promotions but primarily relies on weekend specials. Service is moderate, more than A provides, but far less than C.

Three of these supermarket chains are existing fairly comfortably in their market area; one is rapidly losing ground. Which is the weak one? You probably surmise correctly that it is D. It has found no unique niche for itself; no distinctive image; no service, price, merchandise, or promotional package attractive enough to win and hold sufficient customers.

In Chapter 5 we discussed the need to develop a retailing mix that will appeal to target customers. When this is not done, a store is vulnerable. In food retailing, a "blah" or imageless store will attract some customers because of its location. But with no competitive draw, its market is limited and sales per store tend to be lower than competitors'. The result is a chain of marginal units. A&P had reached this point in many market areas. They embarked on their program of WEO ("Where Economy Originates") prices in order to gain an image of a best-values store. The efforts cost them horrendous losses and the lasting effect of their image-changing attempt is questionable.

INCOME-PRODUCING SERVICES

Major retailers are becoming aware that they can sell service as well as tangible goods. The diversification of Penney into life insurance seems a radical move for a company that not much more than a decade ago was reluctantly considering credit, and was primarily a dry-goods firm that did not even carry appliances, sporting goods, or housewares, much less furniture and auto supplies. Ward had gone strongly into money-making services: charm and self-improvement courses, beauty salons, floral services, and rentals are some of these services. Sears long has been the leader in merchandising services ranging from mutual funds, insurance, home cleaning and repairs, and appliance servicing to eye-glass fitting.

Some retailers have discovered the profitability of renting out items such as floor polishers, electric power tools, ladders, fence post diggers, and so on. Even small retailers, such as hardware stores, can gain extra business from renting out. Larger retailers have sometimes set up separate rental departments.

Although merchandising services and rentals may seem far afield from traditional retailing, in some ways they are natural areas for expansion, especially for the firm with a tradition of dependability behind it and a sizable body of loyal customers with active charge accounts. Much of the success of Sears in promoting its home repair and appliance servicing, and even its auto service, has been due to its image of reliability, honest work, and guaranteed satisfaction. Many consumers see these characteristics sorely needed in repair industries, where honest work and dependability are far from universal.

BROADENING THE SCOPE OF RETAILING

Although the merchandising of some services, such as auto servicing and mutual funds, may be important steps in the direction of sound retailer diversification, the range of possibilities has been barely tapped. Opportunities for expanding retailing activities and customer offerings lie in a wide variety of hitherto unconsidered areas. E. B. Weiss, an "idea man," has suggested these possibilities for major department stores and chains to broaden the scope of their activities:

Exercise chains and fitness clubs

Child-care centers—tied in with sales of garments, footwear, toys, and other products

Tennis facilities on store roofs—tied in with sales of tennis paraphernalia and apparel

Art schools, stockbroker services, travel services—also closely related
to merchandise sales

Full-service truck-servicing facilities. Penney is experimenting with this

Home security services

Cooking schools—tied in with gourmet cooking equipment, small
appliance sales, and so on

Home catering service

Party services, especially for children's parties—tied in with sales of
toys, gifts, and the like

Home and apartment maintenance services[5]

Although all the above suggestions involve expanding via service
merchandising rather than specific goods, the tie-in with sales of regular
goods should make such expansion alternatives attractive. Far from
being a staid and traditional business, retailing today has the promise of
being a great growth industry of the coming decades.

■ Summary

Customers have come to expect retailers to provide them with an array
of services. Even most discount stores today have credit and delivery
(for large items), check cashing, and miscellaneous other services.
Some services are income producing, or have the potential to be, such
as credit and various repair services. Others, such as delivery, are an
added cost, and issues are raised whether they indeed need to be
provided, and, if so, how they should be funded. The importance of
good customer relations should be recognized by all retailers, but
improvements often can be made in handling customer complaints and
grievances, and in such simple ego-satisfying services as courtesy and
respect, prompt attention, and consideration. An efficient operation is
also an aspect of customer service, and this is described in the next
chapter, along with the nagging problems of shoplifting and employee
pilferage.

■ Key Terms

Aging the receivables

Centralized adjustment
handling

Decentralized adjustment
handling

Fraud by consumers

[5] E. B. Weiss, "Lip Service for Service Merchandising," *Stores*, September 1972, pp. 47–48.

Garnishment
Income-producing services
Installment credit
Intangible customer services,
   or overtones

Layaway plan
Open-account credit
Retail credit bureau
Return-goods privilege
Revolving credit

■ **Discussion Questions**

1. Contrast the desirability of a layaway plan versus the availability of credit, from the firm's viewpoint and that of the customer.
2. How do you explain the fact that the typical interest charge of 18 percent on retail credit has apparently had little negative effect on the use of credit? Does it bother you to pay 18 percent interest?
3. Why is credit so necessary to do business in the ghetto? Would not a layaway plan be sufficient, less risky, and better tailored to the needs and resources of the ghetto consumer?
4. How important are customer complaints in providing feedback about customer satisfaction with a store?
5. Why is the retail firm, especially the larger one, in a good position to expand into income-producing services? Do you see any limitations to such expansion?
6. How would you evaluate the customer-service policies of a store? What factors or criteria would you use regarding which services are desirable and which should be discontinued or not added?
7. Can you give examples of some services that are promotional and at the same time perform a service for customers?
8. Should a store be concerned with "silent complainers"? Why?

■ **Project**

Ascertain what income-producing services the major retailers in your community are offering. Also determine if a sample of small retailers are offering any such services. Draw up a list of income-producing services that would be appropriate for small retailers to offer, along with your reasons for such recommendations.

■ **Exercise in Creativity**

You have been transferred to a store that has had a declining sales and profit pattern for several years. Specific causes of this situation are not obvious, since merchandise, prices, and promotional efforts are similar to those of other successful stores in the chain. Through your own observation over a period of several weeks, you have gained the impression that the personnel of the store—many of whom have been with it for years—take customers for granted and often are impatient and even rude to them. Consequently, you see an urgent need to improve the customer-relations climate of the store, before more customers are driven away.

Develop as many ideas as you can for stimulating good customer overtones among the employees of the store.

■ Retailing in Action

"Because of the energy crisis and the soaring costs of delivery," your boss says, "we will have to cut our deliveries in half. I want you to develop new policies that will enable us to do this. You will probably have to put some size and distance limitations on what we will or will not deliver. And you better prepare signs and publicity releases to explain to our customers why we are cutting back on this service."

18 Store Operation: Requirements and Problems

Store operation consists of miscellaneous activities—many of them behind the scenes and not readily evident to customers. In large stores operation is usually headed up by a major executive, perhaps with the title store manager, store superintendent, or operating superintendent. Few retailing texts and articles give more than minimal attention to this aspect of retailing. It is taken for granted. Standard operating procedures, which may be well prescribed in some stores and implicit or ill-defined in others, are assumed to make most operational activities simple, repetitive, uninspired. But this viewpoint represents careless thinking.

At best, most operations proceed smoothly enough that no major complaints reach the ear of responsible executives, but we may suspect that efficiency might be improved, leading to reduced costs and better service. At worst, careless or badly planned and supervised operations may result in unbearable losses from theft, long delays and many errors in receiving and marking merchandise, a dirty store, equipment breakdowns, and a host of other problems that can lose sales and customers and add greatly to the cost of doing business.

IMPORTANCE OF STORE OPERATION

Although most store-operation activities are less visible than merchandising and promotional activities, their importance lies in enhancing and not detracting from the merchandise and the efforts to pull customers into the store. Store operation is secondary to the revenue-producing role of merchandising; its purpose is to be helpful. For this reason, buyers and merchandise managers usually receive higher salaries than comparable-level executives in the operations division. Consequently, operation tends to attract a somewhat lower caliber of trainee and executive than the merchandising division and has the added handicap of being less glamorous.

The tendency to take store operation for granted has sometimes led to inattention to possibilities that improvements in efficiency can be made that can translate directly into added profits. The need to improve operational efficiency was brought rather forcefully to some retailers' attention when discount stores came on the scene with significantly lower operating costs. Today with shoplifting and employee theft increasing, better and more sophisticated protection is essential.

In this chapter we will view the store operation function as important to the health and safety of a store. As such, creative diagnosis seems needed to cope with emerging problems and with opportunities to develop better efficiency. For example, problems such as increased shoplifting and employee theft, or increasing delivery mistakes and delays must be quickly noticed and corrective action taken. And a store should be alert to new processes and equipment that can speed the flow of goods through receiving and marking room bottlenecks.

RESPONSIBILITIES OF STORE OPERATION—A SUMMARY

The following may be classified as *store operation responsibilities:*

1. Store maintenance. This includes such diverse and specialized activities as repairs and renovations to building and parking lot, to

fixtures and equipment (including plumbing, heating, and air conditioning). It also includes the mundane but necessary janitorial and cleaning services.

2. Merchandise handling and controlling. Included here are the receiving, checking, and marking of all goods coming into the store, and all goods leaving it. This involves warehouses, loading docks, shipping rooms, and stockrooms.

3. Purchasing supplies and equipment for the store. A large store consumes a huge amount of supplies and equipment, ranging from paper bags, light bulbs, and fuel, to such major purchases as delivery trucks.

4. Store security. All-night guards and store detectives are a large part of the staff in some stores. But more than manpower is involved. Store security policies, procedures, and equipment should minimize dangers of theft, fire, and other hazards.

5. Workrooms. Most large stores have a number of nonmerchandise departments and workrooms that are the responsibility of store operation. Examples are restaurants, beauty shops, drapery workrooms, apparel alterations, laundries, and employee cafeterias. Some may be manufacturing departments, such as candy and ice cream making, and bakeries.

6. Customer service. Some customer services are under the operating division. Adjustments, delivery, and wrapping usually are. General supervision of the salesfloors is sometimes the responsibility of store operations, with floor or section managers assigning and scheduling salespeople, approving refunds, checks, and merchandise exchanges, and in general dealing with any emergencies that arise on the salesfloor.

Certain of these functional areas will be examined in more detail, especially where they pose unusual problems or opportunities for greater efficiency. Although the breakdown of activities follows that customary in large stores, we should recognize that they are just as important to the small store. Perhaps the store manager or proprietor assumes responsibility for these duties in the small store. But neglect or careless handling of these activities can hurt any retailer, big or small.[1]

---

[1] Although not commonplace, both natural and manmade disasters can also challenge the resourcefulness of retailers: for example, blizzards, power failures, floods, looting, arson, bombings, and kidnappings. See Marian Burk Rothman, "Handling Disasters," *Stores*, April 1978, pp. 41–44.

STORE MAINTENANCE

Although the complexities of certain aspects of store maintenance, such as servicing air conditioning equipment or elevators, are certainly far beyond the scope of this book, one aspect of store maintenance deserves our attention: *housekeeping.* This means keeping the store clean, uncluttered, pleasant to shop in, and the merchandise protected as much as possible from becoming soiled and shopworn.

In a big store, overall housekeeping maintenance is not difficult to keep up to desirable standards. With a large staff and someone definitely responsible for the organizing, scheduling, and supervision of such activities as window cleaning, store and sidewalk sweeping, regular collections of trash, cleaning of restrooms, and so on, housekeeping is usually taken for granted. But intradepartmental housekeeping is another matter.

Department personnel, rather than operating people, are responsible for these department maintenance duties: having signs on merchandise, dusting counters, shelves, and merchandise; keeping wrapping and cash register counters uncluttered; straightening, repackaging, refolding, and replenishing merchandise; and keeping merchandise and understocks orderly so that sizes, colors, and styles can be easily located. These are simple and necessary tasks, yet because of their drudgery and repetitiveness, they are often given short shrift. A trainee or junior executive's first supervisory responsibility often is to see that such departmental housekeeping is done promptly and completely. Otherwise, the appearance of the department and its merchandise suffers, and there may occur that worst sin of all sins—losing a sale when the item the customer wanted was in stock but couldn't be located immediately.

ROLE PLAY—*Improving Housekeeping*

You know that the buyer will be livid when he finds out about the lost sales that have been occurring all week because you could not find any more size 15½, 33 dress shirts in the most popular style number. Four more dozen of this, the most common size, have been found misplaced and under the wrong counter.

You have recently been transferred as assistant buyer to one of the largest departments in the store. The buyer is known to be demanding, but fair. It seemed reasonable to expect that if you could measure up to his standards, you would be in line for an early promotion to buyer of some smaller department.

When you finally approach him about the lost sales he is more sad than angry. "We have lost upward of $400 in shirt sales this week, and who knows how much in accessory sales because of these misplaced goods. We can't bring these sales back—that's over with—and we'll probably lose some of the customers too. But let's forget about that part of it, Jim. Let's just be sure our housekeeping is improved enough so that such a thing doesn't happen again. Okay?"

You nod soberly. Although the fault was not directly yours—as both the buyer and you know—you still, as the major floor supervisor, can hardly escape the responsibility for poor housekeeping by the newer and part-time employees.

For Thought and Discussion What would you do at this point to insure that such costly housekeeping snafus would not occur again?

In a small store, housekeeping tends to be less systematized and more erratic. This is not surprising since so many other matters intrude for attention. It is helpful to have a work schedule of maintenance activities to be performed: how often and by whom. For example, sidewalks should be swept the first thing every morning; but outside windows washed only every three days, and the inside of the display windows may need to be washed only every ten days. Sometimes inattention to certain aspects of maintenance can be embarrassing. The author remembers his first assignment as manager of a small Penney store. A few weeks after taking the assignment, the zone manager (who was responsible for supervising some fifty stores) paid a visit. As he made his tour through the store, several times he reached his hand to touch rather inaccessible shelves and displays. His fingers came away dark with dust. Silently he held them up for all of us to see.

MERCHANDISE HANDLING AND CONTROLLING

Need for Good Merchandise Handling

The time it takes for an order to be received in the store, processed, and sent to the sales floor can be crucial in maximizing sales, in preventing merchandise outs, and in achieving a good merchandise turn-over rate. The accuracy with which the receiving and processing job is done affects shrinkage and profits. You can see how taking a week to ten days to get merchandise to the salesfloor can mean considerable lost business and may force the buying of larger quantities because of the long replenishment time. Especially for seasonal goods, delays of this kind can be serious.

Another profit drain resulting from slow receiving room service is delay in paying bills. If a shipment is not checked promptly and the invoice forwarded to the accounting office for payment, the store loses the cash discount and anticipation that is allowed for prompt payment. (Some stores, in order to insure the cash discount, pay invoices as received without waiting for the goods to be checked in.)

The task of promptly handling incoming goods would not be par-ticularly difficult if their flow into a store was fairly uniform. But it is not. Building up stock for fall and Christmas peak selling activity can strain the resources for merchandise handling to the utmost and force the use of inexperienced workers who are slower and more error prone. Thus the ground is laid for delays and costly mistakes.

Steps Involved in Handling Incoming Goods

The *receiving process* involves these steps:

1. Checking the number of cartons received against the freight bill of the transportation firm or carrier; paying the freight charges
2. Checking the contents of the shipment and verifying that the mer-chandise received is that ordered and is in good condition
3. Marking the individual items with prices and other information (unless they are to be bulk marked)
4. Paying the vendor's invoice
5. Moving the goods from the receiving room to the sales floor and/or the stockroom, warehouse, and/or branch stores

Figure 18.1 depicts the physical movement of goods into a large store and its branches and warehouses. Inefficiencies and costly errors can occur at each of these stages. Furthermore, goods need to be protected, both from damage and from theft, in this movement through the system.

CHECKING AT THE DOCK   Goods are unloaded from trucks at the store or warehouse dock. The first possibility for error and carelessness

FIGURE **18.1** FLOW OF GOODS INTO THE STORE SYSTEM

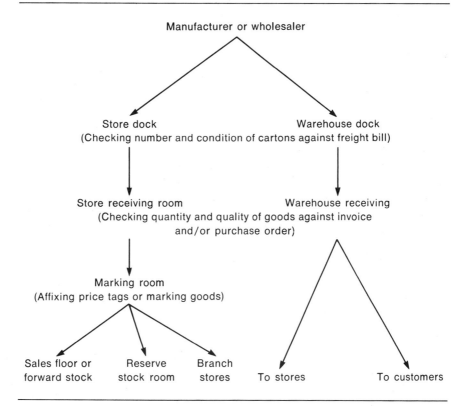

occurs at this point. If the receiving clerk signs the freight bill without verifying the number of cartons received, any subsequently discovered shortages will not be reimbursable. At this time the cartons must be examined for visible signs of damage, such as being crushed, opened, or stained (suggesting breakage inside.) Any damaged containers should be noted on the freight bill; otherwise damage claims are difficult to prove. At this point the goods are ready to move into the receiving room to await further processing.

CHECKING IN THE RECEIVING ROOM   After cartons are opened, the goods must be compared in quantity and quality against those ordered. There are three common methods of checking quantities of incoming merchandise: (1) the direct check, (2) the blind check, and (3) a combination of the two.

The *direct check* is most common. It involves checking a shipment against a vendor's bill, which is known as an *invoice,* or against a copy of the buyer's purchase order. Matching of quantities received against quantities billed and ordered can be done rather quickly, which accounts for the popularity of this method. However, the direct check does offer the temptation to "assume" that the quantities received are correct without rigorously verifying it. Hence some managers prefer the *blind check,* in which the checker works with a blank form and fills in the style numbers and quantities in the shipment; these figures are later checked against the invoice or purchase order by clerical personnel. But this is more costly and time consuming, and may not be worth the extra assurance of checking accuracy. The combination plan uses the direct check whenever the invoice and purchase documents are available; when they are not, a blind check is used so that merchandise is not detained in the receiving room.

Receiving room operation can often be made more efficient by updating equipment, facilities, and the general procedure and layout. Stationery and movable tables can sometimes be relocated and increased. Even conveyor systems are used in big stores to move merchandise from the receiving point through the checking and marking operations. Handling equipment may include hydraulic platforms, forklift trucks, and even overhead monorails used for hanging merchandise.

MARKING   One can readily see how important accuracy is in marking merchandise. If the wrong price is affixed to a certain lot of goods, serious shrinkage can result if the price is below the prescribed price; if the price is higher than it should be, the merchandise may not sell. But other information such as stock control information, and sometimes sizes, is included on most price tickets. Errors in style numbers can disrupt buying and unit control records, and errors in marking sizes invariably result in excessive merchandise returns and customer dissatisfaction.

The information on prices may be put on the purchase order or invoice by the buyer after he has seen the goods. *Preretailing* is often done, with the buyer determining prices and recording them on the purchase order at the time the order is written up. Preretailing expedites checking and marking goods, since this can proceed without waiting for the buyer to come to the marking room.

Sometimes goods are *group* or *bulk marked* without price marking each individual unit. This is commonly done for items of low unit value that can be conveniently displayed in bins or tables with a price sign. Examples are many hardware items, candy, notions, and toiletries. Large retailers have been pressuring manufacturers to premark merchandise before it is shipped, thus minimizing handling in the store.

Bulk marking is common for items of low unit value that can be conveniently displayed with a price sign in bins or on tables. Here the signs are crude but still convey the image of discount prices and attractive bargains. (Alex Webb/Magnum)

Desired price and other information can be placed on merchandise in a number of ways with varying degrees of sophistication: writing with an ordinary pencil or a grease pencil; a rubber stamp may be used; or various labels, tickets, or printed tags can be affixed either by hand or by machine. Tags can even be of the print-punch type used in an electronic data processing system for stock control and sales feedback. A wide range of equipment and machinery is available for this process and can aid efficiency.

PAYING INVOICES The bookkeeping job of processing and paying invoices is usually the least error prone and most efficient aspect of the receiving process. The greatest waste that can occur here is that cash discounts and any anticipation allowed are not taken advantage of, either because of delays in getting invoices up from the receiving room, or delays in processing them in the accounts payable office. Even if money has to be borrowed, invoices ought to be paid promptly enough to get the discount. To illustrate the desirability of taking this discount, assume that an invoice of $5,000 has terms of 2/10, net 30, which means that the retailer is saving $100 by paying in ten days. Such a saving is equivalent to an interest rate of 36 percent and is given by the seller because the firm is getting the money twenty days before the net period ends.[2]

Accordingly, care should be taken that no discounts are wasted. Close supervision, or at least periodic spot checks, may be necessary here. In order to take advantage of all such discounts, sometimes invoices may have to be paid before the merchandise is actually checked (as noted earlier). In such cases, any discrepancies of actual versus billed quantities can usually be straightened out by a claim to the vendor, even after the invoice has been paid.

INTRACOMPANY DISTRIBUTION OF GOODS   After incoming goods have been checked and marked, they usually are sent to the salesfloor and forward stock or to the reserve stockroom, or perhaps both. Many retailers today attempt to limit reserve stockkeeping for many goods and keep all backup stocks near the goods at the selling point. These backup goods become *forward stock.* Emphasis on leaner stocks and faster merchandise turnover partially accounts for this; better fixture design and space allocation are also factors.

Some goods of necessity cannot be accommodated on the selling floor. Bedspreads, pillows, lawn and garden suppliers, and other bulky goods are examples. And some merchandise has to be sold by sample, with most of the stock warehoused, examples being major appliances, furniture, and carpeting. Such goods are usually delivered from the warehouse directly to the customer. Warehouses typically are located in low-rent areas, often some distance from the store. Warehouse sales are big promotional events for many retailers, and such merchandise can be priced very attractively because of reduced selling and handling costs.

Most chains have found it desirable to have regional warehouses serving perhaps hundreds of stores. These afford faster replenishment time than when individual stores go directly to manufacturers. They also permit purchasing in huge quantities with consequent cost savings. Warehouses or distribution centers often incorporate the newest equipment and techniques for merchandise handling. Some are highly automated and use computers in filling orders and in maintaining inventory levels and replenishing stocks.

Interstore transfers of merchandise are a common practice of multiunit firms, whether chain outlets or branches of department stores. Thereby, stocks can be evenly balanced with demand in the various

---

[2] The 36 percent is derived from: $\dfrac{360 \text{ days in a year}}{20 \text{ days}} \times 2 \text{ percent}$

units: overstocks in one store can be transferred to other stores; merchandise outs can be quickly corrected. A large department store may have all incoming orders shipped to the main store for checking and marking and then relay them to the various branches, thus saving costs of branch receiving, checking, and marking facilities. Of course, careful supervision and control are necessary to make interstore transfers with a minimum of errors and delays.

COST-SAVING OPPORTUNITIES IN MERCHANDISE HANDLING   Cost-saving opportunities in the physical handling and processing of merchandise may be categorized as:

1. Speeding up checking and marking of incoming goods by:
    a. Close supervision and training of workers
    b. Analyzing bottlenecks and improving the system where possible
    c. Equipment improvement, such as conveyor systems and faster ticket-making machines
    d. Preretailing and premarking where possible
2. Paying all invoices promptly in order to take advantage of cash discounts and anticipation
3. Concentrating purchases among fewer vendors
4. Minimizing transportation charges by selecting best routes and modes of transportation and by prompt filing of loss and damage claims

We discussed the first two categories earlier in this section. The latter fall under the control of the merchandising division rather than of operations.

When a buyer deals with fewer vendors, this results in fewer shipments, especially small shipments. It is these small shipments that typically add to the costs and delays of receiving and processing, since more orders and invoices are involved and the cartons are often smaller (which means more have to be inspected, recorded, and opened). Furthermore, smaller shipments result in shorter jobs on ticket-making equipment, which means more type has to be set. The greater the number of shipments and separate invoices that have to be handled, the more chance for errors, and the less likelihood that errors will be caught.

Savings in transportation costs can be made by specifying appropriate routing on purchase orders. Large stores usually have a traffic department to assist buyers in finding least-cost routes. However, when a buyer habitually orders late or "by crisis," fastest routing rather than some cheaper mode of transportation must be specified. Some cost-conscious stores audit freight bills periodically to make sure that goods were shipped at the proper rate and by the specified routing. Where instructions were not followed, vendors can be billed for any resulting overcharges. Filing of loss and damage claims is automatic in most stores. But sometimes carelessness and delays occur and result in a store's not getting a legitimate claim.

PURCHASING STORE SUPPLIES AND EQUIPMENT

Some equipment purchases are highly technical and may require trained engineers or top-level executive committee authorization. Many other purchases are commonplace, but substantial money may be spent on such things as paper bags and other wrapping supplies, light bulbs, and cleaning supplies.

Routine purchasing of staple items is not difficult, since previous years' usage should be a good guide. But costs can be unnecessarily increased by the practice of (1) sticking with old sources of supply, whereas some shopping around might disclose cost or delivery advantage in dealing with another supplier; or (2) buying too much and having too large a supply tying up space and investment. More frequent orders in smaller amounts are desirable.

For the small store, the purchase of supplies often presents an unexciting task, neglected as long as possible and then handled with a minimum of attention. Often no regular schedule is laid out for checking and ordering such goods. The result is "feast and famine": some items are on the threshold of being used up before a rush order is placed; and others are available in a six-month supply.

A frequent source of extra costs is using larger-size bags or containers than the merchandise warrants. Giving a customer a large bag when a smaller one would suffice may represent an extra supply cost of 50 percent and even more. It is not uncommon for a store to be out of stock for several weeks of the most popular size paper bag (since this one is used up the fastest), and to be forced to use larger ones until another shipment is received.

STORE SECURITY

The Problem of Invisible Shrinkage

Store security concerns the protection of a store and its contents. As we noted in Chapter 14, the need for protection against pilferage (by both customers and employees) is of major importance. Complicating the task of protection from theft is the fact that no store really knows how much it is losing in this way. Invisible shrinkage, which is the difference between what the books show should be on hand and what the physical count shows to be actually on hand, is composed of many things, from actual theft to careless clerical and receiving room errors. Even the physical inventory itself is error prone and may distort the calculation of this invisible shrinkage. But we know that pilferage today is a growing problem and one that is a significant drain on profits.

Consumer fraudulent practices or dishonesty undoubtedly account for a large part of invisible shrinkage problems. Some of this dishonesty is as simple as changing price tags on items so that a purchase can be made at a lower price, or buying a product on sale and taking it back for a full regular price refund at another store, or not informing a store clerk of an error made in the customer's favor. On the other hand, more overt and bold methods may be used by both amateurs and professionals.[3]

An indication of the worsening of security problems is the increase in department store inventory shortages, which rose from 2.01 percent to 2.13 percent in 1976, according to the National Retail Merchants Association. Total retail losses in 1976 were estimated at $7.2 billion, according to the Bureau of Domestic Commerce.[4]

The drain on business profits can come from a variety of criminal offences. These crimes can be classified as:

Visible crimes: burglary and robbery
                 shoplifting
                 arson
                 vandalism

Invisible crimes: pilferage of merchandise and supplies by employees
                 embezzlement by employees
                 credit and payment frauds—counterfeit money, bad checks, counterfeit credit cards, unauthorized purchases
                 kickbacks
                 computer fraud and manipulation

Retail establishments fall victim to burglary and robbery more often than other businesses, with retail burglaries—illegal entry of the

[3] For more specifics, see "Rip offs—New American Way of Life," *U. S. News and World Report,* May 31, 1976, pp. 29–32; Stuart C. Hadden, John M. Steiner, and Len Herkomer, "Price Tag Switching," *International Journal of Criminology and Penology,* May 1976, pp. 129–143; and Charles H. McCaghy, *Crime, Conflict, and Interest Groups* (New York: Macmillan, 1976).

[4] As cited in Marian Burk Rothman, "Internal and External Theft, What It Costs," *Stores,* January 1978, pp. 44–46.

premises—outstripping robberies four to one. Shoplifting has received the most attention, and according to the Small Business Administration, accounts for the largest proportion of retail losses, some 28 percent. An estimated four million shoplifters are apprehended each year, but it is thought that only one in thirty-five offenders is caught.[5] Arson and vandalism are more prevalent in the inner city, but suburban stores are also victimized.

Some observers single out internal theft by employees as even more costly than shoplifting. Such internal theft has been credited with direct blame for about 7 percent of business failures, and some experts think such theft by insiders may cost businesses several billion dollars a year more than burglary and robbery losses.

Retailers are particularly vulnerable to counterfeit operations. It has been estimated that $4.8 million in bogus bills are passed to retailers each year, with the $5 bill the one most frequently copied.[6] In recent years counterfeit and stolen credit cards plague both small and large retailers. Kickbacks and bribes have been revealed in all levels of commercial enterprises. But the computer has the potential for being the most dangerous. By manipulating computer systems, physical shortages of inventory or cash can be covered up, duplicate paychecks can be issued. As well, other ingenious and sophisticated crimes can be perpetrated and can be extremely difficult to detect. The dollar amounts for a single episode involving computers can far exceed those for any other single crime.[7]

RETAILING PROBLEMS—*Examples of Pilferage*

Pilferers come in all sorts of guises, from the rank amateur to the smooth professional. For example:

1. A teen-ager stops at the cosmetic counter. Another customer is buying perfume and looks at several brands before deciding on one. As the salesperson goes to the cash register, the teen-ager notices that one of the boxes of perfume has been left on the counter. Furtively glancing around, she slips it into her coat pocket and wanders away.
2. A pleasant, matronly woman takes several dresses into the fitting room.

---

[5] Ibid.
[6] Ibid., pp. 44–45.
[7] Ibid.; "Computer Fraud: Growing Retail Menace," *Chain Store Age, Executive Edition,* June 1978, pp. 27–30.

Emerging, she hands one to a salesperson, remarking that she can't decide today. She leaves the department wearing two dresses.

3. A clerk in the radio, stereo, and TV department opens the carton of a color TV set and puts the set on display. During the noon hour when everybody is busy, he quietly fills the carton with a variety of expensive stereo components and radios from the stockroom, and reseals the carton. An accomplice comes in later in the day, buys the $300 "set" from him and he puts the delivery tag on $1,000 worth of merchandise.

4. The sale is $4.96. However, unknown to the customer or to fellow workers, the salesperson rings up 96¢. Then she brings the package and the change to the customer, but deliberately neglects to put the incorrect sales ticket in the bag. Later in the day when no one is around she pulls out $4 from the cash drawer, in addition to more money resulting from several other under-rings.

For Thought and Discussion   As the manager, what would you do to try to minimize or prevent each of these occasions of shoplifting?

One can see from the above examples the challenges confronting store security forces. There are many opportunities for theft, both by customers and by employees, and complete surveillance is practically impossible. Furthermore, until recently in most states the retailer who apprehended a suspected shoplifter could be sued for false arrest or false imprisonment. Now a number of states have enacted laws stating that the merchant cannot be sued successfully if there was probable cause for suspicion, even if a mistake was made. Usually apprehension must be delayed until the shoplifter leaves the store, but some states are beginning to waive this requirement also. Such laws designed to give better protection to the retailer are by no means universal as yet.

What Can Be Done?

It is essential that stores experiencing high shrinkage tighten their controls. This may not eliminate the problem, but it will reduce it. Since shrinkage can be due to a combination of many factors, controls must be comprehensive.

In order to lessen carelessness or overt manipulation of records, supervision needs to be tight not only in the receiving rooms where goods are checked in, but also on the salesfloor and even in the offices

Store security workers must be on the lookout not only for shoplifters, but also for fire hazards and pilferage of goods by employees. (Cliff Garboden/Stock, Boston)

where the books are maintained and cost and price computations are made.

In order to lessen temptations for employees, both selection procedures and supervision should be tight. Checking references of new employees is necessary in order to catch any who were discharged under suspicious circumstances. Employees need to be carefully checked when leaving the store. Handbags and packages brought into the store by employees should be checked and not permitted in the department.

In the previous example of the salesperson who under-rang the cash register and pocketed the difference, this pilferage would not be detected by the cash register tape since the under-ring would balance the money in the till with the amount recorded.[8] Many stores, in order to combat this, subscribe to shopping services, of which *Willmark* is the most common. These detection services send unobtrusive "customers" to stores periodically. They ostensibly make purchases and observe

[8] By no means are all cash register misrings indications of pilferage. Most are due to carelessness. A recent study found that 15 percent of all cash register rings were inaccurate, but the misrings were split almost equally between undercharges and overcharges. See Noel B. Zabriskie and Joe L. Welch, "Retail Cashier Accuracy: Misrings and Some Factors Related to Them," *Journal of Retailing,* Spring 1978, pp. 43–50.

whether salespeople ring up the correct amounts. Unfortunately, Willmark and other detection services can operate only periodically in a store, otherwise employees will become suspicious. Alert and observant store management perhaps is the best preventative of employee dishonesty.

A store can reduce its stock shortage by training and motivating employees to be shortage-minded and observant of carelessness that leads to shortages, as well as alert to suspicious customers and unguarded merchandise. For example, the perfume in the first example should not have been left on the counter.

Although shoplifting is not the only source of shrinkage, it tends to be the one most frightening to retailers. Stores have beefed up security departments, increased the number of store detectives, and have even hired guards for fitting rooms. Some stores have turned to electronic gadgetry such as TV systems, electronic alarms, and lie detectors.

Citywide antishoplifting efforts have proved promising. For example, Philadelphia-area retailers combined public-service radio, TV, print, and outdoor advertising in a $100,000 campaign aimed at teen-age shoplifters, many of whom steal for the "thrill."

"Shoplifting is no joke," stressed a typical ad. "It's a serious crime. No more getting off with a slap on the wrist. Now shoplifters are being arrested and convicted. This means a criminal record. It could keep you out of college. Kill your chances for a decent job. Cause you to get a thumbs-down when you need a loan . . ."[9]

Although much of the security department's time is taken up in surveillance and apprehension of shoplifters, care must be taken that other major opportunities for pilferage are not permitted. In particular, the movement of goods through a store and to branches and warehouses leads to vulnerability at various points along the line. More to be feared here is the professional team, which can get away with a great amount of high-value merchandise if the system is not completely tight. And if documents can be falsified, such losses may not be discovered for some time.

ROLE PLAY—Covering Up Shrinkage

You are a management trainee assigned to the men's clothing department in a medium-size chain store.

[9] "Philadelphia's Way of Stopping the Shoplifter," *Business Week*, May 6, 1972, p. 58. Also advocating public exposure of shoplifters is Robert E. Wilkes, "Fraudulent Behavior by Consumers," *Journal of Marketing*, October 1978, p. 74.

One day you notice that an entire group of slacks is marked up at over two dollars more than the correct price. You call this to the attention of Bill Jericho, the experienced department manager. He tells you that the mistake will have to stand as is, "It will be too complicated to try to correct it now."

Later you find out that many such "mistakes" occur. Stockroom employees are often asked to mark up merchandise to compensate for "later markdowns in price." For this the employees receive price reductions on merchandise they want. As you become more familiar with the store, you find that other department managers follow similar practices (which are against company policy). "If we don't do this, the quarterly results will reflect unfavorably on us," you are told.

For Thought and Discussion

1. Why would this practice be against company policy? (In some firms, such action done deliberately is cause for instant dismissal.)
2. Is the real motive for these practices to compensate for markdowns?
3. What would you do at this point?
4. When you get to be a store manager, what would you do about this type of practice?

An additional responsibility of security must be continued alertness to any fire hazards or other potentially dangerous situations. Fire extinguishers should be properly serviced and positioned. More than this, employees should be instructed in their use, especially in areas of great fire hazard, such as part of the receiving room, kitchens, and the like. Smoking by employees and by customers may be forbidden in retail stores by local ordinances. Often this is not enforced, and especially at peak traffic times such as Christmas, fire precautions should be intensified.

WORKROOMS

Most large stores have a variety of workroom or manufacturing departments that do not come under the supervision of the merchandising division. Even small stores may have one or more such departments, such as an alteration or tailoring department. These departments are diverse and often require specialists if they are to operate efficiently. For example, the operation of a tire and auto service department requires an expert in this area; so does the food service operation; and employees in such departments as candy- and ice-cream–making and bakeries need competence and experience.

Unfortunately, the tendency for higher management is to rely on the "experts" for the running of these departments, and not to exercise as active supervision and control as might be desirable. Unless some follow-up is periodically made of these various operations, less-than-desirable practices may become commonplace. For example, the auto service department may be using bait-and-switch tactics to an extreme degree in their selling of tires and batteries. Repairs that are not really needed may be foisted on customers. Even used parts may be placed in cars as new. And customer relations may be gradually deteriorating.

The food or restaurant operation in particular can be a source of problems. The restaurants of a store often are bellwether departments. That is, the customer's perception of the whole store may be at least partly based on the quality, prices, and service found there. The operation of food services can be either a major profit-maker or a drain on profits. Restaurants tend to have both the highest gross margin and the highest expenses. Slight volume changes or miscalculations can play havoc. Equipment breakdowns and employee absenteeism assume more serious roles than in other departments.

RESPONSIBILITY FOR CUSTOMER SERVICES

Customer services were discussed in the previous chapter. It is worth noting here, however, that most customer services are the responsibility of the operating division (a major exception is credit, which is usually under the control division). These services should be performed as efficiently and economically as possible, just as the receiving operation should run smoothly.

Customer service is also provided by salespeople. Although personal selling was discussed in Chapter 15, another aspect of it deserves mention at this time: assignment, scheduling, and supervision of the sales staff. This relates to the larger question: how much sales staff? In the range of alternatives, the extremes are self-service with no sales personnel, and full service with enough salespeople to wait on customers promptly even during peak times. In the interests of maximum productivity, most stores compromise between these extreme positions.

We have noted before that in some department stores the buyer and his or her assistant do not actively supervise salespeople. They have many other responsibilities and often are not able to spend much time on the salesfloor. Sales supervision may then be handled by the operating division (although it sometimes is a responsibility of the personnel division). There are several factors that make the job of salesperson scheduling and supervision difficult.

1. Customer traffic typically is extremely erratic. Not only are there tremendous seasonal peaks and valleys of business, but there can also be wide day-to-day and hour-to-hour fluctuations. Consequently, a sales force adequate for peak traffic may be virtually wasted during slower periods.
2. Customer traffic is usually heavier during noon hours, because many office and other workers shop during their lunch break. But this is precisely the time when the store has its leanest staff.
3. A great difference exists between some salespersons and others in the speed of handling customers, the number that can be waited on at one time—the overall efficiency. This complicates the scheduling problem.
4. Salespeople often are young and poorly motivated (partly because of low salaries in retailing). Continual supervision is required if they are to approach customers promptly.
5. The long hours that many retailers are open make scheduling the shifts with the right blend of experienced and inexperienced workers complicated.

Although many customers do not like to be pounced on as soon as they enter a department, in most stores today a scarcity of salespeople is more annoying. Customers may grow tired of waiting for service and walk out. Just as serious is the temptation presented the shoplifter at seeing an unguarded counter.

■ Summary

Store operation is concerned with efficiency. An efficient operation is one that has lower operating costs than less efficient operations and also produces a minimum of mistakes and snafus that can result in costly efforts to correct, in lost sales, and in disgruntled customers. Store maintenance, merchandise handling, purchasing supplies and equipment for the store, workrooms, certain customer services, and store security are the major activities of the operating division. Considerable attention in this chapter has been given to store security and the twin problems of pilferage by customers and by employees. These deserve maximum attention because they can result in a horrendous drain on profits.

■ Key Terms

Blind check	Invoice
Bulk marking	Preretailing
Direct check	Receiving process
Forward stock	Store operation responsibilities
Housekeeping	Visible crimes
Interstore transfers	Willmark
Invisible crimes	

■ Discussion Questions

1. Discuss the importance of prompt handling of incoming goods in the receiving room.
2. What are the relative advantages and disadvantages of direct checking versus blind checking?
3. Under what circumstances would you advocate bulk marking of merchandise? What are the dangers here?
4. What are the advantages of having a traffic department or a traffic manager?
5. In what ways can the receiving and checking of incoming goods be speeded up? Which way do you think is the most difficult to accomplish, and why?
6. Why is the exact amount of loss attributable to shoplifting impossible to pinpoint?
7. How would you build managerial controls for a restaurant operation and an auto service department that are being managed by specialists?
8. What steps can a store take to minimize employee theft? Is it likely that employee theft can be entirely eliminated?
9. What steps can a store take to minimize customer theft? How successful are these steps likely to be?

■ Project

What steps are retailers in your community taking to lessen shoplifting? You will want to observe any signs and advertisements relating to this. In addition, you may want to query store protection people in several firms about the problem and their success in coping with it.

■   **Exercise in Creativity**

You have been transferred to a small Woolworth store on the edge of a ghetto. It has experienced serious shortages in the past. Describe as many ways as you can for tightening up security in this store.

■   **Retailing in Action**

One of the more difficult problems for a small store bent on expansion and wishing to open other stores concerns the honesty of management in such additional outlets. Since such managers will operate somewhat independently and at some distance from the owner, dishonesty and theft are more difficult to detect than under a close supervisory environment.

What would you do to minimize the probability of such management theft? (Hint: How would you design the procedures and controls so that the opportunity for theft is lessened and that prompt detection of any theft is possible?)

Cases for Part Five

THE NOR'EASTER SHOP—*Promoting and Stocking a Small Store*

Miss Gertrude Delavie conceived the Nor'easter Shop in the summer of 1976, while vacationing in a small Maine resort town. The town had been a prosperous family resort area before World War II, but had been going downhill ever since; it was located near the tip of a small peninsula and off the main stream of tourist traffic, and there was no longer any public transportation into the town (at the height of its popularity, trains carried many vacationers into town for the resorts located close by). Miss Delavie, a teacher, had spent her summers in the town for a number of years, and had become attached to it and rather saddened by its decay. By 1976, there were eight empty storefronts on the main street and the dilemma of this small hinterland town was similar to hundreds of small towns elsewhere.

Miss Delavie thought that a new business might provide some spur to the economy of the town and she decided to open a small gift shop that would appeal both to the small band of faithful summer visitors and to the year-round inhabitants. She also envisioned the town reviving in subsequent years as more people sought to escape the congestion of major vacation areas and looked for quieter surroundings. She rented and renovated an old but picturesque building, and she created a rather distinctive "character" sign to highlight the building and the new shop.

She spent the fall and winter of 1976 shopping for goods with which to stock the store. New York City, where Miss Delavie taught, of course provided ample sources of goods, but she looked elsewhere as well. She prided herself in being a knowledgeable shopper and had years of experience in collecting various artifacts and antiques for her own use. Acquiring merchandise for the store was therefore no particular problem, but rather a source of real enjoyment and challenge. The shop was to carry toys, provincial artifacts, local effort (such as hand-knitted items and carvings), costume jewelry, belts and ties, and some antiques and reproductions. Most of the items were bought to sell for under $25, although some antiques were relatively expensive.

The shop opened in June 1977, and several local teen-agers were hired to help out. Miss Delavie held an open house for the town's other retail merchants to convince them that she was not carrying any items that might compete with any of theirs, and to elicit their support and encourage them to recommend her store to their customers. This good will gesture, the fact that local teen-agers were being hired, and Miss Delavie's long support of the town, easily gained the cooperation of the other merchants.

However, sales the first year did not come up to expectations (or else the sales forecast had been too optimistic), and a loss of $1,700 resulted. Miss Delavie, in retrospect, was inclined to think her promotional efforts had been ineffective. She had shunned billboards, thinking they should be banned from highways because they detract from the scenery. She had used brochures and flyers (distributed rather aimlessly), and some local newspaper ads. She had attempted to change window displays every few weeks. No price reductions or sales were announced until the final 20 percent off September clearance sale. The store was closed down for the winter months—because for the most part tourists departed by Labor Day, and Miss Delavie had to leave for her school term by the middle of September.

A few changes were instituted the following year. One major change was longer hours. Other stores along Main Street were open until 9:00 P.M. and catered to many browsers during the long summer evenings. Miss Delavie hoped this next year that by following suit some of these customers would find their way to the Nor'easter. An optimistic omen for future business was a growing percentage of customers who had come from some distance on the recommendation of their friends and acquaintances: word-of-mouth publicity was beginning to be effective.

By the end of the 1978 season, a 30 percent sales increase had been recorded, and the store had earned a small profit.

		1977		1978
Sales		$24,800		$32,200
Beginning inventory	14,500		4,000	
Purchases	4,000		17,700	
Less ending inventory	− 4,000		− 6,500	
Cost of goods sold		14,500		15,200
Gross margin		10,300		17,000
Expenses		12,000		12,600
Net Profit (loss)		(1,700)		4,400

Miss Delavie still at this point could not afford to give up teaching and devote full time to the store (although if the store could have been operated as a year-round business, this might have been feasible). However, she seemed to be approaching a crossroads: whether to devote aggressive efforts to making the store a major success (and perhaps even expanding it, or opening another store), or to be content with a profitable summertime hobby. She recognized that she lacked an adequate business know-how, especially in budgeting and record keeping, and also in controlling her inventories. For example, the first year she had carried $4,000 worth of inventory through the winter months when the shop was closed; and by the end of the 1978 selling season, she had $6,500 worth of such unsold goods.

However, she believed her buying ability for this type of merchandise was excellent. She was especially enthusiastic about her ability to renovate junk. For example, a chair had been purchased for $9 and after refurbishing, sold for $70; similarly, an old desk that she acquired for $10 had been sold for almost $100.

Questions

1. Should Miss Delavie attempt to expand the operation of the Nor'easter?
2. How should the retailing mix be designed to be more effective? In particular, should promotional, merchandising, and pricing efforts be changed?
3. What problems do you see in this particular operation?
4. In retrospect, do you consider Miss Delavie's preopening planning and research adequate? How might it have been improved?

JONATHAN'S—A Cause for Concern: Invisible Shrinkage

Bill Scarpino, general manager of Jonathan's, a medium-size department store in a Western city, wearily massaged his forehead. He had been studying the profit-and-loss figures for the last twelve months' operation, and the results were appalling. Everything had seemed to be going along so fine. Sales were up substantially over the previous year, the gross margin was right on plan, and markdowns were even slightly below expectations. This should have resulted in a very satisfactory profit picture. Except for one thing!

"Tell Jamison I'd like to see him right away," he told his secretary.

It took Jeff Jamison, vice president of operations, a bare three minutes to reach his boss's office. "I think I know what you want to see me about. I've been looking over the profit-and-loss statement too."

"How can we have incurred a 4.2-percent shrinkage, Jeff? What on earth happened?"

"I wish I knew, boss. When I first saw these figures, I called some of my friends in several other stores to see if they have been encountering a much higher level of shoplifting than usual."

"And . . . ?"

"As far as they can tell, shoplifting is no higher than normal."

"Have you been able to analyze what departments are incurring most of the shrinkage?"

"There seems to be less pattern than one would think. Almost all departments are up considerably over other years. Two of the worst departments—and this sure surprises me—are lamps and furniture." Jamison shook his head in bewilderment.

Scarpino's frown lines deepened. "You don't mean to say that shoplifters are walking out of here carrying table and floor lamps and pieces of furniture?"

"I know, boss. It's a strange one. At first I thought the physical inventory must be fouled up—that some merchandise was not counted. But spot checking on this shows no significant discrepancies."

Scarpino sighed and turned his chair toward the window. He had never had a shrinkage problem nearly this serious in his twenty-five years in retailing. He rapidly calculated in his head: 4.2 percent of $16,000,000 in sales amounted to shrinkage of $672,000—unaccounted for merchandise and loss. What on earth could explain so much slipping away? Instead of the $500,000 profit that they reasonably could have expected, there was almost a $200,000 loss. Damn!

Scarpino swiveled his chair around. "Jeff, I want you to investigate this thing as thoroughly as possible. It must never happen again. If employees are stealing from us, if professional shoplifters are robbing us blind, we have to pin this down and eliminate it, before it happens again next year. This takes priority over everything else. Can you give me and the board of directors a complete report, both on the probable causes, and what we can do about correcting the situation in two weeks?"

Questions

1. How would you go about tracking down information on the probable causes of the shrinkage?
2. What probable causes would you speculate might account for much of this shrinkage, given the facts presented in the case?
3. How would you propose to tighten up security and any other aspects of the operation that might be contributing to this problem?

6

Controlling the Operation and Improving Decision Making

19 Retail Accounting and Expense Control

In a large firm the accounting calculations and reports are prepared by specialists. And, unless you move into the accounting or control division, you will probably not be directly involved with them. But at whatever executive level you may find yourself, you will need to understand reports and the vital information they contain. Profitability of your operation and your own success and promotion will depend on the performance depicted by accounting reports.

The small retailer has an even closer relationship with accounting. Such a merchant may have to prepare some or all of the store's reports (although bookkeeping-by-mail services have been formed to assist small merchants in handling their accounting problems and reports). Providing complete data is essential to the continued existence of the small firm. Small businesses have been criticized often for their poor recordkeeping and inadequate appreciation of the importance of sound accounting practices. For example, in studies of small-business failures, inadequate and undercontrolled financial records have been a prime contributor, and the following factors have been ignored until too late:

Diminishing cash
Declining sales
Excessive inventory
Increasing uncollectible customer accounts
Mounting debt accumulation[1]

Since you probably have had a basic course in accounting, we will cover general accounting only superficially.[2] However, there are some accounting practices that are unique to retailing. These warrant a deeper discussion, in order for you to learn certain terms and their implications, which may affect your future as a retail executive.

ACCOUNTING REPORTS

Purposes Served by Accounting Reports

Any business, retailing or otherwise, needs accounting records for these reasons:

1. Records have to be maintained if bills are to be paid on time, payrolls met, and customers billed correctly.
2. Evaluating performance of the firm, the department, and the executives responsible depends on records and statements that summarize the results of current operations and permit a comparison with previous periods and with plans.
3. Certain outsiders require complete and up-to-date financial statements: creditors, especially before granting loans; various local,

---

[1] Janet M. Pomeranz and Leonard W. Prestwich, *Meeting the Problems of Very Small Enterprises* (Washington, D.C.: Small Business Administration, 1962), p. 145.
[2] For readers not familiar with basic accounting principles, any standard beginning textbook on accounting can be consulted. For a short discussion of the major accounting statements, see "Basic Financial Statements" in the *Values of Total System Reports for Retailers* (Dayton, Ohio: National Cash Register Co., n.d.), pp. 4–10.

state, and federal government agencies, requiring reports on taxable income, sales taxes collected, social security and unemployment insurance taxes collected, and others; and stockholders, if the firm is publicly owned.

Balance Sheet

A simplified version of a *balance sheet* is shown in Table 19.1. Such a balance sheet shows the financial position of a firm on a given date. In a

TABLE 19.1   BALANCE SHEET (FOR SMALL STORE) AS OF DECEMBER 31, 1979

Assets		
Current Assets		
Cash on hand and in bank	$ 2,500	
Accounts receivable	10,000	
Merchandise inventory	42,000	
Supplies	2,000	
Total current assets		56,500
Fixed Assets		
Building less depreciation reserve	30,000	
Store fixtures less depreciation reserve	6,000	36,000
Total Assets		92,500
Liabilities and Net Worth		
Current Liabilities		
Accounts payable	10,000	
Payroll payable	4,000	
Taxes payable	4,000	
Total current liabilities		18,000
Fixed Liabilities		
Mortgage due 1985		22,000
Net Worth		
Capital account		43,000
Net profit for 1979 added to capital		9,500
Total Liabilities and Net Worth		92,500

balance sheet, the assets = the liabilities + net worth. In Table 19.1, therefore, assets of $92,500 = liabilities of $40,000 + net worth of $52,500. The liabilities, of course, are the claims of creditors, whereas the net worth represents the owner's claim on the assets of the business based on investment or equity.

Income Statement

Whereas the balance sheet shows financial condition at a given date, the *income statement* gives operating performance reflected as profitability over a given period of time. For the store manager or department manager this is an important measure of the effectiveness of merchandising operations, and bonuses and/or profit-sharing provisions are based on income statement figures. Table 19.2 shows a simplified income or profit-and-loss statement for the year 1979.

Expenses are discussed in more detail later in this chapter. The calculation of the cost of goods sold, and especially the valuation of the inventory, presents some complexities unique to retailing. Table 19.3 shows the derivation of the cost of goods sold.

In Chapter 14 we discussed some problems in taking physical inventories and the effects on profits of errors here, particularly in regard

TABLE 19.2   INCOME STATEMENT FOR YEAR ENDED DECEMBER 31, 1979

Gross Sales	$160,000	
Less returns and allowances	10,000	
Net Sales		150,000
Less cost of goods sold		90,000
Gross Margin		60,000
Less operating expenses		
Salaries	36,000	
Advertising	4,000	
Delivery expenses (other than salaries)	2,500	
Loss from bad debts	2,000	
Miscellaneous other expenses, including		
rent, depreciation, and utilities	6,000	50,500
Net Profit		9,500

TABLE 19.3   FINDING THE COST OF GOODS SOLD

Opening Inventory at Cost, January 1, 1979		33,000
Purchases at cost	$96,000	
Freight and other transportation charges	2,000	
Workroom costs and alterations	1,000	99,000
Total Cost of Goods Handled		132,000
Less closing inventory at cost, December 31, 1979		42,000
Cost of Goods Sold		90,000

to the current period and the succeeding one. This should be of deep concern to any manager or buyer, who will be judged on the profitability of the store or department. (You may wish to review this section of Chapter 14.) Here is a brief summary of the effects of incorrect inventory valuation:

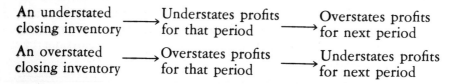

An understated closing inventory ——→ Understates profits for that period ——→ Overstates profits for next period

An overstated closing inventory ——→ Overstates profits for that period ——→ Understates profits for next period

Ratio Analysis

A number of ratios have been developed, based on balance sheet and income statement data, to reveal quickly the financial condition of a firm and its profitability. If you go to work for a big firm you will probably not be too concerned with such ratios—except for the profit on sales ratio—until you become a top executive or financial manager. If you go with a small firm or start your own business, these ratios become of vital concern.

NET PROFIT ON SALES RATIO   This ratio is the common measure of performance and profitability, and it shows what part of every sales dollar goes into profit.

$$\text{Net profit on sales} = \frac{\text{Net profit}}{\text{Net sales}}$$

From Table 19.2, this ratio is

$$\frac{9,500}{150,000} = 6.3 \text{ percent}$$

The higher the percentage, of course, the greater the efficiency and profitability of operation. However, the best measure of profitability is the net profit on net worth ratio.

NET PROFIT ON NET WORTH   This ratio provides the real measure of profitability, since the return on invested funds is what really defines profitability for any business (and not percent of profits to sales).

$$\text{Net profit on net worth} = \frac{\text{Net profit}}{\text{Net worth (or capital account)}}$$

In Table 19.1, this ratio is

$$\frac{9,500}{43,000} = 22 \text{ percent}$$

This is a high return, especially when one can realize about 5 percent from a savings account or 8 to 10 percent from corporation bonds.

CURRENT RATIO   The most widely used ratio for determining financial stability is *current ratio* and it indicates the number of times current assets exceed current liabilities.

$$\text{Current ratio} = \frac{\text{Current assets}}{\text{Current liabilities}}$$

Using the data in Table 19.1, the current ratio is

$$\frac{56,500}{18,000} = 3.1$$

A current ratio of 2 is usually considered satisfactory and indicates a strong financial position, able to withstand emergencies. A ratio of less than 2 suggests that a firm might be in danger of liquidation, since in an emergency forcing payment of all current obligations or liabilities, current assets might be insufficient (especially since the inventory is unlikely to be quickly convertible to cash).

ACID TEST OR NET QUICK RATIO   The current ratio is not the only, or even the best, indicator of liquidity, since some of the current assets (inventory, in particular) may not be easily liquidated and might suffer serious loss in valuation in the event of a sudden forced liquidation.

The *acid test or net quick ratio* is better. It is similar to the current ratio except that inventory (and any prepaid expenses, such as insurance premiums) is not included.

Using the data in Table 19.1, the net quick ratio is

$$\frac{12,500}{18,000} = .7$$

This suggests that the firm's liquidity is not particularly good; most bankers and creditors like to see 1.0 or better.

A number of other ratios are in common use. But the above are among the most important and are sufficient for our purposes here. For more detail and depth of treatment, refer to any financial management or corporation finance textbook.

Comparative Analysis

Comparing a firm's present situation and performance with its past experience, and also with that of comparable firms, provides an important measure of how the business is doing. In *comparative analysis,* the following questions should be answered:

Is the situation of the firm improving, or is it worsening?

Is the situation of the firm better or worse than the average of similar firms?

Are the operations of the firm showing improvement over previous periods, or are they deteriorating?

Are the operations of the firm better, similar, or worse than those of comparable firms?

The first two questions can be answered by examining balance sheet statistics and ratios; the last two questions by examining income statement items.

BALANCE SHEET COMPARISONS   A store (or department, or company) can note the percentage increase or decrease in various asset and liability accounts. It can determine what percentage of total assets or total liabilities and net worth each item is, and how this has changed. For example, again taking 1979 figures from Table 19.1:

| | December 31 | | Percentage | Percent of total assets | |
	1978	1979	increase	1978	1979
Inventory	33,000	42,000	27	38	45
Total assets	87,000	92,500	6	100	100

In this example, the rise in inventory indicates a worsening situation that may require some drastic action, such as markdowns and strong clearance efforts, to correct. In particular, the increase of investment in inventory from 38 percent of total assets in 1978 to 45 percent in 1979 is not healthy. If the current ratio and the acid test are compared for the two years, the decline in the store's liquidity is even more clear.

| | December 31 | |
	1978	1979
Current assets w/o inventory of merchandise and supplies	12,000	12,500
Inventory	33,000	42,000
Supplies	2,000	2,000
Total current assets	47,000	56,500
Total current liabilities	13,500	18,000
Current ratio	$\frac{47,000}{13,500} = 3.5$	$\frac{56,500}{18,000} = 3.1$
Acid test	$\frac{12,000}{13,500} = .9$	$\frac{12,500}{18,000} = .7$

The various ratios can also be compared with average or median ratios for similar stores. Such ratios are available from field offices of the U.S. Department of Commerce, from many trade associations, Dun & Bradstreet, and other sources. As well as spotlighting possible emerging problems, such comparisons are necessary to obtain credit and for other financial matters.

INCOME STATEMENT COMPARISONS   Just as the data on the balance sheet can be compared with previous periods as well as with comparable firms, so can the *income statement* items. Comparing the income and expense items is important to any retail executive, whether in a small or big firm, since the trend of performance can be measured: Are things getting better or worse?

For example, taking the following data from Table 19.2 and comparing them with the previous year:

| | Year ended December 31 | | Percent of net sales | |
	1978	1979	1978	1979
Net sales	$140,000	$150,000	100.0	100.0
Cost of goods sold	82,000	90,000	58.6	60.0
Gross margin	58,000	60,000	41.4	40.0
Expenses				
Salaries	34,000	36,000	24.3	24.0
Advertising	3,500	4,000	2.5	2.7
Delivery	2,500	2,500	1.7	1.7
Loss from bad debts	1,000	2,000	.7	1.3
Miscellaneous	5,500	6,000	3.9	4.0
Total expenses	46,500	50,500	33.1	33.7
Net profit	11,500	9,500	8.3	6.3

In making these comparisons it is best to express all items as percentages of sales, as we have done in the two right-hand columns. We can see that although sales increased in 1979, both dollar profits and percent of profits declined from those of 1978. In analyzing what happened, we note that the gross margin percentage was lower in 1979, indicating that less markup was obtained on purchases or that markdowns were higher, or both.

Comparing expenses as a percentage of net sales, we find nothing particularly different in 1979 except loss from bad debts, which has shot up 0.6 percent. This, along with the lower gross margin, is enough to reduce net profit percentage from 8.3 to 6.3.

Similar comparisons can be made using industry figures as compiled by a trade association or other stores in a chain.

INVENTORY VALUATION

The value of the closing inventory can be established in two ways. The *cost method* simplifies recordkeeping, but taking the physical inventory is more time consuming. The *retail method* is in common use, especially by large retailers, although it is not without some disadvantages. We will examine each in more detail.

The Cost Method

The cost method is easy to understand, and requires only simple record keeping. The retailer does need to record the cost of all items entering the store.

Usually the cost of each item is marked in code on the price ticket. There are many variations of such cost codes. For example, MAKE PROFIT, MONEY TALKS, and REPUBLICAN are common codes, each comprised of ten different letters that can be used in place of numbers such as the following:

$$\text{R E P U B L I C A N}$$
$$1 \quad 2 \quad 3 \quad 4 \quad 5 \quad 6 \quad 7 \quad 8 \quad 9 \quad 0$$

An item with a cost of $8.40 then would be coded CUN. A number code is sometimes used with the cost price placed in the middle of a string of numbers, omitting the decimal point. The numbers before and after the cost figures then might be used to show when the merchandise was obtained, such as in the following example for: an item costing $8.40 bought in March 1979

$$\text{number code} = 7984003$$

When a physical inventory is taken, the cost price is the one recorded.

Most firms using the cost method don't maintain a running count or *book inventory* of all changes in the value of the goods on hand. Only once or twice a year, when a physical inventory is taken, are all the costs of the stock on hand added up. On the other hand, the retail method of inventory valuation does furnish a continuous book inventory.

Why is a book inventory desirable? Without it, there is no way to determine stock shortages, since one does not know the value of the goods that *should* be in stock. A merchant knows from a physical inventory what *is* actually on hand, but as we saw in the last chapter, theft, errors, and carelessness usually result in actual goods on hand being less than book inventory.

The cost method has several other disadvantages. It is difficult to determine any depreciation in inventory value. As we know, some goods will never be sold at their original prices. The merchant fearful of overstating his inventory may use some "aging" formula according to the number of months an item has been in stock. For example, goods three months old might be valued at 25 percent less than original cost; stock six months old at 50 percent less. But these arbitrary figures may not coincide with actual selling prices that can be realized.

Frequent financial statements, monthly ones, for example, may be lacking under the cost method, since a physical inventory—usually taken only once or twice a year because of the time and expense involved—is needed to prepare financial statements, unless a book inventory system is maintained.[3]

Retail Inventory Method

In the retail method, physical inventories are taken only at the selling prices that appear on the tickets; there is no need to decipher coded costs. The storewide markup percentage of the total merchandise handled is determined and the cost value of the inventory is calculated from the retail value by means of this markup percent. Actually this is done by multiplying the total retail value of the inventory by the complement of the markup percent.

Complement of markup = 100 percent − Markup percent

For example, if the markup percent is 38, the complement is

100 percent − 38 percent = 62 percent

The following example shows how the cost value of the closing inventory is calculated by a small retailer using the retail method. A small dress merchant took her inventory at retail prices at the end of her first year of operation, and found a stock of $30,000 on hand. Purchases as determined by the invoices on file totaled $60,000 at cost. She had also calculated the retail value of each invoice, which came to a total of $100,000. The cost value of the inventory was then found as follows:

$100,000 − $60,000 = $40,000, the markup in dollars

$$\frac{40,000}{100,000} = 40 \text{ percent, the markup percent}$$

100 percent − 40 percent = 60 percent, the complement
of the markup

30,000 × 60 percent = $18,000, the cost value of the inventory

Actually, some other factors also affect the cumulative markup percent from which the complement is derived. Freight and any additional markups are the principal ones. In general, any deductions from and additions to the stock must be completely and accurately recorded at retail prices.

Calculating the cost by the retail method can be done only if the

---

[3] Some retailers try to approximate a closing inventory at cost for monthly financial statements by estimating gross margin figures. Then from sales information they can work back to an estimated inventory figure.

original markups are known, as in the above dress shop example. Furthermore, this cost should be determined for related merchandise having markups similar to what is normally handled. Otherwise the goods being inventoried might not be a representative sample of all goods handled during the period. This method is best used in stores that carry related items or that are departmentalized, as most large stores are.

THE BOOK INVENTORY OF THE RETAIL METHOD   A major advantage of the retail method is that a perpetual book inventory is easily calculated and can be used as a basis for preparing monthly accounting statements, without a complete physical count. For example, in the previous dress shop example, the inventory at the end of the period could be calculated from book figures without taking a physical count, as follows:

Merchandise available at retail	$100,000
Less sales and reductions of stock (markdowns, employee discounts)	68,000
Inventory at retail	32,000

Using the complement of the markup, the cost value of the inventory is 32,000 × 60 percent = $19,200. Notice in this example that we have assumed $2,000 shrinkage, the difference between the $32,000 inventory that the books show should be on hand, and the $30,000 that actually was on hand according to the physical count.

Such a book inventory figure is often made more accurate (when used for calculating interim financial reports) by adding estimated shortages (usually based on previous years' experience) to reductions of stock and sales.

ADVANTAGES OF THE RETAIL METHOD   There are several advantages in being able to derive a book inventory figure at any time. In the event of theft or loss of goods because of fire, flood, and so on, the book value of the goods can be determined. As noted in the above example, shortages can be accurately calculated whenever a physical inventory is taken and compared with the book figure. Being able to prepare financial statements monthly (using the book inventory figure for these assets) without having to take a physical inventory or make a crude estimation is most desirable.

The retail method has certain other advantages. Taking the physical count is much easier when goods simply can be recorded at their selling prices without having to decode to get cost prices. Another advantage may be less obvious. The inventory can be figured realistically at the present market value—the price at which the merchandise is actually being sold. If the market value has become less than when the goods were originally received, this would be reflected through markdowns into a lower selling price. In the cost method, how much to depreciate the inventory is always a problem; unless certain individual items are arbitrarily depreciated for the inventory, it may be overstated.

DISADVANTAGES OF THE RETAIL METHOD   Despite its advantages, some problems and limitations do exist with the retail method.[4] The smaller retailer may shun it because it involves more records and more effort to insure that all price changes (such as markdowns, additional markups, cancellations of markdowns), are accurately and systematically recorded. With the cost method, cost of goods and sales are all that need to be recorded. For the small merchant there is usually little gain in using the more tedious, albeit sophisticated, retail method when the store has to take a physical inventory anyway.

The retail method is essentially a method of using averages to derive the cost of the ending inventory—in this case, the average markups of the goods on hand at the beginning of the period and of all purchases received throughout the period. The assumption is that the goods remaining are a reasonable representation of all goods that had been available for sale. But if individual items have widely varying markups and rather different rates of turnover, this average figure may not be an accurate estimate of the cost price. It may present too high an inventory figure, since fast-moving, low-markup items handled throughout the year (especially if a store has used many price promotions) may not be represented adequately in the closing inventory. The cumulative markup complement then tends to increase the valuation of the inventory.

For certain departments the retail method cannot be used. It is not suitable for manufacturing or processing departments in which merchandise is changed in form or has certain labor inputs that make a selling price impossible to determine when merchandise is received. A number of such departments exist in most large stores: restaurants, bakeries, prescriptions, drapery workrooms, furniture refinishing, and

[4]The shortcomings of the cost method and retail method have led to another method of merchandising and pricing called *merchandise management accounting*. While it is beyond the scope of this book to discuss this not very widely used approach, we can note that it basically seeks to improve dollar profit (rather than percentage profit) through attempting to determine costs by individual items. For more detail, see: M. P. McNair and E. G. May, "Pricing for Profit: A Revolutionary Approach to Retail Accounting," *Harvard Business Review*, May-June 1957, pp. 108–11; Roger Dickinson, "Marginalism in Retailing: The Lessons of a Failure," *Journal of Business*, July 1966, pp. 353–58; and Harvey E. Kapnick, Jr., "Merchandise Management Accounting," in *Frontiers of Marketing Thought and Science*, ed. Frank M. Bass (Chicago: American Marketing Assoc., 1958), pp. 120–34.

the like. Usually such departments are operated on the cost method and are known as *cost departments*, even though the rest of the store may use the retail method.

RETAILING TOOL—*Exercise in Retail Method of Inventory Valuation*

Problem: You are a new department manager. When you took over the department you had a retail inventory of $16,200 that cost $12,700. During your first month you purchased an additional $3,000, which was priced into retail at $4,100. Net sales for your first month were $12,000.

Calculate: Total merchandise handled at retail
Total merchandise handled at cost
Cumulative markup percentage
Ending inventory at retail
Ending inventory at cost
Cost of goods sold
Gross margin
Stock turnover for the month

Solution

	Cost	Retail
Beginning inventory	12,700	16,200
Purchases	3,000	4,100
Total mdse. handled	15,700	20,300

Cumulative markup % $\dfrac{R-C}{R} = \dfrac{20,300 - 15,700}{20,300} = 23\%$

	Cost	Retail	
Net sales		12,000	
Ending inventory (retail)		8,300	
Ending inventory (cost)	6,391		$(8,300 \times .77) = 6,391$
Cost of goods sold	9,309		
Gross margin	2,691		(Sales − cost of goods sold)

$$\text{Stock turnover} = \frac{\text{Sales}}{\text{Average Inventory}} = \frac{12,000}{\dfrac{16,200 + 8,300}{2}} = .9796$$

Source: Problem suggested by Professor Dale E. Helwick, Lorain County Community College.

For Further Analysis Make the same calculations if purchases were
$6,200 for the first month, and you were able to achieve a 41-percent
markup of these purchases, and sales were $14,400.

FIFO and LIFO Methods of Determining Inventory Costs

If wholesale prices remain constant, there is no problem in determining
inventory costs or valuation since unit costs for the same items will not
vary from shipment to shipment. But in the situation of constantly
rising prices we commonly face today, there is the need to decide
whether the goods on hand for the end-of-period inventory should be
valued at the cost of the most recent purchases or the cost of the
purchases at the beginning of the period. The two valuation alternatives
are *FIFO* (First-in First-out), and *LIFO* (Last-in First-out).

FIFO METHOD   It has been traditional in retailing to try to sell those
goods that were bought first, before selling the newer goods. This
keeps stocks fresh and minimizes shopworn merchandise. Some merchants even insist that older merchandise be brought to the front of
displays and bins, and the newer goods placed behind them. However,
in preparing corporate earnings statements the FIFO method results in
higher inventory valuations and overstates profits for periods when
prices are rising, as shown by the following:

A buyer of men's white shirts made the following purchases during the last six months

	Quantity	*Cost*	*Total cost*
August	1,600 units	$5.00 each	$ 8,000
October	2,200	5.00	11,000
November	3,000	5.50	16,500
Totals	6,800		35,500

Average cost during the period: $\frac{35,500}{6,800} = \$5.22$

The inventory in January showed 1,400 shirts left. What should
these be costed at? Under FIFO we assume that all the earlier
shipments at lower costs have been sold, so that the cost of the
remaining 1,400 is $5.50 each, for a total inventory valuation of
$7,700.

As we will see shortly, this gives a higher valuation to the inventory
than LIFO, which would lead to a lower cost of goods and more profit.

You may reasonably ask: What is wrong with more profit—isn't this what every business is seeking? The problem is that during rising prices these profits tend to be "paper" profits and only make the firm subject to higher taxes. With replacement costs rising over those of goods purchased earlier, the paper profits in reality are absorbed in purchasing higher cost goods.

LIFO METHOD In 1947, the Internal Revenue Service approved the use of LIFO by retailers. LIFO had been used by certain manufacturers for a long time, especially in the extractive industries such as minerals and petroleum. A firm is not permitted to switch from one method to another without good reason and would hardly be permitted to switch back to FIFO just because prices had begun falling rather than rising.

Using the men's white shirts example, we can compare the two methods as follows:

	FIFO			LIFO	
Sales					
(5,400 @ $10)		$54,000			$54,000
Cost of goods sold					
3,800 @ $5	19,000		3,000 @ $5.50	16,500	
1,600 @ 5.50	8,800	27,800	2,400 @ 5	12,000	28,500
Gross margin (profit)		26,200			25,500
Ending inventory					
1,400 @ 5.50		7,700	1,400 @ 5		7,000

Therefore, when wholesale prices are rising, LIFO results in lower profits before taxes and therefore less taxes. Furthermore, the merchandise valuation for the ending inventory is lower, more conservative. When prices are falling, the opposite occurs: LIFO inflates profits, taxes, and ending inventory; FIFO now would show lower profits, lower taxes, and lower inventory value. During periods of stable prices, there is no advantage of one method over the other. But with the prevalence of inflation today, some large firms have found a significant tax break by switching to LIFO.[5]

We should note here that where LIFO is used, this is primarily for corporate accounting statements. It has little effect or consequence on departmental operations and it certainly does not change the traditional physical flow of merchandise.

[5] For more detail see: "The Facts of LIFO," *Fortune,* December 1951, p. 198; Malcolm P. McNair and Anita C. Hersum, *The Retail Inventory Method and LIFO* (New York: McGraw-Hill, 1952), chap. VIII; Maurice Moonitz, "The Case Against LIFO as an Inventory Pricing Formula," in *Significant Accounting Essays,* ed. Maurice Moonitz and A. C. Littleton (Englewood Cliffs, N.J.: Prentice-Hall, 1965), pp. 439–49.

EXPENSE ANALYSIS AND MANAGEMENT

Expenses are a necessary part of doing business. As noted in Table 19.2, expenses are deducted from gross margin to yield net profit (or loss). Unlike the other two factors affecting profits, sales and cost of goods, expenses are more directly under the control of management. This does not mean that expenses often can be eliminated or even reduced; but they can be planned and controlled in a way that maximizes the efforts of the company. In particular, judgment can be made as to whether the expenses involved in doing a certain thing, such as providing delivery, are generating enough additional sales to be worthwhile.

Classification of Expenses

Expenses hardly can be analyzed and controlled unless they are classified in some reasonable way. Although this is usually the job of accountants, certain industrywide classifications have been designated that enable a retailer to compare expenses with those of similar stores. But such comparisons can be made only if all stores classify their expenses in the same way.

The National Retail Merchants Association suggests two types of expense classifications, one for smaller stores, the other for larger. For small department stores the following seventeen-point natural classification of operating expenses is recommended:[6]

Payroll   Pensions
Fringe benefits   Insurance
Advertising   Depreciation
Taxes   Professional services
Supplies   Donations
Services purchased   Bad debts
Unclassified   Equipment costs
Traveling   Property rentals
Communications

For larger stores, it is recommended that expenses be classified according to so-called *expense center* groupings, such as the following:

[6] *Retail Accounting Manual* (New York: National Retail Merchants Assoc., Controllers' Congress, 1962), pp. 111-1 to 111-5.

General management costs
Real estate costs
Control and accounting expenses
Accounts receivable and credit expenses
Sales promotion costs
Maintenance and building operation costs

Up to twenty-three expense centers are recommended, and these can be subdivided further for large stores.

Allocation of Expenses

Once a system for classifying them has been established, expenses can be distributed to the various selling departments or, in the case of small chain stores, to the store outlets. Therein lies the prime ingredient in the attractiveness of retailing to many ambitious and confident people: retailing permits evaluating performance by *profit centers,* so that executives who do above-average jobs can be recognized quickly by the sales and profits of their semi-autonomous units.

METHODS OF ALLOCATING TO PROFIT CENTERS   Some expenses are easily chargeable to a department because they were incurred by the department and would disappear if the department were dropped. These are called direct expenses. Salaries of the employees who work in the department, the supplies they use, and advertising costs of the department are examples. Other expenses are not so easily assignable: they would exist even without a particular department. These indirect expenses include general rental for the entire building, heat and light, central office expense, receiving and marking expenses, and taxes. There are two common approaches for allocating indirect expenses to selling departments: (1) net profit method, and (2) contribution method.

Net Profit Method   Here all expenses, both direct and indirect, are assigned to the department or selling unit. Direct expenses present no problem, of course. But indirect expenses need to be assigned on a predetermined basis, such as by sales, floor space occupied, number of invoices involved, and number of pieces delivered. For example, general administrative expenses may be divided among the various profit centers of a store in ratio to the sales of those centers. The costs of the accounts payable department may be allocated on the basis of number of invoices involved. Building rent or maintenance may be divided according to sales or to floor space occupied.

However, this method of prorating expenses may cause some controversy and may not accurately reflect departmental performance. It may penalize some operations and subsidize others. For example, allocating rent expense on the basis of square feet occupied by a department would penalize an upper-floor department and work to the advantage of a main-floor department, since a main-floor location is more valuable because of greater customer traffic. The temptation in allocating indirect expenses is to do so according to sales. But this leads to some real inequities. To charge delivery expenses on the basis of sales would harshly penalize a notions or cosmetics department, which ordinarily has few deliveries, whereas a furniture department would pay only a small fraction of its true contribution to these expenses. Some of the advantages of profit centers in providing a measure of performance and a strong incentive to produce are diluted when an executive is held responsible for indirect expenses over which he or she has no control.

Contribution Method In an attempt to overcome the major drawbacks of the net profit method, a department may instead be judged on its contribution to profits and overhead. Direct expenses chargeable to the department are deducted from departmental gross margin. But indirect expenses are not allocated and deducted. Consequently, the department does not come up with a net profit but with a controllable margin or contribution, as follows:

Net sales		$200,000
Cost of goods sold		150,000
Gross margin		50,000
Direct expenses		
Selling	10,000	
Advertising	1,200	
Supervision	4,200	
Stock maintenance	2,000	
Buying	12,000	29,400
Controllable margin (Contribution)		20,600

A major disadvantage of the contribution method is that selling department managers often tend to make heavy demands for credit, delivery, and other sales-supporting services, since they are not charged for using these services. Also, since no total expense figure is derived for the department, it is difficult to judge how much markup or what price levels are really needed to achieve a reasonable profitability goal.

As a result of the inherent drawbacks of both plans, a compromise method may be used. Departments are evaluated primarily by their contribution, but indirect expenses are also distributed to the department to obtain the net profit figure.

Budgeting Expenses

If the various categories of expenses are to be kept in line, some guide or plan for present and future charges should be developed and maintained. Otherwise, expenses are incurred without any particular coordination or understanding of how they fit into the total profit picture. It is difficult to realize good profit performance without such plans. Inevitably, expenses will creep out of line, or such a penny-pinching atmosphere may prevail that sales suffer.

A *budget* is this guide or plan. It expresses in numerical terms the anticipated results of operations in the future. It is usually planned for six months or a year, and then further broken down into months and weeks. In a small store, a budget can be prepared for the entire store without much difficulty. For a large department store, not only will the entire store have a budget, but it will be composed of individual departmental or organizational unit budgets.

PREPARING THE BUDGET   Just as in preparing a household or family budget, in which one starts with expected income, so in the business budget estimated sales is the starting point. In arriving at this expected sales figure one is guided by results of the previous year as well as the trend of sales over several years. If one anticipates unusual circumstances that may affect sales, such as a labor contract running out with a strike likely, they should of course be taken into account in making the sales forecast.

The gross margin is then estimated, and the various expense categories that are under direct control of the store or department can be budgeted. If indirect expenses are to be allocated, they also can be estimated. The balance then is planned net profit. After the overall budget is prepared, it needs to be further broken down into shorter periods (months and weeks), so that progress toward the budget goals can be watched and any adjustments made as needed during the period.

It is helpful to break down expense figures into fixed expenses and controllable or variable expenses. Fixed expenses include rent, depreciation, insurance, taxes, heat, and electricity—in other words, expenses that are incurred regardless of sales. Variable expenses tend to vary with the level of sales and include salaries, advertising, and display. More judgment can of course be used in planning variable expense items.

DANGERS IN BUDGETING   Overbudgeting can occur. This may be due to top management's preoccupation with reports and sophisticated management tools. Budgeting can become cumbersome, meaningless, and unduly expensive. Even worse, it can destroy flexibility and freedom of action, so that exceeding some budgeted expense figure (even though certain profitable opportunities might be tapped thereby) would be disapproved.

To gain the most benefit from budgets, sales and other estimates should be realistic. Executives who are affected by the budget, such as department managers, should participate in its preparation. Such involvement furnishes needed input for the budgeted figures, and also tends to bring about more commitment by the executives to achieve budget goals.

Much of the success of the budget in being a reasonable guide for future operations depends on the sales forecast. If this is badly off, the whole budget will be thrown out of kilter. For example, if sales miss their mark by 10 percent, salaries, advertising, and other variable expenses will be too high, since they are often based on some percentage of estimated sales. On the other hand, if sales are much higher than planned, some lost business will probably result because the staff is too lean to handle the extra business, and the advertising budget is too low. Consequently, if basic conditions change, the budget should be revised.

ADVANTAGES OF BUDGETS   Despite dangers in unrealistic and inflexible budgets, the advantages are substantial. Budgeting tends to improve the quality of planning. It forces executives to look ahead beyond immediate, day-to-day problems. A better balance and coordination of different operations results.

Budgeting places definite goals and fixes responsibilities on individuals. Their performance in reaching these goals can be evaluated. The budget can become a strong motivating tool if the goals are reasonable and attainable.

A further advantage of expense budgeting is that it focuses attention and analysis on each expense classification at the time the budget is prepared and also when the actual costs are incurred. Any deviations can then be studied and overall efficiency improved.

Expense Comparison and Evaluation

Two comparisons are possible with the various categories of expenses.[7] If expenses are to be controlled and kept lean but not too lean, the following comparisons are desirable:

1. Comparing long-run trends in expenses, perhaps over a three- to five-year period, although some retailers do so over ten years. Such trend comparisons are best made when the expense figures are expressed as a percentage of sales, as was done earlier in this chapter.
2. Comparing the retailer's expenses with those of similar firms.

In examining trends in expenses, the retailer may find some that are rising disproportionately. There may be good reasons for this—about which not much can be done. An example would be rising salary expenses, reflecting that labor costs are rising faster than productivity (or maybe only catching up with overall wage levels). But sometimes steps can be taken to bring certain mushrooming expenses back into line. The importance of this analysis is to spot possible problem areas so that they can be examined to determine their causes.

Through trade associations, affiliated stores, and various other sources[8] a retailer can compare the store's detailed statistics with those of similar stores. These data usually are published in the form of ratios or percentage figures. From these, merchants can learn whether their expenses are out of line. Yet, an individual retailer with an expense picture that is somewhat different from those of average stores should not necessarily trim expenses to match industry norms. (Sometimes an expense, such as salaries, advertising, or insurance may show up below industry norms and suggest that the store is not sufficiently reaching for sales or is not adequately protecting its assets.) The store's situation, type of customer, or store image may dictate a different allocation of expenses. But at least attention can be focused on questionable comparisons and a justification recognized or corrective action taken.

POSSIBILITIES FOR REDUCING EXPENSES   Rare is the retail store that does not have some opportunities for expense reduction. Savings can

---

[7] Another method of reviewing a firm's own long-run expense trends by making expense comparisons with other firms is *production unit accounting.* This is used by some department and chain stores, but is too complex for discussion here. For details and implications, see *Retail Accounting Manual* (New York: National Merchants Assoc., Controllers' Congress, 1962), chap. XII.

[8] Such as National Cash Register Company, *Expenses in Retail Businesses,* rev. ed. (Dayton, Ohio: National Cash Register Co., n.d.).

result simply from instructing or motivating salespeople to economize. For example, conserving such supplies as paper bags by using proper sizes can affect considerable savings. In Chapter 18 we looked at some operating division areas where economies are often possible, either through a change in the system or through certain equipment improvements. Sometimes real detective work and ingenuity are required to find a key to reducing costs in a particular area.

Two examples of how some costs can be reduced through careful analysis of the situation follow: in one department store the floor space of the book department was reduced by 40 percent, yet the same display and counter space was maintained through an improved bookcase design, and sales did not suffer; a variety chain developed a method for simplifying and speeding up in-store sign making, so that a salesperson could assemble a counter sign in seconds, thus eliminating the expense as well as the time delays of having a separate sign department.[9] Analysis and some ingenuity can sometimes pay rich dividends. Where a store has a suggestion box in which employees can turn in suggestions for cost savings or other possible improvements, and are given recognition and perhaps monetary rewards for doing so, surprising savings may result, as well as increased employee morale.

On the other hand, keeping too tight a rein on expenses may not be best for long-term profitability. There is sometimes a thin line between penny-pinching in a damaging sense, and tight expense control. Sometimes tight expense control becomes vulnerable when, for example, an employee becomes sick and no trained replacement is available. An operation that seemed lean and profitable then becomes inadequate. (See the penny-pinching case at the end of Part 6.)

■ Summary

The necessity of accounting records cannot be escaped by any business, no matter how small: the government and other outsiders, such as creditors, require complete and up-to-date operational information. But the various records and reports are also management tools, and necessary for meeting payrolls, bills, and evaluating the performance of the firm and identifying areas on which improvement is possible and potential problems are looming. The balance sheet and income statement are vital financial reports. Various financial ratios and comparisons of operational results with prior periods help identify problems and improve decision making. The retailer must make a merchandise

[9] These examples are taken from Robert F. Hartley, "Effective Expansion of Research by Large Retailers," *Journal of Retailing,* Winter 1969–1970, pp. 36–44.

inventory valuation at the close of each period in order to determine the profitability of the business, which, as we have seen, can be done by the cost method or by the retail inventory method. The latter is more widely used, especially by large firms, because it enables the physical inventory to be taken at selling prices without having to worry about costs of each item to be inventoried. The retail method makes it possible to calculate the book inventory at any time, without waiting for a complete physical count, which is advantageous in preparing monthly accounting statements and for insurance purposes in case of loss of goods by fire, theft, and so on. Control of expenses is necessary if reasonable profits are to be insured. Budgeting or planning future expenses is an important part of sound expense control; so are expense comparisons with previous selling periods and with similar firms. In the next chapter, other tools for improving decision making are examined.

■ **Key Terms**

Acid test, or Net quick ratio	Expense center
Balance sheet	FIFO
Book inventory	Income statement
Budget	LIFO
Comparative analysis	Net profit method of allocating expenses
Contribution method of allocating expenses	Profit center
Cost department	Retail method of inventory valuation
Cost method of inventory valuation	Return on investment
Current ratio	

■ **Discussion Questions**

1. Why are carefully kept accounting records necessary for a business?
2. Differentiate between an inventory valuation based on cost and one based on retail.
3. Why is it desirable to have a book inventory?
4. Why should expenses be budgeted?
5. Although comparison of one store's expenses with those of another is a useful evaluation, what can be some dangers in using industry norms as goals?
6. What dangers are there in tightly controlling expenses?

7. What is meant by "aging the inventory"? Are there any drawbacks to this?

8. What are some of the problems in allocating indirect expenses to profit centers? How would you eliminate these problems or controversies?

9. The retail method of inventory permits insurance claims to be more easily settled. Why do you think this is true?

10. If your advertising budget for this period is all used up and you have just received a new shipment of top-selling merchandise, what arguments would you raise for being permitted to exceed your budget? As a merchandise manager who is concerned with adhering to budgets, what rationale would you give for refusing such a request?

11. Based on the income statement comparisons given in the chapter, what would you recommend for improving performance in 1980?

■ Project

Visit your local Internal Revenue Service, and also any state or municipal taxing authority, and ascertain from them what records a small retailer must keep in order to satisfy their requirements.

■ Exercise in Creativity

You are the operations manager of a medium-size department store. Because of the energy crisis and the increasing costs of energy you have been asked to present to top management for approval as many ways to curb the use of energy as possible. Of course, you cannot sacrifice employee health or customer patronage. Develop such a list as well as recommended priorities for the various alternatives.

■ Retailing in Action: Role Play

You are the manager of a lingerie department and your salary is partly dependent on the profitability of your operation. Lately you have become increasingly upset by some indirect expenses that are being charged to your department. For example, delivery expenses have been greatly increasing in the last several years, and these are charged to your department as a percent of sales. Yet your use of delivery is negligible. Similarly, you know that interstore transfers of goods by your department to branch stores are far below those of many other departments. Yet, these expenses too are charged to you on the basis of sales.

What bases for allocation would you suggest for these two expense categories? What counterarguments would you expect?

■ **Retail Math**

1. Calculate the ending book inventory at cost:

Opening inventory at retail	$40,000
Purchases	60,000
Freight	4,000
Average markup percent (on retail)	33
Sales	72,000
Markdowns	6,000

2. Allocate expenses to the Men's, Boys', and Shoe Departments, and determine their net profits:

	Men's	*Boy's*	*Shoes*
Sales	120,000	$70,000	$50,000
Gross margin	50,000	30,000	25,000
Direct expenses			
Sales salaries	15,000	10,000	10,000
Miscellaneous	10,000	7,000	7,000

Indirect expenses
   Store supplies (total of $8,000; allocate on basis of sales)
   Office salaries (total of $10,000; allocate on basis of sales)
   Rent (total of $5,000; allocate on basis of square feet of floor space, which is 8,000 for men's, 4,000 for boys', and 6,000 for shoes)
   Delivery (total of $4,000; allocate on basis of sales)

3. If, in the example of the firm described in Table 19.1, the inventory were $20,000 and the other figures were the same, how would this affect the current ratio and the net quick ratio? As a lender, how would you feel about the liquidity of the firm and the risks in lending to it?

20 The Role of the Computer and Retail Research

In today's competitive and rapidly changing environment, aggressive retailers need more information faster, and better tools to assist them in making decisions. Electronic data-processing systems (EDP) and the computer equipment required can provide voluminous data and complex analyses in seconds. Through time-sharing even small retailers can make use of such systems. Another source of information, and a sometimes unappreciated decision-making tool, is retail research.

THE COMPUTER AND RETAIL MANAGEMENT

Although the complexities of data processing and computer technology cannot be described here in much detail, some of their terms are so frequently encountered that they need clarification.

The computer requires a special language to permit the precise level of communication that is needed. Technicians or programmers have to write the instructions or programs so that the computer can solve particular problems. The most common computer languages are COBOL (an acronym for "*c*ommon *b*usiness-*o*riented *l*anguage"), and FORTRAN (*for*mula *tran*slator). Small and medium-size retailers can make better use of RPG (Report Program Generator), which requires less-sophisticated programming skills and is quicker and easier to use.

The Nature of Computer Systems

In a computer information system, data are (1) collected, (2) stored, (3) analyzed, and (4) retrieved. The simplest system is called a *first-level information system,* and it provides information for only one organizational unit, the store. A *second-level information system* involves two units or entities, perhaps a store and a warehouse, or a store and its branches, tied together. A *third-level information system* might tie the parent store, its branches, and a warehouse together. More levels are possible.

Computer information systems are further categorized as on-line real-time systems, and off-line systems. The *on-line real-time system* (OLRT) is by far the more expensive of the two. With it, various decentralized computer terminals (points where information enters and leaves the system) are in direct and continuous contact with the central computer bank, so that a dialogue can take place. For example, such a system enables a salesperson to check on a credit sale, using the salesfloor terminal to connect with the central computer, and receive an answer in seconds. Or a salesperson may check the in-stock condition at a central warehouse and receive a near-immediate response.

In the *off-line system* there are no connecting terminals with the central computer. Any dialogue has to be handled by an intermediary at the central computer. Of course, a similar credit query from the salesfloor could be made by phone to the central computer bank. But this is not instantaneous and may involve delays during busy periods.

Computer *hardware* refers to the components of a computer system. The first computers (referred to as first-generation) used vacuum tube circuitry. Second-generation hardware uses solid-state circuitry.

A clerk uses an optical scanner to record Universal Product Codes at a supermarket check-out. The UPC check-out process can be faster and more accurate than the traditional method of ringing cash registers. (Photo furnished by the Food and Drug Administration, Department of HEW)

Third-generation systems are based on integrated circuitry, which combines greater capacity and speed with smaller physical size.

The best-known forms of data input for computers are key-punched cards. But input forms have evolved considerably beyond that. Punched tape is popular, but it requires manual punching (or keyboarding) of data prior to feeding the computer. Magnetic tape requires no such manual punching; it is used by banks in the processing of millions of checks, with the data "read" through magnetic ink on checks.

The most advanced input device is the *optical scanner* or reader. It is capable of translating specially shaped characters into electrical impulses, which are transmitted to the computer. For example, such a scanner at a retail checkout counter can "read" prices on goods without a cash register being punched.

RETAILING CONTROVERSY—*Optical Scanners, the Universal Product Code, and the Controversy Over an Innovation*

By waving a hand-held electrical optical scanner over the price tags or over the little band of parallel lines that make up the *Universal Product Code* (see below), a coded description of each item is recorded not only on the adjacent point-of-sale electronic cash register, but also on a retail-control processor (at some other location) where the information on sales is available for merchandise analysis—all this can be done in seconds, including providing a totaled receipt for the customer.

0   13000 00814

The first set of five digits at the bottom of the bars identifies the manufacturer: about 100,000 variations are possible. The second set of five digits designates each of the manufacturer's products. The widths of the dark bars and the white spaces between them are different for each product. As most consumers today know, the symbol, distinctive for each manufacturer and product, is printed on the product's label.

This innovation can eliminate the costly need to mark the price on each item. As a tool for speeding check-out time, for eliminating item-price marking, as well as being an important facet in inventory control, the process seemed an unassailable innovation. But alas, it is not true.

Consumer groups protested that the code was aimed at not letting customers know the prices of the product they select until they are checked out—thereby, so the critics maintained, it would be easy to surreptitiously hike up prices. Consumer outcries reached such proportions that half a dozen states, including California and New York, passed laws forcing stores to retain item pricing. Labor, worried over loss of jobs, joined with consumers to lobby successfully for item-pricing laws.

The costs of converting a ten–check-out lane supermarket from manual registers to scanners range from $100,000 to $300,000. Denied the 20 percent in savings expected from eliminating item pricing, it becomes too expensive for most supermarkets. Although, in 1978, 170 billion packages of grocery products were coded, fewer than 40 million a week got decoded.

Other retailers, particularly Penney's and Sears, have also been testing scanners in some of their stores. Although the scanners eliminate the inaccuracies of the old-fashioned nonelectronic cash registers that had to have information manually punched, at this writing their cost effectiveness has not been definitively proven.

Sources: "Scanners in Stores Are Making Waves in the Retail Trade," *Wall Street Journal,* August 30, 1977, p. 9; "Supermarket Scanning . . . and You," *Progressive Grocer,* December 1975, pp. 56ff; "Issues '76/Scanning," *Progressive Grocer,* April 1976, pp. 66ff; and "Breaking the Code," *Forbes,* March 6, 1978, p. 50.

For Thought and Discussion

1. How would you as a retailer answer the customer's objection that the Universal Product Code (UPC) will lead to higher prices because of the high cost of scanner systems?
2. That it will prevent comparison shopping for best values?
3. That it will replace retail workers?

Retailing Backwardness in Use of Computers

Although most large retailers have turned wholeheartedly to this new technology, other retailers still shun the computer as too costly and impractical. Part of the blame for this may lie with conservative managements and their notion that retailing, and especially merchandising, is an art that cannot be improved upon even with new technology.

Part of the backwardness reflects the relatively low wages in retailing and the large number of part-time, imperfectly trained people, who are prone to make mistakes. For example, if merchandise classification information is punched incorrectly at the check-out register, the resulting computer sales analysis will be incorrect and misleading. And any computer system is only as accurate as the input.

Some aspects of the retail operation that could benefit most from the application of computer technology, such as merchandise control, often can be adapted to such a system only with difficulty and considerable possibility of error. In addition to errors from careless recording, there are other problems. If merchandise data are placed into the system from price tags, then these tags should be standardized; yet the many different sizes, shapes, and materials of merchandise handled make this no easy task. And what of the lost tag? If the merchandise data are to be placed into the system through a point-of-sale recorder, such as an electronic cash register, it takes longer to do all this recording. In a supermarket or other busy store where numerous transactions must be handled quickly, this is a serious limitation. The optical scanner or wand described earlier shows considerable promise in speeding this transaction recording as well as reducing recording errors.

The costs in switching to a computer system can be awesome. Small and medium-size installations range from $25,000 to $5 million. Most such equipment is rented, but rental charges are not small: one of IBM's smallest computer systems rents for $1,000 a month; a medium-size System 370 Model 145 rents for almost $15,000 per month. But costs do not stop with equipment purchase or rental. A year or two of study, preparation, and employee training is usually necessary prior to the selection of the equipment. Furthermore, there is a breaking-in period after the equipment has been installed. With such massive costs involved for large retailers, it is no wonder that some retailers question whether the greater flow of information is worth the cost. It should be noted, however, that smaller retailers can obtain some of the advantages of computers by renting their services for a few hours at a time instead of installing a complete system for their own use.

RETAILING ERRORS—*Too Much Data*

A computer can provide so much data and such detailed reports that it becomes wasteful. For example, one department-store corporation once furnished its executives with an eighty-one page report each morning that, for each of the company's nine stores, gave the previous day's sales by store, by department, by dollar amounts, and a comparison with the previous year-to-date and the trend of sales. It also gave a record of sales for selected items.

One wonders how many busy executives had time to review such daily compilations. How much of this information was unused?

Source: Example taken from "The Computer's Newest Conquest: Marketing," *Business Week* Special Report, April 17, 1965.

For Thought and Discussion

1. As a merchandise manager in the above firm, what data might you instruct computer services to provide for your buyers, daily, weekly, and monthly?
2. What would you eliminate? Why?

Current Uses of EDP in Retailing

Typically, the first uses of EDP in retailing were in the most routine clerical activities, where there were a large number of transactions. Payroll was often the first choice for computer experimentation because of the large number of employees, the differing number of hours worked and pay scales, the need to record the commissions of some employees, and the seasonal peaks of payrolls, which always present greater burdens to a payroll clerical staff. Computerizing accounts payable was often a next step in the progression of computerization. As the computer proved its usefulness and was gradually operated with more understanding and with fewer bugs, attention was turned to customers' accounts, the accounts receivable.

ACCOUNTS RECEIVABLE   In a typical large store with several hundred thousand customers' accounts, processing is a highly repetitive procedure and one involving the accumulation, tabulation, and billing of vast amounts of data. EDP provides much faster service than a hand operation. Floor authorization on credit sales can be speeded up and bad accounts quickly identified. Many analyses can be made of customer accounts: which ones are becoming inactive; where customers live; their characteristics such as age, marital status, and so on; and which departments are not being frequented by certain categories of customers. The computer also permits considerable payroll savings in the credit and billing department by eliminating manual operations.

But, as we have noted before, the computer can be a major source of trouble with customer accounts. Until difficulties are eliminated from the system, numerous errors in posting and billing can result. A small error in programming, for example, can cause thousands of customers to be incorrectly billed. Other customer resentment arises from the impersonality of some computer systems and the difficulty encountered in trying to get a mistake corrected.

MERCHANDISE MANAGEMENT   The use of EDP for the management and control of merchandise has been one of the more intriguing areas of retail experimentation. By receiving sales information, recorded through a punched price ticket or on a cash register, the computer can produce printed records of the current inventory on hand by units for each stock control factor, the dollar inventory, and current open-to-buy for departments. For staple goods, when the quantity on hand reaches a certain minimum level, the computer can print up a new order, and a new on-order total will be entered on the unit-control record for that item.

Fashion goods buying can also benefit from the computer. Because of the rapid feedback of sales and trend information, critical points in the sales curve of styles may be observed. This of course permits faster reordering, and items that are markdown candidates are flagged.

Retail chains in particular have found EDP of great help in merchandise management and in better coordinating warehouse stocks with stores' needs. It is possible to tie the inventory management, physical distribution, and merchandising of all units into a centralized system for better overall planning and control. In the process, leaner stocks and higher turnover can be achieved.

OTHER USES Once a firm acquires or rents a computer to perform certain clerical and/or analytical tasks, it is only natural that more and more uses are found for it. The computer can be used to forecast sales and make projections based on historical data. Analyses of many kinds are possible with a computer and can give management a better grasp of emerging problem areas as well as opportunities. For example, analyzing return goods may furnish useful information from which corrective action can be taken regarding vendors, departments, merchandise categories, salespeople, sales events, and so on. Analysis of vendors can spot those who are poorer than average in merchandise quality, delivery time, return goods, shortages, and markdowns.

Special research studies can use the computer to perform complex computations. Indeed, the presence of a computer tends to have these side effects: research studies and analyses that never would have been thought of are stimulated. A new perspective is generated in an organization when people start looking for imaginative ways to use the computer. The result is that computers tend to be put to work twenty-four hours a day. A desirable situation when one considers their high rental costs.

EDP in Smaller Firms

The benefits of a computer are not limited entirely to large firms; small retailers can rent time for their needs. This is known as *time-sharing,* and commercial computer centers are rapidly spreading throughout the country to service those firms too small to afford their own installations. Such service companies supply programmers, operators, and computer time on an hourly basis.

Unfortunately, many small retailers are ignorant both of the advantages EDP can offer their operation and of its availability at a practical cost. Retail trade publications and trade associations are striving to motivate and educate smaller retailers toward the computer. The firm with the prompt sales, merchandise, and customer information that the computer can provide has a decided advantage over a firm that does not have computer service.

Probable Future Role of Computer Systems in Retailing

Technological advances are occurring rapidly. We briefly looked at one earlier in this chapter, the optical scanner, which, with the Universal Product Code for the food industry, may have the potential to greatly increase the efficiency of retailing. The optical character recognition, font A (OCR-A), promises the same for general merchandise stores. The cost of these systems, of course, does not make them practical yet for smaller retailers, and there is still considerable consumer and governmental agitation against the idea of not having individual items price marked. Point-of-service (POS) terminals, which can capture sales data and funnel it to central processing points where all kinds of analyses are possible, are becoming more and more sophisticated and useful.

Another technological advance that is also on the threshold of significant contribution to retailing is *electronic funds transfer* (EFT). Let us briefly examine this. With a terminal at the point-of-service on the retailer's premises tied in with a financial institution, credit authorization, credit card transactions, data capture, check verification, and funds transfers could be quickly handled. Such an instant authorization of credit would make more feasible the acceptance of credit by supermarkets, where delays for credit authorization at check-out counters now virtually preclude credit. EFT also will reduce the "float," the time that elapses between the presentation of a check and the debiting of funds to the retailer's account. Since a retailer may face a number of different credit cards from customers, there can be the drawback of needing several terminals linked to different banks; this will probably eventually be solved by having a universal card developed for EFT. Consumers also stand to benefit from EFT by having automatic payroll and check deposits, eliminating check writing and the costs of mailing bill payments, as well as reducing the risk of checks being lost or stolen. However, the consumer also loses the several days' float before his or her check is processed and the money transferred to a merchant's or payee's account.[1]

---

[1] For more information on EFT, see "EFT: The Unanswered Questions," *Chain Store Age Executive,* February 1977, p. 19; "EFT Banking into Clouds," *Chain Store Age Executive,* February 1976, p. 19; and Anthony M. Dilorio, "EFT Today," *Computer Decisions*, March 1976, p. 21.

It is true that some retailers' first exposure to computer technology has left a bad taste; they have been oversold on the benefits of EDP and have had too elaborate and costly a system installed. Just as the eighty-one-page daily report mentioned earlier in this chapter was a waste, so many other possible applications of the computer may not be of much practical value. The costs of a system certainly must be carefully weighed against the benefits; however, the possible competitive advantage that the firm with the more sophisticated system might have should not be overlooked.

Retailing may be at the threshold of a new stage of computer utilization, with the traditional bases for making decisions by intuition and subjective judgment being repudiated. The computer also holds the promise of serving as the foundation of corporate long-range strategic planning through better use of the information and analyses it can provide.

RETAIL RESEARCH

Just as some retailers have lagged in adopting computer technology, so many have lagged in using the type of marketing research techniques long standard in nonretail firms. A number of studies through the years have found that even among the largest retailers in the United States, only a bare majority have a research department. Furthermore, most retail research departments have apparently played a minor decision-making role, being concerned with such routine, clerical-type activities as information exchange with noncompeting stores, forms control, supervision of unit stock controls, comparison shopping, and checking of staple stocks.[2]

Purpose of Research

Research is a staff activity for management. It provides information and analyses to aid judgment and decision making. In its ultimate role,

[2] For example, Joseph M. Goloff, "Research in Retailing," *Journal of Retailing,* Summer 1949, pp. 80–85; Theodore D. Ellsworth, "Research Management in Large-Scale Retail Firms," (Ph.D. diss., Graduate School of Business Administration, New York University, 1955); Robert F. Hartley, "Effective Expansion of Research by Large Retailers," *Journal of Retailing,* Winter 1969–1970, pp. 36–44; Dik Warren Twedt, ed., *1973 Survey of Marketing Research* (Chicago: American Marketing Association, 1973); and Peter M. Golding, "The Use of Marketing Research by Large General Merchandise Retailers" (MBA thesis, Bernard M. Baruch College of the City University of New York, 1975).

research becomes part of the intelligence system of a firm (along with the computer system), used to conduct special inquiries into problems and also into immediate and long-term opportunities.

Although a researcher can and often does make recommendations as the result of a particular study, they can be accepted or rejected. The researcher makes no decisions. But this has been one of the misunderstandings of some executives regarding research: they have feared that it would take away some of their authority and reduce their importance. For this reason some have tended to oppose it.

Just as computer technology is gradually being seen as a necessity in order to compete effectively, so attitudes toward the role of research in retailing are gradually becoming more positive. The functions of research are being expanded, although few retailers are using it to its full potential. The alternative to research is decision making by hunch, by intuition, by the "way we have always done it."

Limitations of Research

Research is no panacea. The most we generally can expect is to improve the "batting average" of decisions. For example, instead of a 60-percent chance of making a correct decision on a particular matter, the use of research may raise the probability to 75 percent. Although it seldom points to the optimum solution, increasing the odds in the decision-maker's favor can be an important contribution—especially where the stakes (in investment and/or manpower time) are high.

Research can be expensive and time-consuming, which rules out rigorous research efforts for many retail problems. A single decision may not be of sufficient importance to warrant the time and expense necessary to research the alternatives adequately. This is especially true with many advertising and merchandising decisions.

For other problems, the tools and techniques to make valid research conclusions are not always available. Some of the factors involved may be intangible and incapable of precise measurement. Attempts to find optimum allocations for promotional and merchandising efforts are examples of such problems. For example, how does one determine what is the most effective advertisement or the best amount to spend? The answers to these questions are elusive.

A further limitation on many research efforts is that the data obtained must be interpreted to discover what they mean and what should be done about them. Customer preference statements and information on customer characteristics do not directly point the way to actual sales. Imagination is still needed to turn this information into sales.

But far from being discouraging, such limitations make the art of decision making more challenging. Any tools that can shed some light ought to be welcomed. In the following section, the more fruitful areas for retail research are discussed.

Areas for Research Application

The greatest potential for using research lies in the following areas:

Merchandising and promotional decisions
    Customer analysis
    Sales analysis
    "Sick department" studies
    Vendor analysis
    Determining customer attitudes and satisfaction
    Analysis of market share and sales potential
    Advertising research
Personnel decisions
Operational problems
Store location studies
Long-range problems and opportunities

Some of these research activities involve special problem-solving studies; others, such as sales analysis and analysis of market share are more continuing activities. As such, research can perform a dual role: (1) it can help detect trouble spots, and (2) it can provide the thorough and exhaustive investigation needed to determine the cause of the trouble, as well as suggesting possibilities for corrective action.

What are some trouble spots that need detection? The following are typical:

Fewer customers
High percent of walkouts (without buying)
Lower average sale than previously
Declining sales per square foot
Slow turnover of merchandise
Decreasing charge-account sales
Market share—either for the entire store or for certain departments—
    declining, as competitors grow stronger

Unsuccessful promotions (or an increasing percentage of unsuccessful
    ones)
Increase in customer complaints (and perhaps in returned goods)
High personnel turnover
Decline in number of qualified job applicants
Slow collection of receivables

These trouble spots may be typical of the entire store or of only
certain departments. But they are often symptoms of illness. Especially
if trend information is available—that is, does a comparison with data
from previous periods indicate that the situation is growing worse or
improving?—such symptoms need prompt and probing analysis. We
can seldom wait for them to go away; they tend instead to get so much
worse if left unattended that no effective remedy may be possible. Lost
customers are not easily won back, and a store's deteriorating image
and reputation are often lasting.

Not all of these trouble spots or symptoms will necessarily be detected by research. Executives should become increasingly aware of
some. But executives tend to be too close to the operation, too involved with day-to-day problems to see a deteriorating situation until
too late. Certain continuing analyses or sensors and the greater objectivity that a research department provides can help detect trouble spots
before they become too serious.

RESEARCH FOR MERCHANDISING AND PROMOTIONAL DECISIONS
Merchandising and promotional problems and decisions concern the
basic ingredients of retail success: Who are our customers? How can we
best appeal to them? How well are we doing this?

Customer Analysis   Plotting where customers live provides valuable
information about the characteristics of a store's present customers.
This data can be tabulated by census tract areas (or also by the larger
postal zip code areas). Since a census tract is small, it usually consists of
rather similar dwellings and people. The population characteristics of
specific census tracts—such as average income, age, family size, education, car and home ownership—depict the characteristics of a store's
customers who live in the area. This information is readily available
through census data. From such an analysis, a store can determine if it is
appealing to its target customers. It can discover if there are gaps in its
coverage or appeal. If, for example, it is not appealing sufficiently to
young families, this fact may warrant additional outlets or changed
promotional and merchandising efforts.

A customer analysis can easily be made by sampling charge accounts and by plotting the addresses of a small percentage of charge customers on a map of the city. However, it is desirable to ascertain if there are significant differences in cash and charge customers. If such differences are suspected, it may be necessary to analyze store deliveries or to sample cash saleschecks. The latter can be done simply by obtaining names and addresses of customers making cash purchases and plotting some of these.

Important to all such studies is trend information—information on how things are changing, whether a store is gaining or losing certain types of customers. Studies that are conducted once and never again may allow a slowly deteriorating situation to go unnoticed and uncorrected.

Sales Analysis   Sales by merchandise classifications can yield valuable information. We have noted before that a store's and department's sales can be evaluated in relation to national and regional sales of the same merchandise lines. Such an analysis can pinpoint areas for further study. This may justify a "sick department" analysis. A further objective of sales analysis is to uncover possible latent demand and to identify new consumption patterns and subtle changes in the social or economic environment.

Sick Department Analysis   A sick department analysis is a problem-solving task concerned with analyzing certain aspects of poorly performing departments. All aspects of such a department may be examined: its merchandise, personnel, service and operations, attitudes of customers toward it, status in terms of competition, physical layout, and so on.

Vendor Analysis   Vendors can be evaluated for such performance factors as contribution to markdowns and markups, amount of returns and allowances, delivery time, and dependability. Some vendors may be eliminated or commitments with them reduced. Data necessary for such analyses usually are routinely recorded on various forms. To be usable, they need to be centrally accumulated. As mentioned before, computerized data processing is making this more feasible for large retailers.

Customer-Attitude Survey   Small store owners and managers have little difficulty keeping attuned to customers' attitudes since they necessarily are in close contact with their customers. Determining how satisfied customers are with a store becomes much more difficult for larger retailers. In order to maintain a better contact with customers, it has long been customary for buyers and even high-level executives to spend a certain amount of time on the salesfloor, observing and receiving customer comments. Yet, such information is seldom representative and unbiased. More systematic and objective techniques are desirable, such as described in the following Retailing Tool.

RETAILING TOOL—Measuring Customer Satisfaction

Customer attitudes and satisfaction with a store, its service and merchandise, can be determined objectively in several practical ways. Interviews can systematically be made of people leaving the store or department without a package in order to determine what is at fault. A follow-up of customer opinions of garment alterations can bring with it significant responses regarding the entire store. Short questionnaires can be particularly effective when inserted in packages or with monthly credit billing statements. These should be simple and can be used to solicit specific or general comments or complaints, such as in the following sample:

Sample Customer Satisfaction Questionnaire
(for use as package or credit statement insert)

Your opinion of our service and merchandise is important to us. So that we may serve you better, please answer the following questions:

	Very Satisfied	Satisfied	Dissatisfied
How satisfied are you with			
your purchase(s)?			
the service?			

If dissatisfied, in what way? _____

How often do you shop at our store? _____

What particularly do you like about it? _____

_____

Can you suggest how we may serve you better? _____

_____

An ideal measurement technique should provide, at low cost, responses from a high percentage of customers who have had recent experience with the store and its merchandise and service. Unfortunately, even a simple consumer feedback system will generally be used by only a small proportion of customers, and some of these will be the chronic complainers. However, with this flaw in mind, the assumption can be made that those customers with the more serious complaints or strongest feelings are more likely to return the questionnaire; those customers reasonably satisfied are less likely to respond. Such feedback then is usually far superior to the distortions and biases of other customer-satisfaction measurement techniques, such as opinions of executives and other personnel, customer complaints, and financial results, the weaknesses of which were discussed in Chapter 4.

Sometimes a customer-attitude survey can yield unexpected results, results that may reveal the need for major policy changes. For example, Woodward & Lothrop, a major department-store corporation in Washington, D.C., as a matter of routine interviews customers at all newly opened stores. A store was opened in a predominantly working-class lower-income area, and because of its location, the merchandising of this branch was altered to carry more budget-priced goods, with self-service emphasized. However, the interviews showed pronounced negative reactions to this modification. Woodward & Lothrop quickly adapted to the expressed preferences of its customers and revamped the store to be more conventional in merchandise and service.

Sources: For more ideas and specifics on measuring customer satisfaction, see: Ernest R. Cadotte and Larry M. Robinson, "Measurement of Consumer Satisfaction: An Innovation," *Journal of Marketing,* July 1978, pp. 8 and 58; H. Keith Hunt, ed., *Conceptualization and Measurement of Consumer Satisfaction and Dissatisfaction* (Cambridge, Mass.: Marketing Science Institute, 1977); Ralph L. Day, ed., *Consumer Satisfaction, Dissatisfaction, and Complaining Behavior* (Bloomington, Ind.: Indiana University, 1977).

For Thought and Discussion

1. How would you handle the possible biasing due to chronic complainers in customer-attitude surveys?
2. Would you rely entirely on customer statements of what they like or dislike about a store? Are there other investigations you might want to make?

Customer-attitude surveys are not widely used by retailers. This can be a serious deficiency. In general, such studies have the following advantages:

1. Trends can be established for customer satisfaction and disatisfaction, and problem areas detected early before they become serious.

2. Good will can be fostered by continuing efforts of this kind, and the store may gain a reputation as "the store that cares."
3. Unfilled customer needs and wants may be revealed, and opportunities to be tapped by innovation may be suggested.
4. The time and expense involved in such surveys can be modest.

RETAILING TOOL—Studies of Customer Walkouts

Related to surveys of customer attitudes are customer-walkout studies. A walkout takes place when a customer enters a department or a store, ostensibly for the purpose of making a purchase, and then does not. Analyses of walkouts are perhaps the most neglected research in retailing. Many merchants are quick to make excuses for customer walkouts: "They were just looking." "Customers today insist on comparison shopping." "Consumerism makes them hard to please. . . ."

The sheer percentage of such walkouts is shocking, however. Several studies have found median walkout figures to be slightly over 90 percent. If this figure could be reduced to a still miserable 85 percent, sales would increase 50 percent without the addition of a single customer. A new operating statistic, called by one consultant a Traffic Conversion Ratio (TCR), seems worth developing. By observation, periodic studies can be made of the number of customers buying out of every 100 customers entering the department or store. Although such a TCR would vary with departments, when used over a period of time, the trend of ratios could pinpoint a worsening situation early so that corrective action could be taken. Furthermore, such data showing a poor TCR could be a challenge and a motivating tool for salespeople and management alike to improve customer service.

Source: George C. Engel, "Semantics and Profits," *Stores,* May 1972, pp. 14, 33.

For Thought and Discussion   What recommendations could you make to a department manager to help lessen the percentage of walkouts?

Sales and Market Share Analysis   A firm's sales by merchandise lines can be analyzed relative to those of other firms in its market area. For example, a department store may find its share of total men's clothing sales in its market to be 12 percent. For multiunit firms, sales of merchandise lines can be compared from one market to another. If one outlet has 12 percent of the market in one area and another outlet only 6 percent, further analysis may be desirable to ascertain the reason for this difference. Standards and goals for measuring sales productivity, sales penetration, and for market planning can also be developed. Such studies also should be made on a continuing basis so that change as well as present position can be measured.

Advertising Research A single retail advertisement seldom warrants research efforts, and the time element usually would permit only superficial research at best. But where research is applied to a series of promotional efforts, it can be worthwhile. Testing of slogans may result in a theme that can be used in all advertisements for an entire season. Finding the best circulation for advertising circulars, and determining the most effective medium to reach certain types of customers are worthwhile objectives for research efforts.

Centrally recording data about customer reactions to promotions and related information, such as weather, and about competitors' efforts can narrow the uncertainty of advertising decisions and isolate significant factors. Empirical information on advertising effectiveness usually is diffused throughout the organization. Each buyer or division may accumulate some data, but this is fragmented and often sporadic. A more systematic accumulation of data is desirable.

RESEARCH FOR PERSONNEL DECISIONS As we have discussed before, high employee turnover is a common problem in retailing. Research can aid in selecting people with more stable characteristics. A weighted application blank, in particular, can help select better people for numerous sales and clerical jobs. This is not particularly difficult to develop, but it does require a systematic analysis of the characteristics that differentiate good and poor workers.

Other possibilities for research in the personnel area include: developing programmed learning manuals for training purposes, conducting morale surveys, validating tests to be used for hiring purposes, evaluating the house organ, and making salary comparisons with other companies.

RESEARCH FOR OPERATING PROBLEMS Studies to improve methods and procedures can range from special projects, such as improving the flow of goods through receiving rooms, docks, stockrooms, and other merchandise-handling bottlenecks, to routine assignments like service checks and forms control. The possibilities are almost limitless in this area. Usually the value of such research is evident almost immediately in greater efficiency and reduced time and expense of operation.

STORE LOCATION STUDIES   Decisions regarding location of new branches and outlets carry considerable risk; certainly the stakes are high in the investment required. It is not surprising that some research efforts are involved in most location decisions (although a major supermarket chain until a few years ago did no location research, relying instead on the arguments and persuasion of real-estate developers), but their range and exhaustiveness vary greatly. A serious weakness of most store-location research is that no follow-up studies are made to evaluate the correctness of past decisions. Such lack of follow-up prevents development of more meaningful criteria for location research.

This innovative roof of translucent fabric can reduce energy costs for lighting, heating, and air conditioning by as much as 40 percent. At the same time, it imparts an exciting shopping environment. Retailers need to look for ways to reduce costs and increase the appeal of the shoppers' surroundings. In the process, they can gain a competitive advantage. (Photo courtesy of Owens-Corning)

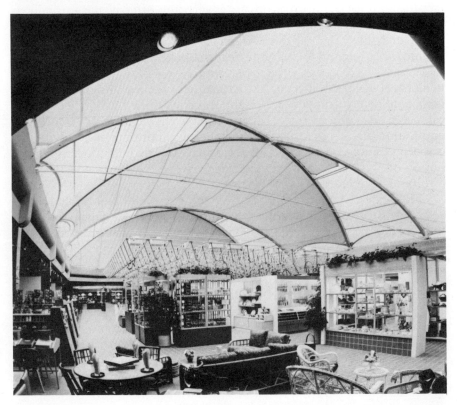

LONG-RANGE PROBLEMS AND OPPORTUNITIES   We will look at the need for long-range research and at the contribution it can make to innovation within the firm in the last section of this chapter. Most retail research can be described as "fire fighting," being totally concerned with day-to-day problems. This immediate type of research is more tangible and the value is more evident to management than studies dealing with long-range problems and opportunities. Yet there is danger in failing to adapt to changing market conditions. We do not have to look far to see examples of major firms that failed to adapt as quickly as conditions warranted. Two examples of such firms are Woolworth's long insistence on sticking with 5¢ and 10¢ items, and Penney's reluctance to offer credit. Both static positions in a changing environment undoubtedly caused these firms millions in lost business. Often changes occur so gradually that they go undetected until serious inroads have been made by innovative competition.

Organization for Retail Research

Research can be done informally or formally. An individual executive or his or her assistant can do some fact-finding and analysis for certain decisions. However, such busy executives seldom have the time or the research skills to make any exhaustive studies. Many large retailing firms have a special department assigned to do research. Where continuing analyses are used to develop trend data, such a formal responsibility is necessary. A research department, in addition to doing various continuing analyses, is available for special studies for top executives, as well as helping with fact-finding activities for department managers and buyers as needed.

Not all of what we think of as research activities necessarily is done by a research department. In some firms analytical studies, especially of the continuing kind, may be spread to four or five departments, such as industrial engineering, comparison shopping, unit control, long-range planning, store development, and systems and procedures.

Outside research and consulting firms may sometimes be called in, even when a firm has its own research department. Some of these consultants are far more expert and specialized than store personnel can be. They may be called in for special problems such as store location, merchandise handling, and organizational changes.

The small retailer will hardly have a separate research staff. Except for extraordinary problems or decisions, such a merchant cannot afford the expense of outside consulting help. The small retailer, however, being in closer contact with customers and supposedly better attuned to the nuances of the market place, can constantly sift and analyze information about customers, their reactions to various merchandise, and promotions. And if the small store is not alert to competition—what other stores are doing and what changes may be forthcoming—it will be vulnerable.

Statistics and information provided by trade associations, wholesalers, and sometimes manufacturers can be helpful. Many metropolitan areas supply data to all interested parties on population composition and trends, economic projections, planned highway changes, shopping center statistics, and other relevant material.

LONG-RANGE RESEARCH AND INNOVATION

The idea of long-range research is rather fascinating. It has an aura of promise, a hint that the future may be plotted. And long-range research can help a firm (1) to cope better with competitive changes, and (2) to seek change—that is, to anticipate and to adjust more quickly.

Long-range research implies a formal and systematic study of matters that are not of immediate importance. Innovative thinking, on the other hand, suggests a more informal, perhaps creative, approach. Innovative thinking may mean being receptive to new ideas or being willing to imitate, and it may involve genuine creativity. As such, it can come from a variety of sources both inside and outside the organization, such as an executive, a committee, a consultant, a trade association, a manufacturer, even a customer. Creative ideas may be developed by brainstorming, by accident, from exposure to other operations, even from sitting in an armchair.

Marketing research is compatible with innovative thinking. Although it may contribute an idea, more likely its role is to explore feasibility of ideas and alternatives. The research department can work closely with idea generation and testing, especially of long-range plans. It provides some important characteristics for this: objectivity that comes from detachment from operating responsibilities; its members have the expertise and familiarity with research techniques and sources of information needed for comprehensive studies. Furthermore, the questioning mind of the researcher counters the kind of thinking that tends to develop where tradition and the hunch-based-on-experience are customary aids to decision making.

Unfortunately, many retailers are shortsighted and do not encourage long-range research. The payoff of such research is often impossible to determine, at least in the near term. But where perspectives can be enlarged and fire fighting reduced to a minimum, the opportunities for long-range growth are enhanced.

■ Summary

Computer technology has greatly broadened the horizons of retail operations. Faced with thousands of transactions in a single day, large retailers have found their accounts payable, accounts receivable, payrolls, merchandise control, and sales forecasting to be greatly facilitated. Newer utilizations of computer technology, such as optical scanners and the Universal Product Code, optical character recognition, and electronic funds transfer, offer intriguing promises of things yet to come. Even small retailers can benefit from the new technology through time-sharing. Retail research also offers intriguing promise, although its potential has long been overlooked by many retailers. Almost all retail functional areas can benefit from problem-solving studies, or from more continuing activities such as sales and market share analyses. Trouble spots in particular can be researched so as to determine the reasons they exist and suggest possibilities for corrective action. Long-range research can enable those progressive firms utilizing research an opportunity to be more innovative and to take better advantage of future environmental changes.

■ Key Terms

Advertising research	Optical scanner
Computer languages	Sales analysis
Customer analysis	Sales and market share analysis
Customer-attitude surveys	
Customer-walkout studies	Second-level information system
Electronic funds transfer (EFT)	Sick department analysis
First-level information system	Third-level information system
Hardware	
Off-line system	Time sharing
On-line real-time (OLRT) system	Universal Product Code
	Vendor analysis

■ Discussion Questions

1. What is the difference between a first-level information system and a third-level system? Under what conditions would you recommend each?

2. What is the difference between an on-line real-time system and an off-line system? Which would you recommend for a medium-size

(sales $15 million) department store? For a large furniture store? Why?

3. In what way has the caliber of the retail work force possibly impeded the adoption of computer systems in retailing?

4. What do you think is the major advantage promised by an optical scanner?

5. Can you offer an explanation of why research has lagged so much in retailing as compared with manufacturing?

6. How can a vendor analysis be useful to a retailer? A customer analysis?

7. Would you recommend that all retailers with sales over $100,000 have a separate research department? Why or why not?

8. How would you research how many of your present customers would continue to shop in your store if you moved a mile and a half away, into a new shopping center?

9. In what way would a decline in number of qualified job applicants suggest that something is wrong with the store? Does a lower average sale per customer necessarily mean that something is wrong?

■ Projects

1. Visit the major retail firms in your area and ask to talk to the research director (if there is such a position). Try to determine the type and extent of formal research being conducted by the store (or company). If there is a research department, find out how big it is and how long it has been in operation. Perhaps you can draw some conclusions about the state of research among retailers in your locality.

2. Visit several commercial computer firms that provide time-sharing geared to providing service for those firms too small to afford their own installations. Determine the costs involved and what advantages such services can provide for the small retailer.

■ Exercise in Creativity

You think it would be desirable for your store to have a profile of present customers—that is, the characteristics of the average customer. How would you recommend that the research department go about determining this? What practical usefulness would such a profile have?

■ **Retailing in Action: Role Play**

1. Sales for a housewares department are down for the last six months (compared to the same six months a year ago). As the research director of the store, you are asked to ascertain how many lost sales the department is experiencing and what the reasons are. How would you design research to determine this?

2. Your department-store corporation is asking for a major research effort to help top management with location-policy decisions. Specifically, the question to be answered is: Would it be better to open future stores in shopping centers (as is being done now), or in freestanding sites at some distance from other stores? How would you suggest this problem be approached?

3. You are the credit manager of a large department store. For several years the accounts receivable (customer charge accounts) have been computerized. Although there were some bugs at first, you are rather certain they have been eliminated. Of course, there will always be the problem of employee error in recording data for the computer.

   You have just been called into the office of the general manager.

   "Jane, how is the computer operation going?" he asks.

   "Fine, Bob," you reply.

   There is a slight pause. He frowns. Then he says quietly, "At the last meeting of my wife's bridge group several people said they had been billed incorrectly. Now, Jane, I understand these things can happen—after all, your people are only human. But the problem is that customers can't get mistakes on their bills corrected without a helluva time. What do you propose to do to remedy this situation? I want your written recommendations on my desk by tomorrow."

   What recommendations would you make? How would you propose to implement them? Do you think the experiences mentioned indicate a widespread problem?

Cases for Part Six

PENNY-PINCHING

Frank Pfeiffer managed a chain store in a small town in central Minnesota. This was his second store, and the size (sales $600,000) made it a distinct advancement from his first store, which barely did $300,000. Frank was considered by many of his fellow managers in the Dakota-Minnesota-Iowa district to be a comer; and indeed his performance in his first store and his rapid advancement—in only two years—seemed to confirm this. Accordingly, some of the other store managers occasionally sent one of their management trainees to talk to Frank, perhaps for inspiration, but certainly for advice on what they might expect when they got their first store.

Stan Pomeranz was such a trainee. He had been with the company for above five years and could reasonably expect to be promoted to manager of a small store in a few more years. He was, however, becoming somewhat impatient, and his boss thought a day spent with Frank Pfeiffer might curb any inclinations toward restlessness.

Frank quickly got to the point with Stan. "First of all, let me say that I'm not content to stay here. I want to manage a class-A store [one having over $1 million in sales] in a few more years. But I'm not going to work as hard as I did with the first store."

"How was that?"

"I knew in this business that you start out with a small store in a small town, and gradually work your way up to bigger stores and bigger towns. I didn't mind that idea—my family and I rather like small towns. And as a chain store manager you can be a big fish in a small pond. But that first store and town, Stan . . . it was just too much. The town was on the edge of a desert in South Dakota, the streets—even the main street—were not even paved and we were constantly contending with dust. The worst thing, though, was the school . . . the students were mostly poor kids who couldn't even read, and the teachers could care less. Well, I made up my mind that if I had to work like a dog to get my family out of that town, I would."

After handling a customer adjustment, Frank went on. "I knew there was little likelihood of increasing sales enough to get a promotion out of that depressed community. But maybe I could achieve a sparkling profit performance."

"Are there that many expenses you can really control?" Stan asked.

"More than you might think, if you're willing to take over more duties yourself. For example, I got by without any stockroom help. I did the receiving and checking of merchandise myself. I pared the sales and office salaries to the bone, again by doing some of this work myself. I was able to effect savings with store supplies such as boxes and bags, and used low-wattage light bulbs in the stockroom. I found we could get by with lower temperatures in the winter and still be comfortable enough for customers. During the slow times of the day, such as before noon on weekdays, I didn't turn on all the lights. On weekday evenings, especially in the winter when there were few people on the streets, I wouldn't turn on the window lights. Furthermore, I refused to make any donations to little league, or scouts, or any of the many organizations that are always soliciting merchants. Oh, I made a few contributions out of my own pocket, but nothing was charged to store expense. You know, there are a lot of ways you can cut costs if you carefully analyze the situation. Anyway, my store had the highest net profit percentage of any store in the district, and the net profit dollars were higher than for some stores twice as large. Although I had virtually exhausted myself, we got a good promotion and a much nicer place to live."

"Did you cut out advertising?"

"No, but I was very careful about how I spent the money. I found that a smaller ad could be just as effective as a larger one. And I did quite a bit less advertising at Christmas than had been done before, since I figured people would be shopping anyway."

"With such a skeleton crew, what did you do if someone got sick?"

"Ah, that can be a real problem," Frank admitted.

Questions

1. Is there any way that the risk of unexpected illnesses and absences in a highly pared down work force can be met without disrupting job performance?
2. Do you think Frank was wise in all of his efforts at reducing expenses?
3. Would you personally be inclined to do as Frank did?
4. Do you think his superiors would approve all of these efforts at expense cutting?

THE NEED FOR RETAIL RESEARCH

It had always bothered Beth Aronson that her company made so many decisions without adequately researching them. She had come a long way in the last ten years with Pruitt Stores, and she knew it and was grateful. And yet, they did so many things wrong, or at least made so many decisions without due reflection or analysis. Now as the director of planning she should be in a position to initiate better-considered actions than had been the rule in the past.

Part of the problem was that her firm, a regional supermarket chain in Mississippi and Alabama comprised of some 67 stores, was relatively successful. In several major cities in which they did business they were the dominant food marketer. But now they were thinking of acquiring an ailing supermarket chain on the West Coast that was almost as big as they were, but with minuscule profits. At the last executive committee meeting, Beth had argued against making the acquisition decision so quickly, and succeeded in getting it tabled for a few weeks. But she knew that the Costello brothers who owned the company were anxious to make the move. They had a Messianic complex, she sadly reflected, that they could do no wrong, that because they were successful in the South, they had only to wave their hands and any sick enterprises they acquired would immediately achieve profitability. And Beth couldn't buy this reasoning.

"We need to do more research into this firm, as well as concerning the business and competitive environment in California," she had told Ted Costello, the executive vice president.

"What kind of further research can we possibly need?" he had countered. "After all, we know the financial picture of the firm, and we also know that because of their problems we can pick them up at a real bargain. What else is there to research? These opportunities do not come around all the time, you know."

"Give me just a few weeks to research the situation in the California market," she had pleaded. "After all, this is a big move for Costello enterprises."

Ted Costello was not a quiet man. He had come up through hard work and a willingness to take risks, and he and his brother were recognized by friends and opponents alike as being aggressive and vigorous. Now he slammed his fist on his desk. "Very well, Beth. I'll give you a week to come up with data and recommendations for this acquisition. We'll make a decision at that time whether or not you have developed any useful information."

Questions

1. What kind of information do you think should be developed for an acquisition decision of this kind?
2. How can such information be obtained?
3. Develop a research plan for acquiring all desired information for such an acquisition decision, recognizing the time constraints.

Glossary

Absolute Sale   Buyer and seller agree to a sale with no restrictions on either party.

Accessories   In women's apparel departments and stores, items, such as gloves, hosiery, handbags, jewelry, and perhaps shoes, that are considered subsidiary to dresses, coats, or suits.

Account   A formal record, maintained for bookkeeping purposes, of a particular type of transaction.

Accounting Period   The period of time for which an income statement is customarily prepared, usually one month or one year.

Account Payable   A liability to a creditor.

Account Receivable   A claim against a customer.

Acid Test Ratio   A ratio that indicates the ability of a firm to meet its current obligations. The formula is:

$$\frac{\text{Cash } + \text{ receivables } + \text{ marketable securities}}{\text{Current liabilities}}$$

A ratio of 1 to 1 is usually considered satisfactory.

Adjustment   The handling of a customer's complaint to the satisfaction of both the customer and the store.

Advance Order   An order placed well in advance of the desired shipment date, often to obtain a lower price by enabling a supplier to maintain production during slack periods.

Advertising Allowance   A commitment made by a vendor to share with the retailer advertising costs, up to a certain percentage of purchases, for specific items.

Anchor Store   A large store in a shopping center that serves as a major customer-attracting force for the center. Also called generator store.

Anticipation   A discount added to the cash discount when a bill is paid before the expiration of the cash discount period.

AOG   Arrival of goods. With AOG terms, the cash discount granted if payment is made within the number of days specified is calculated from the time the goods arrive on the retailer's premises. This is primarily to accommodate distant customers.

Approval Sale   A sale made to a customer subject to later approval, thereby giving the customer unlimited return privileges.

Arrears   A charge account behind in its payment is in arrears.

Assortment   The range of choice offered a customer within a particular classification of goods, such as the range of prices, colors, styles, patterns, and materials.

Automatic Reorder   The reorder of staple stocks on the basis of a predetermined minimum stock and specified reorder quantities. This can be done, without the buyer's intervention, manually by reorder clerks or automatically by a computer system.

Back Order A part of an order that is not filled by the vendor on time, but is expected to be shipped as soon as the goods are available.

Back-up Stock Additional merchandise available in the stockroom or warehouse. This is especially important for fast-moving goods.

Bait and Switch Promoting a product at an extremely low price to attract customers to the store where they are switched to other higher-priced goods either because the advertised item is not available or is hardly suitable.

Balance Sheet A statement of a firm's financial position at a given point in time, usually the end of the month or year. Balance sheets are broken down into assets, liabilities, and ownership equity.

Balanced Stock Merchandise in the assortment characteristics that will satisfy customer wants while keeping the investment in inventory reasonable, in keeping with store objectives.

Basic Stock List The planned assortment for staple items that are to be continuously maintained in stock.

Better Business Bureaus Voluntary, nonprofit organizations formed by local business firms to encourage honesty and fair dealings with customers.

Bill of Lading A receipt issued by a carrier (transportation company) for merchandise to be delivered to a customer. The bill of lading acts as evidence that the carrier has received the shipment. In air shipping this is called a waybill.

Blanket Order A general order placed with a vendor that does not specify sizes, colors, and so on, with these to be furnished later.

Blind Check A procedure wherein the receiving room checker counts and lists the items being received without the aid of the invoice or purchase order.

BOM Inventory Beginning-of-month inventory.

Book Inventory A compilation of the amount of inventory on hand according to a perpetual inventory system by which the value of incoming goods is added to previous inventory figures, and the value of outgoing goods is deducted.

Boutique A small shop or department selling rather unique merchandise with an imaginative and informal decor and personalized service. From the French word meaning "little shop."

Branch Store An outlet store usually administered by executives of the main or parent store.

Brand A name, mark, symbol, or combination of these that identifies the product or service offered by a seller.

Brand Image The impression that a consumer has of a particular brand.

Brand Loyalty The degree of consumer preference for one brand over its close substitutes.

Brand Share The market share that one brand has.

Breadth of Merchandise Offering The number of different lines and departments that a store offers.

Breakeven Point The point at which the sales volume will just cover costs. Below this point, the firm will incur a loss; above it, a profit.

Broken Lot A less-than-standard unit of sale.

Budgeting An expense plan for the forthcoming time period that is in accord with the sales forecast.

Bulk Marking Placing the price only on original shipping containers or other bulk packages, without marking individual units of merchandise.

Buying Group An organization representing a group of noncompeting stores formed for the purpose of buying merchandise and sharing market information.

Buying Plan A breakdown of the dollar open-to-buy figure for a department or merchandise classification into the number of units to buy for specific merchandise categories.

Buying Power Index A weighted average of each market's strength, as measured in terms of its proportion to U.S. retail sales, U.S. population, and U.S. effective buying income. The BPI is published annually in *Sales and Marketing Management's* Survey of Buying Power. It provides an estimate of the ability of an area to purchase consumer goods of rather broad appeal.

Carrier Any commercial transportation firm that moves merchandise from a vendor to a purchaser.

Carrying Charges Interest charged on the unpaid balance of a charge account.

Carry-Outs Merchandise carried from the store by the customer, thereby saving on store delivery costs.

Carry-Over Merchandise Goods left over from one selling season to the next season.

Cash Discount A reduction in price offered the buyer for paying before the due date. The most common cash discount is 2 percent, which is generally given for payment within the first 10 days of a 30 day obligation.

Catalog Showroom A retail outlet that provides merchandise depicted in catalogs, usually at discount prices.

Census Tracts Small, fairly homogeneous geographical areas of a city, usually between 3,000 and 6,000 people, for which detailed population characteristics are available.

Centralized Adjustment System A centralized desk or office for handling customer complaints, adjustments, and refunds.

Centralized Buying Buying done exclusively by a central merchandise staff, usually located at corporate headquarters. This is a common organizational arrangement with some chains.

Chain An organization with two or more centrally owned stores handling substantially the same merchandise.

Cherry Picking Selection by a buyer of only a few items from a vendor's line, presumably the best items.

Classification Grouping goods into a homogeneous category, such as men's sport shirts, women's dressy blouses, and jogging apparel.

Clearance Sale A price reduction and sale of slow-moving, shopworn, broken-sized, and end-of-season goods.

Clipping Bureau An agency that clips and provides files of news stories and advertisements to clients.

Close-out Merchandise offered at reduced prices because of incomplete stock or a discontinued line.

COD   Collect on delivery. The buyer must pay for the goods at the time they are delivered.

Collection Period   A ratio of accounts receivables to the number of days it takes to obtain that volume of sales, an indication of the size of customers' accounts.

Commissary Store   A retail outlet owned and operated by the military to sell food and related products at greatly reduced prices to military and some governmental personnel and their dependents.

Committee Buying   Buying decisions made by a group of people rather than a single buyer; this is most likely to be encountered in multiunit firms.

Common Carrier   Transportation firms required to accept shipments from any party, and to maintain regular service over established routes and at published rates.

Community Shopping Center   A medium sized shopping center, usually with total floor space of 100,000 to 300,000 square feet, with a variety store or junior department store as anchor tenant, and with a trading area comprised chiefly of the community in which the center is located.

Comparative Balance Sheet   Two or more balance sheets for the same operation over two or more time periods, set up with parallel columns for easy comparison of changes.

Comparative Prices   Promotional prices shown in advertisements or signs comparing present prices with previous prices or prices goods are estimated to be worth.

Comparison Shopping   Visiting competing stores to ascertain prices and operational and promotional efforts.

Complement of Markup Percentage   One hundred percent less markup percentage on retail.

Confirmation of Order   The official order of a store for goods. It is made out on the store order form and usually countersigned by both buyer and merchandise manager.

Consignment   Goods shipped to a store for which title remains with the vendor until they are sold.

Consumer Cooperative   A marketing organization owned by consumers and operated for their benefit.

Consumerism   An attempt by consumers—sometimes organized, often not—to exert influence in the marketplace to uphold rights regarding safety, information, quality assurance, and so on.

Controllable Costs   Those costs that within certain limits can be controlled by the organizational unit, thereby capable of being raised or lowered according to management expectations and planned strategy of operation.

Convenience Store   A retail store offering consumers geographical or time convenience, but usually charging higher prices for goods.

Cooperative   An establishment owned by an association of customers and giving patronage dividends based on the volume of expenditures by members.

Cooperative Advertising   Advertising in which the vendor offers to pay some portion (usually 50 percent) of the cost that the retailer incurs in advertising the vendor's items in a local medium.

Cost Department   A manufacturing or processing department that operates on the cost method of accounting within a retail store. Examples are bakery or candy-making departments, or certain departments selling mostly services, such as restaurants, and beauty parlors, where no inventories at retail value are carried.

Cost Method of Inventory   The determination of inventory on hand by marking the actual cost on each price ticket in code and computing inventory value using these unit cost prices.

Coupons   A sales promotion technique in which cards or cut-outs are distributed to consumers and can be redeemed for certain items at reduced prices.

Creative Selling   A kind of high-level selling in which customers' needs and wants are ascertained and goods are persuasively presented to best satisfy those needs and wants. Creative selling is the opposite of routine order taking.

Credit   In retailing, obtaining goods now in exchange for a commitment to pay later. *Credit* is also an accounting term denoting an entry to the right side of a ledger.

Credit Bureau   An organization that provides credit information on prospective as well as current customers.

Credit Limit   The maximum amount of credit allowed to be outstanding on each individual customer account.

Cross Selling   The practice of individual salespeople selling in more than a single department, thereby achieving a larger total sales transaction with each customer and providing more convenience to customers.

Cumulative or Maintained Markup (or Markon)   The difference between the total cost and the total original retail value (before markdowns) of all goods handled to date. This is usually expressed as a percentage of the cumulative original retail.

Cumulative Quantity Discount   A reduction in price based on total amount purchased during the period, rather than any single order.

Current Asset   Cash and other assets readily convertible into cash within, usually, one year. Inventory and accounts receivable are current assets.

Current Liability   Short-term debt to be paid within a relatively short period, usually one year or less.

Current Ratio   The ratio of current assets to current liabilities.

Customer Service   Fringe benefits provided by a store to induce customer patronage. Some services may be free while others may not.

Custom Selling   Contacting a customer in the home and customizing merchandise to order rather than selling off the rack.

Dating   Setting the time limits for when retailers should pay for their purchases.

Dealership   Conventional type of franchise giving a dealer or franchisee an exclusive marketing territory.

Decentralized Adjustment System   A procedure whereby customer complaints, adjustments, and refunds are handled at the selling department involved.

Delicatessen Buying   Sampling many different lines of merchandise, but with little depth in any line. Not a recommended merchandising technique.

527

Delivered Price A quoted price that includes delivery costs to the F.O.B. point.

Delivery Period The normal time between placing an order and actual receipt of goods.

Demographics The distinguishing characteristics of a particular population in terms of age, educational level, occupation, income, and so on.

Department Manager The person responsible for the operation of a department. In a department or specialty store, this person may be responsible for both the buying and selling of merchandise; in chain organizations and where the buying and selling functions are separated, the department manager may primarily be responsible for the sale of merchandise purchased by the central buyer.

Department Store A retail store offering a large variety of goods under one roof, having at least twenty-five employees and merchandise including apparel, appliances, home furnishings, and dry goods.

Department Store Ownership Group An organization with department store outlets that are individually merchandised and operated subject only to broad central policies and controls.

Depreciation The loss in value of an asset with the passage of time and use.

Depth The number of sizes, colors, and other choices offered within a single merchandise line.

Derived Cost Inventory The cost of goods on hand as determined from their retail value by using the complement of the initial markup percentage.

Direct Buying Buying directly from a manufacturer rather than going through a middleman.

Direct Check Checking goods received against the vendor's invoice to ensure that quantities billed equals quantities received.

Direct (Controllable) Expenses Expenses that can easily be directly allocated to various departments, store outlets, or other profit centers. These expenses are usually controllable to some extent, and would be eliminated if the profit center were discontinued. Common direct expenses are sales salaries, buying expenses, departmental advertising, and supplies used.

Direct Selling Organizations Nonstore retailing firms that distribute their products door-to-door.

Discount Store A store that operates on a lower margin than conventional stores selling the same type of merchandise. It is usually self-service, offers only limited customer services, and emphasizes its discount prices.

Distress Merchandise Goods presumably marked down drastically for rapid disposal, often because of a financial emergency; it may also be merchandise reclaimed by a vendor for lack of payment.

Dollar Control Analyzing and planning sales, stocks, markdowns, and markups in terms of dollars rather than units.

Drop Shipper (Desk Jobber) A wholesaler who arranges shipments of goods directly from manufacturer to retailer. While he takes title to the goods, he does not handle them.

Early Markdown A markdown taken early in the season while demand should still be strong.

EDP Electronic data processing. The use of computer technology in the processing of data.

EFT Electronic funds transfer. A computerized banking system to speed up credit transactions, verification of checks, and funds transfer.

Elasticity of Demand A ratio of the percentage change in quantity sold (or demand) to the percentage change in price. The more demand is affected by price, the more elasticity there is.

Employee Discount A discount on the retail price offered to employees, usually practiced by general merchandise retailers but not by food retailers.

EOM End of month. This term can refer to an end-of-month inventory; it can also refer to end-of-month dating, in which the cash discount and the net credit periods begin on the first day of the following month, rather than on the invoice date.

Equity The interest of the owner in a business, subject to the prior claim of creditors.

Exclusive Distribution An agreement by a vendor to sell goods in a particular geographical area only through a single retailer or a selected few.

Expense Control Classifying and analyzing expenses so as to achieve the most profitable spending.

Extra Dating A type of deferred dating in which the purchaser is allowed a certain number of extra days before the regular dating period begins. For example, 2/10–30 days extra means that the buyer has 30 days plus 10 days, or 40 days, from the invoice date in which to pay the bill and still take the cash discount.

Eyeball Control A means of controlling stock and reorder points by visually examining stock to see how much is on hand.

Factoring Selling accounts receivable to financial institutions so that the retailer can have more liquidity.

Fad A style that becomes popular quickly, but is likely to disappear just as quickly.

Fashion A style that is currently popular.

Fashion Cycle The tendency of all fashions to increase in popularity, to plateau, and then decline.

Fifth Season A midwinter selling season, primarily characterized by clearance sales, white sales, and some demand for cruisewear.

Fill-in An order to complete or replenish the stock on hand.

FIFO First-in, first-out. A method of valuing inventory in which it is assumed that the oldest acquisitions were disposed of first, so that what remains represents more recent purchase costs.

Fixtures The various furniture pieces, tables, and counters that are necessary to stock and display merchandise for sale in a store.

Flagship Store Usually, the downtown store that serves as the buying headquarters of a department store and its branches.

Flash Report A prompt and unaudited report giving the day's sales figures to management.

Flying Squad A group of salespeople who are flexible and available to fill in in a number of different departments whenever needed.

F.O.B.   Free on board. A shipping term that signifies that the shipper retains title and pays all transportation charges to the f.o.b. point.

Forced Sale   A sale of goods at less than market price carried out because of an urgent need to liquidate the merchandise assets, often to meet the demands of creditors.

Forward Stock   Merchandise on the selling floor, rather than in a reserve stockroom.

Franchising   A contractual arrangement in which the franchisor extends to independent franchisees the right to conduct a certain kind of business according to a particular format.

Free Flow Layout   A layout characterized by irregular, curving aisles, a deliberate absence of uniformity, and considerable open space.

Free Goods   A type of concession sometimes offered by a vendor in lieu of a special discount. For example, the retailer may be offered one extra item free with every dozen purchased.

Free-standing Location   A site that is not adjacent to other retailing businesses.

Fringe Sizes   Sizes at the end of the assortment, either very large or very small, which face a very limited demand.

Full Line   Stock in a particular classification of goods that is offered in all reasonable sizes, colors, styles, fabrics, and so on.

Future Dating   Designating a specific future date when the terms of sale become applicable. For example, in the case of goods shipped in August with the terms 2/10, net 30 as of November 1, the discount and net period would be calculated from November 1.

Garnishment   A court-directed allocation of all or part of the salary of a debtor who is delinquent in paying bills.

Good Will   Intangible assets such as customer loyalty and a good reputation.

Green River Ordinances   Municipal ordinances regulating house-to-house selling, canvassing, or soliciting of business.

Grid Layout   A store layout in which fixtures and aisles are uniform and usually in a rectangular pattern.

Gross Margin   The difference between net sales and total cost of goods sold.

Gross Sales   Total sales before deducting any returns and allowances, but after subtracting trade discounts and sometimes cash discounts.

Guarantee (Warranty)   An assurance by the seller that if merchandise proves to be defective or does not perform as specified the problem will be corrected.

Hand-to-Mouth Buying   Buying in the smallest feasible quantities for immediate requirements.

Hard Goods   Hard goods comprise mostly hardware, home furnishings, furniture, and appliances, as opposed to soft goods which are textiles.

Head of Stock   The person in large, departmentalized stores who is responsible for the maintenance of reserve and forward stocks. This person is at the first executive or training level and usually reports to the assistant buyer.

Heart Sizes   The sizes in most demand and carried in the greatest depth.

House Brand   One brand carried for all items in a line.

Housekeeping A function that involves keeping the stock in the most sales-presentable form possible.

House Organ A paper or magazine published by the employer and distributed to employees.

Hypermarket A combination discount store, supermarket, and warehouse under one roof. A European phenomenon, hypermarkets are characterized by merchandise stacked as high as ten feet and super-low discount prices.

Impulse Goods Items that are frequently bought as a result of unplanned decisions.

Incentive Pay A compensation plan whereby the salesperson is given extra pay according to sales production.

Income Statement A financial statement showing the profit and loss results of a period's operation. Sometimes called a *profit and loss statement*.

Independent Store A retail store owned individually and not part of a chain, branch store, or ownership group.

Indirect Expenses Those expenses that would exist even if the department, store, or other profit center were eliminated, for example, administrative overhead.

Initial Markup The difference between the cost of merchandise and the original retail price placed on goods. This is often expressed as a percentage of the retail price.

Insolvency An inability to pay debts as they become due. Bankruptcy results when the liabilities exceed the fair value of the assets available for their settlement.

Installment Sale A sale in which a series of payments is made over a period of time.

Institutional Advertising Advertising designed to promote good will for the firm rather than immediate and specific product sales.

Institutional Sales Selling merchandise to such institutions as hospitals, schools, and restaurants.

Intensive Distribution Distributing a product to as many retailers as can be induced to handle it. A classic example of intensive distribution is cigarettes.

Inventory The value of merchandise on hand at cost or retail.

Inventory Valuation A determination for accounting and tax purposes of the proper value of goods on hand.

Invoice A document prepared by the seller itemizing all articles bought and the amount due for payment.

Job Analysis A study of a job to determine requirements, duties, and responsibilities.

Job Lot Promotional grouping of merchandise by which some vendors dispose of end-of-season surpluses and incomplete stocks.

Jobber Another word for wholesaler.

Key Items Best-selling items that are in great demand.

Keystone Markup Double the cost price, which results in a markup on the selling price of 50 percent.

Kickback An unethical practice in which a vendor gives a buyer some payment or gift in return for business.

Landed Cost An item's invoiced cost plus transportation charges.

Layaway A purchase plan by which an item is bought with a downpayment. The store retains possession until the full payment is made, usually in a series of installment payments.

Leader Pricing Pricing certain goods at attractively low prices in order to draw customers into the store, where they may buy other goods at regular prices.

Lead Time The time expected to elapse between order placement and receipt of goods.

Leased Departments An area within a store operated by a company other than the one that operates the store. Usually customers are not aware of this arrangement.

Liability An obligation to pay a certain amount to another party, usually because of some contractual arrangement.

Lien The right of one person to satisfy a claim against another, usually by legally seizing the other's property as security.

LIFO Last-in, first-out. A method of valuing inventory in which it is assumed that the most recent purchases are disposed of first, thus making the ending inventory valuation based on the oldest purchase costs.

Line of Credit Permission granted by a financial institution for a firm to borrow up to an established amount.

Liquidation Converting goods and other assets into cash in order to satisfy the claims of creditors.

Liquidity A determination of the solvency of a firm measured by how readily assets are likely to be converted into cash.

List Price The gross billed price, subject to a trade discount. Sometimes the list price is the retail price suggested by the manufacturer.

Loading Increasing the amount charged to a selling department for a purchase by the difference between some arbitrary cash discount rate set by the store and the cash discount actually obtained from the vendor.

Loss Leader An item that is sold below cost in order to generate store traffic.

Mail-Order House A firm primarily engaged in selling through the mail.

Maintained Markup The difference between the cost of goods sold and net sales.

Mall Shopping Center A group of stores that face a mall or pedestrian shopping area, with parking surrounding the store concentration.

Manufacturer's Representative A selling agent who sells the goods of a number of client manufacturers, usually noncompeting, in a given area.

Markdown A price reduction from the previous retail price of an item.

Markdown Cancellation An upward price adjustment offset against a former markdown. The most common example is the restoration of the previous selling price for goods that were marked down for a specific sales event.

Markdown Control An evaluation of markdowns taken. The aim is to determine causes of excessive markdowns and to institute corrective action if needed.

Market Share The sales position of a firm, department, or category of merchandise relative to other firms in the same geographical area, usually expressed as a percent of total sales for that market.

Markup (or Margin)   The difference between merchandise cost and the retail price.

Markup Percentage   The difference between cost and retail, expressed either as a percentage of cost, or, more commonly, as a percentage of the selling price.

Mass Merchandising   The type of merchandising practiced by self-service stores that display and sell all kinds of merchandise, usually at discount prices.

Memorandum Buying   An arrangement in which the merchant has the right to return unsold items to the vendor or pay for the goods only after they are sold. However, the title of the merchandise passes to the buyer, who assumes all risks of ownership.

Merchandise Classification   Subdividing a selling department's inventory, purchases, and sales figures for the purpose of closer control.

Merchandise Control   Monitoring the movement of inventory investment in light of customer demand and investment constraints.

Merchandise Marts   Showrooms for manufacturers and importers where buyers can inspect many lines conveniently.

Merchandise Mix   The breadth of merchandise carried by a retailing firm.

Merchandising   The planning involved in trying to have the right merchandise, at the right place, at the right time, in the right quantities, and at the right price, even though the optimum will probably never be achieved.

Middlemen   Firms that stand between producers and consumers. Most often middlemen are thought of as wholesalers, but retailers are also middlemen.

Missionary Salespersons   Representatives employed by manufacturers to help retailers arrange sales promotions, handle any problems, and in general promote the manufacturer's goods. The main function of missionary salespeople is not to write up orders, but to assist the sales efforts of retailers.

Model Stock   A planned assortment of goods balanced according to anticipated customer demand.

Multiple Pricing   Combining several units of a product as a package of one, such as 4 for $1. This method gives the appearance of a better value, but sometimes it actually involves a higher markup than when only one item is sold.

National Brands   Manufacturers' brands that are promoted and distributed nation-wide.

National Retail Merchants Association (NRMA)   A national trade association formed to promote the interests of department, chain, and specialty stores.

Neighborhood Shopping Center   A usually small strip of stores, predominantly of the convenience and service type, often with a single supermarket as a major tenant, and servicing chiefly the surrounding neighborhood.

Net   The amount realized after the various costs, discounts, or return goods have been deducted from the gross figure, as in net sales, net alteration costs, net purchases, and net profit.

Net Worth   The owner's equity in the firm, computed as the difference between assets and liabilities.

Never-Out Merchandise Key items and best sellers that should always be in stock because of perpetually high customer demand.

Nonselling Departments Departments in a store involved in activities other than direct selling of merchandise. The receiving department is an example.

Nonstore Retailing A type of retailing in which consumer contact is made outside the retail store. Telephone shopping, catalog sales, and door-to-door selling are examples.

Notions Department A department carrying small sundries, such as needles, thread, ribbons, and the like.

Obsolescence Loss of value of assets because of technological or style changes.

Occupancy Costs Expenses related to the use of property, such as rent, utilities, and general upkeep.

Odd Lots Broken lots or unbalanced assortments of discontinued merchandise reduced for clearance.

Odd Pricing Pricing at other than even prices, such as $4.98 rather than $5.00.

One-cent Sale Selling two items of a certain line of merchandise for one cent more than the price of one.

100 Percent Location The retail site that has the greatest exposure to the store's target customers.

One-Price Policy Charging all customers the same price for the same merchandise.

On-Orders Goods that have been formally ordered, but have not yet been received. Such on-orders must be considered in calculating open-to-buy.

Opening Inventory Value of the goods on hand at the beginning of an accounting period.

Open Order An order without a price or delivery stipulation placed with a resident buyer when merchandise is needed in a hurry. The resident buyer is given authority to seek out and negotiate the best merchandise and terms.

Open-to-Buy (OTB) The amount of merchandise that may be ordered for delivery during a control period. It represents the difference between merchandise on hand and on order, and planned requirements.

Open Stock Patterns of china, glassware, and silverware sold either in complete sets or in separate pieces.

Operating Expenses Costs incurred in operation of the business, as opposed to outlays to finance the business.

Optical Scanner A device that permits the reading of prices and other merchandise information by machine. Optical scanners are used with the Universal Product Code for mechanized check-outs in supermarkets.

Other Income Income from sources other than the sale of merchandise, such as interest and dividend income.

Out-of-Stock A lack of a particular item of merchandise that is commonly carried.

Outsizes The extremes on any size scale that are seldom ordered in depth, although certain stores, such as Lane Bryant, specialize in offering such goods to the hard-to-fit.

Overage The amount by which a physical inventory exceeds the book inventory figure, as opposed to a shortage.

Overbought The condition in which the buyer has made purchase commitments in excess of the planned purchase allotment for a particular time period.

Overhead Another word for fixed expenses, those that do not vary with sales.

Overstored The condition in which a given area has more stores than are needed to satisfy consumer demand.

Parasite Stores Stores that live off traffic generated by other stores.

Patronage Motives The reasons why customers shop in various stores.

Performance Appraisal Evaluating the work performance of an individual, often by comparing results against predetermined standards or goals.

Periodic Inventory Determining the specifics of the goods on hand by periodic physical counts.

Perpetual Inventory Keeping track of the specifics of the goods on hand by continuous recording of the movement of items into and out of the stock.

Physical Inventory The value of the merchandise on hand at a given time, based on an actual count.

Piece Goods Fabrics that are usually sold by the yard.

Pilferage Stealing a store's merchandise.

Planned Stock The physical inventory a store wants to have on hand at a given time for a certain department, merchandise classification, price line, or other control unit.

Point-of-Purchase Display Merchandise displays and signs at the point where the goods are sold to the customer.

Premarking Price marking on goods done by the vendor before goods are shipped to the store.

Premium Something given free or at an especially attractive price to promote the sale of a product.

Preretailing Placing selling prices on a copy of the purchase order at the time the goods are bought.

Price Guarantee An inducement offered by a vendor to encourage larger orders and commitments made in advance of the selling season. The vendor agrees to reimburse the retailer for any losses incurred should the market price for the merchandise fall between the date of purchase and the normal selling period.

Price Lining A limited number of price points at which a particular category of merchandise will be offered for sale.

Price Zone A range of prices within which to maintain an assortment. For example, a buyer may want to maintain a good assortment of dresses between $35 and $50, but the particular price line within that zone may change with market conditions.

Private (or Distributor) Brands Brands of retailers or other middlemen, in contrast with the national brands of manufacturers.

Professional Discount A discount granted to people in a particular field or profession, such as special discounts given to physicians by drugstores, or to contractors by hardware stores and lumber dealers.

Promotional Allowance An amount given by a vendor to a store to cover all or part of the store's cost of advertising or displaying the vendor's goods.

Puffing An exaggerated claim that adds to a product's appeal. Such unsubstantiated claims are now vulnerable to governmental scrutiny and possible restrictive action.

Purchase Order The written document made out by the buyer, and often countersigned by the merchandise manager, authorizing a vendor to deliver a certain quantity of specified goods at a designated price.

Push Money (PM) A special bonus given salespeople for selling particular goods. PM is used as an incentive to push slow-selling or overstocked merchandise.

PX Post exchange. A general-merchandise store operated by the armed forces offering low prices for military and diplomatic personnel and their families.

Quantity Discount A discount based upon the quantity of goods purchased that is used as an inducement to buy a larger amount.

Quota Used in compensation plans as a sales goal or target that must be reached before any commission is paid.

Rack Jobber A wholesaler, operating primarily in supermarkets and other self-service outlets, who takes over the maintenance of certain categories of merchandise, such as notions and hardware, to relieve retailers of tedious stockkeeping and reordering.

Receivables The accounts receivable (or customers' accounts) owned by a business.

Regional Shopping Center The largest class of shopping center, usually having several major department stores, 50 to 150 or more smaller establishments. Regional centers draw from a wide geographical area.

Repossession The recovery of merchandise sold to a customer who has failed to complete payment for it.

Reserve Stock Stock kept in the stockroom until needed on the selling floor.

Resident Buying Office A facility maintained in the central market—usually New York City—that provides contacts, information, and guidance in purchasing for its retailer clients.

Retailing Mix The controllable variables of an operation that a retail firm can combine in many alternative ways to arrive at a strategy for attracting customers. Such variables include price, promotion, merchandise assortment, and service.

Retail Method of Inventory A method of determining the cost of an inventory by summing the goods on hand at current retail prices and translating this retail total into cost by using the complement of the cumulative markup percentage.

Retail Reductions The total of markdowns, employee and customer discounts, and stock shortages.

Return on Investment (ROI) The true measure of the profitability of any venture, ROI is determined by dividing net profit by the amount of investment.

Return per Square Foot The amount of sales contribution that is obtained from a square foot of selling space. For a department, this is calculated by dividing total sales by the number of square feet of space comprising the department.

Returns and Allowances The dollar total of goods returned, either to vendors, or by customers.

Revolving Credit A credit plan whereby the customer can pay a minimum amount per month plus a finance charge, and continue adding new purchases to the account up to the credit limit.

ROG Dating Receipt-of-goods dating, which denotes that the discount period begins, not from the invoice date, but from the date the customer receives the goods.

Routing The selection of a preferred mode of transportation for shipping goods from the vendor to the store, usually specified by the store.

Runner A style, usually in fashion apparel, for which there are many repeat orders.

Sales Forecast An estimate of sales for a specified future period, taking into account the contemplated selling efforts and economic conditions.

Sales Promotion Marketing activities geared to stimulating sales, usually those other than advertising and personal selling, such as displays, shows, and demonstrations.

Sampling A type of sales promotion in which a customer is given a small amount of the product, such as a taste of a food product.

Scrambled Merchandising Selling merchandise that is unrelated to the traditional and regular lines carried by the store. A common example is supermarkets carrying nonfood items.

Seasonal Dating A type of advance dating allowed on seasonal merchandise to induce early buying of such goods, thereby eliminating some of the extreme peaks and valleys of production.

Seasonal Discount A discount offered for ordering seasonal goods well in advance of the normal buying period.

Seasonal Merchandise Goods with temporary demand that cannot normally be sold at regular prices once a set time has passed.

Season Letter A code placed on a price ticket to identify when goods arrived in the store and when clearance action may be needed.

Second-Line Merchandise A lower-price line added to a manufacturer's regular line of goods. This should not be confused with "seconds."

Seconds Merchandise that is slightly damaged or flawed and is offered by some stores, particularly bargain basements, at substantially lower prices than first quality goods of the same type.

Selective Distribution The practice by some manufacturers of limiting the outlets for their products to those retailers who will contribute the most to profits and prestige.

Self-service A type of retail operation where the customer is exposed to merchandise that may be examined and taken to a checkout without sales assistance.

Sell-and-Lease Arrangement An arrangement whereby a retailer occupying real estate sells it to an investor and then leases it back, thereby freeing up funds for more rapid expansion.

Service Desk A place where customers take merchandise for exchange or credit, or may possibly obtain other store-provided services.

Services Things that a store offers customers aside from actual goods. Some of these services may be provided free or at cost; others may be money making.

Shopping Center A geographic cluster of stores distinct from the downtown business district.

Shopping Goods Those goods that customers typically like to exert some shopping effort to obtain, because they want to consider alternative choices.

Shrinkage (Shortage) The difference between actual stock on hand and the book inventory. This loss can be caused by employee theft, by shoplifting, or by carelessness in store procedures.

Single-Line Stores Stores that carry only one line or, at most, a very few related lines of merchandise, but maintain great depth and variety in the lines carried.

Size Lining Selection of size points at which merchandise will be offered. Such sizes are grouped together, as in junior or subteen sizes.

Skip Loss Credit loss due to a customer who has disappeared.

Soft Goods Merchandise basically derived from textiles and typically non-durable.

Special Order An order sent to a vendor, usually at the request of a customer, for merchandise not regularly carried in stock.

Specialty Goods Consumer products for which some customers will exert the greatest shopping effort.

Specialty Store A store that handles only a limited variety of goods, but usually somewhat more lines than a single-line store.

Specification Buying Sometimes done with private-brand (store-brand) goods, with the buyer dictating the product features and standards for the manufacturer to produce.

Split Shipment The vendor ships only part of the order, with the rest back-ordered to be shipped when the goods are available.

Sponsoring A method of training new employees in which a current employee assists the newcomer in becoming accustomed to the store, its people, and the regulations and procedures.

Spot Check A receiving procedure in which certain cartons are opened in the central distribution point and spot checked for quality and quantity before being reshipped to branch stores or other outlets.

Staffing The function of maintaining personnel for a store. Staffing includes determining personnel needs, recruiting, selecting, orientation and training, compensation, and performance evaluation.

Standard Metropolitan Statistical Area (SMSA) Areas designated by the U.S. Census of Business, consisting of central cities of 50,000 or more inhabitants and their adjacent suburbs, for which considerable statistical data have been compiled.

Standing Order Arrangement with a vendor to make shipments periodically in specified quantities.

Staple Stock An item that is in continuous fairly active demand. It is desirable to carry staples in stock at all times.

Staple Stock List   List of staple items that are to be carried in stock.

Stock Balance   Having the right merchandise on hand in sufficient quantity to meet expected demand, while at the same time staying within designated investment constraints.

Stock-Keeping Unit (SKU)   One distinct type of item carried in stock.

Stock-Out   The lack of an item that is not carried in sufficient quantity to meet customer demand.

Stock-Sales Ratio   The ratio between retail stock on the first of the month and sales for that month. This is differentiated from turnover which involves the average stock for the period of time.

Store Audit   A service, usually purchased by a manufacturer from a marketing research firm, in which field auditors regularly check the stock of cooperating retail outlets to determine sales of the manufacturer's own and competing brands, and other related information.

Store Image   The overall personality of a store from the consumers' viewpoint.

Store Layout   The internal arrangement of departments, placement of merchandise, aisles, fixtures, displays, and the like.

Strip Shopping Center   A center in which stores are aligned along a major street, usually with parking spaces provided in front.

Style   The distinguishing characteristics of an article. A style does not become a fashion until it achieves a degree of popularity.

Style-out   A method of pinpointing emerging fashions by evaluating early sales trends.

Suggestion (or Suggestive) Selling   Recommendations by salespeople of additional items, usually related in nature, to those just purchased by a customer.

Supermarket   A large food store laid out for self-service. It can be a unit of a chain or independent.

Target Market   The particular segment of the population toward which a firm wishes to cater its marketing strategy.

Tear Sheets   Advertisements torn from newspapers and magazines and used as evidence of the insertion and as a record of past ads.

Terms of Sale   The conditions under which a product is sold, such as discounts, date of delivery, and methods of payment.

Token Order   Placing a small sample order with the possibility of ordering more later.

Tracer   Person in a traffic department who checks into lost or delayed shipments, both from vendors and to customers.

Trade Association   A group of firms with common business interests who meet to discuss problems and share operating and market information, and sometimes attempt to influence public opinion and legislation.

Trade (Functional) Discount   A discount given to middlemen for performing distributive services that would otherwise have to be performed by the manufacturer. These discounts are given regardless of quantities purchased.

Trade Show   A meeting where many different vendors having related goods come together to show their wares, thus expediting the buyers' search for goods, especially the newest offerings.

Trading Area   The geographical area surrounding a store or shopping center from which most of the retail trade is drawn.

Trading Stamps   Stamps purchased by retailers from trading stamp companies and distributed to customers in proportion to their purchases. Redemption may be for cash, but more commonly it is for merchandise.

Trading-Up   Introducing better-quality, higher-priced merchandise to store assortments in order to improve the store image and profits. This term is also used when a salesperson attempts to sell a customer a higher priced item than the customer originally intended to buy.

Traffic   The customers or potential customers who frequent a store within a particular period of time.

Traffic Items   Items that regularly bring traffic to a store.

Transfers   Moving goods from one profit center to another, usually done only with the approval of both parties.

Turnover   The number of times within a given period that a stock of goods is sold and replaced. Turnover can also refer to personnel.

Twig Store   A department-store outlet that is smaller and not as complete as a branch store. Instead a twig store carries only a few specialized lines.

Understored   Refers to a condition that exists when an area has too few stores to meet the needs of consumers.

Uneven Exchange   An exchange of goods by a customer when the value of the goods returned is different from the value of the new goods received.

Unfair Competition   Business practices that are not considered ethical, and may be illegal in a given community. Generally, severe loss-leader merchandising may be considered unfair competition by other firms, and some states have unfair practices acts that are designed to prohibit severe price cutting.

Unit Control   The control of stock in terms of merchandise units rather than dollar figures.

Unit Pricing   Showing prices of items to include the price per unit, such as per pound or per quart, in addition to the price of the product as packaged.

Universal Product Code (UPC)   A code identification system placed on most packaged food products today (and a number of nonfood items as well), that can be read by an electronic scanner at a checkout counter. The scanner transmits price and other information to a computer that controls the cash register.

Upgrading   Increasing price lines by offering better quality and assortments in a particular category of goods.

Variable Costs   Operating expenses that are affected by changes in sales volume. Expenses for delivery and for supplies are examples.

Variable Price Policy   A policy of adjusting selling prices for different customers, often according to their perceived ability to pay.

Variety   The number of different classifications of goods carried by a department or store.

Variety Store   Originally "five and ten" stores and "dime" stores, variety stores sell a wide range of goods in the low and popular price categories.

Vendor   An individual or firm from whom purchases are made. Also called a supplier and a resource.

Vendor Analysis   An analysis of the performance of a vendor, in such areas as markups, markdowns, customer complaints, promptness of delivery, and the like.

Visual Check Controlling merchandise by "eyeball" checks rather than by periodic or perpetual inventory control methods.

Voluntary Chain A group of independent retailers that form an association with a wholesaler or manufacturer to carry on joint merchandising activities. Voluntary chains usually exhibit some uniformity of store image and operational strategy.

Want Slip (Want Book) A slip or notebook for recording customer requests for merchandise not presently handled by a store.

Warehouse Retailing Retailing of certain types of products, such as food or furniture, in low-rent, isolated buildings (often former warehouses or even barns) with few services but very attractive prices.

Warranty A synonym for *guarantee.*

Waybill The bill of lading for air shipments. It is a receipt from the carrier and a contract between the carrier and the shipper.

Wheel of Retailing A theory describing and predicting change in retail institutions. Major retailer innovations are seen as occurring on a low price, minimum service foundation.

Wholesaler A business concerned with selling to those who buy for resale or industrial use.

Will Call Products ordered by customers in advance of the time delivery is desired.

Working Capital The excess of current assets over current liabilities that represents the capital immediately available to a business.

Workrooms Service departments of a store, such as alterations rooms, drapery workrooms, and furniture repair shops.

Index